Trefoil
Round the World

'In a world fraught with uncertainty and fear our Movement shines out as a golden chain against a dark background. The links in the chain are forged out of the finest gold, our Promise and Law. Each has its special and individual decoration, its national characteristics, to enrich and beautify the whole. The chain is getting longer with each new link and stronger as each country increases in spirit and in numbers.'

Olave, Lady Baden-Powell
World Chief Guide

World Association of Girl Guides and Girl Scouts
World Bureau, Olave Centre
12c Lyndhurst Road
London NW3 5PQ, England

First Edition June 1958
Second Edition March 1959
Third Edition January 1961
Fourth Edition March 1964
Fifth Edition August 1967
Sixth Edition 1973
Seventh Edition 1977
Reprinted 1979 with Supplement
Reprinted 1984 with Addendum
Eighth Edition 1986
Reprinted 1988 with Supplement
Ninth Edition 1992
Tenth Edition 1994

ISBN 0 900827 64 5

Note

In the case of Member Organizations in countries where English is not the mother tongue, the English version of the Promise and Law is a translation of the text adopted by the National Organization; it should be noted that without knowledge of the language or culture of the country it is often difficult to comprehend fully the true meaning and significance of the words chosen by an Association.

The membership figures for each Member Organization have been taken from the 26th Triennial Report and Update. In some instances, census information is currently either unavailable or incomplete and estimates have been made. In these cases, the figures have been marked with †.

We offer our sincere thanks to the Girl Scouts of the USA, whose idea it was that this book should replace HANDS AROUND THE WORLD, *published in the United States of America in 1949.*

The World Bureau expresses its sincere thanks to all Member Organizations who assisted with information and photographs for this publication. WAGGGS makes every effort to assure the accuracy of each submission. Information is the best available at the time of printing. WAGGGS regrets any errors or omissions. Please send corrections to the Head of Communications and Public Relations at the World Bureau.

Produced by the World Bureau, World Association of Girl Guides and Girl Scouts.
Co-ordinated by Banson, 3 Turville Street, London E2 7HR.
P rinted in Great Britan

Contents

** Indicates Associate Membership*

Introduction

Girl Guides and Girl Scouts on the Move

From a handful of founding members, the Girl Guide/Girl Scout Movement has become the largest, worldwide voluntary organization for girls and young women, offering them opportunities to develop character, become responsible citizens, and give service in their communities. More than 8.5 million strong in 128 countries around the globe, it continues to grow, providing its members with stable values in a changing world.

The Roots of the Movement

The roots of the Girl Guide/Girl Scout Movement go back to the early days, when its extraordinary founder, Robert Baden-Powell, started the Boy Scout Movement in 1908. Almost at once a number of girls appeared declaring themselves Girl Scouts, and Baden-Powell decided that they should have their own movement. By November 1909, a scheme had been formulated to suit the specific needs of girls and young women. Today these World Movements continue to be separate and independent, collaborating at various levels, exchanging information, and sharing activities and projects.

Initially the Movement for girls was known as the Girl Guides, after the famous corps of guides in India who were "distinguished for their general handiness and resourcefulness under difficulties, and their keenness and courage... The word Guide meant one who embodies all these desirable qualities, including industry, practical common sense, and self reliance."

In 1910, Baden-Powell asked his sister Agnes to adapt his book *Scouting for Boys* for use with girls. In the same year, the Girl Guides Association (United Kingdom) was officially established under Agnes's presidency, and interest in the Movement began to grow.

Baden-Powell understood the importance of special language, signs and ritual, which contribute to a sense of group membership. The symbols and their meanings, now an integral part of the World Association of Girl Guides and Girl Scouts (WAGGGS), are explained in Appendix C (page 319).

The Partnership

Baden-Powell retired from the army in 1910, devoting himself to Scouting and Guiding. He attended camps, rallies and jamborees all over the world. It was at the start of a world tour on the *Arcadian*, bound for the West Indies, that he met his future wife, Olave St Clair Soames.

Although 32 years separated them in age, they were united by mutual interests, a similar attitude to life, and a common birthday – 22 February. After a brief courtship carried out mainly by correspondence, the couple were married at a country church in Dorset, England.

Olave accompanied her husband on visits and tours and joined his enthusiasm for the new youth organizations. She began the Girl Guide Movement in Sussex, England. In 1916, at the first gathering of Commissioners, Olave was elected to the Office of Chief Commissioner and, in 1918, she was made Chief Guide.

The following year, Olave formed the International Council to provide a means of keeping in touch with members of the Movement around the world. In 1920 the Council had its first International Conference in Oxford, England, attended by delegates and visitors from 15 countries. That same year Baden-Powell was elected World Chief Scout.

At a rally in 1908 in London, these girls arrived, declaring themselves to be Girl Scouts. The Girl Guide/Girl Scout Movement began officially in 1909.

Growing Worldwide

The next three years were busy ones for the Baden-Powells, spent visiting Girl Guide/Girl Scout and Boy Scout events all over the world.

In July 1924 the first World Camp, combined with the 3rd International Conference, took place at Foxlease, in the United Kingdom. The following year saw the publication of *The World Bulletin*, a magazine for Girl Guides/Girl Scouts throughout the world. It was later renamed several times, and now exists as *Our World News*.

At the 4th International Conference (USA, 1926), delegates designated a special day each year which members would devote to thinking of one another with love and friendship. The date chosen was 22 February, the joint birthday of the Baden-Powells, and the name adopted was Thinking Day.

Today Thinking Day encourages Girl Guides and Girl Scouts to think of other members of the Movement around the world. Thoughts are translated into action by participating in international activities and contributing money for the promotion of Girl Guiding/Girl Scouting. Thinking Day contributions are a vital part of the World Association's resources, and the Day itself has provided Girl Guides/Girl Scouts with greater opportunitites to help others.

Two years later, at the 5th International Conference (Hungary, 1928) delegates formed the World Association of Girl Guides and Girl Scouts (WAGGGS), which replaced the International Council. The International Conferences were renamed World Conferences. Today the World Conference is held every three years in a different region of the world, and it continues to set policy for the world Movement.

Today's girls take action on issues to improve their world, such as advancement of girls and young women, the environment and peace.

In 1930 Olave was appointed World Chief Guide. The previous year Baden-Powell had been created Baron Baden-Powell of Gilwell, and in 1932 Olave was created Dame Grand Cross of the Order of the British Empire.

Expansion and the World Centres

During the early thirties the Movements enjoyed phenomenal success. In 1931 WAGGGS' membership exceeded one million girls and women around the globe. Today there are 8.5 million members, and the Movement has reached millions more over the years.

In July 1932, Our Chalet became WAGGGS' first World Centre, opening in Adelboden, Switzerland. Today there are four World Centres: Our Chalet; Pax Lodge (London, England); Sangam (Pune, India); and Our Cabaña (Cuernavaca, Mexico).

One of the first events at Our Chalet was the Juliette Low gathering, held to honour the founder of Girl Scouts of the USA. The Juliette Low Memorial Fund, now known as the Juliette Low Friendship Fund, has enhanced international friendship and understanding among many Girl Guides and Girl Scouts.

On 2 May 1939, the second World Centre, Our Ark, was opened in Palace Street, London. The ark has always been a symbol of security and, in its early years, Our Ark offered refuge to many members of the Movement forced to abandon their homes during the Second World War.

The summer of 1939 saw Pax-Ting, the first Girl Guide/Girl Scout World Camp, held in Hungary and attended by some 4,000 girls. International activities and World Committee meetings were suspended during the Second World War, but in 1946, World Conferences resumed.

Meanwhile, Baden-Powell's failing health brought the couple to the warmer, more therapeutic climate of Kenya. Their Kenyan home was called Paxtu (Pax the Second, or, in Swahili, "Complete Peace"), and it was here that Baden-Powell died on 8 January 1941. Though devastated by her husband's death, Olave soon resumed her lifelong work. She travelled the world, encouraging and inspiring girls and women everywhere. She opened the doors of Our Cabaña, the third World Centre, in Mexico on 24 July 1957.

Over the years, the Our Ark premises proved too small, and in 1957 an appeal was launched to rehouse Our Ark. A new building was found in Longbridge Road, Earls Court, London and the World Centre was renamed Olave House. WAGGGS was rapidly gaining strength, and in 1959 introduced regional world gatherings in Finland, Fiji, Mexico and Pakistan. In 1963 the Mutual Aid Scheme was set up so Member Organizations could help each other in their work.

On 16 October 1966, WAGGGS' fourth World Centre opened in Pune, India. The Centre was named Sangam, which means "coming together" (as of small rivers which flow into one main stream).

In March 1991, the newest World Centre, Pax Lodge, opened its doors for the first time. It forms part of the Olave Centre and adjoins the World Bureau. Several years in its planning and construction, Pax Lodge was the result of a huge worldwide fundraising effort. It replaces Olave House and joins the other three World Centres in welcoming Girl Guides and Girl Scouts from all over the world.

The World Centres continue to operate today under the direction of a Guider-in-Charge and sub-committees, appointed by the World Committee to supervise their administration. They offer programmes and conferences designed to give young women a chance to learn more about other people and cultures, and to share friendship and understanding.

Baden-Powell's Legacy Continues

In 1970, health reasons prevented Olave from travelling overseas, but from then on she entertained Girl Guides/Girl Scouts at her home in Hampton Court Palace, England. Olave Baden-Powell died peacefully in her sleep on 25 June 1977. Millions mourned throughout the world, united in the grief felt at the loss of the World Chief Guide.

In 1979 the Olave Award was established for outstanding service to the community by a single patrol or pack, company or troop of any age group. It continues to be made annually. The World Bureau, previously housed in Ebury Street, moved in 1984 to larger premises at 12c Lyndhurst Road, Hampstead, London. This move was the first phase of a plan to create Olave Centre, a permanent memorial to the World Chief Guide. The new World Bureau was officially opened in 1985.

The WAGGGS' Way

WAGGGS operates through a system of democratic governance – through co-operation, action and respect. This system is known as WAGGGS' Way. Its methods and philosophy have been effective and long-lasting.
The World Bureau, first set up in London in 1928 as the international secretariat for the Movement, is the heart of the World Association, providing day-to-day support for the World Movement. It serves as a link to all the Member Organizations. The World Bureau is headed by a Director, who is responsible to the World Committee for the Bureau's proper management and administration. The World Bureau staff assist with the overall planning of World Conferences and World Committee meetings, support the World Committee in co-ordinating the work of its sub-committees, and help implement decisions taken at World Conferences.

Member Organizations, also known as national Associations, agree to abide by WAGGGS' Constitution and Bye-Laws. To be recognized as a Member Organization, a national Association must have a constitution approved by the World Committee, adopt the method of the Girl Guide/Girl Scout Movement, incorporate the Trefoil in its badge and develop programmes suited to the needs of the girls in its country. It must have sound finances and a structure which can support further development. It must also pay an annual quota (a sum of money determined on a proportional basis) and send an annual report of its work to the World Bureau, WAGGGS' secretariat in London. There are now 128 Member Organizations providing services to over 8.5 million members.

There are two categories of membership: Associate and Full. Associate Members are national Associations accepted into WAGGGS while continuing to work towards Full Membership.

WAGGGS' World Conference is its policy-making body, meeting every three years to determine policies and standards of the Movement. Each Member Organization may send up to two delegates, who may be supported by a number of observers determined proportionally by membership. The World Committee may invite visitors and guests at its discretion.

The World Committee is composed of 12 members elected by the World Conference and acts on behalf of the Conference between triennial meetings. World Committee members represent the interests of the Movement as a whole. They serve one nine-year term. Four new members are elected each triennium to replace four who are retiring.

The World Committee appoints its own sub-committees, considering names submitted by Member Organizations, and, in the case of the Regional Committees, recommendations from the Regions. There are sub-committees for Constitutions; Finance; Promotion; each of the four World Centres (Our Chalet, Pax Lodge, Our Cabaña and Sangam); each of the four Regions (the Western Hemisphere, Asia Pacific, Europe and Africa); and a Youth Committee. Although not appointed by the World Committee, the Arab Regional Group operates in North Africa.

On the Move Today

The last few years have been busy ones for the Movement. Its activities have expanded within the Regions and Arab Regional Group. In Central and Eastern Europe, WAGGGS has helped to develop new Girl Guide/Girl Scout organizations in countries where the Movement was dormant or forbidden during the Communist era. Many of these countries are now Associate Members. Similarly, WAGGGS is working to help the Movement develop in the Commonwealth of Independent States.

To recognize the importance of high standards of training for leaders, WAGGGS created a worldwide Training Accreditation Scheme. It was designed to encourage the development of "Training for Trainers" Programmes by Member Organizations. A Programme Pack was introduced to help new organizations develop their programme for girls.

As part of a campaign to emphasize the importance of clean and safe water, a worldwide campaign called "Water is Life" began in 1990. The UN Environment Programme provided a grant to produce two books, which set out the problems of water supply, sanitation and preservation, and offered practical examples of what Member Organizations could do. WAGGGS then developed its first worldwide badge system to offer recognition for Girl Guide/Girl Scout efforts to keep their water supplies safe and clean.

Rangers and Rovers from Italy had a powerful experience of discovery and change by volunteering to help children in Albania – many of whom are refugees from Croatia and Slovenia.

In order to be able to meet the challenges posed by an ever-growing Movement, in 1990 at the 27th World Conference the WAGGGS Constitution and Bye-Laws were updated to make membership more accessible. At the 28th World Conference in Denmark nine new countries became members, and about 20 others are working towards membership.

Challenges for the Future

As the world continues to evolve at an ever-increasing rate, the need for information is growing. WAGGGS meets this challenge by providing help and guidance for its Member Organizations. It also produces a series of booklets on world issues, such as AIDS, Food and Nutrition, Street Children, Trade in Women, and Refugees. These publications provide information and project ideas.

WAGGGS works with the UN and its specialized agencies on various projects to create a better world. In 1993 WAGGGS' membership voted to reaffirm its long-standing commitment to peace through a three-year intitiative – CREATE PEACE WORLDWIDE – THE WAGGGS INITIATIVE. Through training, projects and personal commitment WAGGGS' members will work in their own way to build peace. Whether through the assembly of Peace Packs for refugee children, advocacy, personal development or direct action, Girl Guides and Girl Scouts will be heard and will make a difference.

The original Promise and Law continue to provide the fundamental principles that link the world of Girl Guiding and Girl Scouting together. Every national Association has a Promise and Law approved by WAGGGS' World Committee, which contains the essential elements of that developed by Baden-Powell, even though it is adapted to the country's needs and culture.

In every country the Movement is open to all girls and young women without distinction as to creed, race, nationality or any other circumstance. And national Associations remain independent of any political organization or political party, free to govern themselves and to formulate and put into practice their own policies. WAGGGS' flexibility in a changing world allows new approaches to today's challenges, making it an effective voice for girls and young women for the future.

Antigua and Barbuda

The Girl Guides Association of Antigua and Barbuda

Girl Guiding/Girl Scouting introduced: 1931
Became Associate Member of WAGGGS: 1984
Membership 1992: 690
Membership as % of female population: 2.0%
WAGGGS Region: Western Hemisphere

Promise

I promise that I will do my best:
To do my duty to God
To serve the Queen and my country and help other people and
To keep the Guide Law.

Law

1 A Guide is loyal and can be trusted.
2 A Guide is helpful.
3 A Guide is polite and considerate.
4 A Guide is friendly and a sister to all Guides.
5 A Guide is kind to animals and respects all living things.
6 A Guide is obedient.
7 A Guide has courage and is cheerful in all difficulties.
8 A Guide makes good use of her time.
9 A Guide takes care of her own possessions and those of other people.
10 A Guide is self-controlled in all she thinks, says and does.

Brownie Guide Promise

I promise I will do my best:
To do my duty to God
To serve the Queen and my country and help other people and
To keep the Brownie Guide Law.

Brownie Guide Law

A Brownie Guide thinks of others before herself and
Does a good turn every day.

Development of the Movement in Antigua and Barbuda

Guide

In 1931 the first two Guide companies in Antigua were registered with the Girl Guides Association (United Kingdom), a step that was rapidly followed by an expansion in the number of units.

Two visits from the World Chief Guide, and contact with trainers from the Girl Guides Association (United Kingdom), in the following years helped to boost the development of the Movement. In 1969 the first trainer from the islands officially qualified and this led to the development of residential trainings for Guide leaders.

In 1983 The Girl Guides Association (United Kingdom) approved a deed of transfer making the Girl Guides Association of Antigua and Barbuda self-governing in all areas of work.

Brownie Guide

The Programme

Antigua and Barbuda uses an eight-point programme based on keeping fit, becoming a homemaker, giving service, keeping the Guide Law, getting to know people, enjoying the outdoors, thinking for yourself and exploring the arts.

Working with the Community

Hurricane Hugo caused much damage in Antigua and Barbuda in 1989, largely destroying the Association's headquarters. Guides helped victims of the hurricane by offering emergency support.

Training

Antigua and Barbuda has two certified trainers and three prospective trainers. Training is on an ad hoc basis and includes training weekends and sub-regional trainings.

Communication and Co-operation

Guides in Antigua have strong overseas links through frequent participation in international camps. Antigua and Barbuda forms part of the Caribbean Link set up for mutual aid and consultation among Guide Associations in the Commonwealth countries and islands of the Caribbean.

The Association has good relations with the community, the government and the Scout Association, the Chief Commissioner being a member of its Executive. Most units are attached to churches and the Guides work closely with these religious bodies.

Argentina

Asociación Guías Argentinas

Girl Guiding/Girl Scouting introduced:	**1915**
Became Associate Member of WAGGGS:	**1958**
Became Full Member of WAGGGS:	**1963**
Membership 1992:	**5,751**
Membership as % of female population:	**0.03%**
WAGGGS Region:	**Western Hemisphere**

Guide

Promesa
Por mi honor y con la gracia de Dios prometo hacer todo lo posible para cumplir mis deberes para con Dios y mi Patria, ayudar al prójimo en todas las circunstancias y observar la Ley Guía.

Ley
1 La guía es digna de toda confianza.
2 La guía es leal y responsable.
3 La guía sirve y ayuda al prójimo sin esperar recompensas ni alabanzas.
4 La guía considera a todos como hermanos.
5 La guía es cortés.
6 La guía ve en la naturaleza la obra de Dios y la respeta.
7 La guía es obediente y disciplinada y nada hace a medias.
8 La guía es alegre y enfrenta las dificultades con serenidad.
9 La guía es económica y respeta el bien ajeno.
10 La guía es pura en sus pensamientos, palabras y obras.

Lema
Siempre lista	(Guía en Caravana)
Siempre adelante	(Guía del Sol)
Servir	(Guía Mayor)

Promesa de la Alita
Prometo hacer todo lo posible para cumplir mis deberes para con Dios, mi Patria, mis padres y observar la Ley de la Ronda.

Ley de la Alita
La Alita es activa y observadora.
La Alita está limpia y bien arreglada.
La Alita es alegre.
La Alita dice la verdad.
La Alita piensa siempre en los demás.

Lema de la Alita
Siempre mejor

Promise
On my honour and with the help of God,
I promise to do my best to do my duty to God and my Country,
to help other people at all times and to obey the Guide Law.

Law
1 A Guide is to be trusted.
2 A Guide is loyal and responsible.
3 A Guide serves and helps other people without expecting rewards or praise.
4 A Guide sees herself as a sister to all.
5 A Guide is courteous.
6 A Guide respects nature for in it she sees the work of God.
7 A Guide is obedient and disciplined and does nothing by halves.
8 A Guide is cheerful and faces difficulties serenely.
9 A Guide is thrifty and respects other people's property.
10 A Guide is pure in thought, words and deeds.

Motto
Always ready	(Caravan Guide)
Always forward	(Sun Guide)
Serve	(Ranger)

Little Wing

Little Wing Promise
I promise to do my best to fulfil my duties to God, my country, my parents and to obey the Law of the Pack.

Little Wing Law
The Little Wing is active and observant.
The Little Wing is clean and tidy.
The Little Wing is cheerful.

The Little Wing tells the truth.
The Little Wing always thinks of others.

Little Wing Motto
Always better

Age Groups

Guía Mayor	Ranger	16 - 19
Guía del Sol	Sun Guide	13 - 15
Guía en Caravana	Caravan Guide	10 - 12
Alita	Little Wing	7 - 9

Development of the Movement in Argentina

When Guiding began in Argentina in 1915 it was confined to English schools and companies and packs were registered with the Girl Guides Association (United Kingdom). During the first 40 years the development of the Movement was hindered by many difficulties, including a governmental ban on all uniformed groups of foreign origin in 1939. The situation changed when an autonomous Guide Movement was started in 1953 and the Asociación Guías Argentinas was officially founded. In 1956 the Association was granted legal status by the government.

The Programme
The Guide programme is centred on four main areas: the community, the outdoors, culture and the world of Girl Guiding/ Girl Scouting. The aim of the programme is to encourage girls to become active members of their community; to become conscious of the environment and to protect it; to develop skills and means of expression; and to further international understanding through the principles of Girl Guiding/Girl Scouting.

Working with the Community
The Association carries out vaccination, hygiene and literacy campaigns, and runs libraries, nurseries and school canteens. Members determine areas of need within their own communities and carry out community development projects, sometimes in co-operation with other organizations concerned with youth.

The WAGGGS Olave Award 1984, for achievement in community development or community service, was won by a Senior Guide company for a project involving the establishment and running of a canteen for local needy children. A second canteen was set up for homeless elderly people in the district. The project has now been extended to review the needs of those with mental and physical disabilities, teenagers in need of support, and low-income families.

Another Argentine Senior Guide group won the Olave Award in 1991. This was the Senior Guide group "Juan Pablo II", from Tandil, Province of Buenos Aires, who carried on a project in a mapuche community in Lago Rosario, Province of Chubut in the south of Argentina. The Guides interested their own community and the community of Lago Rosario and received their co-operation in order to build a playing ground for children of the Indian community. They continue motivating both communities in order to promote the knowledge and development of that isolated community of indigenous people.

Outdoor and Environmental Activities
The Asociación Guías Argentinas holds regular camps and encourages members to learn about the countryside and the geographical features of the country. Members participate in outdoor games, sports and outings, and are involved in conservation projects.

Training
The Asociación Guías Argentinas reviews training methods at national seminars in order to keep abreast of current trends. Training methods used include gatherings, workshops and correspondence courses for isolated groups. Over 300 members receive training each year at local, regional and national level from a training team of approximately 30 members.

Communication and Co-operation
The Asociación Guías Argentinas encourages its members to participate in international events, and a special committee dedicated to public relations ensures press coverage for special, newsworthy events.

Aruba
Het Arubaanse Padvindsters Gilde

Girl Guiding/Girl Scouting introduced:	**1941**
Became Associate Member of WAGGGS:	**1993**
Membership 1992:	**246**
Membership as % of female population:	**0.82%**
WAGGGS Region:	**Western Hemisphere**

Promise
Ik zal ernstig trachten God en mijn land te dienen iedereen te helpen waar ik kan en de Padvindsterswet na te leven.

Law
Een Padvindster is eerlijk
Een Padvindster is trouw
Een Padvindster is hulpvaardig
Een Padvindster is vriendelijk voor ieder en een zuster voor alle Padvindsters
Een Padvindster is beleefd en voorkomend
Een Padvindster is goed voor planten en dieren
Een Padvindster weet te gehoorzamen
Een Padvindster draagt teleurstellingen met opgewektheid
Een Padvindster is spaarzaam
Een Padvindster is rein in gedachten, woord en daad.

Brownie Promise
Ik zal mijn best doen om een echte Kabouter te zijn, iedereen te helpen waar ik kan, wooral thuis.

Brownie Law
Een Kabouter is eerlijk
Een Kabouter is gehoorzaam
Een Kabouter is vriendelijk
Een Kabouter is goed voor planten en dieren.

Promise
I will earnestly strive to serve God and my country,
To help everyone wherever I can,
and to live by the Girl Guide Law.

Law
A Guide is honest
A Guide is loyal
A Guide is useful and helps others
A Guide is a friend to all and a sister to every Guide
A Guide is courteous
A Guide is kind to animals and enjoys the beauty in nature
A Guide is obedient
A Guide bears disappointments cheerfully
A Guide is thrifty
A Guide is pure in thought, word and deed.

Brownie Promise
I will do my best to be a true Brownie and to help everyone wherever I can, especially at home.

Brownie Law
A Brownie is honest.
A Brownie is obedient.
A Brownie is friendly.
A Brownie is good for plants and animals.

Age Groups

Pioneers	17-21
Guides	11-17
Brownies	7-11

Guide

Brownie

Development of the Movement in Aruba

In 1941 a group of women, inspired by the Guide Silver Jubilee celebrations in the Netherlands, decided to introduce girls in Aruba to Girl Guiding. In the early years the Girl Guides of Aruba worked alone, using manuals produced by the Nederlands Padvinsters Gilde (NPG). In 1946 they officially joined NPG and became part of the Region of Curaçao. In 1953 Aruba became an autonomous Region and in 1972 an independent Association within the Netherlands Antilles.

In the early 1970s and through the early 1980s, Guiding activities on the island waned but in 1986 a revival provoked new interest in Guiding in Aruba. The Association had a new Constitution; a new name: Het Arubaanse Padvindsters Gilde (APG). Closed groups, which had restricted group membership to one denomination, were replaced with open Guiding.

Former leaders reacted to newspaper advertisements requesting help and Guiding started to grow. In 1992 the APG was invited to the Western Hemisphere Conference. Guiding is now active in most of the country, and the APG is planning to start more groups around the island.

The Programme
The aim of the APG is to help girls and young women to become responsible citizens who are able to give leadership and service to the community, through the promotion of the fundamental principles of Girl Guiding. The programme is devised to suit the needs of each age group and to enable its members to meet these aims. The Association has introduced a programme to suit the Aruban girl, by combining elements of its original Dutch programme with ideas from the programmes used by the Padvindsters Nederlandse Antillen and Girl Guides of Canada-Guides du Canada.

Working with the Community
The APG take part in the on-going "Keep Aruba Clean Campaign" and the annual sale of "Children's Stamps" for charity. They also make visits to the aged in "Homes at Christmas" and donate food baskets.

Outdoor and Environmental Activities
The APG help with clean-up activities such as the "Keep Aruba Clean Campaign".

Training
Three trainers form a Training Committee responsible for preparing the Association's training programme and for training potential trainers. Training seminars are held for leaders on a regular basis.

Communication and Co-operation
The Association has a good relationship with the National Government, religious authorities, other organizations and the general public. The Girl Guides and Brownies form Guards of Honour for all important visitors to the island and participate in national parades, together with other youth organizations.

In 1991 the Association produced its first publication, a songbook.

Brownies enjoy a crafts session at camp in Aruba.

Australia

Girl Guides Association of Australia Incorporated

Founder Member of WAGGGS
Girl Guiding/Girl Scouting introduced: 1911
Membership 1992: 87,660
Membership as % of female population: 1.4%
WAGGGS Region: Asia Pacific

Promise
I promise that I will do my best:
To do my duty to God, to serve the Queen and my country,
To help other people and
To keep the Guide Law.

Law
1 A Guide is loyal and can be trusted.
2 A Guide is helpful.
3 A Guide is polite and considerate.
4 A Guide is friendly and a sister to all Guides.
5 A Guide is kind to animals and respects all living things.
6 A Guide is obedient.
7 A Guide has courage and is cheerful in all difficulties.
8 A Guide makes good use of her time.
9 A Guide takes care of her own possessions and those of other people.
10 A Guide is self-controlled in all she thinks, says and does.

Motto
Be Prepared

Brownie Guide Promise
I promise that I will do my best:
To do my duty to God, to serve the Queen and my country,
To help other people and
To keep the Brownie Guide Law.

Brownie Guide Law
A Brownie Guide thinks of others before herself and does a good turn every day.

Brownie Guide Motto
Lend a Hand

Gumnut Guides Special Saying
Gumnut Guides care and share.

Age Groups

Ranger	17-25
Ranger Guide	14-18
Guide	10-15
Brownie Guide	7-11
Gumnut Guide	6-7½

Guide

Development of the Movement in Australia

Guiding began spontaneously in many parts of Australia from 1911 onwards. Soon after the end of the First World War in 1918, each state established its own organization and headquarters. In 1926, a Federal Council was formed linking the states together as the Girl Guides Association of Australia. In 1928, Australia became a founder member of WAGGGS. The constitution was amended in 1958 to include an Australian executive, which enabled Australia to act as a national body. The Association was incorporated in 1980.

Brownie Guide

The Programme
The programme, based on eight points, is reviewed regularly to ensure that it is relevant to the needs of girls in today's changing society. The programme gives each girl an opportunity to develop her potential in the following areas: mind, physical fitness, character, creative ability, relationships with others, readiness and ability to serve others, home management skills and enjoyment of the outdoors.

Gumnut Guide

The Gumnut Guide programme was launched in 1990, enabling six-year-olds to enjoy the fun of Guiding and develop an

Guide learning car maintenance in Western Australia.

awareness of the world around them while learning to care and share.

Girls isolated from active units participate in Lone Guiding. Their unit meeting is in the form of a circular letter or audio-tape, and training aids are sent regularly to patrol leaders. Lone gatherings and camps give members an opportunity to meet each other. In some remote areas of Australia, they are linked through the School of the Air and The Royal Flying Doctor Service.

Girls with special needs are integrated into local units in most instances. These members are encouraged to participate fully in the programme, sometimes with the assistance of an able helper as a companion.

Australia is a multicultural society with almost 30% of its population born abroad. Guiding has welcomed members from over 50 different ethnic backgrounds in recent years. It recognizes the contribution these culturally diverse members are making to Guiding, and is working towards increasing membership.

Working with the Community

Being of service and developing a positive attitude towards community responsibility are important parts of the programme in all sections. The girls are encouraged to initiate service projects and give practical assistance when needed.

This includes helping those who are disadvantaged, the elderly and patients in hospitals. Service projects involving care of the environment, such as tree-planting and the 'Clean Up Australia' campaign are popular.

Many groups are involved in fundraising for a variety of community causes. Significant amounts of money have been raised using innovative ideas for Save the Koala Foundation, The National Heart Foundation, Guide Dogs for the Blind, as well as for medical research and care of disadvantaged or sick young people.

Outdoor and Environmental Activities

State associations own and operate a number of campsites, indoor accommodation, training and conference centres, as well as having facilities for water, air and snow activities.

Outdoor and adventure activities offer fun and challenge and the opportunity for girls and leaders to develop skills and self-reliance, as well as a caring concern for the environment. Earth Education camps have been established in various centres around Australia.

Australia is the only country in the world to recycle corks, and members in all states are collecting corks to help save the world's cork trees.

Training

The Australian Leadership Training Programme gives guidelines for a national training scheme for adult leaders. Pre-training support is given through the use of a *Leaders Logbook* and the personal assistance of a *Guiding Partner*. Cross crediting of prior knowledge is encouraged, as is self-evaluation and goal setting. A leaders' handbook supplements formal training sessions. Special courses are offered to potential trainers and they are encouraged to assess their own strengths and weaknesses as they progress.
The Australian Leadership Training

Programme is accredited with the World Association of Girl Guides and Girl Scouts training scheme and accredited trainers wear the World Association training pin.

The Junior Leaders Scheme, for girls ages 14½ to 18, provides leadership training and experience for those wishing to work with the younger age groups.

Communication and Co-operation
The Australian Association is an active member of WAGGGS and is involved regularly with other Member Organizations, particularly those of the Asia Pacific Region. Many opportunities to attend international camps and other events both abroad and in Australia are available to girls and leaders. Australia also participates in exchange programmes and other informal visits. Mutual Aid, Jamboree-on-the-Air and Post Box provide other links with WAGGGS Member Organizations.

The Ranger Section and leaders are encouraged to participate in international service projects which are arranged on a regular basis.

Members are encouraged to financially support the Thinking Day Fund and the Four World Centres. Some financial assistance is sometimes available to help members who represent Australia at international events.

The Girl Guides Association of Australia identifies with the United Nations' special years, and special programmes are planned around these themes. Projects are organized at local and national level. Many units celebrate other special UN days such as World Environment Day, International Day of Peace and Universal Children's Day with special activities.

The Girl Guides Association of Australia maintains contact with other organizations at state and national level and is an active member of the Conference of Australian Youth Organizations and Australian Youth Policy and Action Coalition. Members of the Ranger Section and young leaders attend forums, conferences and workshops and contribute to the decision-making process of the Association. They also represent the Association on various state and national committees which focus on the social and health issues facing today's youth.

The Girl Guides Association of Australia and Scout Association of Australia have a co-operative working relationship especially through informal networks in the local community. Joint and shared activities take place at all levels.

A monthly magazine, *Guiding in Australia*, gives activity ideas and news of Guiding both nationally and internationally.

A new uniform with a variety of options for all sections has helped to give Guiding a modern and flexible image.

The Australian Association is working on a communications plan to create a greater awareness of Guiding in the community and to assist in recruiting new girls and leaders. Recruitment videos, posters, leaflets and radio advertisements, as well as articles in newspapers are helping to achieve these objectives.

Rangers share a sailing adventure in a tall ship.

Austria

Pfadfinder und Pfadfinderinnen Österreichs
(Boy Scouts and Girl Guides of Austria)

Girl Guiding/Girl Scouting introduced:	**pre-1914**
Became Associate Member of WAGGGS:	**1957**
Became Full Member of WAGGGS:	**1969**
Membership 1992:	**10,957**
Membership as % of female population:	**0.27%**
WAGGGS Region:	**Europe**

Guide

Brownie

Versprechen
Ich verspreche bei meiner Ehre, dass ich mein Bestes tun will, Gott und meinem Lande zu dienen, meinen Mitmenschen zu helfen und nach unserem Gesetz zu leben.

Gesetz
1 Die Pfadfinderin sucht den Weg zu Gott.
2 Die Pfadfinderin ist treu und hilft, wo sie kann.
3 Die Pfadfinderin achtet alle Menschen und sucht sie zu verstehen.
4 Die Pfadfinderin überlegt, entscheidet sich und handelt danach.
5 Die Pfadfinderin lebt einfach und schützt die Natur.
6 Die Pfadfinderin ist fröhlich und unverzagt.
7 Die Pfadfinderin nützt ihre Fähigkeiten.
8 Die Pfadfinderin führt ein gesundes Leben

Motto
Allzeit bereit

Brownie Promise
Ich verspreche, so gut ich kann, ein gutes Wichtel zu sein, nach unserem Gesetz zu leben, und bitte Gott, mir dabei zu helfen.

Brownie Law
1 Das Wichtel tut sein Bestes.
2 Das Wichtel hilft freudig, wo es kann.

Brownie Motto
So gut ich kann

Promise
I promise on my honour that I will do my best to serve God and my country, to help my fellow man and to live by our Law.

Law
1 The Guide seeks the way to God.
2 The Guide is loyal and helps where she can.
3 The Guide pays attention to all human beings and seeks to understand them.
4 The Guide considers, decides for herself and acts accordingly.
5 The Guide lives simply and protects nature.
6 The Guide is happy and does not despair.
7 The Guide uses her abilities.
8 The Guide leads a healthy life.

Motto
Always Prepared

Brownie Promise
I promise as well as I can, to be a good Brownie, to live by our Law and, God willing, to thereby help myself.

Brownie Law
1 The Brownie does her best.
2 The Brownie helps cheerfully wherever she can.

Brownie Motto
As well as I can

Age Groups

Ranger	Ranger	16-19
Caravelle	Caravelle	13-16
Pfadfinderin	Guide	10-13
Wichtel	Brownie	7-10

Development of the Movement in Austria

Girl Guiding in Austria began before the First World War and a National Organization was formed in 1924. But due to an increasingly difficult political situation, all Guiding activities had ceased by 1938. After the Second World War Guiding activities began again throughout the country.

The Österreichischer Pfadfinderinnen-verband St Georg merged with the Pfadfinder Österreichs in 1976 to form the Pfadfinder und Pfadfinderinnen Österreichs.

The Programme

With the merging of the two Associations in 1976 a new common programme for Guides and Scouts was introduced, retaining valuable contents and material from the recently renewed girls programme, which met the needs of both girls and boys. After 15 years working as a merged association and in order to be able to lead the way into the 21st century, the social structure and changing values in our society was studied. Working with young people, new programmes were developed and adopted.

The programme has eight points, each linked to a clause of the Law. There are compulsory challenges for each clause, and further challenges which may be chosen by the individual from a wide selection of options. Disabled members of the Association are integrated into units. Development in Central and Eastern Europe is opening up new contacts and possibilities for the Association. Pfadfinder und Pfadfinderinnen Österreichs is the Link Member to our sisters in Hungary.

Working with the Community

In addition to the service projects to the elderly, disabled and refugees in Austria, in 1985 the Pfadfinder und Pfadfinderinnen Österreichs created the 'George Week'. Every year all units work during this week and the money earned is used for Community Development projects. This has brought help for projects in Haiti, Senegal, Guatemala, Nepal, several African countries, 'Help Children Grow' in Egypt for two years, the Philippines, and India, where a school is under construction in the leprosy village near Sangam.

Outdoor and Environmental Activities

Camps for all age groups are held throughout the year and the Association welcomes Girl Guides/Girl Scouts from other countries. In 1981 the merged Association held its first international camp with 6,000 participants, including guests from 30 countries. In 1991 the second international camp of that size was organized. In 1993 the Association hosted Eurofolk.

Training

The training of youth leaders and trainers has priority within the Association and is regularly offered at district and national levels.

The Association has published a series of handbooks for each age group and for the leaders. The handbooks cover training, leading a unit, spiritual dimension, and international education.

Communication and Co-operation

The Pfadfinder und Pfadfinderinnen Österreichs enjoys good relations with the community. The media is kept informed and events are publicized. The Pfadfinder und Pfadfinderinnen Österreichs published a set of posters and folders, including a press information pack. *Ja*, *PPÖ-Brief* and *Units news* caters to young people and leaders.

Austrian Brownies, or Wichtels, are ages 7 to 10 years.

Bahamas

The Bahamas Girl Guides Association

Girl Guiding/Girl Scouting introduced: 1915
Became Associate Member of WAGGGS: 1975
Became Full Member of WAGGGS: 1978
Membership 1992: 2,744
Membership as % of female population: 2.08%
WAGGGS Region: Western Hemisphere

Guide

Promise

I promise that I will do my best:
To do my duty to God;
To serve the Queen, my Country and help other people;
and
To keep the Guide Law.

Law

1 A Guide is loyal and can be trusted.
2 A Guide is helpful.
3 A Guide is polite and considerate.
4 A Guide is friendly and a sister to all Guides.
5 A Guide is kind to animals and respects all living things.
6 A Guide is obedient.
7 A Guide has courage and is cheerful in all difficulties.
8 A Guide makes good use of her time.
9 A Guide takes care of her own possessions and those of other people.
10 A Guide is self-controlled in all she thinks, says and does.

Brownie Guide

Brownie Guide Promise

I promise that I will do my best:
To do my duty to God;
To serve the Queen, my Country and help other people;
and
To keep the Brownie Guide Law.

Brownie Guide Law

A Brownie Guide thinks of others before herself and does a good turn every day.

Development of the Movement in the Bahamas

Guiding was introduced to the Bahamas in 1915 and functioned in schools, playing an important part in the life of the colony.

Guiding activities continued from 1915 to 1935, but were then suspended for a time due to a lack of leaders. In 1946 Guiding was restarted in Nassau with the introduction of five units. In the same year the Association was visited by the World Chief Guide, who helped to inspire the girls and their leaders, resulting in the establishment of many new companies in Nassau and an increase in membership.

In the following years trainers from the Girl Guides Association (United Kingdom) visited the Association to help leaders to set up new companies and packs. The Association's headquarters were opened in Nassau in 1952.

The Programme

The majority of units in the Bahamas are attached to schools and the leaders are mainly teachers. Efforts are being made to encourage more young adults to join the Movement.

Working with the Community

Service is a very important part of the programme, in both the Guide and Ranger age groups. Members help out in hospitals and centres for the deaf, collect for the needy and visit the elderly and the disabled in their homes. Brownies also help with parties for underprivileged children.

Outdoor and Environmental Activities

Camping is a popular activity among members of the Association and Guides have been involved in environmental protection through tree planting projects.

Training

The Association holds one or two training sessions each year for leaders.

Communication and Co-operation

In 1952 the Association was represented abroad for the first time when two Guides attended an international camp in England. Since then Guides, leaders and commissioners have attended international trainings and events in other countries as well as welcoming visitors to the islands.

The Association informs the general public about Guiding through newspapers, radio and television.

The Association takes part in activities organized to celebrate the United Nations' International Years. The Bahamas Girl Guides Association works closely with the Scout Association, the Red Cross Society and the Salvation Army.

Bahrain

The Girl Guides Association of Bahrain

Girl Guiding/Girl Scouting introduced: 1970
Became Associate Member of WAGGGS: 1981
Became Full Member of WAGGGS: 1984
Membership 1992: 1,878
Membership as % of female population: 0.9%
Member: Arab Regional Group

Guide

Promise

On my honour, I promise that I will do my best
To do my duty to God and my country
To help other people in all circumstances
To obey the Guide Law.

Law

1 A Guide's honour is to be trusted.
2 A Guide is loyal to God, her country, her parents and to all those who are older than she.
3 A Guide's duty is to be useful and to help others.
4 A Guide is a friend to all and a sister to every other Guide.
5 A Guide is courteous.
6 A Guide is a friend to animals.
7 A Guide obeys fully the orders of her parents, the head of her division and her team's leader.
8 A Guide smiles under all difficulties and accepts them with patience and perseverance.
9 A Guide is thrifty and economical.
10 A Guide is pure in thought, in word and in deed.

Brownie

Brownie Promise

On my honour, I promise
To do my duty to God and my country
To help other people every day especially my parents
To obey the Brownies' Law.

Brownie Law

1 She is obedient to her elders.
2 Her head rules her heart.

Motto

Be Prepared

Age Groups

Ranger	18 - 23
Senior	16 - 18
Guide	12 - 15
Brownie	7 - 11

Development of the Movement in Bahrain

The Girl Guides Association of Bahrain was formed in 1970 when Guide companies were started in three secondary schools. By 1973 additional groups and six Brownie packs had been set up in primary and intermediate schools. The Association, one of the few organizations for girls in Bahrain, continues to expand and benefits from the support of Sheika Noura Isa Al-Kalifa, the daughter of the Emir. All companies and packs in Bahrain are attached to schools.

The Programme

The programme aims to prepare Bahraini girls to be useful and active citizens. It is designed to meet the needs of the country and includes duty to God; sincerity and respect for other people; respect for all living things and responsibility to oneself. Much of the programme is based on ideas taken from the WAGGGS' publication, *International Education: A Pathway to Understanding*, which has been translated into Arabic. Each age group has a specific programme encouraging members to develop creative abilities.

Working with the Community

Members of the Association carry out a variety of service projects including the distribution of equipment and dissemination of information during a national health week. Guides also help to

organize an annual traffic week.
Guides offer help in hospitals and nurseries and visit the elderly and disabled. The Association undertook a three-year child welfare project in co-operation with the Child Welfare Centre (supervised by the Ministry of Labour and Social Affairs) from 1987 to date. The programme focuses on entertaining the children and supplying necessary clothing and toys.

The Girl Guides Association of Bahrain organizes fundraising activities to support the Bahraini Guide Fund which helps the underprivileged.

In 1973 the Association established a national literacy programme. This ongoing programme has proved highly successful, particularly during 1990, International Literacy Year.

The Association distributes Eid (feast) dresses for the poor every year. The Guides also visit different villages every month to check all medicines and inoculation certificates.

Outdoor and Environmental Activities

Camping activities in Bahrain are often linked to service projects and are seen as being important in training girls in self-confidence and enjoyment of nature. The Association promotes environmental awareness through tree-planting projects, and cleaning public gardens and beaches. The first outdoor camp in the area took place over four days.

Training

The Girl Guides Association of Bahrain shares a training centre and facilities with the Scout Association but trainings are held separately. The Association has a training team responsible for preparing the training scheme and supervising its implementation. Basic trainings are held for new leaders and patrol leaders, and refresher courses for experienced leaders. Trainings are carried out at regional and national level, and Bahraini Guides also participate in Arab Regional trainings.

Bahrain is now able to translate material from the World Bureau and other Member Organizations into Arabic. This has enabled the training team to learn from the example of others and has greatly improved the quality of training in Bahrain.

Communication and Co-operation

Guiding is well accepted in the country and the public recognizes the contribution that it has made to the development of girls and women. All the Association's activities are reported in the newspapers. Bahrain has published many books on training, camping, outdoor activities, environment, fundraising and handicrafts, including translated documents.

Leaders have attended many international camps in different parts of the world as well as attending Arab Jamborees with their Guides and Brownies. In 1988 Bahrain became the home of the Arab Regional Bureau for Girl Guides, when the Bahraini Chief Commissioner was elected as Secretary General of the Bureau.

Guides learn first aid as part of the skills needed to carry out work in the community.

Bangladesh

Bangladesh Girl Guides Association

Founder Member of WAGGGS	
Girl Guiding/Girl Scouting introduced:	**1928**
Became Full Member of WAGGGS (under the name Bangladesh):	**1973**
Membership 1992†:	**31,196**
Membership as % of female population:	**0.05%**
WAGGGS Region:	**Asia Pacific**

Guide

Promise

On my honour, I promise that I will do my best:

1 To do my duty to God, and my country.
2 To help other people at all times.
3 To obey the Guide Laws.

Law

1 A Guide's honour is to be trusted.
2 A Guide is loyal.
3 A Guide's duty is to be useful and to help others.
4 A Guide is a friend to all, and a sister to every other Guide, no matter to what creed, country or class the other belongs.
5 A Guide is courteous.
6 A Guide is a friend to animals.
7 A Guide obeys orders.
8 A Guide smiles and sings under all difficulties.
9 A Guide is thrifty.
10 A Guide is pure in thought, word and deed.

Yellowbird

Yellowbird Promise

I promise to do my best:

1 To do my duty to God and my country.
2 To help other people every day especially those at home.

Yellowbird Law

1 The Yellowbird gives in to the older folk.
2 The Yellowbird does not give in to herself.

Age Groups

Rangers	17 - 25
Guides	11 - 16
Yellowbirds	6 - 10

Development of the Movement in Bangladesh

Since 1928 Girl Guides have been active in the area which is now Bangladesh. The Bangladesh Girl Guides Association was welcomed as a separate member of WAGGGS in 1973 and is now the country's largest national organization offering leadership training to girls and young women.

In addition, Guiding has been incorporated into the student curriculum at the college of physical education and at the institute for primary teachers' training, and every year more than 80 young women participate in training. Guiding is also an integral part of the secondary school curriculum for girls.

The Programme

Bangladesh Girl Guides Association uses an eight-point programme in all three branches under the headings: mind, character, physical fitness, outdoor enjoyment, relationships with people, creativity, readiness to help others and homecraft skills. The aim is to develop the full potential of each girl and encourage her to actively participate in the life of her community.

Working with the Community

Members of the Association are involved in many types of service including adult education, planting trees, digging canals, running campaigns to grow more food, launching nutrition projects, and farming fish and poultry.

Rangers are involved in community development in rural villages where they help to administer injections, distribute medicine, run courses on hygiene and family life education, and conduct surveys in slum areas.

Members give service, for example distributing relief materials and medicines, during and after natural disasters, sometimes in co-operation with other organizations. A special Guides Relief Fund was established after the floods and cyclone of 1988.

Bangladesh Girl Guides Association is well known for its youth welfare work and runs a primary school for the children of low-income families. The school has a special class for children with mental disabilities, and members organize social activities and sports days for the children. Bangladesh also operates a child day-care centre and a home for vagrant girls and orphans in Dhaka. The home was established to minimize the problem of vagrancy and to encourage the girls to be useful members of the community by offering them vocational skills training to help them achieve self-sufficiency. In addition to formal education, the girls are instructed in social skills and encouraged to take part in leisure activities.

Outdoor and Environmental Activities

District and regional camps are held each year and national camps every two years while special camps are organized for underprivileged Guides and for members of shelter homes. Guides also participate in cross-country walking, skiing, outdoor photography, and assist the organizers of sports federations.

The Association is involved in regular tree-planting projects in co-operation with the Bangladesh Forestry Department. In the summer Guides throughout the country organize programmes to plant and maintain trees at school premises, at roadsides, and in villages.

Training

In order to extend Guiding to every part of the country, the Association has trained 24 junior trainers to spread Guiding to villages under the leadership of the district commissioners. Training is also carried out at the Association's National Training Centre in Dhaka for leaders from remote villages.

The Association organizes many training courses on specialized subjects including batik print, cutting vegetables, and making and arranging artificial flowers. Training camps for patrol leaders and

Guides used these posters to educate the community in a village outside Dhaka about the benefits of planting trees.

adults are arranged as part of the camping programme.

Communication and Co-operation
Bangladesh Girl Guides Association encourages its members to take part in international events whenever possible. Bangladesh is twinned with the Girl Guides Association of Australia Incorporated on the Bangladesh-Australia Child Health project. It also works in co-operation with other national Girl Guide/Girl Scout organizations, receiving support for such projects as its home for vagrant children.

The Association liaises with the government and with national and international non-governmental organizations involved in work with children, young people and women. Activities include workshops, seminars and combined rallies and festivals. The association makes every effort to observe United Nations designated years.

Guiding in Bangladesh is well received by the authorities and the public. The Association organizes radio and television programmes for each age group, and Guides take part in cultural evenings of dance, music and drama to promote contact between members of the Movement and the public. The Association has produced a film show on Guiding in Bangladesh. Posters and banners on Guiding are featured on public display and the Association also publishes a quarterly periodical, *Sangbad Bichitra*.

Peace march in Dhaka, 1993.

Barbados

The Girl Guide Association of Barbados, (Inc.)

Girl Guiding/Girl Scouting introduced: 1918
Became Associate Member of WAGGGS: 1969
Became Full Member of WAGGGS: 1972
Membership 1992†: 3,158
Membership as % of female population: 2.43%
WAGGGS Region: Western Hemisphere

Promise
I promise that I will do my best:
To do my duty to God;
To serve the Queen and my Country and help other people; and
To keep the Guide Law.

Law
1 A Guide is loyal and can be trusted.
2 A Guide is helpful.
3 A Guide is polite and considerate.
4 A Guide is friendly and a sister to all Guides.
5 A Guide is kind to animals and respects all living things.
6 A Guide is obedient.
7 A Guide has courage and is cheerful in all difficulties.
8 A Guide makes good use of her time.
9 A Guide takes care of her own possessions and those of other people.
10 A Guide is self-controlled in all she thinks, says and does.

Motto
Be Prepared

Brownie Guide Promise
I promise I will do my best:
To do my duty to God;
To serve the Queen and my Country and help other people;
To keep the Brownie Guide Law.

Brownie Guide Law
A Brownie Guide thinks of others before herself and does a good turn every day.

Brownie Guide Motto
Lend a Hand

Age Groups

Ranger	16 - 21
Guide	11 - 16
Brownie Guide	6 - 11

Development of the Movement in Barbados

Guiding started in Barbados in 1918 and the following year the first rally was held at Government House. The Association was given impetus when Lord and Lady Baden-Powell visited the island in 1930 and on a return visit in 1964 when Lady Baden-Powell opened the new headquarters, Pax Hill (the hill of peace), after the Founder's home.

The first National Assembly was held in 1968 and has been an annual event ever since. A junior council was formed in 1976 with one young leader from each district providing a communications link at national level.

The Programme
In 1969 the Association introduced an eight-point programme incorporating physical fitness, the mind, outdoors enjoyment, homecraft skills, service to others, human relations, creativity and character. Guides also participate in the Duke of Edinburgh's Award Scheme.
The Association encourages the integration of girls with special needs into existing units whenever possible, although it has two units for girls with mental disabilities.

Guide

Brownie Guide

Working with the Community

The programme stresses the importance of community service, and Guides and Guiders have participated as counsellors and directors at government summer camps for children since 1989. Other service projects include helping at homes for children and the elderly, giving gifts of food to veterans of the First and Second World Wars, entertaining patients in hospital, and running errands for the housebound and elderly. The Barbados Association also works with migrants and immigrants.

Outdoor and Environmental Activities

The Association has a campsite at the northern end of the island and organizes many camping and hiking activities including pack holidays. Members also take an active part in conservation projects.

Training

The Association places much emphasis on training patrol leaders – both active and potential – and regular trainings are held, including three weekend sessions a year. Active interest is maintained through representation on the Caribbean Link Training Committee, and trainers conduct training sessions in neighbouring islands when requested.

Communication and Co-operation

Barbados is part of the Caribbean Link, set up for the purposes of consultation and mutual aid among countries of the Commonwealth and Caribbean islands. International education plays a major part in the programme, and girls visit Our Cabaña and international camps whenever possible. The Association has good relations with other organizations in Barbados and publicizes Guiding through the newspapers, radio and television. The Guide Association holds a joint national church service with the Scout Association every year on Thinking Day. Ranger Guides and Venture Scouts work closely together, and a special committee has been set up to further co-operation.

Belgium

Guidisme et Scoutisme en Belgique (GSB), Gidsen en Scoutsbeweging in Belgie (GSB)

Component Associations:
Scouts et Guides Pluralistes de Belgique (SGP)
Federatie voor Open Scoutisme (FOS)
Fédération des Guides Catholiques de Belgique (GCB)
Vlaams Verbond van de Katholieke Scouts en Meisjesgidsen (VVKSM)

Founder Member of WAGGGS	
Girl Guiding/Girl Scouting introduced:	**1915**
Membership 1992:	**50,910**
Membership as % of female population:	**1.01%**
WAGGGS Region:	**Europe**

Scouts et Guides Pluralistes de Belgique (SGP)

Promesse

Je promets sur mon honneur de m'efforcer:
de servir Dieu,
mon pays et l'amitié entre les hommes,
d'aider mon prochain en toute occasion,
de vivre la Loi de l'Eclaireuse.
ou
Je promets sur mon honneur de m'efforcer:
de servir un Idéal Elevé,
mon pays et l'amitié entre les hommes,
d'aider mon prochain en toute occasion,
de vivre la Loi de l'Eclaireuse.

Loi

L'éclaireuse:
1 dit la vérité et tient parole.
2 respecte les autres dans leurs convictions.
3 se rend utile.
4 travaille en équipe, offre son amitié.
5 fait preuve de courtoisie.
6 aime et protège la nature.
7 sait obéir.
8 aime l'effort et ne fait rien à moitié.
9 respecte le travail et le bien de tous.
10 reste maître de ses paroles, de ses actes, de ses pensées.

Devise

Toujours prête

Promesse des louveteaux

Je promets, avec l'aide de Dieu, de faire de mon mieux pour observer la loi des louveteaux et faire un bon tour chaque jour.
ou
Je promets de faire de mon mieux pour observer la loi des louveteaux et faire un bon tour chaque jour.

Loi des louveteaux

Un louveteau offre sa joie aux autres, puise sa force dans le clan et va jusqu'au bout de ses chasses.

Devise des louveteaux

De notre mieux

Promise

I promise on my honour to endeavour:
to serve God,
my country and friendship between people,
to help others on all occasions,
to live by the Girl Scout Law.
or
I promise on my honour to endeavour:
to serve a high ideal,
my country and friendship between people,
to help others on all occasions,
to live by the Girl Scout Law.

SGP Girl Scout

SGP Cub

FOS Guide

Law

A Girl Scout:
1 tells the truth and keeps her word;
2 respects the convictions of others;
3 makes herself useful;
4 is a good team member and is friendly to others;
5 shows courtesy;
6 loves and protects nature;
7 knows how to obey;
8 likes endeavour and does nothing by halves;
9 respects the work and belongings of all;
10 controls her words, acts and thoughts.

Motto

Be Prepared

Cub Promise

I promise, with God's help, to do my best to keep the Cub Law and to do a good turn every day.
or
I promise to do my best to keep the Cub Law and to do a good turn every day.

Cub Law

A Cub is cheerful with others, draws his strength from the Pack and does all he can.

Cub Motto

The best we can

Age Groups

Aînée	Ranger	16+
Eclaireuse	Girl Scout	11 - 17
Louveteau	Cub	8 - 12
Castor	Beaver	5 - 8

Federatie voor Open Scoutisme (FOS)

Belofte

Ik beloof, op mijn eer, te trachten:
trouw te zijn aan God, Koning, Land en troep,
de gidsenwet na te leven,
elke dag een goede daad te stellen.
of
Ik beloof, op mijn eer, te trachten:
trouw te zijn aan een Hoger Ideaal, Koning, Land en troep,
de gidsenwet na te leven,
elke dag een goede daad te stellen.

Wet

1 Een gids is oprecht en heeft maar één woord.
2 Een gids eerbiedigt de overtuiging van de anderen.
3 Een gids maakt zich nuttig.
4 Een gids is een vriend van allen.
5 Een gids is hoffelijk.
6 Een gids kan gehoorzamen.
7 Een gids staat open voor de natuur.
8 Een gids laat zich niet ontmoedigen.
9 Een gids is ijverig.
10 Een gids heeft eerbied voor zichzelf en voor de anderen.

Leuze

Steeds bereid

Cub Promise

Akela,
Graag wil ik welp zijn van onze horde.
Daarom wil ik mijn best doen om flink mee te spelen met alle welpen en oude wolven.

Cub Law

Als welp speel ik samen met de anderen in de jungle.
Ik luister naar de oude wolven.
Ik ben eerlijk, vriendelijk en ik hou vol.

Cub Motto

Wij doen ons best

Promise

I promise, on my honour, to try:
to be true to God, King, Country and company,
to live up to the Guide Law,
to do a good deed every day.
or
I promise, on my honour, to try:
to be true to a Higher Ideal, King, Country and company,
to live up to the Guide Law,
to do a good deed every day.

Law

1 A Guide is loyal and speaks the truth.
2 A Guide respects the convictions of others.
3 A Guide is useful.
4 A Guide is a friend to all.
5 A Guide is courteous.
6 A Guide knows how to obey.
7 A Guide appreciates nature.
8 A Guide does not become discouraged.
9 A Guide is good a worker.
10 A Guide respects herself and others.

Motto

Be prepared

Cub Promise
Akela,
I would like to be a cub in our pack.
Therefore I will do my best to play with all the cubs and wolves.

Cub Law
As a cub I play together with the others in the jungle.
I listen to the old wolves
I am honest, friendly and perseverant.

Cub Motto
We do our best

FOS Cub

Age Groups

Senior	Senior	16+
Gids	Guide	14 - 16
Jonggids	Junior Guide	11 - 13
Welp	Cub	8 - 10
Bever	Beaver	5 - 7

Fédération des Guides Catholiques de Belgique (GCB)

Promesse
Sûre de votre amitié,
je promets de vivre selon la Loi des guides:
pour aimer davantage les autres,
être active dans toutes les communautés,
et répondre ainsi à l'appel de Dieu.

La Loi
1 La guide est vraie, elle mérite et fait confiance.
2 La guide est loyale, elle tient ses engagements.
3 La guide rend service.
4 La guide veut être l'amie de tous.
5 La guide est courtoise, elle est attentionnée.
6 La guide aime la nature et protège la vie, elle peut y découvrir l'oeuvre de Dieu.
7 La guide sait obéir, elle va jusqu'au bout.
8 La guide partage sa joie de vivre.
9 La guide respecte le bien commun et participe à l'effort de tous.
10 La guide est simple, elle a du respect pour elle-même et les autres.

Devise
Toujours prête

Promesse des lutins
Avec l'aide du Seigneur Jésus
Je promets de faire de mon mieux et je choisis d'être ... ou de faire ... pour vivre selon les règles d'or des lutins.

Le Lutin est invité à personnaliser son engagement en le précisant au moyen d'un commentaire qui lui sera propre.

Loi des lutins
Quand un lutin écoute Jésus et les autres
- Le lutin pense d'abord aux autres
- Le lutin cherche toujours à faire plaisir
- Le lutin sème toujours la joie
- Le lutin est toujours vrai.

Devise des lutins
De notre mieux

Promise
Sure of your friendship,
I promise to live according to the Guide Law:
in order to love others more,
to be active throughout the community,
and thus to respond to God's call.

Law
1 A Guide is truthful, she can be trusted and trusts others.
2 A Guide is loyal, she honours her obligations.
3 A Guide is helpful and gives service.
4 A Guide wishes to be the friend of all.
5 A Guide is courteous, she is considerate.
6 A Guide loves nature and protects life, she is able to see in it the work of God.
7 A Guide knows how to obey, she carries things through to the end.
8 A Guide shares her delight in life.
9 A Guide respects the common good and participates in the endeavours of all.
10 A Guide is unaffected, she knows how to respect herself and others.

GCB Guide

Motto
Be prepared

Brownie Promise
With the help of the Lord Jesus
I promise to do my best and I choose to be ... or to do ... in order to live according to the Brownie Golden Rules.

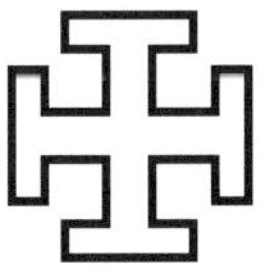

GCB Brownie

The Brownie may if she wishes insert her own words to make the Promise personal.

Brownie Law
When a Brownie listens to Jesus and others:
- The Brownie thinks first of others
- The Brownie always seeks to give happiness.

- The Brownie always spreads joy
- The Brownie is always truthful.

Brownie Motto
The best we can

Age Groups

Eclaireuse	Ranger	17+
Guide 'Horizon'	Horizon Guide	15-17
Guide 'Aventure'	Adventure Guide	11-14
Lutin	Brownie	7-11
Nuton	Nuton	5-7

VVKSM Guide

Vlaams Verbond van Katholieke Scouts en Meisjesgidsen (VVKSM)

Promise
The Association no longer uses a formulated Promise. Each member uses their own words to express their individual commitment to the Movement.

Gidsenwet
A text adapted to today's needs replaces the Girl Guide Law.

Als gids-verkenner wil ik leven:

Ik doe niet mee
met 't geprogrammeerde spel van de lunaparken.
Ik wil mezelf op een nieuwe manier ontdekken in wat ik kan,
in wat ik wil.
Ik durf geloven in de anderen en zoeken naar God.

Ik wil spelen, praten, lachen, vliegen en stil zijn.
Zomaar... of toch niet altidj zomaar.
Ik wil niet verstrikt geraken in de dagelijkse sleur en vastgeroeste ideeën
maar samen met de groep uit ons warme nest kruipen
en opkomen voor wereldvrede en solidair zijn met...
Ik pak niet enkel de kansen die voor 't grijpen liggen.
Ik neem zelf initiatief, soms risico's.
Dat weet ik.
Ik weet ook dat ik hierin niet alleen sta.
Ik ben geen eenzaat,
maar een stukje groep...
Een groep waar grote monden niet alles te zeggen hebben,
een groep waar ook ik mee beslis.
Ik ben mee verantwoordelijk.

Geregeld wil ik tijd maken
om met de ganse groep eens terug te blikken.
Niet als een pletwals door te drammen
Maar te zoeken welke richting we verder uitwillen.

Hiervoor zet ik me in
morgen en ook vandaag.

Jonggidsenwet
Wij zijn jongverkenners/jonggidsen/sheepsmakkers
Wij wagen het avontuur
Wij zijn kameraden en willen eerlijk zijn met elkaar
Wij willen samen werken en beslissen
Wij zeggen onze mening en luisteren naar die van anderen.

Zelf zet ik al eens de eerste stap
Ik help graag waar ik kan
Ik wil winnen en kan verliezen
Ik respecteer wat waardevol is: de mens, de natuur en het materiaal
Jezus' voorbeeld zal ons hierbij helpen.

Motto
Wees bereid

Kabouterswet
Wij doen ons best om het hier plezant te maken.
Wij willen eerlijk met de anderen spelen
hen geen pijn doen, geen verdriet
want dat helpt de vrede niet.
Zo wil God het graag en wij ook,
dus dat komt goed uit.
Toch is het niet gemakkelijk
en lukt het niet in één keer
dan is dat niet erg
want we zien elkaar véél meer.

Brownie Motto
Op ons best

Promise
The Association no longer uses a formulated Promise. Each member uses their own words to express their individual commitment to the Movement.

Guide Law
A text adapted to today's needs replaces the Girl Guide Law.

I am a Girl Guide and I want to live:

I choose
not to take part in programmed leisure;
I want to take a different look at myself.
What am I able to do?
What do I want to do?
I dare believe in the others and look for God.

I want to play, to laugh, to fly and to be quiet.
Without any reason at all... or still not always.
I do not want to get trapped in everyday routine and rusty ideas
but I want to get out of my cosy cover together with the group and fight for peace in the world and declare solidarity with...

I do not only take chances within my grips.
I take initiative,
sometimes I run risks, I know.
I also know I am not alone.
I am not a lonely girl,
but I am part of the group...
A group where not only Mr Big mouth has a say,
a group where I decide as well.
I am co-responsible.

At regular intervals I want to free up some time
to look back, together with the whole group.
Not to pull everything down
but to find which way we want to take.

That's what I want to work for
not only tomorrow but also today.

Junior Guide Law
We are junior Guides (junior boy scouts)
We challenge adventure
We are friends and we want to be honest with each other.
We want to work and decide together.
We say what we think and we listen to the others.

It happens that I take the first step.
I like to help wherever I can.
I want to win but I can lose.
I respect valuable objects and subjects:
Men, nature and matter.

Jesus' example will be our guide.

Motto
Be prepared

Brownie Law
We do our utmost to make it nice here.
We want to play fairly with the others.
We do not want to hurt them,
We do not want to cause them pain,
as it does not help peace.
God wants it this way and so do we,
hence that fits in very well.
Still, it is not easy
and it does not always work at once
but then, it does not matter
as we see each other many times more.

Brownie Motto
Do our best

Age Groups

Jin	Ranger	17+
Gids	Guide	14 - 17
Jonggids	Junior Guide	11 - 14
Kabouter	Brownie	8 - 11
Kapoen	Beaver	6 - 8

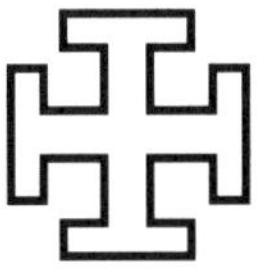
VVKSM Brownie

Development of the Movement in Belgium

Guiding in Belgium was officially registered in Brussels in 1915, although there were active groups before that date. In 1919, Belgium became a member of the International Council, and in 1928 a Founder Member of WAGGGS.
Belgian Guiding reflects the nature of the country. There are two linguistic communities – Flemish in the north and French in the south.

In 1979, its three merged Associations, together with the Guides Catholiques de Belgique and the Fédération des Scouts Catholiques de Belgique (five Associations in all) created a new co-ordinating committee to facilitate the exchange of ideas and promote the fundamental principles of Guiding and Scouting, while at the same time respecting the individual characteristics of each Association.

Guiding in Belgium is linked together by Guidisme et Scoutisme en Belgique, Gidsen en Scoutsbeweging in Belgie. GSB presents a united image to the public through the press.

Scouts et Guides Pluralistes de Belgique (SGP) and Federatie voor Open Scoutisme (FOS)

The former Boy Scouts of Belgium and Girl Guides of Belgium, which were non-denominational, merged in 1945 and Fédération des Eclaireuses et Eclaireurs (FEE) was formed for French-speaking members, and FOS for Flemish-speaking members. In 1992 the FEE was renamed the Scouts et Guides Pluralistes de Belgique (SGP). Apart from language, the differences between SGP and FOS are to be found mainly in the age groups.

The Programme
Both Associations' aim is to encourage young people to be open-minded socially, politically and ideologically. Any sincere philosophical or religious opinion is accepted and members are encouraged to express their opinions and to accept and respect those of others. The programmes are designed to prepare members to live in a pluralist society and to develop their own views.

Communication and Co-operation
Both Associations have prepared brochures on international aspects of Girl Guiding/Girl Scouting and both have good contacts with the press. SGP publishes three periodicals: *Point Barre* and *Relex-Echo* for leaders, *Plein Vent* for Girl Scouts and *Yaou* for Cubs. FOS publishes two periodicals: a monthly magazine, *Informatieblad*, for leaders; and a bi-monthly, *Totem*, for all members.

Fédération des Guides Catholiques de Belgique (GCB)

GCB is a single-sex organization, French-speaking and Roman Catholic. It has three main objectives: to recognize the needs of girls and young women, to increase participation, and to involve leaders in planning the programme and activities.

The Programme
As a result of a survey conducted at regional and district level, the programme for each age group has been updated and new guidelines have been published. Programmes are centred upon current issues, and the United Nations' International Years are observed. Work has centred on the community, women, peace, and on the partnership between different groups such as rich and poor, young people and adults, men and women. Much attention has been given to the importance of education of girls and young women.

Working with the Community
As part of its work with developing countries, the Association has provided training for refugees from Southeast Asia at its training centre at Mozet and has co-operated with the other Belgian Catholic Guide and Scout Associations and the Association des Girl Guides Luxembourgeoises in a twinning project with the Association des Guides du Rwanda.

Communication and Co-operation
International education is included in training programmes for leaders. GCB has increased its efforts to attend international gatherings and seminars and has prepared a brochure on international aspects of Girl Guiding/Girl Scouting.

GCB is often featured in the press and, on occasion, gives press conferences. The Association publishes a magazine for each age group: *Envoi*, published quarterly for leaders and those over 17; *Horiscope*, for Horizon Guides, *Tréfle* for Adventure Guides; and *Echo* for Brownies.

Brownies from the GCB.

Vlaams Verbond van Katholieke Scouts en Meisjesgidsen (VVKSM)

In 1972, VVKM, Flemish-speaking and Catholic, merged with the parallel Scout Association, VVKS, and became the Vlaams Verbond van Katholieke Scouts en Meisjesgidsen (VVKSM). Units are free to merge or to work separately. All teams are merged at district, regional and national level.

The Programme

The programme is the same for girls and boys, whether in merged units or not, and can be adapted by the leaders according to the needs of the unit. The Association aims to contribute to a total, social and personal, education of its members. The programme stresses community development, peace, environment and working with people with special needs. Education for Faith is integrated into the Association's programme and activities. The Association encourages the integration of members with special needs into existing units wherever possible although special units do exist.

Working with the Community

VVKSM has formed the Jeunesse Outremer (Youth Overseas) with GCB and the Fédération des Scouts Catholiques to help community development projects undertaken by other Member Organizations. They have a special interest in Rwanda. VVKSM emphasizes the integration of minorities such as the underprivileged and immigrants.

Outdoor and Environmental Activities

The Association sees camping as a valuable method of bringing young people into contact with nature and environmental concerns, with peace and with God.

Communication and Co-operation

International education is included in training programmes for leaders. VVKSM has a brochure on international aspects of Girl Guiding/Girl Scouting. VVKSM has contacts with the press and publishes a magazine for leaders: *Over en Weer*, and a magazine for each age group.

Belize

The Girl Guides Association of Belize

Girl Guiding/Girl Scouting introduced:	**1937**
Became Associate Member of WAGGGS:	**1987**
Became Full Member of WAGGGS:	**1993**
Membership 1992:	**1,083**
Membership as % of female population:	**1.14%**
WAGGGS Region:	**Western Hemisphere**

Guide

Promise

I promise that I will do my best;
To do my duty to God
To serve the Queen and my
Country and help other people and
To keep the Guide Law.

Law

1 A Guide is loyal and can be trusted.
2 A Guide is helpful.
3 A Guide is polite and considerate.
4 A Guide is friendly and a sister to all Guides.
5 A Guide is kind to animals and respects all living things.
6 A Guide is obedient.
7 A Guide has courage and is cheerful in all difficulties.
8 A Guide makes good use of her time.
9 A Guide takes care of her own possessions and those of other people.
10 A Guide is self-controlled in all she thinks, says and does.

Motto

Be prepared

Brownie Guide

Brownie Guide Promise

I promise I will do my best;
To do my duty to God
To serve the Queen and my
Country and help other people and
To keep the Brownie Guide Law.

Brownie Guide Law

A Brownie Guide thinks of others before herself and does a good turn every day.

Brownie Guide Motto

Lend a hand

Age Groups

Ranger Guides	14 - 19
Guides	11 - 14
Brownies	7 - 11

Development of the Movement in Belize

Guiding was introduced in British Honduras (now known as Belize) in 1937, when six companies were formed in Belize City under church sponsorship. In the same year the Association was registered with The Girl Guides Association (United Kingdom) as the British Honduras Branch of the Girl Guides Association.

A rally held in Belize City in 1938 attracted many more girls to Guiding. By 1939 Guide groups had been established at Stann Creek with sponsorship from the Methodist, Anglican and Roman Catholic churches. The first Brownie packs were formed in 1948 in Belize City and the first Ranger company in 1949.

In 1973, when the country changed its name to Belize, the Association became known as the Belize Branch of the Girl Guides Association. The Association grew steadily, helped in its development by trainers from the United Kingdom and the Caribbean Link. In 1986 The Girl Guides Association (United Kingdom) signed a Deed of Transfer, giving the Girl Guides Association of Belize self-government in all areas of work.

The Programme

The programme is based on an eight-point programme incorporating physical fitness, the mind, outdoors enjoyment, homecraft skills, service to others, human relations, creativity and character.

One company in Belize city makes a particular effort to welcome girls with disabilities and has forged links with a local special school.

Working with the Community

The Rangers of Belize City run a pre-school 'Sunshine Stimulation Centre' for approximately 40 children, funded by contributions from members. Guides also participate in clean-up campaigns in their communities, keep church halls and compounds clean, and give service in local institutions.

Outdoor and Environmental Activities

The government has given the Association a five-acre plot of land to be used as a permanent campsite and training centre. A special fund has been established to finance its development. National and training camps for Guides, Rangers and adult leaders are held annually.

Training

Leaders' training incorporates an understanding of Guide methods, programmes and badge schemes, as well as leadership skills. Training sessions are carried out regularly in Belize City and at least once every three months in the districts. A training programme operating at a teacher training college has led to the recruitment of many young teachers into the Movement. Friends of the Movement assist with training, especially in areas such as first aid, camping and outdoor activities.

Communication and Co-operation

The Association makes every effort to participate in international events and is a member of the Caribbean Link, set up for the purposes of consultation and mutual aid among Guide Associations in Commonwealth countries and islands of the Caribbean. Guides and leaders have attended several events at Our Cabaña, WAGGGS' World Centre in Mexico, and, when possible, take part in activities organized by neighbouring Caribbean islands, and other Associations.

Guiding is well received by the general public. Both national and local governments are very supportive of the Movement and the national government provides the Association with a small grant. Guides in Belize receive support from the churches which provide meeting places for some companies.

The Association's monthly newsletter, started in 1985, is valuable both as a training tool and as a means of communication. Belize also publicizes its activities on radio and television.

The Girl Guides Association of Belize has undertaken several projects with the Scout Association in Belize and is a member of the Council of Voluntary Social Services (CVSS).

Brownies, Guides and Guiders welcome Martha M. de Hernandez, Western Hemisphere Committee, at the entrance of Belize City.

People's Republic of Benin

Scoutisme Beninois
(Guides du Bénin)

Girl Guiding/Girl Scouting introduced: 1954
Became Associate Member of WAGGGS: 1963
Membership 1992: 407
Membership as % of female population: 0.02%
WAGGGS Region: Africa

Guide

Promesse
Sur mon honneur je m'engage à servir Dieu et mon pays en toute circonstance à aider mon prochain et à observer la loi des guides.

Loi
1 La guide n'a qu'une parole.
2 La guide est loyale.
3 La guide est utile à ses parents, ses camarades et son pays.
4 La guide est l'amie de tous.
5 La guide est courtoise et sait obéir.
6 La guide découvre la nature et la protège.
7 La guide est toujours de bonne humeur.
8 La guide est économe et travailleuse.
9 La guide est propre dans ses pensées, ses paroles et ses actes.
10 La guide est civiquement consciente et sert les intérêts du peuple béninois.

Devise
Toujours prête

Brownie

Promesse des Jeannettes
Je promets de faire de mon mieux: pour être fidèle à Dieu, à la Patrie, à mes parents, à la loi de la ronde, et pour faire chaque jour un plaisir à quelqu'un.

Loi des Jeannettes
Une jeannette est toujours propre.
Une jeannette est toujours active.
Une jeannette est toujours gaie.
Une jeannette dit toujours vrai.
Une jeannette pense d'abord aux autres.

Devise des Jeannettes
De notre mieux

Promise
On my honour, I undertake to serve God and my country in all circumstances to help others and to keep the Guide Law.

Law
1 A Guide keeps her word.
2 A Guide is loyal.
3 A Guide is useful to her parents, friends and country.
4 A Guide is a friend to all.
5 A Guide is courteous and knows how to obey.
6 A Guide learns about Nature and protects it.
7 A Guide is always good-tempered.
8 A Guide is thrifty and hardworking.
9 A Guide is pure in her thoughts, her words and her deeds.
10 A Guide is a responsible citizen and acts for the good of the people of Benin.

Motto
Always prepared

Brownie Promise
I promise to do my best: to be faithful to God, my Country, my parents and the Law of the Pack, and to do a good turn to someone every day.

Brownie Law
A Brownie is always clean.
A Brownie is always active.
A Brownie is always cheerful.
A Brownie always tells the truth.
A Brownie thinks first of others.

Brownie Motto
The best we can

Age Groups

Guide aînée	Ranger	16+
Guide	Guide	11 - 16
Jeannette	Brownie	8 - 11

Development of the Movement in Benin

Guiding in Benin began in 1954 in a girls' secondary school at Porto Novo. Two years later a Guide camp was held, and in 1956 the 1st Cotonou Guide company was officially registered. During the following year several other companies were formed, and by 1957 Brownie packs and Ranger units had also been introduced. The Association was officially established by the end of 1960. About the same time Guide companies began to adopt villages where they carried out service projects with the community. Guiding has now developed in both urban and rural areas.

The Programme

Guides du Benin adopt a theme each year, to be used as a basis for its programme for all age groups.

Working with the Community

Rangers help women in rural villages by organizing classes in literacy, childcare, hygiene and needlecraft. The Association has also worked with a national home economics organization to provide a training course in home economics for girls from rural areas, which is funded by UNESCO.

Outdoor and Environmental Activities

Camps and holiday camps are popular amongst members of the Association.

Training

Regional training camps are held at least twice a year for leaders and weekend trainings are regularly organized by the Association's training team.

Communication and Co-operation

The Association has co-operated with other organizations at national level on specific projects and has worked with UNICEF.

Bolivia

Asociación de Guías Scouts de Bolivia

Girl Guiding/Girl Scouting introduced:	**1915**
Became Associate Member of WAGGGS:	**1966**
Became Full Member of WAGGGS:	**1978**
Membership 1992†:	**700**
Membership as % of female population:	**0.01%**
WAGGGS Region:	**Western Hemisphere**

Girl Scout

Intermediate

Little Wing

Promesa

Yo prometo, por mi honor, hacer cuanto de mí dependa, para:
Cumplir con mi deber hacia Dios y mi Patria; Ser útil al prójimo en todo momento y obedecer la Ley Guía-Scout.

Ley

1 La Guía-Scout es persona en cuyo honor se puede confiar.
2 La Guía-Scout es leal.
3 El deber de la Guía-Scout es ser útil y ayudar a otros.
4 La Guía-Scout es amiga de todos y hermana de toda Guía-Scout.
5 La Guía-Scout es cortés.
6 La Guía-Scout es buena con los animales.
7 La Guía-Scout obedece órdenes.
8 La Guía-Scout sonríe y canta en todas las dificultades.
9 La Guía-Scout es económica.
10 La Guía-Scout es pura de pensamiento, palabra y obra.

Lema

Siempre Lista

Promesa de la Alita

Yo prometo hacer lo mejor por amor a Dios y a mi Patria, ayudar a todos, y en especial a los de mi casa.

Lema de la Alita

Ayudar a todos

Promise

I promise, on my honour, to do my best:
To do my duty to God and my Country;
To help other people at all times, and to obey the Guide-Scout Law.

Law

1 A Guide-Scout is a person whose honour is to be trusted.
2 A Guide-Scout is loyal.
3 A Guide-Scout's duty is to be useful and to help others.
4 A Guide-Scout is a friend to all and a sister to every other Guide-Scout.
5 A Guide-Scout is courteous.
6 A Guide-Scout is kind to animals.
7 A Guide-Scout obeys orders.
8 A Guide-Scout smiles and sings under all difficulties.
9 A Guide-Scout is thrifty.
10 A Guide-Scout is pure in thought, word and deed.

Motto

Be prepared

Little Wing Promise

I promise to do my best for the love of God and my Country, to help everyone, especially those at home.

Little Wing Motto

Help everyone

Age Groups

Guía Mayor	Senior Guide	15-18
Intermedias	Intermediates	13-14
Pre Intermedias	Pre-Intermediates	11-12
Alita	Little Wing	6-10

Development of the Movement in Bolivia

Although the Movement was introduced in Bolivia in 1915 the first contact with WAGGGS was not made until 1954 when the Western Hemisphere Travelling

Commissioner visited Bolivia. The Asociación de Muchachas Guías de Bolivia was established in 1958.

The Association is working hard to develop units in other regions and to strengthen the Movement in other areas.

In 1990 the Girl Scouts in Bolivia received a very special 75th anniversary present from the Bolivian Government, 'The Condor of the Andes Jewel'. The Jewel represents the greatest honour awarded by the Bolivian Government to outstanding people or organizations.

The Programme
The Asociación de Guías Scouts de Bolivia is adapting its programme to meet the changing needs of its members and their country, and to help them overcome the problems of modern society.

Working with the Community
The Association encourages its members to render service to the community. Various projects have been undertaken such as the construction of a health centre in Tiraque (Cochabamba), a library in Villazón and a pharmacy in Cotagaita (Potosí).

Outdoor and Environmental Activities
Girl Scouts in Bolivia are involved in tree-planting activities and the Association has also launched a water project supported by German Association Bund der Pfadfinderinnen un Pfadfinder (BdP).

Training
The Association's Manual for Guiders has recently been revised, as have the training programmes for each of the branches. A National Training Event is held each year, supported by training courses within local Councils. A National Team of Trainers has been established to form a permanent training workshop to introduce trainers to all areas.

Communication and Co-operation
In recent years many Bolivian Guides have been encouraged to attend international events and to visit the World Centres. This international experience has greatly influenced the Association's activities within the country.

The Association has been a member of La Coordinadora de la Mujer (the Co-ordinating Committee for Women), a co-ordination agency for non-governmental organizations, since 1989. The agency works with women in education, health and production projects. For the last 20 years, the Asociación de Guías Scouts de Bolivia has also sold cards and calendars for UNICEF.

Guides prepare a song during training session.

Botswana

Botswana Girl Guides Association

Girl Guiding/Girl Scouting introduced:	**1924**
Became Associate Member of WAGGGS:	**1969**
Became Full Member of WAGGGS:	**1984**
Membership 1992:	**4,281**
Membership as % of female population:	**0.62%**
WAGGGS Region:	**Africa**

Girl Guide

Tsholofetso ya bokaedi

Ke solofetsa gore ke tlaa dira bojotlhe jwa me:
Go direla Modimo tshwanelo ya me,
Go direla lefatshe la gaetsho le go thusa batho ba bangwe
le
Go tshegetsa molao wa Bokaedi.

Melao ya Bokaedi

1 Mokaedi o boineelo, gape o ka ikanngwa.
2 Mokaedi o na le thuso.
3 Mokaedi o maitseo, gape o a akanyetsa.
4 Mokaedi o na le botsalano, e bile ke ngwana wa ga mma-Bakaedi ba bangwe.
5 Mokaedi o pelotlhomogi mo diphologolong gape o dibela dilo tsotlhe tse di tshelang.
6 Mokaedi o na le kutlo.
7 Mokaedi o pelokgale e bile o nna pelotshweu mo gare ga mathata otlhe.
8 Mokaedi o sola nako ya gagwe molemo.
9 Mokaedi o tlhokomela ditsa-gagwe le tsa batho ba bangwe.
10 Mokaedi o ikefa mo go tsotlhe tse o di akanyang, tse o di buang le tse o di dirang.

Sekao

Nna o ipaakantse

Sunbeam

Sunbeam Promise

Ke solofetsa gore ke tlaa dira bojotlhe jwa me: Go direla Modimo tshwanelo ya me,
Go direla lefatshe la gaetsho le go thusa batho ba bangwe; le
Go tshegetsa molao wa Marang a Letsatsi.

Sunbeam Law

Lerang la Letsatsi le boammaaruri, le boikokobetso, le tletse boitumelo,
Lerang la Letsatsi le akanyetsa ba bangwe pele le ikgopola.

Sunbeam Motto

Kwa godimo – dimo – dimo

Promise

I promise that I will do my best:
To do my duty to God,
To serve my country and to help other people
and
To keep the Guide Law.

Law

1 A Guide is loyal and can be trusted.
2 A Guide is helpful.
3 A Guide is polite and considerate.
4 A Guide is friendly and a sister to every other Guide.
5 A Guide is kind to animals and respects all living things.
6 A Guide is obedient.
7 A Guide has courage and is cheerful in all difficulties.
8 A Guide makes good use of her time.
9 A Guide takes care of her own possessions and those of other people.
10 A Guide is self-controlled in all she thinks, says and does.

Motto

Be Prepared

Sunbeam Promise

I promise that I will do my best:
To do my duty to God,
To serve my country and to help other people; and
To keep the Sunbeam Law.

Sunbeam Law

A Sunbeam is truthful, obedient and cheerful,
A Sunbeam thinks of others before herself.

Sunbeam Motto

Up, up, upwards

Age Groups

Senior	16-21
Girl Guide	11-15
Sunbeam	7-10

Development of the Movement in Botswana

Guiding in Botswana (then called Bechuanaland Protectorate) began in 1924 after a young girl, returning home to Kanye from boarding school in England, contacted other girls and interested them in the Movement. The Poppy patrol, with six members, was formed and by the end of the year a Brownie six had also started.

In 1928 a company of Girl Wayfarers, an organization for African girls working on similar lines to Guiding, was started by the wife of a missionary living in Kanye. Numbers grew steadily and interest in the Movement spread throughout the country. In 1936 the Girl Wayfarers, by affiliation with WAGGGS, became Wayfarer Guides, and by 1945 there was one Movement for all the girls in Botswana whose members were known as Girl Guides and Sunbeams. The Girl Guides Association (United Kingdom), the Girl Guides Association of South Africa and members of the Movement in Belgium gave valuable training assistance to the developing Movement in Botswana.

In 1966 the country became independent and the Girl Guides Association (United Kingdom) approved a deed of transfer making the Botswana Girl Guides Association self-governing in all areas of work.

The Programme

The Association uses an eight-point programme under the headings keeping fit, becoming a homemaker, giving service, keeping the Guide Law, getting to know people, enjoying the outdoors, thinking for oneself, and exploring the arts.

Working with the Community

The Association operates two centres offering skills training to school-leavers in Serowe and Gaborone. The centres aim to help girls, mostly from rural areas, to be self-sufficient and to support themselves on a self-employed basis. Instruction is offered in food and nutrition, sewing, crafts, laundry work and home management as well as English. In 1993 two student teachers from the University of Botswana were at the centre for three months doing their practice teaching, one in agriculture and the other in English.

The Bakaedi Literacy School for children is another noteworthy project undertaken by the Guides. Since it was introduced in 1976 more than 200 children have progressed through the school to take up places in schools within the regular education system. In 1986 Botswana was awarded an Honourable Mention in the UNESCO International Reading Association Literacy Prize for this project.

The Ramotswa Guides have an on-going project with a destitute woman. They put up a flat with a toilet and fenced the yard. The Guides keep the place neat and tidy all the time and look after her.

The Association is frequently asked to perform traditional dances, issue programmes and clean up at National Celebrations. Some local hotels use the Gaborone Centre students when catering major events. They have also been used by the Health Clinics when they have special activities, like publicising the AIDS Campaign.

Outdoor and Environmental Activities

Apart from tree-planting, which is plagued by constant droughts, some groups of Sunbeams have been working on the "Water is Life" Project. One group had a lot of support from the Westwood Primary School which allowed them to have a week-long exhibition. The Association continues to support tree-planting activities.

Training

Training is on-going, but needs to increase. The Executive Committee has decided to review training and camping. The Senior Branch is targeted to reflect renewed support from secondary schools. Guiding is still scattered all over the country, but adult leaders are still in demand.

Communication and Co-operation

The Botswana Girl Guides Association corresponds with several Girl Guide/Girl Scout Associations and has sent representatives to international trainings and gatherings. In addition, the Gabarone Girl Guides Youth Centre is a product of a twinning relationship with Girl Guides in New Brunswick, Canada.

The activities of the Botswana Girl Guides Association are reported in the national press and on the radio, and the Association, which is held in high esteem by the general public, also publicizes its activities through a biennial newsletter.

The Botswana Girl Guides Association is a member of the Youth Council and co-operates with the Red Cross Society, the YWCA, Botswana Christian Council, Botswana Council of Women and other voluntary and governmental organizations.

The Association still co-operates with other non-governmental organizations in the country. It is also a member of the committee that is co-ordinated by the Women's Affairs Unit of the Ministry of Labour and Home Affairs, under which non-governmental organizations are listed.

Brazil

Federação das Bandeirantes do Brasil
(Federation of Girl Guides of Brazil)

Girl Guiding/Girl Scouting introduced: 1919
Became Full Member of WAGGGS: 1930
Membership 1992: 5,846
Membership as % of female population: 0.01%
WAGGGS Region: Western Hemisphere

Promise
I will do my best:
To achieve personal improvement;
To participate actively and responsibly in my community;
To seek a faith in God and
To live according to the Guide Law.

Law
A Guide shall strive for universal brotherhood, duty to others, self-discipline, respect for nature, to overcome egotism, pessimism, racial prejudice, religious intolerance, class distinction.

This Guide Promise and Law is based on the concept of the original Promise and Law. If she prefers, a Guide may choose to make the Promise and accept the Law in its original form as laid down by the Founder.

Motto
Semper Parata* Be Prepared

**An interpretation in Latin of Be Prepared.*

Age Groups

Guia	Ranger	15-18
Bandeirante 2	Guide	12-15
Bandeirante 1	Junior Guide	9-12
Ciranda	Brownie	6-9

Development of the Movement in Brazil

Guiding in Brazil began in Rio de Janeiro in 1919 following a letter from Olave, Lady Baden-Powell, to the authorities responsible for the education of girls. The Federação celebrates 13 August as Foundation Day, the date on which the first 11 Guides (Bandeirantes) made their Promise in 1919. In 1930 Brazil became the first South American association to be a member of WAGGGS.

Guide

The Programme
The Federação has developed an educational programme which is divided into four age groups corresponding to stages of development of girls and young women. The programmes are reviewed and updated on a yearly basis in order to maintain the girls' interest in the method and principles of the Movement. Programme elements include activities such as camping, games, handicrafts, domestic skills and art.

The Federação das Bandeirantes do Brasil is an organization for girls and young women, however there have been experimental co-education groups in some regions since 1970.

Working with the Community
Community development is an important part of the Federation's activities.

The Brasilia Community Project, involving communities around the country's capital, aims to provide inhabitants with a means of achieving self-sufficiency and relief from housing problems, malnutrition and disease. The project includes handicraft courses, and two nurseries which provide food and education for young children and free their mothers for work. In addition, the project provides occupational therapy for the elderly, advice to pregnant women, and medical consultations and recreational activities for children and young people. The project is run by

Brownie

Guides, who are aided by volunteers from Brasilia and members of the Trefoil Guild. Handicrafts produced are sold in bazaars organized by Guides elsewhere, and the resulting revenue helps to finance the project.

Bandeirantes cut and prepare the leaves for the Tree of Life during the Global Forum held by the UN in Rio de Janeiro, 1992.

Outdoor and Environmental Activities

Guides participate in campaigns against air and water pollution, and protect trees and wildlife. Their camp training includes nature preservation and conservation. A national environmental project 'Nature: How to Know and Love It' focusing on pollution, forest damage, flora and fauna, and water has been in progress since 1989.

A four-year national Ranger project, Health and Environmental Preservation, was also implemented in 1989 aiming to promote national awareness about health and environmental preservation among young people.

Communication and Co-operation

Members of the Federação das Bandeirantes do Brasil participate in international activities whenever possible, and international education is an integral part of the programme.

Brazil co-operates with Norway on a series of community programmes, including projects focusing on children, the elderly and expectant mothers.

The Federação utilizes the media to promote Guiding within the country and publishes a bimonthly periodical, *Bandeirantes*.

Whenever possible the Federação co-operates with other organizations involved in welfare and education. The Federação's work is recognized by government agencies which often provide funding. The Federação supports the United Nations' International Years and related projects are incorporated into the programme. Many members support UNICEF by selling Christmas cards and calendars produced by the agency.
The Movement participated and was very active during the 1992 Earth Summit & Global Forum in Rio de Janeiro.

Brunei Darussalam

Persatuan Pandu Puteri Negara Brunei Darussalam
(Girl Guides Association of Negara Brunei Darussalam)

Girl Guiding/Girl Scouting introduced:	**1951**
Became Associate Member of WAGGGS:	**1987**
Membership 1992†:	**994**
Membership as % of female population:	**0.78%**
WAGGGS Region:	**Asia Pacific**

Promise

Bahawa dengan sesungguhnya saya
berjanji dengan sedaya upaya:
Menunaikan kewajipan saya kepada
Allah, taat setia kepada Kebawah
Duli Yang Maha Mulia Paduka Seri
Baginda Sultan dan Yang Dipertuan
Negara Brunei Darussalam,
Menolong orang setiap masa dan
Mematuhi undang-undang Pandu Puteri.

Law

1 Seorang Pandu Puteri boleh dipercayai.
2 Seorang Pandu Puteri suka membantu orang
3 Seorang Pandu Puteri berbudi bahasa dan bertimbang rasa.
4 Seorang Pandu Puteri adalah sahabat kepada semua orang dan semua Pandu Puteri yang lain.
5 Seorang Pandu Puteri sayang kepada binatang dan hormat kepada benda hidup.
6 Seorang Pandu Puteri sentiasa menurut perintah.
7 Seorang Pandu Puteri mempunyai keazaman dan riang dalam menghadapi kesusahan.
8 Seorang Pandu Puteri berjimat cermat dan menggunakan masanya dengan baik.
9 Seorang Pandu Puteri memelihara harta bendanya dan kepunyaan orang lain.
10 Seorang Pandu Puteri dapat mengawal diri dalam apa jua yang difikirkan, dikatakan dan dilakukan.

Motto

Selalu sedia.

Promise

I promise that I will do my best;
To do my duty to Allah
To serve His Majesty the Sultan
and Yang DiPertuan Negara Brunei
Darussalam
and help other people and
To keep the Guide Law.

Law

1 A Guide is loyal and can be trusted.
2 A Guide is helpful.
3 A Guide is polite and considerate.
4 A Guide is friendly and a sister to all Guides.
5 A Guide is kind to animals and respects all living things.
6 A Guide is obedient.
7 A Guide has courage and is cheerful in all difficulties.
8 A Guide makes good use of her time.
9 A Guide takes care of her own possessions and those of other people.
10 A Guide is self-controlled in all she thinks, says and does.

Motto

Be prepared

Guide

Brownie Guide Promise

Bahawa dengan sesungguhnya saya
berjanji dengan sedaya upaya:
Menunaikan kewajipan saya kepada
Allah, taat setia kepada Kebawah
Duli Yang Maha Mulia Paduka Seri
Baginda Sultan dan Yang Dipertuan
Negara Brunei Darussalam,
Menolong orang setiap masa dan
Mematuhu undang-undang Tunas Puteri.

Brownie Guide Law

Tunas Puteri mementingkan orang lain lebih dari dirinya sendiri dan menolong orang setiap masa.

Brownie Guide

Brownie shows her badges and patches.

Brownie Guide Motto
Sentiasa menolong.

Brownie Guide Promise
I promise I will do my best;
To do my duty to Allah
To serve His Majesty the Sultan
and Yang DiPertuan Negara Brunei Darussalam
and help other people and
To keep the Brownie Guide Law.

Brownie Guide Law
A Brownie Guide thinks of others before herself and does a good turn every day.

Brownie Guide Motto
Lend a hand

Development of the Movement in Negara Brunei Darussalam

In 1951 the Brunei branch of the Girl Guides Association was registered in the United Kingdom. Following a training camp in Singapore in 1954, the first Guide company was formed in the capital, Brunei Town. A Brownie pack was started in Brunei Town in the same year.

More new companies were formed following a visit by a trainer from the United Kingdom in 1964, and that year Her Highness Pengiran Anak Puteri Noor Ehsan accepted the position of State Commissioner, which greatly encouraged the members. In 1966 the position of Organization Commissioner for the Association was established within the State Education Department and this further helped to promote Guiding.

Following the resignation of the Association's President in 1972, membership dropped, and companies and packs closed. But in September 1983 Her Royal Highness Paduka Seri Pengiran Anak Puteri Masna became President of the Association. She instigated new activities and programmes which began to revitalize Guiding. A major campaign for membership was launched which was very successful.

Brunei Darussalam became independent in 1984, and in 1986 the Girl Guides Association (United Kingdom) signed a Deed of Transfer, giving the Girl Guides Association of Negara Brunei Darussalam self-government in all areas of work.

The Programme
The Association uses an eight-point programme based on keeping fit, becoming a homemaker, giving service, keeping the Guide Law, getting to know people, enjoying the outdoors, thinking for yourself and exploring the arts.

Working with the Community
Guides and Brownies give community service by visiting hospitals and a home for children with special needs where they entertain the residents. Members also help at national sports meetings and with school activities. The Association organizes an annual reading competition for its members, and Guides and Brownies help members of the community in the course of the annual job week.

Outdoor and Environmental Activities
The Guiding year in Negara Brunei Darussalam revolves around several annual activities, including many outdoor activities such as annual games and rallies, annual badminton and volley ball tournaments, and state camps.

Communication and Co-operation
The Association makes every effort to send participants to international events. Guides and leaders regularly attend camps held in neighbouring countries and in the United Kingdom.

The Guides are held in high esteem by the general public and government authorities. They are frequently invited to participate in national activities such as National Day Celebrations and Royal Birthdays. A State Rally is held annually when Guides, Brownies and leaders from all areas of the country gather in the capital to compete for various awards offered by the Association. In 1988 the Association launched a quarterly newsletter, *Warta Pandu Puteri.*

The Association participates with other youth organizations, in particular with the national Scout Association.

The Association is one of the founder members of the Council of Women of Brunei Darussalam, which is a member of the ASEAN Confederation of Women's Organizations.

Burkina Faso

L'Association des Guides du Burkina Faso

Girl Guiding/Girl Scouting introduced: 1955
Became Associate Member of WAGGGS: 1972
Membership 1992: 2,289
Membership as % of female population: 0.05%
WAGGGS Region: Africa

Guide

Promesse
Sur mon honneur et avec la grâce de Dieu, je m'engage à servir de mon mieux Dieu, l'Eglise, ma Patrie, à aider mon prochain en toute circonstance et à observer la Loi des Guides.

Loi
1 La Guide est croyante, elle vit sa foi
2 La Guide est serviable et obéissante
3 La Guide est soeur de toute autre Guide et ouverte à tous
4 La Guide est respectueuse et accueillante
5 La Guide respecte et améliore la nature
6 La Guide ne craint pas l'effort, elle ne fait rien à moitié
7 La Guide garde courage et sourit même dans les difficultés
8 La Guide est économe et a le sens du bien commun
9 La Guide se respecte, elle est droite dans des pensées, ses paroles et ses actes.

Promise
On my honour and with God's help, I commit myself to do my best to serve God, the Church and my country; to help my neighbour in all circumstances and to observe the Guide Law.

Law
1 A Girl Guide believes in God and her faith guides her life
2 A Girl Guide is helpful and obedient
3 A Girl Guide is a sister to every other Guide and open to all
4 A Girl Guide is respectful and friendly
5 A Girl Guide respects and improves nature
6 A Girl Guide is not afraid of hard work and never does anything half-heartedly
7 A Girl Guide keeps calm and smiles even when in difficulties
8 A Girl Guide is thrifty and has a sense of the common good
9 A Girl Guide respects herself, and is pure in thought, word and deed.

Development of the Movement in Burkina Faso

Guiding in Burkina Faso, formerly known as Upper Volta, began in 1955, but for almost 15 years it was confined to towns, where it existed mostly in schools. In 1971 Guiding started to become established in rural areas, and the Association, l'Association des Guides de Haute-Volta, was organized into provinces, districts and companies. In 1984 the Association changed its name to the Association des Guides du Burkina Faso.

The Programme
The programme is reviewed annually and is based on four signposts: giving girls and young women the opportunity to become active and happy citizens; involving them in the life of their community; strengthening the bonds of solidarity within the country; and creating international goodwill. Collaboration is encouraged between Guides living in rural areas and towns. Projects include the twinning of companies, joint camps and exchange visits.

Working with the Community
Guides in Burkina Faso are active in many areas of community service and development, including hygiene campaigns, first aid, childcare and market gardening projects. Ninety-two wells have been constructed as part of a major water project since 1980. A vocational training project has been operating at the Association's national centre since 1989,

offering skills training to local women. Health has been another major programme thrust and members have been involved in seminars on AIDS, nutrition, sanitation and associated subjects.

Outdoor and Environmental Activities
Camping is a popular activity among members of the Association, and Guides have been involved in tree planting as part of a service project.

Training
Qualified training instructors conduct special training camps. National or international leaders' training camps are held every year.

Communication and Co-operation
Burkina Faso co-operates with other national Girl Guide/Girl Scout Associations on specific projects. The well-construction project is a twinning project with the Girl Guides of Canada - Guides du Canada and the vocational training project at the national centre is a result of close co-operation with Guides and Scouts in Italy.

The Association publishes a quarterly newsletter called *Info-Guides* and has worked with UNESCO in preparing an audio-visual presentation on the lives of African women.

Burundi

Association des Guides du Burundi

Girl Guiding/Girl Scouting introduced: 1954
Became Associate Member of WAGGGS: 1972
Membership 1992[†]: 600
Membership as % of female population: 0.02%
WAGGGS Region: Africa

Guide

Promesse

Sur mon honneur (et avec la grâce de Dieu)[‡]
je m'engage à remplir de mon mieux mes devoirs envers (Dieu, l'Eglise et)[‡] la Patrie;
à aider mon prochain en toutes circonstances,
et à observer la loi guide.

[‡]La mention entre parenthèses est facultative; elle peut être modifiée si nécessaire suivant les croyances.

Loi

1 La Guide est vraie, elle mérite confiance.
2 La Guide est fidèle, elle tient ses engagements.
3 La Guide se rend utile et aide les autres.
4 La Guide est l'amie de tous et la soeur de toute autre Guide.
5 La Guide est courtoise.
6 La Guide aime et respecte la nature (oeuvre de Dieu)[‡].
7 La Guide obéit joyeusement et ne fait rien à moitié.
8 La Guide est toujours de bonne humeur et courageuse dans les difficultés.
9 La Guide est économe et respecte le bien d'autrui.
10 La Guide est simple et pure.

Devise

Toujours prête

Promesse des Bergeronnettes

Je promets d'être fidèle (à Jésus)[‡], à mes parents, à la loi de la ronde, et de faire chaque jour un plaisir à quelqu'un.

Loi des Bergeronnettes

La Bergeronnette écoute les Grands Oiseaux.
La Bergeronnette ne s'écoute pas elle-même.

Devise des Bergeronnettes

De notre mieux

Promise

On my honour (and with the grace of God)[‡]
I undertake to do my best to fulfil my duties towards (God, the Church and)[‡] my Country;
to help other people in all circumstances,
and to keep the Guide Law.

[‡]Words in brackets are optional; they can be modified if necessary according to beliefs.

Law

1 A Guide is truthful, she can be trusted.
2 A Guide is faithful, she keeps her promises.
3 A Guide makes herself useful and helps others.
4 A Guide is a friend to all and a sister to every other Guide.
5 A Guide is courteous.
6 A Guide loves and respects nature (work of God)[‡].
7 A Guide obeys cheerfully and does nothing by halves.
8 A Guide is always good-tempered and is courageous under difficulties.
9 A Guide is thrifty and respects other people's belongings.
10 A Guide is unaffected and pure.

Motto

Always prepared

Wagtail Promise
I promise to be faithful (to Jesus)‡, my parents, the Wagtail Law, and to do a good turn to someone every day.

Wagtail Law
The Wagtail listens to the fully fledged birds.
The Wagtail does not pay too much attention to herself.

Wagtail Motto
The best we can.

Age Groups

Eclaireuse (Guide aînée)	Ranger	16+
Guide	Guide (Senior)	13 - 16
Guide	Guide (Junior)	10 - 13
Bergeronnette	Wagtail	7 - 10

Development of the Movement in Burundi

Guiding in Burundi was started in 1954-55 by Belgian social workers as part of the Catholic Guides of Belgian Congo, Rwanda-Urundi. After the country's independence in 1962 an Association was formed which has since grown steadily.

The Programme
The programme is drawn up for four age groups under the headings general knowledge, self-expression, traditional arts of Burundi, service, health, home economics, faith, the techniques and spirit of Girl Guiding/Girl Scouting, nature and camping.

Working with the Community
Great importance is given to service as a means of contributing to the development of Burundi. Senior Guides provide cover for hospital staff allowing them to take holidays, as well as helping the elderly. Under the leadership of a full-time trainer, girls have cultivated land and sold the crops grown to raise funds. Guides and their leaders also organize literacy courses for other Guides and young women outside the Movement.

Outdoor and Environmental Activities
The Association owns a campsite, Charles de Foucauld, where members enjoy regular camping activities.

Training
All leaders receive regular training, and training camps are held for leaders, and members of the Association occasionally attend training events in other countries.

Communication and Co-operation
The Association strives to make itself known both to government bodies and to women's organizations in Burundi. It co-operates with the Scout Association, and Guides receive instruction in first aid from the Red Cross Society in Burundi.

United Republic of Cameroon

Association des Guides du Cameroun

Girl Guiding/Girl Scouting introduced: 1943
Became Associate Member of WAGGGS: 1972
Membership 1992†: 2,070
Membership as % of female population: 0.03%
WAGGGS Region: Africa

Guide

Promesse
Je promets sur mon honneur et avec la grâce de Dieu de faire tout mon possible pour:
servir Dieu et ma patrie,
aider les autres en tout temps,
obéir à la Loi des Guides.

Loi
1 La Guide est sincère.
2 Elle est loyale.
3 Elle est serviable.
4 Elle est l'amie de tous et la soeur de toutes les autres Guides.
5 Elle est polie.
6 Elle respecte la nature et y voit l'oeuvre de Dieu.
7 Elle est obéissante.
8 Elle sourit et chante malgré les difficultés.
9 Elle est active et économe.
10 Elle sait se dominer dans ses pensées, ses paroles et ses actes.

Devise
Sois Prête

Promise
I promise on my honour and with the grace of God to do everything possible to:
serve God and my country,
help others at all times,
obey the Guide Law.

Law
1 A Guide is sincere.
2 She is loyal.
3 She is helpful.
4 She is a friend to all and a sister to every other Guide.
5 She is polite.
6 She respects nature in which she sees the work of God.
7 She is obedient.
8 She smiles and sings in spite of difficulties.
9 She is active and thrifty.
10 She can control her thoughts, her words and her deeds.

Motto
Be Prepared

Development of the Movement in Cameroon

Guiding began in West Cameroon in 1943 with the formation of a Girl Guide company in Victoria. The Movement spread to other areas of the country and by 1947 Brownie packs had been formed. However, until the country's independence in 1961, Guiding activities were carried out in conjunction with the Nigerian Girl Guides Association. The West Cameroon Girl Guides Association was subsequently formed as an independent association.

Guiding in East Cameroon was officially established in 1963 when Les Guides du Cameroun was formed, although in some areas of the region Guiding activities had already been taking place for two years.

A Cameroon National Guide Council was formed in 1970, followed a year later by the creation of the Cameroon Union of Girl Guides and Girl Scouts consisting of the West Cameroon Girl Guides Association and Les Guides du Cameroun.

After the creation of the United Republic of Cameroon, which replaced the Federal Republic, and with the expansion of

Guiding in the country, in 1974 it was decided to dissolve the union and to establish in its place a single Guide association, the Cameroon Girl Guides Association/Association des Guides du Cameroun.

The Programme

The programme incorporates a range of activities designed to assist girls in the development of character, civic responsibility and community service.

Working with the Community

During school holidays the Association organizes activities for young children, teenagers and adults. The Association runs a Craft Training Centre for unemployed girls, which is also attended by local women and workers in their free time, and provides training in handicrafts and cookery.

Outdoor and Environmental Activities

National camps are held for Guides and Brownies, often at schools and colleges.

Communication and Co-operation

Cameroon Girl Guides have been represented at international camps and conferences, have attended trainings abroad, and have participated in exchange visits with other Girl Guide/Girl Scout Associations in the Africa Region.

The Cameroon Girl Guides Association co-operates with the Boy Scouts Association and maintains close contact with the Ministry of Youth and Sports.

A Guide and leader – mentoring is one way young women learn skills and self-confidence.

Canada

Girl Guides of Canada - Guides du Canada

Founder Member of WAGGGS
Girl Guiding/Girl Scouting introduced: 1910
Membership 1992: 273,681
Membership as % of female population: 2.02%
WAGGGS Region: Western Hemisphere

Guide

Promise

I promise, on my honour, to do my best:
To do my duty to God, the Queen and my country;
To help other people at all times;
To obey the Guide Law.

Law

1 A Guide's honour is to be trusted.
2 A Guide is loyal.
3 A Guide is useful and helps others.
4 A Guide is a friend to all, and a sister to every Guide.
5 A Guide is courteous.
6 A Guide is kind to animals and enjoys the beauty in nature.
7 A Guide is obedient.
8 A Guide smiles and sings even under difficulty.
9 A Guide is thrifty.
10 A Guide is pure in thought, word and deed.

Motto

Be Prepared

Demonstrating a solar cooker.

Brownie

Brownie Promise
I promise to do my best:
To do my duty to God, the Queen and my country;
To help other people every day, especially those at home.

Brownie Law
A Brownie is cheerful and obedient.
A Brownie thinks of other people before herself.

Brownie Motto
Lend a Hand

Age Groups

Ranger, Cadet, Junior Leader (senior branches)	15 - 17+
Pathfinder	12 - 15
Guide	9 - 12
Brownie	6 - 9
Spark	5

GFC Guide

Guides francophones du Canada

Promesse
Avec vous toutes,
Confiante dans le Seigneur
Je m'engage
à rendre les autres plus heureux
à servir avec audace mon pays
et à partager l'idéal de toutes les guides du monde.

Loi
1 La Guide est vraie et joyeuse.
2 La Guide est accueillante et fraternelle.
3 La Guide acquiert la maîtrise d'elle-même.
4 La Guide surmonte les difficultés.
5 La Guide aime la nature.
6 La Guide vit et fait vivre.
7 La Guide mérite et fait confiance.
8 La Guide partage l'effort de tous.
9 La Guide rend service.
10 La Guide apprend à vivre avec le Seigneur.

GFC Jeannette

Devise
Sois prête

Promesse des Jeannettes
Je promets de faire de mon mieux, pour être fidèle à Dieu, à mes parents et à la loi de la Ronde; pour faire chaque jour un plaisir à quelqu'un.

Loi des Jeannettes
Une jeannette est propre.
Une jeannette est joyeuse.
Une jeannette est active.
Une jeannette dit vrai.
La jeannette est l'amie de l'autre.

Devise des Jeannettes
De notre mieux

Promise
With you all,
Trusting in the Lord
I undertake
to make others happier
to serve my country with boldness
and to share the ideal of all the Guides of the world.

Law
1 A Guide is truthful and cheerful.
2 A Guide is welcoming and sisterly.
3 A Guide is self-controlled.
4 A Guide overcomes difficulties.
5 A Guide loves nature.
6 A Guide lives and makes live.
7 A Guide deserves and gives her trust.
8 A Guide shares in the endeavours of all.
9 A Guide renders service.
10 A Guide learns to live with the Lord.

Motto
Be Prepared

Jeannette Promise
I promise to do my best, to be faithful to God, my parents and the law of the pack; to do someone a good turn every day.

Jeannette Law
A Jeannette is clean.
A Jeannette is cheerful.
A Jeannette is active.
A Jeannette tells the truth.
A Jeannette is a friend to others.

Jeannette Motto
The best we can

Age Groups

Aînée	17+
Kamsok	14-17
Guide	11-14
Jeannette	8-11
Étincelle	6-8

Development of the Movement in Canada

The first Canadian Guide companies were established in 1910 in Ontario, and by 1912 Guiding had spread across Canada. Five years later the Dominion Government granted incorporation to the Canadian Girl Guide Association. In 1961 the Association's name was changed to the Girl Guides of Canada - Guides du Canada.

The Salvation Army adopted the Girl Guide programme for its girl members, becoming a Co-operating Society of the Girl Guides of Canada – Guides du Canada in 1937.

Since 1962 Guides francophones du Canada has been affiliated with the Girl Guides of Canada - Guides du Canada by special agreement which grants them the right to autonomy in matters of programme, training, appointment of officers and finance. Their programme, training and literature are designed to suit particular needs of French-speaking girls. Guides francophones have their own uniform and adhere to the policies of the Girl Guides of Canada. They have representation on the National Council of the Girl Guides of Canada and participate in national and international events.

The Aim of Canadian Guiding is to help girls and young women to become responsible citizens, able to give leadership and service to the community, whether local, national or global. The National Council is committed to achieving this aim through a series of goals which recognize the need to respond to the demands of a rapidly changing society.

The Programme

The programme for girls is reviewed regularly to meet the changing needs of girls. In 1989 Sparks were introduced, a pre-Brownie section for five-year-olds. The Spark Promise is 'I promise to share and be a friend'.

Home, community, the world, camping and the outdoors are stressed in the programmes in each age group. 'Home' focuses on the development of life skills and the awareness of self and includes nutrition, arts, technologies, careers, dealing with change, taking responsibility, and physical and emotional well-being. 'Community' focuses on awareness of people and incorporates building pride in heritage, respect for self and others, and giving service. 'World' focuses on the appreciation and knowledge of culture and customs around the world, including international friendship, stewardship, understanding and experience. 'Camping and the outdoors' focuses on enjoyment and appreciation of the outdoors and incorporates caring for the environment, camping with friends, keeping fit, learning new skills and sharing adventure.

Working with the Community

In keeping with the Promise, Canadian Guides help other people and serve their communities. They help in hospitals and at blood donor clinics, 'adopt' disabled or elderly people and perform many useful services for them. Members sometimes sponsor a child in another country by assuming all financial responsibilities. The organization has participated in anti-drug abuse campaigns.

Water activities are part of Canada's programme opportunities.

Outdoor and Environmental Activities
Camps take place in all seasons and may bring members together from a very wide area. Camp activities include hiking, canoeing, swimming, cycling, riding, snowshoeing and service.

A national environmental project was launched in 1990. Water for Tomorrow aims to promote the preservation of water resources through education and service. In 1993 Canada hosted Guelph '93, an international event with participants from over 40 countries.

Training
The Leadership Development Programme for adults is reviewed regularly to meet the changing needs of girls and leaders.

Communication and Co-operation
The Girl Guides of Canada - Guides du Canada contributes to world understanding and peace by establishing and maintaining contacts with other WAGGGS' Member Organizations, through correspondence and exchanges. Canadian Guiding is involved directly in partnership projects with many other WAGGGS' Member Organizations. In 1979 a water project was initiated with Burkina Faso. Since 1984 the Girl Guides of Canada has been involved in a Twinning Project scheme, based on sustainable community development. Separate provinces in Canada are twinned with several member countries including Saint Lucia, The Gambia, Tanzania, Sierra Leone and the Solomon Islands.

The Girl Guides of Canada - Guides du Canada has a special fund dedicated to international Girl Guiding/Girl Scouting. The Canadian World Friendship Fund, made up of voluntary contributions, is used to support WAGGGS through the four World Centres, the Thinking Day Fund and the Mutual Aid Scheme. Money from the Fund is used to help meet the expenses of members travelling to, and coming from, other countries. It also provides assistance to Girl Guides/Girl Scouts in countries suffering from natural disasters.

The official magazine of the organization is *Canadian Guider*, published five times a year. Numerous books and promotional materials are also available. The organization works through the media to build and retain community awareness about Guiding activities.

Girl Guides of Canada – Guides du Canada co-operates with other organizations with mutual interests, including Scouts Canada, Young Women's Christian Association, Boys and Girls Club of Canada, Canadian Girls in Training, Canadian Red Cross, Canadian Council of Children and Youth, Canadian 4H Council and Duke of Edinburgh's Award Young Canadians Challenge. Co-operation also takes place with many national women's organizations, organizations concerned with international development and those involved with fitness. Girl Guides of Canada - Guides du Canada actively supports designated United Nations' International Years.

Central African Republic

Guides de la République centrafricaine

Component Associations:
Association des guides catholiques de la République centrafricaine
Association des éclaireuses laîques de la République centrafricaine

Girl Guiding/Girl Scouting introduced:	**1952**
Became Associate Member of WAGGGS:	**1963**
Membership 1992†:	**1,400**
Membership as % of female population:	**0.08%**
WAGGGS Region:	**Africa**

Promesse
Sur mon honneur, avec l'aide de Dieu, je promets de servir de mon mieux: Dieu (l'Eglise si la guide est catholique ou son église si elle est protestante); d'aider mon prochain en toutes circonstances, d'observer la loi des guides.

Loi
1 La guide a un seul coeur et une parole.
2 La guide pense d'abord aux autres.
3 La guide met son coeur et ses mains au service des autres.
4 La guide est soeur des guides de toutes races, elle a l'esprit d'équipe.
5 La guide est accueillante, elle est là pour tous.
6 La guide respecte la nature, elle découvre l'oeuvre de Dieu.
7 La guide sait obéir.
8 La guide sourit dans l'effort, elle ne fait rien à moitié.
9 La guide aime son travail et sait employer son argent.
10 La guide garde son corps, sa route est droite dans la joie de Dieu.

Promesse des Jeannettes
Je promets de faire de mon mieux pour être fidèle à Dieu, à mon pays, à mes parents, à la loi de la ronde; et pour faire chaque jour un plaisir à quelqu'un.

Loi des Jeannettes
Une jeannette est toujours propre.
Une jeannette est toujours active.
Une jeannette est toujours gaie.
Une jeannette dit toujours vrai.
Une jeannette pense d'abord aux autres.

Devise des Jeannettes
De notre mieux

Promise
On my honour, with God's help, I promise to do my best to serve: God (the Church if the Guide is Catholic or her church if she is Protestant); to help others in all circumstances and to keep the Guide Law.

Law
1 A Guide has integrity and keeps her word.
2 A Guide thinks first of others.
3 A Guide is willing to help others and be useful to all.
4 A Guide is sister to Guides of all races, she has team spirit.
5 A Guide is welcoming, she is there for all.
6 A Guide respects Nature, she learns about God's work.
7 A Guide knows how to obey.
8 A Guide smiles in her endeavours, she does nothing by halves.
9 A Guide loves her work and knows how to use her money.
10 A Guide is pure, her way is straight in the joy of God.

Brownie Promise
I promise to do my best to be faithful to God, my Country, my parents and the Law of the Pack, and to do a good turn to someone every day.

Brownie Law
A Brownie is always clean.
A Brownie is always active.
A Brownie is always cheerful.
A Brownie always tells the truth.
A Brownie thinks first of others.

Brownie Motto
The best we can

Age Groups

Guide aînée	Ranger	16-21
Guide	Guide	12-16
Jeannette	Brownie	7-11

The Movement in the Central African Republic

Guiding in the Central African Republic began in 1952, and by the following year both Guide companies and Brownie packs had been established in the country. In 1955 a combined Guide and Brownie camp was organized and during the next two years Guiding spread to many rural areas. In 1959 Les Guides Centrafricaines was formally registered, and by 1963 membership in the Association had risen to 1,600 and the first African National Commissioner was elected. In 1979 the Association changed its name to the Association des Guides et Eclaireuses Centrafricaines.

For several years no news was heard of Guiding in the Central African Republic, but in 1991 members combined their efforts to set up a new national team and to bring new life to the Movement.

In June 1993 a federation was established – Fédération du Scoutisme féminin de Centrafrique. The Federation has two component Associations.

Association des guides catholiques de la République centrafricaine

Programme
Each year the Association adopts a different theme as a basis for its programme of activities. The themes chosen are particularly relevant to the problems faced by the youth of today.

Training
A full-time trainer was appointed in 1991 with assistance from WAGGGS. She is working to establish close contacts between Guide units in the country and the national team and to work for the expansion of the Movement. Training camps have been organized and a camp programme has been prepared.

Association des éclaireuses laïques de la République centrafricaine

Information about this Association will be available in a future edition of this publication.

Chile

Asociación de Guías y Scouts de Chile

Girl Guiding/Girl Scouting introduced: 1913
Became Associate Member of WAGGGS: 1957
Became Full Member of WAGGGS: 1981
Membership 1992: 32,588
Membership as % of female population: 0.49%
WAGGGS Region: Western Hemisphere

Promesa
Por mi honor prometo ante todos ustedes hacer todo lo que de mí dependa para servir a Dios y a la Patria, ayudar a los demás en toda circunstancia y vivir la Ley Guía.

Ley
1 La Guía merece confianza porque es responsable.
2 La Guía es leal.
3 La Guía es servicial sin esperar recompensa.
4 La Guía es amiga y comparte con todos.
5 La Guía es atenta y cordial.
6 La Guía ama la naturaleza y en ella descubre la obra de Dios.
7 La Guía sabe obedecer y nada hace a medias.
8 La Guía enfrenta las dificultades con optimismo.
9 La Guía cuida las cosas porque valora el trabajo.
10 La Guía es pura en pensamiento, palabra y obra.

Lema
Siempre Lista

Anhelo de la Alita
Yo anhelo ser una buena Alita, siendo cada día mejor, amar a Dios, la Patria y mis Padres y aceptar la Ley de la Ronda.

Ley de la Alita
1 La Alita escucha y obedece.
2 La Alita trata de vencer las dificultades.
3 La Alita es amable y sincera.
4 La Alita es alegre y generosa.
5 La Alita comparte su felicidad.

Lema de la Alita
Siempre mejor

Promise
On my honour I promise, before all of you, to do my best to serve God and my Country, to help others in any circumstance and to live the Guide Law.

Law
1 A Guide deserves to be trusted because she is a responsible person.
2 A Guide is loyal.
3 A Guide serves others without expecting a reward.
4 A Guide is a friend to all and shares with everyone.
5 A Guide is kind and polite.
6 A Guide loves nature and in it discovers God's work.
7 A Guide knows how to obey and leaves nothing unfinished.
8 A Guide faces difficulties with optimism.
9 A Guide takes care of things because she knows the value of work.
10 A Guide is pure in thought, word and deed.

Motto
Be prepared

Little Wing Great Wish
I wish to be a good Little Wing becoming better every day, loving God, my Country, my parents and accepting the Law of the Pack.

Little Wing Law
1 A Little Wing listens and obeys.
2 A Little Wing tries to overcome difficulties.

Guide

Little Wing

3 A Little Wing is kind and sincere.
4 A Little Wing is cheerful and generous.
5 A Little Wing shares her happiness.

Little Wing Motto
Always better

Age Groups

Walker	18-20
Pioneer	15-17
Guide	11-15
Little Wing	7-11

Development of the Movement in Chile

Guiding began in Chile in 1913 when a Girl Guide company was started in Rancagua and registered with the Scout Association of Chile. Brownie, Guide and Ranger companies were set up throughout the country under the auspices of the Scout Association and activities were mostly carried out in schools with teachers acting as leaders.

In 1953 the Guides formed a separate Association, the Asociación de Guías de Chile and in 1960 it was officially recognized as a national institution of Chile. In the mid-1960s a female section developed within the Federación de Scouts Católicos, and following an agreement for joint action in 1971, these girls were integrated into the Asociación de Guías de Chile in 1974.

In 1974 the Scouts Association of Chile was formed as a result of the merger of Scout Associations in Chile. This Association had a considerable number of girls in its ranks, and by 1977 members of the Asociación de Guías de Chile and the female Scout section were working together on events and courses. Following a study carried out by representatives from both Associations, the Guide and Scout Movements formed a Joint Organization, the Asociación de Guías y Scouts de Chile.

The Programme
The programme has been revised and updated and is now based on an "educational project" which covers six areas of personal development: physical aspects, creativity, character, affection, sociability and spirituality. These are adapted for each age group and approached through a variety of activities such as camping, open air activities, community service, community development projects, games, ceremonies and meetings. Based on the fundamental principles of Girl Guiding/Girl Scouting, learning by doing and group work, the programme as a whole aims to contribute to the development of young people. It helps them to achieve their full physical, intellectual, social and spiritual potential as people, and encourages them to become responsible citizens and members of the local, national and international communities.

Disabled girls are incorporated into existing units under the plan Escultismo Para Todos (Scouting for Everyone).

Working with the Community
The Association has launched a series of projects to strengthen community life and to develop self-help schemes in underprivileged areas. Projects include training people in sewing, cookery, shoe repairs and handicrafts, and looking after poor and delinquent children.

Training
Leadership training is a priority for the Association and is carried out at three levels: basic, intermediate and advanced. The training committee plans, reviews and adapts the training programme, organizes training courses at all levels and supervises follow-up sessions. Training courses are held every year for members of the training committee to enable them to study programmes, try out new methods and exchange ideas.

In addition, the Association offers professional training sessions and courses in subjects such as management, marketing and finance for its staff; sessions in leadership training; and specific courses and workshops on topics of more immediate interest to the organization, such as drug addiction and the integration of returning exiles into the community.

Communication and Co-operation
Chile actively encourages and assists members to participate in Regional and world events. It also receives and entertains Girl Guides/Girl Scouts from neighbouring countries.

The Asociación de Guías y Scouts de Chile informs the general public about Guiding through television, radio and newspapers, and it is gaining recognition for having an impact on Chilean youth.

The Association publishes *Encuentro*, a monthly magazine for leaders, other adult members and sponsors which contains general information and training material. The Association maintains contact with the Ministry of Education, the National Committee for Recreation, the Asociación de Organizaciones No Gubernamentales (ASONG) and the Comité Económico para América Latina (CEPAL). At local and regional level, Guides work with local authorities and organizations interested in community development, and maintain close contact with church authorities.

Guides actively participate in events that further the positive image of the Movement.

Republic of China

National Girl Scouts Association of the Republic of China

Girl Guiding/Girl Scouting introduced:	**1919**
Became Associate Member of WAGGGS:	**1963**
Became Full Member of WAGGGS:	**1966**
Membership 1992:	**42,028**
Membership as % of female population:	**0.07%**
WAGGGS Region:	**Asia Pacific**

Girl Scout

Brownie Scout

Nuoh Yan

Pyng Woo de jen Cheing Woo Yuann duey Shang Tsang her Woo de Gwo jia Jinn Woo de been fenn Woo Yuann Swei Shyr bang juh ta ren Woo Yuann tzuen Shoou Neu torng jiun Guei liuh.

Neu torng jiun Guei liuh

1 Neu torng jiun de rong Yuh Shyh Show ren Shinn Lay de.
2 Neu torng jiun Shyh jong Shin de.
3 Neu torng jiun Shyh juh ren de.
4 Neu torng jiun Shyh Yi Chieh ren de Perng Yeou Shyh Meei Wey Neu torn jiun de tzyy Mey.
5 Neu torng jiun Shyh Chian Gong de.
6 Neu torng jiun Shyh Ay huh dong Wuhn de.
7 Neu torng jiun Shyh fwu tsorng de.
8 Neu torng jiun Shyh Kuay leh de.
9 Neu torng jiun Shyh Chyn jean de.
10 Neu torng jiun de Sy Sheang Yan Yeu jui Shyng dong Shyh dong Shyh Chwen jye de.

Motto

Joen bey
ryh Shyng Yi Shann
ren Sheng Yii Fwu Wuh Wei Muh dih

Promise

On my honour, I promise that I will do my best: To do my duty to God and my Country. To help other people at all times. To obey the Girl Scout Law.

Law

1 A Girl Scout's honour is to be trusted.
2 A Girl Scout is loyal.
3 A Girl Scout's duty is to be useful and helpful to others.
4 A Girl Scout is a friend to all and a sister to every other Girl Scout.
5 A Girl Scout is courteous.
6 A Girl Scout is a friend to animals.
7 A Girl Scout obeys orders.
8 A Girl Scout smiles and sings under all difficulties.
9 A Girl Scout is thrifty.
10 A Girl Scout is pure in thought, in word and in deed.

Motto

Be Prepared
Do a good turn daily
The greatest aim in life is to serve.

Brownie Scout Promise

I promise to do my best:
To do my duty to God and my Country;
To help other people every day, especially those at home.

Girl Scouts together learn, make friends and have fun.

Brownie Scout Law
A Brownie gives in to the older folk.
A Brownie does not give in to herself.

Brownie Scout Motto
Lend a Hand

Age Groups

Tzy Shen Neoh Torng Jiun	Senior Girl Scout	17 - 21
Lan jiee Neoh Torng Jiun	Ranger	15 - 17
Neoh Torng Jiun	Girl Scout	11 - 15
Yeou Neoh Torng Jiun	Brownie Scout	7 - 11

Development of the Movement in the Republic of China

The first Girl Scout troop was organized in Shanghai, China in 1919. At that time it was known as the Boy Scouts of China. The Scout badge was worn by both Boy Scouts and Girl Scouts with no independent section for Girl Scouts. During the war years, 1939 to 1945, the Girl Scouts performed outstanding service, helping in hospitals and schools.

When the political situation changed, the Association was moved from mainland China to Taiwan with the government. It was felt that there was a need to organize a single organization for Girl Scouts. The Chinese Girl Scouts Planning and Training Committee was set up in 1952, and the Girl Scouts Association was formally established on 1 June 1958. The date of 1 June was declared 'Chinese Girl Scouts' Day'.

In 1988 girls and adult leaders representing 21 district branch councils joined in the celebration of the Association's 30th anniversary.

The Programme
The programme has been reviewed to meet the needs of four age groups and features moral, intellectual, physical and group education. It provides girls with the opportunity for self-training, aiming to develop their potential and widen their interests.

Working with the Community
The Association supports projects undertaken by the government and civil organizations such as fundraising and helping the disabled. Girls also visit local nursing homes and collect clothes for the needy. Senior Girl Scouts organize summer camps for aboriginal children in urban areas.

Outdoor and Environmental Activities
Camps and Pack holidays are conducted periodically at district level. Girl Scouts in the Republic of China participate in national environmental conservation projects and tree planting campaigns.

Training
The National Training Team meets regularly and is responsible for the national training scheme for adult leaders. A new training programme handbook gives guidelines for a formal training for four age groups.

Communication and Co-operation
The Association encourages attendance at international events, camps, leaders' trainings and seminars.

A 'Sister Council' relationship with the Girl Scouts of Korea began in 1987, and cultural and sporting exchanges have taken place with Hong Kong in recent years. In 1988 the Republic of China took part in a 'Let Us Share' Project with the Girl Scouts of Japan, enabling many members to establish close international friendships through an exchange programme.

The Association maintains close relations with the Ministry of Education, Ministry of Interior, Boy Scouts of China and other youth organizations, and informs the general public about its activities and services through the press and other media. The Association also has produced a public relations video detailing its activities. The Association is working to promote the role of women in co-operation with the All China Women's Federation.

Girl Scouts on the trail during a programme organized for 'Chinese Girl Scouts' Day.'

Colombia

Asociación de Guías Scouts de Colombia

Girl Guiding/Girl Scouting introduced: 1936
Became Associate Member of WAGGGS: 1954
Became Full Member of WAGGGS: 1957
Membership 1992: 1,429
Membership as % of female population: 0.01%
WAGGGS Region: Western Hemisphere

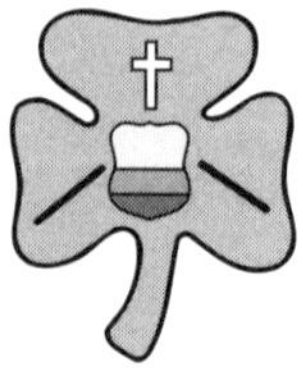

Guide

Promesa
Con la gracia de Dios yo ... prometo por mi honor hacer cuanto de mí dependa para cumplir mis deberes para con Dios, mi Patria y mi familia; ser útil al prójimo en todas las circunstancias; y obedecer la Ley Guía.

Ley
1 La Guía ama la verdad y la vive.
2 La Guía es leal y digna de confianza.
3 La Guía es útil a su comunidad.
4 La Guía es amiga de todos y hermana de las demás Guías.
5 La Guía está abierta al diálogo y respeta las convicciones de los demás.
6 La Guía ama la vida y la naturaleza y al ver en ellas la obra de Dios, procura su conservación y su progreso.
7 La Guía es responsable.
8 La Guía es alegre y optimista ante las dificultades.
9 La Guía cuida sus cosas y respeta las de los demás.
10 La Guía es disciplinada y consciente de lo que piensa, dice y hace.

Lema
Siempre Lista

Fairy

Promesa de la Hadita
Yo ... prometo hacer todo lo posible para cumplir mis deberes para con Dios, mi Patria y mi familia, ayudar a otras personas cada día especialmente en mi casa y mi colegio y obedecer la Ley de la Ronda.

Ley de la Hadita
1 La Hadita es alegre y obediente.
2 La Hadita es generosa y dice siempre la verdad.

Lema de la Hadita
Siempre Mejor

Promise
With the grace of God, I ... promise on my honour that I will do my best to fulfil my duties to God, my country and my family, to help other people in all circumstances and to obey the Guide Law.

Law
1 A Guide loves truth and lives by it.
2 A Guide is loyal and to be trusted.
3 A Guide is useful to her community.
4 A Guide is a friend to all and a sister to all other Guides.
5 A Guide is always ready to talk things over and she respects the convictions of others.
6 A Guide loves life and nature and by seeing in them the work of God tries to conserve and develop them.
7 A Guide is responsible.
8 A Guide is cheerful and optimistic under difficulties.
9 A Guide looks after her things and respects those of others.
10 A Guide is disciplined and aware of all she thinks, says and does.

Motto
Be Prepared

Fairy Promise
I ... promise to do everything possible to fulfil my duties to God, my Country and my family, to help other people every day especially those at home and at school and to obey the Law of the Pack.

Fairy Law
1 A Fairy is cheerful and obedient.
2 A Fairy is generous and always tells the truth.

Fairy Motto
Always better

Age Groups

Guía Mayor	Ranger	16-18
Carabela	Intermediate Guide	13-15
Guía Menor	Junior Guide	10-12
Hadita	Fairy	6-9

Development of the Movement in Colombia

Guiding began in Colombia in 1936, but it was not until 1953 that the National Executive Council was formed, the Association was recognized by the government, and headquarters were set up in Bogotá.

The Programme
The programme is based on the needs and interests of Colombian girls and young women and is extensive and flexible so that it can be developed for use with different geographically-based and socio-cultural groups. It was formulated as a result of a study by sociologists, psychologists, social welfare workers and experts in childcare.

Working with the Community
Development projects have recently been undertaken in four communities on the outskirts of the cities of Barranquilla, Cali, Montería and Manizales. The projects centred around the improvement of hygiene, health and medical services as well as other public amenities including public libraries and a recreational park. Workshops were also set up to enable adult community members to increase their family income.

Outdoor and Environmental Activities
In 1987 the Association focused its attention on tree-planting, and in 1988 on clean air and clean water as part of the Western Hemisphere environmental project. In 1989 attention turned to planning the environment for the future of Colombia. Work centred on children's rights and care of the elderly from 1990 to the present.

Training
Colombia has a National Team of Trainers, co-ordinated by the National Trainer, who is responsible for the training of adult members of the Movement. The training programme is divided into four levels and contains courses in technical and administrative skills, the social sciences and humanities.

A Colombian Guide demonstrates her unit flag at camp. Environmental awareness is a major focus.

Communication and Co-operation
Guides organize raffles, festivals and bazaars to finance international activities. The Association had special ties with Girl Scouts in Pittsburgh, USA and they corresponded and learned about each others' lives and programmes.

The Association has excellent relations with Colombia's government and has received financial aid through COLDEPORTES (Colombian Institute for Youth and Sports).

Cook Islands

The Cook Islands Girl Guides Association (Inc.)

Girl Guiding/Girl Scouting introduced: 1928
Became Associate Member of WAGGGS: 1993
Membership 1991: 864
Membership as % of female population: 0.1%
WAGGGS Region: Asia Pacific

Guide

Promise

Te taputou nei au e ka tauta pakari au i te tavini atu ki te
Atua na roto i taku au angaanga ma te kauraro ki te Ariki
Vaine Ngateitei ma te tauturu i te au tangata tei tumatetenga.
Ko taku teia Taputouanga.

Law

E tu tiratiratu e te pikikaa kore to te Guide te kauraro e te tiama
Kua ki te taeake i te aroa taeake
Kare o te Guide tu akavaavaa e te kopaepae taeke i rotopu i tona au taeake Guides
Ka akono meitaki te Guide i te au manu aaere o te enua e te au mea ora ravarai
E tu kauraro e te ngakau akaaka to te Guide
Kia rava te akakoromaki i te au akaueanga te ka tuku ia kia ratou
Kare te Guide e kaimoumou puapinga kore ua i tona taime
Ka akono meitaki te Guide i te apinga o tetai ke mei tona anake ra apinga
Kare te Guide e rapurapu i tona arero i tana tuatua e te au mea tana ka rave
E akamanako ra oki aia i tona au aerenga katoa.

Motto

Auraka e noo vare ua. E ara.

Promise

I promise on my honour to do my best
To do my duty to God
To serve the Queen and my country and help other people
To keep the Guide Law.

Law

A Guide is loyal and can be trusted.
A Guide is helpful.
A Guide is polite and considerate.
A Guide is friendly and a sister to all Guides.
A Guide is kind to animals and respects all living things.
A Guide is obedient.
A Guide has courage and is cheerful in all difficulties.
A Guide makes good use of her time.
A Guide takes care of her own possessions and those of other people.
A Guide is self-controlled in all she thinks, says and does.

Motto

Be prepared.

Age Groups

Rangers	15-20
Guides	11-15
Brownies	7-11
Pepes	3-6

Development of the Movement in the Cook Islands

1928 marked the beginning of Guiding in the Cook Islands. The first Guide Company opened in the capital, Avarua, on the island of Rarotonga and the Islands were registered as a province of The Girl Guides Association New Zealand (Inc). Ranger patrols were set up in 1935 and the first Brownie pack was registered in 1937.

The first outer island company was started in Aitutaki in 1948. The 1950s were an era of growth with the foundation of new companies both on Rarotonga and the outer islands. The Cook Islands became a Branch Association of the New Zealand Girl Guides, membership increased, and leaders attended overseas trainings and events. UNESCO funded a full-time trainer from 1956 to 1958. With good administration and a more active programme, Guiding became fully accepted by the community and supported by the churches.

In 1986 the Association fulfilled a long-standing ambition by obtaining its own headquarters. Membership continued to grow and in 1992 a Deed of Transfer was signed making the Branch Association of the Cook Islands independent of the Girl Guides Association New Zealand (Inc).

The Programme

The programme used is one developed by the Girl Guides Association of New Zealand for all Pacific Island Associations. It is designed to give girls confidence, training in reliability, responsibility and practical skills. Based on an eight-point programme, it gives girls opportunities to develop physical fitness, the mind, out of doors enjoyment, homecraft skills, service to others, human relations, creativity and character. It is developed according to the needs of each age group.

Working with the Community

The Association participates in a wide variety of service projects and raises funds to support emergency relief demands.

Outdoor and Environmental Activities

Camping and adventurous activities are the most popular aspect of Guiding and annual camps are always well attended. The annual camp is held in the outer islands. Everyone looks forward to attending the camp, as most of the girls from Rarotonga have never been to any of the outer islands. The camp gives them an idea of the different ways of life that the people are living within the Cook Islands.

Training

In the late 1980s the Cook Islands introduced a special Pacific Leadership in the company of other Pacific Island Associations. Part one leads to a warrant and part two offers more advanced individual training.

The Training Adviser and a team of qualified trainers meet regularly to plan trainings and develop an annual training calendar. Leaders of all Branches have trainings together on topics of common interest and separate sessions are held for specific Branch matters.

In 1993 the committee introduced Mobile Trainings to help new leaders in the companies with the planning and running of their weekly meetings until the leaders are confident enough to work on their own. This was introduced specially for new, young and untrained girls who have joined the Movement without any knowledge of Guiding but who are willing to care for the girls and who are very much interested in the activities that the Guiding Movement offers.

Communication and Co-operation

Many Guides participate in major events organized by Girl Guides Association New Zealand (Inc). Even though the Association was not yet a member of the Asia Pacific Region in 1992 it hosted a Regional Workshop on Administration for Member Organizations in the Pacific Islands, co-ordinated by the Girl Guides Association New Zealand (Inc).

The Association is held in high esteem by all in authority. The general public are very aware of the Girl Guides and have expressed their support. The Association has close links with various religious bodies, and combined church parades are held with other youth organizations. Guides also participate in national events such as Independence Day celebrations, South Pacific festivals, Parliament openings and big church conferences and sports tournaments.

The Association does not have publications of its own but uses those prepared for the Islands by New Zealand. The Association is planning to produce a bi-monthly newsletter and to revise the Brownie and Girl Guide handbooks with the assistance of the WAGGGS Field Executive Trainer.

A Ranger carries woven palm baskets, accompanied by a Guide carrying coconuts, at an event in Cook Islands.

Costa Rica

Asociación de Guías y Scouts de Costa Rica

Girl Guiding/Girl Scouting introduced:	**1922**
Became Associate Member of WAGGGS:	**1946**
Became Full Member of WAGGGS:	**1981**
WAGGGS Membership 1992[†]:	**3,101**
Membership as % of female population:	**0.20%**
WAGGGS Region:	**Western Hemisphere**

Guide

Promesa
Por mi honor y con la ayuda de Dios prometo hacer lo posible por cumplir mis deberes para con Dios y la Patria ayudar al prójimo en toda circunstancia y cumplir fielmente la Ley Guía y Scout.

Ley
La Guía es:
El Scout es:

HONORABLE:
Integro (a) ante sí mismo (a) y ante los demás en todos los actos de su vida.

LEAL:
Para con Dios, su Patria, sus padres, sus jefes, subordinados y compañeros.

SERVICIAL:
Ayuda a los demás sin esperar recompensa.

AMIGABLE:
Es amigo (a) de todos y hermano (a) de todo scout y de toda guía, sin distinción de credo, raza, nacionalidad o clase social.

CORTÉS:
Manifiesta su estima y consideración a los demás.

BONDADOSO(A):
Ve en la naturaleza la obra de Dios y la conserva.

OBEDIENTE:
Acepta la legítima autoridad y obedece racionalmente.

ALEGRE:
Es optimista y jovial aún en sus dificultades.

TRABAJADOR(A):
Hace buen uso del producto de su trabajo y es cuidadoso (a) del bien ajeno; hace las cosas en orden y completas.

LIMPIO (A):
Es limpio (a) y sano (a) en sus pensamientos, palabras y acciones.

Principios Guías y Scouts
DEBERES PARA CON DIOS:
Se refiere a la relación de una persona con los valores espirituales de la vida.

DEBERES PARA CON LOS DEMAS:
Se refiere a la relación de una persona con la sociedad, en el sentido más amplio del término.

DEBERES PARA CONSIGO MISMO:
Se refiere a las obligaciones de una persona respecto a sí misma.

Promesa de las Haditas
Prometo hacer cuanto de mi dependa para cumplir mis deberes hacia Dios y mi Patria.
Obedecer la Ley de la Ronda
y ayudar a todos los días, especialmente a los de mi casa.

Ley de las Haditas
La Hadita escucha y obedece a los animalitos consejeros del bosque.
La Hadita se vence a sí misma.

Promise
I promise on my honour to do my best to do my duty to
God and my Country;
To help my neighbours under all circumstances and to obey the Guide/Scout Law.

Law
A Guide is:
A Scout is:

HONOURABLE:
she/he is honest to her/himself and to others in all she/he does.

LOYAL:
she/he is loyal to God, her/his Country, her/his Parents, her/his leaders, her/his subordinates and companions.

HELPFUL:
she/he helps others without expecting a reward.

FRIENDLY:
she/he is a friend to all and a sister/brother to every Guide/Scout without distinction of creed, race, nationality or social class.

COURTEOUS:
she/he shows appreciation and consideration of others.

KIND:
she/he sees the work of God in nature and tries to conserve it.

OBEDIENT:
she/he accepts legitimate authority and obeys in a rational way.

CHEERFUL:
she/he is optimistic and cheerful even in the face of difficulty.

HARDWORKING:
she/he puts to good use the products of her/his own work and is careful with the possessions of others; she/he does things tidily and completely.

PURE:
she/he is pure in her/his thoughts words and deeds.

Guide and Scout principles:
DUTY TO GOD:
Adherence to spiritual principles, loyalty to the religion that expresses them and acceptance of the duties resulting therefrom.

DUTY TO OTHERS
Loyalty to one's country in harmony with the promotion of local, national and international peace, understanding and co-operation.
Participation in the development of society, with recognition and respect for the dignity of one's fellow-man and for the integrity of the natural world.

DUTY TO SELF
Responsibility for the development of oneself.

Brownie Promise
I Promise that I will do my best to do my duty to God
and my Country;
To obey the Brownie Law and to help other people every day,
especially those at home.

Brownie Law
A Brownie listens to and obeys her leader
A Brownie is self-controlled.

Guides assist with a summer camp for children.

Development of the Movement in Costa Rica

Guiding in Costa Rica started in 1922 when a Guide company was opened in the Girls' Secondary School of San José. By 1944 Guiding had spread to other areas of the country and the Asociación de Guías de Costa Rica was established. After a period of decline, fresh impetus was given to the Association in 1965 when a member of the Western Hemisphere Committee visited the country to advise the National Committee. This was followed by a visit from a WAGGGS Travelling Commissioner.

In 1974 talks began with the Boy Scout Association of Costa Rica on a possible merger. A Liaison Committee was set up with representatives from the two National Committees to study possible ways of work and to prepare a draft Constitution and Regulations. After a series of meetings an agreement was drawn up and accepted by both Associations. By 1977 all plans for the merger were implemented and the administrative structure was in operation.

The Programme

In 1977 the programme for each branch was reviewed and a new branch, Tsuris, introduced.

The programme is divided into five main areas: social development, physical development, character development, spiritual development and mental development. It has been developed to suit all age groups and each has its own progress plan, devised to fulfil members' interests and expectations. Particular attention has been paid to adapting the programme to meet the special needs of girls in rural areas with the aim of increasing membership.

Working with the Community

Guides in Costa Rica carry out a number of service activities. They help in orphanages and hospitals, carry out projects with the disabled, organize Christmas parties for the underprivileged, participate as youth leaders in camps for school children, as well as organize youth programmes around the country. The Association is also involved in a literacy project and has organized Brownie packs and Guide companies in homes for the disabled.

The Association participates in a university programme involving students who give voluntary community service. Many students also work as Guide leaders and camp trainers and participate in a special training project for Guides and Scouts with special needs.

Outdoor and Environmental Activities

The Association has its own camping facilities at Campo Escuela, situated 10 kilometres from the capital. It is also engaged in an ongoing marine turtle rescue project which was initiated in 1989. Guides also take part in a national parks project and have worked to improve a zoological park as well as completing tree-planting projects.

Training

The Training Commission, which is responsible for all training, emphasizes the need to make training events enjoyable as well as instructive. Female participation is approximately one third, which is about the same proportion as the female membership of the Association. Brownie and Guide leaders receive separate training from Cub and Scout leaders. Training for leaders of Senior Girl Guides and Rovers is held jointly, although some specialized sessions are conducted separately. Training is also held for administrative staff, committee members and trainers. Most of the training is carried out at the Association's well-equipped training centre, Iztaru, although some sessions are held locally when necessary.

Communication and Co-operation

Costa Rica co-operates with other national Girl Guide/Girl Scout organizations including the USA on a literacy project and Canada and New Zealand on a training and development project.

The Association works to keep the public informed about its activities and the university programme, in particular, has increased public awareness of the Association's work in the community.

The Asociación de Guías y Scouts de Costa Rica has good relations with the churches. The Ministry of Culture, Youth and Sports has assisted it in publishing booklets. Contact with non-governmental organizations is made through the Federation of Voluntary Organizations.

Cyprus

Girl Guides Association of Cyprus

Girl Guiding/Girl Scouting introduced: 1912
Became Associate Member of WAGGGS: 1962
Became Full Member of WAGGGS: 1978
Membership 1992: 4,714
Membership as % of female population: 1.32%
WAGGGS Region: Europe

Promise
I promise on my honour that I will do my best:
To do my duty to God and Cyprus;
To help other people everywhere and always;
To obey the Guide Law.

Law
1 The word of honour of a Guide is to be believed and respected.
2 A Guide is loyal and obedient to her parents and her elders.
3 A Guide is useful and always helps others.
4 A Guide is friendly to all.
5 A Guide is courteous and affable.
6 A Guide loves, respects and protects the environment.
7 A Guide is reliable and punctual.
8 A Guide is calm, optimistic and joyful.
9 A Guide is conscientious, thrifty and tidy.
10 A Guide is pure in her thoughts, words and deeds.

Motto
Be Prepared

Butterfly Promise
I promise to do my best:
To do my duty to God and Cyprus;
To help other people always and bring happiness at home.

Butterfly Law
The Butterfly obeys her elders.
The Butterfly does not think only of herself but is a friend and sister to all other Butterflies.

Butterfly Motto
Help everywhere always

Age Groups

Senior Guide/ Prospective Leaders	16-18
Sea/Forest Guide	13-15
Guide	10-12
Butterfly	7-9
Chrysalides	5-6

Guide

Development of the Movement in Cyprus

Although Lone Guides are known to have existed on the island in 1912, in 1930 Guide Companies began functioning as a branch of The Girl Guides Association (United Kingdom). In 1960 the Cyprus Republic was proclaimed and the Girl Guides Association of Cyprus was officially established. In 1974 the Association was awarded the Walter Donald Ross Certificate of Merit for excellent service rendered to the refugees of Cyprus.

In 1989 the Association hosted the 6th European Scouts and Guides Conference.

The Programme
No branch in Cyprus covers more than a three-year age span in response to girls' rapidly changing abilities and demands. World Association policy and UN programmes are incorporated into the programmes of each branch.

The Association has established some units within refugee settlements. Girls with special needs are incorporated into existing units and the programme is adapted to suit their needs.

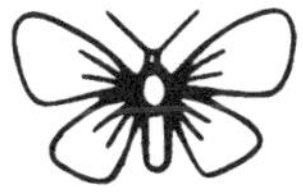
Butterfly

Working with the Community
Much importance is given to community projects and members participate actively in local events. Recent projects include a project on the preservation of cultural heritage and involvement in peace activities based on human rights.

Outdoor and Environmental Activities
The Girl Guides Association of Cyprus owns a campsite in Naados and summer camps have become a regular feature of Guiding in Cyprus. The Association has used camping activities to help integrate children with special needs into society and the Movement. Environmental activities have included a water conservation campaign, tree-planting, a cleaning campaign and a study of the coastline.

Training
The Association holds training sessions, ranging from one to eight days' duration and patrol leaders, prospective and active leaders, camp leaders, prospective trainers and members of committees are asked to participate.

Communication and Co-operation
Cyprus attaches particular importance to the true spirit of Thinking Day and organizes seminars on international problems faced by young people today. Members participate in European seminars and international camps.

The Association maintains good public relations through members' personal conduct, newspaper articles and participation in events organized by the government, the local authorities and other non-governmental organizations.

The Association is an organizing member of the Inter-Ministerial Committee for Youth, the Committee for the Protection and Welfare of the Child, the Thalassaemia Association, the Blood Donation Committee and the Anti-Cancer Association. It also co-operates with other local cultural associations and collaborates with environmental associations and other youth and women's organizations.

Cyprus Guides at camp host Guides from Belarus. Belarus is working towards membership of WAGGGS.

Czech Republic

Junák - Svaz skautů a skautek
(Czech Association of Scouts and Guides)

Founder Member of WAGGGS

Girl Guiding/Girl Scouting introduced:	**1915**
Membership cancelled:	**1950**
Re-admitted as Associate Member of WAGGGS:	**1990**
Membership 1992:	**33,814**
WAGGGS Region:	**Europe**

Guide

Promise

I promise on my honour, as well as I can:
- to serve the Highest Truth and love faithfully at all times
- to fulfill all my own duties and to observe the Scout/Guide laws
- to be prepared to help my country and my neighbours with all my soul and body.

Optional clause: May God help me so.
World Committee approved 1992-1995.

Law

1 A Guide always speaks the truth.
2 A Guide is loyal and trustworthy.
3 A Guide is good and helps others.
4 A Guide is a friend to all people of good will and sister to all guides.
5 A Guide is polite.
6 A Guide protects nature and valuable human products.
7 A Guide obeys her parents, superiors and Guide leaders.
8 A Guide is cheerful.
9 A Guide is thrifty.
10 A Guide is clean in thought, word and deed.

Development of the Movement in the Czech Republic

Guiding started in Bohemia, a part of the Austrian Empire in1915 as a section of the union Junák-Cesky skaut. Shortly after the country proclaimed its independence in 1918, the Czecho-Slovak Boy Scout Association (which included Guides) was established. Czechoslovakia's Association was a founder member of WAGGGS. In 1934 the name was changed to the Czechoslovak Boy and Girl Scouts Association, with independent executive committees created for Scouts and Guides.

In 1939 all youth organizations were required to become members of the official political organization and were forbidden to use the name *skaut* (Scout), only the Czech name *Junák* was allowed. The girls continued to use the name *skautky* (Girl Scouts), but they were not allowed to wear the international Trefoil. Scouting and Guiding continued for a short time, but were forbidden to hold large gatherings. They were forced to stop their activities in 1940 when they were officially forbidden by the Nazi regime and all property was seized for the use of the Nazi Youth Organization.

In 1945, when the country was liberated, Guiding and Scouting re-emerged and the Association was re-established. By the end of the year membership had reached nearly 38,000. Another major setback occurred in 1950 when Guiding and Scouting were once again banned and all possessions were confiscated by the Communist Youth Movement.

Firefly

In 1968 Guiding and Scouting officially resumed, but international contacts were not re-established because the organization was a part of the Federation of Children and Youth Organizations, supported and governed by the state. In 1970, for the third time in its history, the Movement was banned and its possessions were taken over by the Communist Youth Organization.

In 1989 the situation in Czechoslovakia changed once again. With the establishment of democracy, the National Association of Scouts and Guides was recognized. Membership rose quickly despite practical difficulties faced by the organization in finding meeting places and resources.

In 1990 the Association was welcomed back as an Associate Member, but in 1993 the country split, becoming the Czech Republic and the Slovak Republic. Later that year WAGGGS recognized the separate Associations for the newly-formed Republics.

The Programme
The present programme in operation in the Czech Republic focuses on the development of the individual and service. It is currently under revision to ensure that it meets contemporary needs. The Association has also developed a Ranger Section.

The name of Czech Brownies is "Fire-Flies". Their main duty is to "enlighten" the world.

Working with the Community
Service has always played a major part in the Association's programme. Projects will be developed as the Association becomes more firmly established.

Outdoor Activities
The Guides go regularly for hikes during the whole year. Camps, the highlight of the Guide year, last two or three weeks. The Guides build up their camps. The speciality of Czech camps are the wooden bases under tents. Environmental education stands in the centre of the camp programme.

Training
The Association organizes training courses at national level. Leadership training is being further developed and some foreign trainers have taken part in Czech courses. The Czech trainers and commissioners have also attended refresher courses in neighbouring countries, such as Austria.

Communication and Co-operation
The Association has a tradition of international exchanges and is now anxious to participate in events organized by other Member Organizations and the Europe Region. Scouting Nederland has a special link with the Czech Republic involving an exchange programme and exchange visits. These exchanges have also taken place with Guides from the United Kingdom.

A recent development, the teaching of English at Czech camp, has proved to be very popular.

The Association co-operates with other youth organizations. The organization publishes the monthly journal for Scout and Guide leaders – *Skauting*, (Scouting).

Fireflies – the name of the Czech Brownies.

Denmark

Pigespejdernes Fællesråd Danmark
(The Joint Committee of Girl Guides in Denmark)

Component Associations:
Det Danske Spejderkorps
(The Danish Guide and Scout Association)
KFUK-Spejderne i Danmark
(YWCA Girl Guides in Denmark)
Danske Baptisters Spejderkorps
(Danish Baptist Guide and Scout Association)
Kalaallit Nunaanni Spejderit Kattufiat - Grønlands Spejderkorps
(The Guide and Scout Association of Greenland)

Founder Member of WAGGGS

Girl Guiding/Girl Scouting introduced:	**1910**
Membership 1992:	**31,627**
Membership as % of female population:	**1.2%**
WAGGGS Region:	**Europe**

Det Danske Spejderkorps

Spejderløftet
Jeg lover at holde spejderloven.

Spejderloven
Den, der er med i spejdernes Fællesskab gør sit bedste for:
- at finde sin egen tro og have respekt for andres*
- at værne om naturen
- at være en god kammerat, være hensynsfuld og hjælpe andre
- at være til at stole på
- at høre andres meninger og danne sine egne
- at tage medansvar i familie og samfund.

Motto
Vær beredt

Promise
I promise to keep the Guide Law.

Law
The Guide who is part of the Guide fellowship does her best:
- to find her own faith and respect the faith of others*
- to protect nature
- to be a good friend, considerate and helpful to others
- to be trustworthy
- to listen to the opinion of others and to form her own
- to show responsibility in the family and in society (or, to take her share in responsibility for her family and her surroundings).

**Note: These words in Danish mean a spiritual faith, a belief in spiritual principles.*

Motto
Be Prepared

Age Groups

Seniorspejder	Ranger	16-23
Spejder	Guide	12-16
Juniorspejder	Junior Guide	10-12
Minispejder	Mini-Guide	8-10
Mikrospejder	Micro-Guide	6-8

Det Danske Spejderkorps, Association Badge

KFUK–Spejderne i Danmark, Guide

KFUK–Spejderne i Danmark, Brownie

KFUK-Spejderne i Danmark

Spejderløftet
Jeg lover at holde spejderloven.

Spejderlov og spejderløfte
Som spejder lover jeg at gøre mit bedste
for at ære Gud ved at leve efter hans vilje.

Derfor skal en spejder:
- tale sandhed
- stifte fred
- dele med andre
- være en god kammerat
- værne om naturen
- vise hensyn og hjælpe andre
- leve i hjem og samfund med kærlighed og omtanke.

Motto
Værn og tjen‡
‡the international motto
Vær beredt

Brownie Motto
Vi vil stå sammen
Vi vil gøre vort bedste

Guide Promise and Guide Law
As a Guide I promise to do my best
to honour God by living according to his will.

Therefore a Guide should:
speak the truth,
strive for peace,
share with others,
be a true friend,
cherish the living world,
be caring and help others,
show love and thoughtfulness in her home and community.

Motto
Protect and Serve‡
‡the international motto
Be Prepared

Brownie Motto
We will stick together
We will do our best

Age Groups

Ranger	Ranger Guide	17+
Senior spejder	Senior Guide	14+
Spejder	Guide	11-14
Grønsmutte	Brownie	7-10

Danske Baptisters Spejderkorps

Spejderløftet
Jeg lover at gøre mit bedste for at holde spejderloven.

Spejderloven
- Som spejder vil jeg lytte til Guds ord.
- Som spejder har jeg medansvar for det samfund, jeg lever i.
- Som spejder vil jeg være hensynsfuld og hjælpsom.
- Som spejder vil jeg være til at stole på.
- Som spejder vil jeg lytte til andres mening og selv tage standpunkt.
- Som spejder vil jeg lære naturen at kende og værne om den.

Motto
Vær beredt
Spejderflokken: Gør dit bedste

Promise
I promise to do my best to obey the Guide Law.

Law
- Being a Guide I will listen to the word of God.
- Being a Guide I have co-responsibility for the community in which I am living.
- Being a Guide I will be considerate and ready to help.
- Being a Guide I will be reliable.
- Being a Guide I will listen to the opinion of others and make up my mind.
- Being a Guide I will be acquainted with nature and protect it.

Motto
Be Prepared
Guide-packs: Do your Best

Age Groups

Ranger		
RS spejder	Guide/Scout Group	16+
Gruppespejder	Guide/Scout Troop	13-16
Tropspejder	Guide/Scout Pack	10-13
Flokspejder	Guide/Scout Hock	7-10
Klyngespejder	Guide/Scout	5-7

Kalaallit Nunaanni Spejderit Kattufiat - Grønlands Spejderkorps

Spejderlov
Som medlem af spejderbev gelsen vil jeg gøre mit bedste for:
- at være tro mod Gud
- at tage et medansvar for mit land
- at værne naturen og alt levende
- at være hensynsfuld og hjælpe andre
- at være til at stole på
- at lytte til andres mening og finde min egen.

Spejderløfte
Jeg lover at gre mit bedste for at holde spejderloven.

Motto
Vær beredt

Junior Guide Promise
Jeg lover at gøre mit bedste for at holde spejderloven og hver dag gøre en lille ting der kan hjælpe eller glæde en anden.

Junior Guide Law
Klar dig selv og hjælp andre

Promise
I promise to do my best to obey the Guide Law.

Law
As a member of the Guide Movement I will do my best:
- to do my duty to God
- to do my duty as a responsible citizen
- to protect nature and all living creatures
- to be considerate and help others
- to be trustworthy
- to listen to the views held by other people and establish my own.

Motto
Be Prepared

Junior Guide Promise
I promise to do my best to obey the Junior Guide Law and every day do something to help or please others.

Junior Guide Law
Help yourself and help others

Age Groups

Seniorspejdere	Ranger	15+
Spejdere	Guide	10-15
Juniorspejdere	Junior Guide	7-10

Development of the Movement in Denmark

Guiding in Denmark began in 1910 when some girls joined a Boy Scout group. Within a few years the girls had their own organization, Det Danske Pigespejderkorps (The Danish Guide Association), and in 1919 the KFUK-Spejderne i Danmark (YWCA Girl Guides) was formed. These two associations joined in 1928 to form the National Organization, Pigespejdernes Fællesråd Danmark (The Joint Committee of Girl Guides in Denmark) when Denmark became a Founder Member of WAGGGS.

In 1976 the structure of the Joint Committee was changed to include the Danske Baptisters Spejderkorps (Danish Baptist Guide and Scout Association) as a separate association (they had previously been members through the KFUK-Spejderne i Danmark). HRH The Princess Benedikte is the president of the Joint Committee.

Pigespejdernes Fællesråd Danmark presents a united image to the public by issuing press releases for special events. The Joint Committee meets periodically with the Danish Scout Council and holds occasional weekend meetings for members of international committees in Denmark.

In 1993 the Association hosted the World Conference in Nyborg. It was the second time in 30 years that a Conference was held at the Nyborg Strand Hotel. All component Associations contributed to the successful arrangements and support.

Det Danske Spejderkorps

Det Danske Spejderkorps, which is open to girls and boys, was formed in January 1973 when Det Danske Pigesjderkorps merged with Det Danske Spejderkorps (The Danish Scout Association). HM Queen Ingrid is the Patron of the Association. In 1989 membership of the

The Guide and Scout Association of Greenland, Guide

The Guide and Scout Association of Greenland, Junior Guide

Association stood at approximately 32,000, of whom 16,331 were girls.

The Programme

In some instances activities for all age groups are co-educational, in others only Ranger/Rover sections carry out a joint programme. Provisions have been made to ensure equal representation of leaders of both sexes on the National Board, on all committees, and on the staff at regional and local level.

Working with the Community

The Association has worked closely with the Sudan Girl Guides Association since 1976. Projects have included the construction of a poultry farm near the Sudanese capital, and the preparation of a vegetable farm in the southern Sudanese village of Rejaf. Some of the practical work has been carried out at work camps attended by Danish and Sudanese Guides and Scouts. Local workers are employed on both farms and profits are used to continue the project by providing local people with leadership and professional training.

Danske Baptisters, Spejderkorps, Guide

Communication and Co-operation

Det Danske Spejderkorps was involved in a tree-planting project with Nepal Scouts in 1990.

The Association publishes five periodicals: *Spejd*, a monthly magazine for all members; *Tandem*, also published monthly, for patrol leaders; *Broen*, published every fortnight for Rangers/Rovers and leaders; *Gem*, published quarterly for leaders of the three younger age groups; and *Humblebien* (The Bumblebee), also published quarterly, and produced by children for all members of the Association.

Det Danske Spedjerkorps sponsored the WAGGGS/WOSM version of the health education manual *Facts for Life*, produced in co-operation with UNESCO, WHO and UNICEF. The publication was distributed free to all WAGGGS Member Organizations in 1989.

KFUK-Spejderne i Danmark

KFUK-Spejderne i Danmark is open only to girls. HM Queen Ingrid is Patron of the Association. The Metodist Kirkens Spejdere i Danmark (Guides and Scouts of the Methodist Church in Denmark) and the Frelsens Haers Pigespejdere (The Salvation Army Girl Guides) form part of the National Organization through the KFUK-Spejderne i Danmark. In 1992 membership of the Association stood at nearly 12,500.

The Programme

The Association constantly analyses and updates its programme and training scheme and has formed an experimental group, for members aged 6-8. Disabled members are integrated into existing companies.

Communication and Co-operation

KFUK-Spejderne i Danmark is twinned with Zambia.

The Association informs the general public about its activities through magazines and newspapers and produces audio visual displays for use in schools and churches. *Samspil* (Interaction), is the Association's monthly magazine for leaders, and, *Spejderi*, a monthly magazine for children.

Danske Baptisters Spejderkorps

Danske Baptisters Spejderkorps is open to girls and boys in the Danish Baptist Community. In 1992 female members numbered approximately 1,000.

The Programme

The arrangement of activities in the Association varies. Activities for all age groups may be co-educational, or only Ranger/Rover sections may carry out a joint programme. The objectives of the Association are to help children and young people to develop as independent, responsible and democratic citizens with international understanding. The programmes are currently being studied with a view to updating them. All members over 15 years of age may attend the Annual General Assembly.

Working with the Community

Since the beginning of 1984 the Association offered support to four Guide and Scout leaders from Rwanda. Funds for the project are collected by units

Brownie "climbing a mountain" in Denmark at a camp sponsored by the YWCA Girl Guides.

locally, and are sent to Rwanda in co-operation with the Danish Baptist Union.

Communication and Co-operation

The Association informs the general public about its activities, and publishes two monthly periodicals; *Spejdernyt*, for children; and *Forernyt*, for leaders.

Kalaallit Nanaanni Spejderit Kattufiat/Grønlands Spejderkorps

Guiding in Greenland is carried out through the Kalaallit Nanaanni Spejderit Kattufiat - Grønlands Spejderkorps, and this Association, open to girls and boys, has international recognition through the National Organization. Total membership in 1985 was approximately 2,000.

The Programme

In some cases all activities for all age groups are co-educational, sometimes only Ranger/Rover sections carry out a joint programme. The aim of the programme is to offer children and young people the opportunity to participate in Guiding and Scouting activities and thereby become active and positive contributors to the development of their communities. The Association has a group of Guides and Scouts in nearly every town and settlement in the country.

Training

The Association runs a three-tier training scheme: a basic course, run twice a year; an intermediate course, run every other year; and an advanced course, the Gilwell course, run every second or third year.

Communication and Co-operation

The Association publishes a magazine, *Majoriak*, for all members.

Dominica

The Girl Guides Association of Dominica

Girl Guiding/Girl Scouting introduced: 1930
Became Associate Member of WAGGGS: 1987
Membership 1992†: 525
Membership as % of female population: 1.24%
WAGGGS Region: Western Hemisphere

Guide

Promise

I promise that I will do my best;
To do my duty to God
To serve my Country, to help
other people and
To keep the Guide Law.

Law

1 A Guide is loyal and can be trusted.
2 A Guide is helpful.
3 A Guide is polite and considerate.
4 A Guide is friendly and a sister to all Guides.
5 A Guide is kind to animals and respects all living things.
6 A Guide is obedient.
7 A Guide has courage and is cheerful in all difficulties.
8 A Guide makes good use of her time.
9 A Guide takes care of her own possessions and those of other people.
10 A Guide is self-controlled in all she thinks, says and does.

Motto

Be Prepared

Brownie Guide

Brownie Guide Promise

I promise I will do my best;
To do my duty to God
To serve my Country, to help
other people and to
Keep the Brownie Guide Law.

Brownie Guide Law

A Brownie Guide thinks of others before herself and does a good turn every day.

Brownie Guide Motto

Lend a hand

Development of the Movement in Dominica

In 1928 a Guider from neighbouring Barbados visited Dominica and persuaded her friend, who was resident in Dominica, to work towards the establishment of Guiding there.

In 1930 the first Dominica Girl Guide Company was inaugurated, the first Brownie pack soon followed in 1931, and two Ranger companies were started in 1933.

The Association functioned as a Branch Association of the Girl Guides Association (United Kingdom) until 1986 when it became self-governing. Because of the effects of war, there was little Guiding activity during the years 1940 to 1945, but the programme soon resumed in 1946.

After a visit by the World Chief Guide and trainers from the United Kingdom in 1951, new enthusiasm developed and Guiding became firmly established in Dominica.

In 1979 the Association celebrated its Golden Jubilee but in August of the same year, Hurricane David struck the island and caused a major disruption to Guiding due to large scale emigration and a preoccupation with economic recovery and survival. By 1981, however, Guiding had resumed its normal activities and has since continued to grow steadily.

The Programme

The current programme used in Dominica is based on eight-points: keeping fit; becoming a homemaker; keeping the

Guide Law; getting to know people; enjoying the outdoors; thinking for yourself and exploring the arts. New programmes and training schemes are under preparation.

Working with the Community
Community Service is an important part of the Guide programme in Dominica. Guides provide meals for the patients at the infirmary; entertain and care for senior citizens; organize parties for needy children; and visit children's hospital wards.

The Rangers in the North District help at a health centre and in 1986 they started to construct a bus stand at Blenheim with the help of parents and well-wishers.

Communication and Co-operation
The Association actively participates in events organized by other associations in the Caribbean and often takes part in overseas camps.

Dominica is twinned with the State of New Brunswick, Canada. Together they are supporting a self-help scheme for 12 young mothers in the village of Pointe Michel, an economically-depressed fishing village about five miles from Roseau, the capital of Dominica.

The Girl Guides Association of Dominica has been an accepted part of the community for almost 60 years and has good relations with the government.

Dominican Republic

Asociación de Guías Scouts Dominicanas, Inc.

Guiding started: 1961
Became Associate Member of WAGGGS: 1969
Became Full Member of WAGGGS: 1990
Membership 1992: 549
Membership as % of female population: 0.015%
WAGGGS Region: Western Hemisphere

Guide

Promesa

Yo prometo por mi honor hacer cuanto de mí dependa para:
Cumplir con mi deber hacia Dios y mi Patria,
Ser útil al prójimo en todo momento,
Obedecer la Ley Guía.

Ley

1 La Guía es persona en cuyo honor se puede confiar.
2 La Guía es leal.
3 El deber de la Guía es ser útil y ayudar a otros.
4 La Guía es amiga de todos y hermana de toda Guía.
5 La Guía es cortés.
6 La Guía es amiga de los animales.
7 La Guía obedece órdenes.
8 La Guía sonríe y canta en todas las dificultades.
9 La Guía es económica.
10 La Guía es pura de pensamiento, palabra, y obra.

Motto

Siempre Lista

Little Wing

Promesa de la Alita

Prometo hacer todo lo que pueda para cumplir con mi deber hacia Dios y mi Patria y ayudar todos los días a los demás, especialmente a los de mi casa.

Ley de la Alita

La Alita accede a los deseos de sus mayores.
La Alita nunca cede a sí misma.

Motto de la Alita

Dar Ayuda

Promise

I promise, on my honour, to do my best:
To do my duty to God and my country;
To help other people at all times;
To obey the Guide Law.

Law

1 A Guide is a person whose honour is to be trusted.
2 A Guide is loyal.
3 A Guide's duty is to be useful and to help others.
4 A Guide is a friend to all and a sister to every other Guide.
5 A Guide is courteous.
6 A Guide is a friend to animals.
7 A Guide obeys orders.
8 A Guide smiles and sings under all difficulties.
9 A Guide is thrifty.
10 A Guide is pure in thought, word and deed.

Motto

Always ready

Little Wing Promise

I promise to do my best:
To do my duty to God and my Country, and
To help others every day, especially those at home.

Little Wing Law

A Little Wing gives in to the wishes of her elders.
A Little Wing never gives in to herself.

Little Wing Motto

Lend a Hand

Age Groups

Guías Mayores	Senior Guide	15-18
Guías Intermedias	Intermediate Guide	10-14
Alitas	Little Wing	6-9

Development of the Movement in the Dominican Republic

The first company was opened in the Dominican Republic in San Pedro de Macoris in 1961 with the help of representatives from the WAGGGS Western Hemisphere Committee and by April that year Guiding had spread to Santo Domingo. By 1964 the Association had three branches, with the formation of a group of Senior Guides to complement the existing Brownies and Guides.

The Association's National Headquarters were opened in Santiago in 1976 and by 1980 Guiding had spread to the whole country and companies and packs were found in all provinces. In 1988 the National Committee launched an expansion programme with the intention of increasing its membership and improving the quality of Guiding.

The Programme

The Association aims to offer members a programme that provides opportunities for personal growth and development of character through education and fun. A social worker was employed in 1990 to survey the needs of the girls and develop a recruitment plan and revised programmes are currently being tested by leaders. Girls attend discussion groups on such subjects as drug addiction, the Promise and Law, and the young girl and her attitude to the community.

Working with the Community

Service and community development play an important part in the life of the Association. Guides visit hospitals, work in orphanages, and take part in literacy and vaccination campaigns. In 1990, International Literacy Year, Guides and Senior Guides were involved in a literacy programme in several areas of the country.

Outdoor and Environmental Activities

Camping is enjoyed by all and the countryside provides many natural campsites, although schools are also used for camping. The Association organizes an annual "Afternoon of wine and cheese" in order to raise funds. Guides also take part in reafforestation campaigns.

Training

The Dominican Republic has a training team, a training adviser and a national trainer. A training scheme has been prepared which covers training for leaders and girls. A three year development plan has also been devised. Efforts are being made to employ a full-time trainer to take on responsibility for the production of training material and visits to the provinces.

Communication and Co-operation

Members of the Association attend gatherings and seminars abroad whenever possible and input from such events has strengthened Guiding in the Dominican Republic. The Association tries to participate in all Western Hemisphere events and encourages its members to visit Our Cabaña, the WAGGGS World Centre in Mexico.

The Association has an excellent relationship with the general public, the church, the media and the government. Activities are often featured on television in Santiago and Santo Domingo, helping to make the Association widely known. A monthly bulletin containing news and training material is also produced by the Association as well as publicity leaflets on various topics.

Guides enjoy boating as part of the programme of outdoor activities.

Ecuador

Asociación Nacional de Guías Scouts del Ecuador

Girl Guiding/Girl Scouting introduced:	**1919**
Became Associate Member of WAGGGS:	**1966**
Became Full Member of WAGGGS:	**1984**
Membership 1992:	**561**
Membership as % of female population:	**0.01%**
WAGGGS Region:	**Western Hemisphere**

Girl-Scout

Promesa

Yo prometo por mi honor, hacer todo cuanto de mí dependa, para cumplir mis deberes para con Dios y mi Patria, ser útil al prójimo en todo momento y obedecer la Ley Guía-Scout.

Ley

1 La Guía Scout es persona de honor.
2 La Guía Scout es leal.
3 La Guía Scout tiene el deber de ser útil y ayudar al prójimo.
4 La Guía Scout es amiga de todos y hermana de las demás Guías.
5 La Guía Scout es cortés.
6 La Guía Scout ama a los animales y a las plantas y ve la obra de Dios en la naturaleza.
7 La Guía Scout es obediente y disciplinada.
8 La Guía Scout sonríe y canta en las dificultades.
9 La Guía Scout es económica.
10 La Guía Scout es pura en sus pensamientos, palabras y obras.

Lema

Siempre Listas

Little Wing

Promesa de la Alita

Yo prometo hacer lo mejor que pueda para cumplir mis deberes con Dios y mi Patria, ayudar a todos especialmente a los de mi casa.

Ley de la Alita

La Alita dice siempre la verdad.
La Alita es obediente y alegre.

Lema de la Alita

Dar Ayuda con Alegría

Promise

I promise, on my honour, to do my best:
To fulfil my duties to God and my Country;
To help other people at all times; and to obey the Girl-Scout Law.

Law

1 A Girl-Scout is a person whose honour is to be trusted.
2 A Girl-Scout is loyal.
3 A Girl-Scout's duty is to be useful and to help others.
4 A Girl-Scout is a friend to all and a sister to all other Guides.
5 A Girl-Scout is courteous.
6 A Girl-Scout loves animals and plants and sees the work of God in nature.
7 A Girl-Scout is obedient and disciplined.
8 A Girl-Scout smiles and sings under all difficulties.
9 A Girl-Scout is thrifty.
10 A Girl-Scout is pure in her thoughts, words and deeds.

Motto

Always ready

Little Wing Promise

I promise to do my best to do my duty to God and my Country, to help everyone especially those at home.

Little Wing Law

A Little Wing always tells the truth.
A Little Wing is obedient and cheerful.

Little Wing Motto

Lend a Hand Cheerfully

Age Groups

Guía Mayor	Ranger	17-19
Cadete	Cadet	14-16
Junior	Junior	11-13
Alita	Little Wing	7-10

Development of the Movement in Ecuador

The Movement started in Ecuador in 1919 when several companies were formed in the city of Guayaquil, but it was not until 1952 that an Association was established with the help of a WAGGGS' travelling commissioner for the Western Hemisphere. Support from the Western Hemisphere Region helped the Association to develop and it has since extended from the tropical coastal cities to the mountain regions in the interior of the country. Headquarters for the Association are near completion.

The Programme

The programme incorporates alternative sections to suit the varied environments and needs prevalent in Ecuador, reflecting the differences between the coastal regions and the sierra. The programme is designed to make a positive contribution towards the education and development of the girls.

Working with the Community

The Asociación Nacional de Guías Scouts del Ecuador is conscious of community needs and is making efforts to improve the quality of life in Ecuador. Activities include the provision of children's recreation, the organization of holiday camps, and the introduction of literacy schemes and leadership courses for people in isolated areas.

Girl Scouts attend first aid classes to ensure that they are ready to help out in emergency situations. During recent years the Association has worked closely with the Civil Defence in distributing clothes, food and medicines in response to natural disasters such as floods and earthquakes.

Outdoor and Environmental Activities

The Asociación Nacional de Guías Scouts del Ecuador owns three campsites: a campsite and programme centre, Juanita Baca de Dávila, on the outskirts of Quito; the Doña Cary National Campsite near Data in the coastal region; and the Isabel de Ramia campsite in Santo Domingo de los Colorados. Camping is enjoyed by many Girl Scouts and families.
The Association is involved in several ecological schemes including tree-planting and a soil, water and air project.

Training

Seven experienced trainers meet regularly to plan training and programme activities and evaluate work in progress. Training courses are carried out at national and local level for patrol leaders and the leaders of each branch. As the school year in the Sierra is from October to July, and in the coastal regions from May to January, the training courses are held separately, with national training courses held whenever suitable to all.

These girls show the uniform and badges from Ecuador.

Communication and Co-operation

The Asociación Nacional de Guías Scouts del Ecuador actively encourages its members to attend international events and the Association sends delegates to regional and world training events whenever possible. During the late 1980s and early 1990s the association took part in an Experiment in International Living, offering hospitality to a group of members from the United Kingdom for a four-week stay in Ecuador.

The Association takes an active part in Western Hemisphere events and members have attended several events at Our Cabaña, WAGGGS' World Centre in Mexico. One member attended an event at Sangam, WAGGGS' World Centre in India.

The Association is well-known and well-received by the general public. The media is supportive in publicizing its activities and its co-operation with other national voluntary organizations.

Arab Republic of Egypt

Gamiet Morshidat Gomhoriet Misr El Arabiah
(Egyptian Girl Guides Association)

Girl Guiding/Girl Scouting introduced:	**1913**
Became Full Member of WAGGGS:	**1931**
Membership 1992:	**59,652**
Membership as % of female population:	**0.26%**
Member:	**Arab Regional Group**

Guide

Methak

Aedou Besharafi an assaa gohdi lean akoom belwagib alei nahow Allah Thoma alwatan, waan Osaed El Nass fi gamie elzoroof, waan Amel, Bkanoon al morshidat.

Kanoon

1 Sharaf Almorshida iman wathik.
2 Almorshida mokhlisa Lillah walwatan.
3 Wagib Almorshida an takoon nafia waan toeen ghairaha.
4 Almorshida sadikat elgamie wa okht lekol morshida okhra.
5 Almorshida hamidat elsagaya.
6 Almorshida rafika belhayawan.
7 Totei Almorshida awamer walediha wa kaedat ferkatiha wa raissat kesmah.
8 Tabtasim Almorshida lilshadaid watoka belha besabrin wa thabat.
9 Almorshida moddakhira.
10 Almorshida nakiat elsareera tabiyat elkaib wa kareemat elsagaya.

Sheaar

Koony mostaeda

Promise

On my honour I promise to do my duty to God, then my country. To help people in all circumstances. To obey the Guide Law.

Brownie

Law

1 A Guide's honour is to be trusted.
2 A Guide is loyal.
3 A Guide's duty is to be useful and to help others.
4 A Guide is a friend to all and a sister to every other Guide.
5 A Guide is courteous.
6 A Guide is a friend to animals.
7 A Guide obeys orders.
8 A Guide smiles when facing difficulties, and deals with all such difficulties with patience and perseverance.
9 A Guide is thrifty.
10 A Guide is pure in thought, in word and in deed.

Motto

Be Prepared

Brownie Promise

I promise to do my best:
To perform my duty towards God and my dear country;
To help people every day, especially my family.

Brownie Law

Totei Al. Zahra. Kol Man
Yakbarha Senan.
La. Tastslem le Hawa Nafseha

Brownie Motto

Helping people

Age Groups

Gawalat	Ranger	16+
Morshidat	Guide	12-15
Zahrat	Brownie	6-11

Development of the Movement in Egypt

Guiding in Egypt began around 1918 and was introduced to schools in 1925 followed by the formation of the Egyptian Girl Guides Association in 1929. Since then Guiding has expanded into factories and community clubs.

The Programme

Programmes are designed to meet the needs of Egyptian girls and to provide service to the country. The Ranger age group may choose between service projects and activities on land, sea or air.

The Association also works with disabled girls with a view to extending Guiding activities to suit their special needs.

Working with the Community

The Association takes part in hygiene, first aid, literacy and family planning campaigns. In addition, Rangers have worked as literacy teachers as part of a government literacy campaign, receiving high praise from the authorities.

Five vocational training centres have been set up where girls are taught traditional skills including knitting, weaving and embroidery. Some of these centres have received financial support from UNESCO.

Guides from developed areas help other members by preparing training material for leaders; making Brownie, Guide and Ranger uniforms; and supplying school clothing and school bags. Rural camps give Guides the opportunity to co-operate with local people and to participate in organizing welfare projects such as opening nurseries and caring for families in need.

Guide and Scout units attached to colleges and universities work in health caravans in villages around the country bringing health education to rural localities as part of a national immunization campaign.

Outdoor and Environmental Activities

Camping plays a prominent part in training, and camps are frequently organized for leaders. Guides from neighbouring Arab countries often attend camps held in Egypt.

Training

Leadership training is given special priority by the Association, and Guides are encouraged to undertake responsibilities in planning and running camps. Seminars are organized at the Association's headquarters for commissioners and leaders of each age group.

Communication and Co-operation

The Association encourages and assists members to participate in regional and world events and receives and entertains Girl Guides/Girl Scouts from neighbouring countries. The Association's health caravan programme is carried out with both physical and financial support from Guides in Austria. Egypt also co-operates with Liechteinstein on a palm-tree project which aims to establish a factory to turn the raw materials from palm trees into various finished products.

The Egyptian Girl Guides Association has co-operated with UNESCO, UNICEF and WHO on various projects, and has also supported the United Nations' International years.

Finally, members work with people with special needs in co-operation with the Faith and Hope Society.

Guides and Rangers work to clean up their community.

El Salvador

Asociación de Muchachas Guías de El Salvador

Girl Guiding/Girl Scouting introduced: 1944
Became Associate Member of WAGGGS: 1960
Became Full Member of WAGGGS: 1975
Membership 1992: 1,814
Membership as % of female population: 0.07%
WAGGGS Region: Western Hemisphere

Girl Guide

Promesa
Yo prometo por mi honor hacer cuanto de mí dependa para:
cumplir con mi deber hacia Dios y mi patria:
ser útil al projimo en toda circunstancia;
obedecer la Ley Guía.

Ley
1 La Muchacha Guía es persona en cuyo honor se puede confiar.
2 La Muchacha Guía es leal.
3 La Muchacha Guía debe ser útil y ayudar al prójimo.
4 La Muchacha Guía es amiga de todos y hermana de toda Guía.
5 La Muchacha Guía es bien educada y cortés.
6 La Muchacha Guía admira a Dios en la Naturaleza.
7 La Muchacha Guía acepta y cumple órdenes.
8 La Muchacha Guía afronta animosamente las dificultades.
9 La Muchacha Guía es económica.
10 La Muchacha Guía es pura de pensamiento, palabra y obra.

Motto
Siempre Lista

Little Wing

Little Wing Promise
Prometo hacer todo lo que me sea posible, para cumplir con mi deber hacia Dios y mi Patria, ayudar todos los días a los demás, especialmente a los de mi casa.

Little Wing Law
La Alita accede a los deseos de sus mayores.
La Alita nunca cede a sí misma.

Little Wing Motto
Dar Ayuda

Promise
I promise on my honour to do my best;
To do my duty to God and my Country,
To help other people in all circumstances;
to obey the Guide Law.

Law
1 A Girl Guide is a person whose honour is to be trusted.
2 A Girl Guide is loyal.
3 A Girl Guide should be useful and help other people.
4 A Girl Guide is a friend to all and a sister to every other Guide.
5 A Girl Guide is polite and courteous.
6 A Girl Guide admires God in Nature.
7 A Girl Guide accepts and complies with orders.
8 A Girl Guide faces all difficulties with courage.
9 A Girl Guide is thrifty.
10 A Girl Guide is pure in thought, word and deed.

Motto
Always ready

Little Wing Promise
I promise to do everything possible to do my duty to God and my country, help others every day, especially those at home.

Little Wing Law
A Little Wing gives in to the wishes of her elders.
A Little Wing never gives in to herself.

Little Wing Motto
Lend a Hand

Age Groups

Guía Mayor	Senior Guide	15-18
Guía		
Intermedia	Guide	11-15
Alita	Little Wing	7-11

Development of the Movement in El Salvador

Guiding began in El Salvador when a small group of Guides was established at the Bethany Institute of Santa Tecla. The Asociación de Muchachas Guías de El Salvador was founded in 1944 and was officially recognized in 1949.

After a period of decline, a fresh impetus was given to the Association in 1955 when WAGGGS' travelling commissioner for the Western Hemisphere formed an executive committee, and the Guide programme became more educational and geared towards the interests of the girl.

The Programme

The programme provides for a balanced range of activities and offers development for participants as they progress from one stage to the next. Training is an important part of the programme and sessions are held as often as possible.

Working with the Community

Community service programmes are carried out at national level, including courses on literacy and nutrition. Guides visit hospitals and homes for the elderly and take part in clean-up campaigns. In addition to the regular programme, a Guide Week is held every year when members carry out special projects at home, at school and within the community.

The Association has helped homeless war victims by arranging accommodation for them in schools and churches and at its headquarters. Guides collected food and clothing and encouraged the formation of committees among the homeless.

Guides in El Salvador run educational workshops for women in seven different areas of the country. In 1989, 1,250 students attended regular classes in a variety of subjects including tailoring and dressmaking, embroidery, making artificial flowers, working with leather, and managing a small business.

Outdoor and Environmental Activities

Many Guides belonging to the Asociación de Muchachas Guías de El Salvador attend a camp once a year. The Association has a site at Asino, 20 kilometres from the capital.

Environmental awareness is encouraged through national tree-planting and re-afforestation projects.

Girls from Honduras, Colombia and Guatemala attend an International Rangers' Camp in El Salvador.

Training

International training sessions for trainers are held every year with other associations from Central America.

Communication and Co-operation

The Association is keen to exchange experiences with other Associations in the region. El Salvador has taken an active part in a Central American exchange programme which has included exchanges with Honduras and Guatemala.

Leaders and Rangers regularly attend meetings at Our Cabaña, the WAGGGS World Centre in Mexico.

The Association informs the public about its activities through the newspapers, radio and television and publishes an annual training magazine for leaders called *Tahuil*, meaning light.

The El Salvador Association co-operates with many other organizations in its efforts to contribute to the improvement of living standards in the Salvadorian community. These include Plan Godfathers of Salvador, National Commission for Displaced Persons of Salvador, Ministry of Agriculture, Ministry of Education, Centre of Salvadorian Training in Applied Technology, Association for Academic Women of Salvador, Salvadorian Foundation for Development, Salvadorian Cultural Heritage.

In addition the Canadian International Development Agency (CIDA), the Canadian Hunger Foundations, the Hans Seidel Foundation of Germany, UNICEF and FAO all support the Association's work. The Guides also co-operate with the church in religious activities.

Estonia

Eesti Gaidide Maleva Ja Eesti Gaidide Ühenduse Koostööliit

Founder Member of WAGGGS

Girl Guiding/Girl Scouting introduced:	**1919**
Guiding banned:	**1940**
Re-admitted as Associate Member of WAGGGS:	**1993**
Membership 1993:	**1,597**
WAGGGS Region:	**Europe**

Guide

Brownie

Promise

I promise that I will do my best:
To do my duty to God and my country
To help other people at all times and
To obey the Guide Law.

Law

A Guide is to be trusted
A Guide is loyal
A Guide helps other people at all times
A Guide is a friend to all and a sister to every other Guide
A Guide is courteous
A Guide is a friend to nature and animals
A Guide is deferential
A Guide smiles under all difficulties
A Guide is thrifty
A Guide is pure in thought, in word and in deed.

Age Groups

Rangers	18-20/23
Guides	10-18
Brownies	6-10

Development of the Movement in Estonia

Girl Guides were first organized in Tallinn in 1919 as part of the Boy Scout Association. After a Boy Scout Jamboree held in London that same year, the girls separated from the Scouts and became known as Eesti Gaid Maleva (Estonian Guides' Organization).

In 1928, when WAGGGS was formed, Eesti Gaid Maleva became a Founder Member. 1936 brought great changes to the ways of work of the Association when the government formed a new youth department controlling all youth organizations. In 1940, following the establishment of the Soviet Socialist Republic of Estonia, Girl Guiding and Scouting were banned in the country.

In 1988 both Girl Guiding and Scouting were restarted as a result of political changes in Estonia and by 1989 there were five registered Guide and Scout Organizations. In 1992 two Guide Associations, Eesti Gaidide Maleva (EGM) and Eesti Gaidide Ühendus (EGU) formed a federation with a view to re-applying for membership of WAGGGS. The federation works closely with the Guides and Scouts of Finland to develop Guiding and introduce it to more areas of the country. Guiding is now found in most big cities and also in the countryside.

The Programme

The programme is geared towards the development of the girl and young woman and is based around the fundamental principles of Girl Guiding. Leaders are expected to follow a set programme, with freedom to adapt it to the needs of the girls in the group.

Working with the Community

Service has always played a major role in Association programming, and projects will be developed as the Association becomes firmly established.

Outdoor and Environmental Activities

Camping is a popular activity and camps are held throughout the year. Campsites are often given free of charge by the local authorities.

Training

A Training Committee is responsible for all aspects of training including the annual training calendar, incorporating 21 training events. Until 1993 all advanced training was carried out in Finland.

Communication and Co-operation

The organization has a good relationship with religious organizations and the government and meeting places are often provided by religious organizations, as is some financial help.

The relationship with the Scouts is good.

A Guide and Scout Week is held annually in April, an opportunity to inform the general public about the work of the organization. During this week various activities and exhibitions are organized by both Guide and Scout organizations.

The Gaidide Maleva publishes a newsletter five to six times a year and the Gaidide Ühendus has published a Guide programme book and song book. 'The Estonian Guides in Exile' have provided some training material in Estonian and some Finnish, Danish and English publications are also used.

Girl Guides learn to use the media effectively during their unit meeting.

Fiji

Fiji Girl Guides Association

Girl Guiding/Girl Scouting introduced: 1924
Became Associate Member of WAGGGS: 1981
Membership 1992: 6,100
Membership as % of female population: 1.6%
WAGGGS Region: Asia Pacific

Promise
I promise that I will do my best:
To do my duty to God
To serve (the Queen and) my country and help other people and
To keep the Guide Law.

Law
1 A Guide is loyal and can be trusted.
2 A Guide is helpful.
3 A Guide is polite and considerate.
4 A Guide is friendly and a sister to all Guides.
5 A Guide is kind to animals and respects all living things.
6 A Guide is obedient.
7 A Guide has courage and is cheerful in all difficulties.
8 A Guide makes good use of her time.
9 A Guide takes care of her possessions and those of other people.
10 A Guide is self-controlled in all she thinks, says and does.

Motto
Be Prepared

Brownie Guide Promise
I promise that I will do my best:
To do my duty to God,
To serve (the Queen and) my country and help other people and
To keep the Brownie Guide Law.

Brownie Guide Law
A Brownie Guide thinks of others before herself and does a good turn every day.

Brownie Guide Motto
Lend a Hand

Age Groups

Ranger	$14\frac{1}{2}$-22
Guide	$10\frac{1}{2}$-$14\frac{1}{2}$
Brownie Guide	$7\frac{1}{2}$-$10\frac{1}{2}$

Development of the Movement in Fiji

The first Guide company was started in Levuka in 1924 by a Methodist missionary. In 1926 this group of Guides participated in a parade in Suva in honour of a royal visit, and as a result of this public appearance the first Toorak Company was formed in Suva. By 1928 more companies and a Brownie pack had been established in Suva, and all companies had been registered with The Girl Guides Association (United Kingdom). In September 1930 the Girl Guides Association of Fiji was formed.

In 1942 the activities of the growing organization were suspended when Fiji became a military base and schools were used for military purposes. At the end of the Second World War, Guiding was re-established.

Over the years, trainers and other experienced personnel from The Girl Guides Association (United Kingdom) have visited Fiji to assist the Association in the development of its programme and the implementation of its training strategy.

In 1980 The Girl Guides Association (United Kingdom) signed a Deed of Transfer giving the Fiji Girl Guides Association self-government in all areas of work.

The Programme
The programme used in Fiji was prepared by the South Pacific Guide Conference for particular use in the Pacific Islands. The Brownie and Guide programme was introduced in 1976 and the Ranger programme in 1979. Members with special needs are integrated into ordinary units whenever possible.

Guide

Brownie Guide

Working with the Community
Many Guides work in hospitals, caring for patients and cleaning wards. All age groups give service to the community during the annual Guide and Scout Week, when specific projects are carried out. Members also collect firewood and clear gardens for the elderly.

Rangers are involved in a variety of income-generating projects including sewing and vegetable gardening. In urban areas some units learn office skills such as typing, book-keeping and office-management.

Outdoor and Environmental Activities
Residential courses are to be introduced at a training centre and campsite near Suva. The interest that Guides in Fiji take in their environment is demonstrated by their efforts to clear public parks and footpaths and to plant trees.

Training
A training adviser, who heads a training team of 12, has the responsibility for implementing the training programme and supervising all trainings held in the country. Local and national trainings are arranged at regular intervals.

Communication and Co-operation
Fiji is a member of the Caribbean Link set up for the purpose of consultation and mutual aid between Guide Associations in the Commonwealth countries and islands of the Caribbean. Members participate in many international events.

The Association is recognized by the government through the Education Department and the Ministry of Youth and Sport. The Guides are an important part of community life and are often invited to participate in national days and other events.

Every month a 15-minute radio programme on Guiding is broadcast in Fijian, Hindi and English and the Association also publicizes its activities through its periodical, *Fiji Newsletter*.

The Fiji Girl Guides Association combines with the Fiji Scout Association each year to hold a Guide and Scout Week. The Association also works with organizations such as the YWCA, the Red Cross and the St. John's Ambulance Association and is a member of the Fiji National Council of Women.

Brownies in Fiji help out with a local event.

Finland

Suomen Partiolaiset - Finlands Scouter r.y.

(The Guides and Scouts of Finland)

Founder Member of WAGGGS
Girl Guiding/Girl Scouting introduced: 1910
Membership 1992: 47,158
Membership as % of female population: 1.83%
WAGGGS Region: Europe

Promise
Tahdon rakastaa jumalaani ja lähimmäistäni, isänmaatani ja ihmiskuntaa toteuttaen elämässäni partioihanteita.

Ideals
Partiolaisen ihanteena on
- kehittää itseään ihmisenä
- kunnioittaa toista ihmistä
- auttaa ja palvella muita
- tuntea vastuunsa ja velvollisuutensa
- rakastaa ja suojella luontoa
- olla uskollinen ja luotettava
- rakentaa ystävyyttä yli rajojen
- etsiä elämän totuutta.

Motto
Ole valmis

Brownie Promise
Lupaan parhaani mukaan rakastaa Jumalaani, toteuttaa sudenpentujen lakia ja olla toisille avuksi joka päivä.

Brownie Law
Sudenpentu on reipas ja rehellinen.

Brownie Motto
Tahdon tehdä parhaani

Promise
Jag vill älska min Gud och min nästa, mitt land och mänskligheten, i det jag söker förverkliga scoutidealen i mitt liv.

Ideals
En scouts ideal är...
- att utveckla sig själv som människa,
- att känna aktning för andra,
- att hjälpa och tjäna sin nästa,
- att inse sitt ansvar och sina plikter,
- att älska och skydda naturen,
- att vara trofast och pålitlig,
- att främja vänskap över gränserna,
- att söka sanningen i tillvaron.

Motto
Var redo

Brownie Promise
Jag lovar, att efter min bästa förmåga älska min Gud, följa vargungarnas lag och hjälpa andra människor varje dag.

Brownie Law
En vargunge är glad, hjälpsam och ärlig.

Brownie Motto
Jag vill göra mitt bästa

Promise
I will love my God and my neighbour; my native country and mankind by fulfilling the Girl Guide ideals in my life.

Ideals
The ideal of a Girl Guide is...
- to develop herself as a human being
- to respect other human beings
- to help and serve others
- to recognize her responsibility and duties
- to love and protect nature
- to be faithful and reliable
- to build friendships across borders
- to seek for the truth in life.

Motto
Be Prepared

Brownie Promise
I promise to do my best to love my God, to fulfil the Brownie Law and to help others every day.

Brownie Law
A Brownie is cheerful and honest.

Girl Guide

Brownie

Brownie Motto
I will do my best

Age Groups

Vaeltaja (Finnish)		
Seniorscout (Swedish)	Ranger	15-20
Partiolainen (Finnish)		
Flickscout (Swedish)	Guide	10-14
Sudenpentu (Finnish)		
Vargunge (Swedish)	Brownie	7-10

Development of the Movement in Finland

The first Girl Guide company in Finland was formed in 1910, but the years that followed saw great political upheaval resulting in a ban on Girl Guiding. The Movement was officially revived in 1917, and it has expanded steadily and gained strength ever since. The first Brownie pack was started in 1925 and the first Ranger company in 1930. In 1928 three Finnish Associations, Suomalainen Partiotyttöliitto, Finlands Svenska Scoutförbund and Suomen Vapaa Partioryhmä, were recognized together as a Founder Member of WAGGGS.

Interest in the Movement grew fast, and before long there were five active Girl Guide Associations in Finland. In 1934 Girl Guiding was introduced for girls with special needs. The Second World War created the need for closer co-operation, and in 1943 a single Association, the Union of Finnish Girl Guides, was established.

The Union of Finnish Girl Guides worked in co-operation with the Scout Union of Finland, and in 1972 the two unions concluded a formal agreement of co-operation, which preceded the formation of a joint organization. As a result of this, administration for national events and trainings is a combined undertaking and all the Guide and Scout districts work together. At local level many companies still work separately.

In 1973 a study was carried out on the development of Guiding and Scouting in Finland and a long-term planning system for activities and finance established. The two unions were reorganized, new plans were made for strengthening fundraising and public relations, and in 1972, the merged organization, Suomen Partiolaiset - Finlands Scouter r.y. (The Guides and Scouts of Finland) was formed.

The Programme
Guides and Scouts have the same basic programme, with a separate section for each age group. The programme for the Brownies and Cub Scouts is based on eight fairy tales/adventures about various themes. It is sub-divided into three stages: Pikkuhukka (the pet name for a wolf cub), Hukka (the pet name of folk origin for a wolf) and Susi (wolf in Finnish).

The programme for the Guides and Scouts is based on three class stages and it consists of both obligatory activities and optional activity badges. There are three levels of achievement: third class, second class and first class. Implementation of the programme depends upon the interests of each patrol.

The Association's members include Sea Guides and Scouts. Their activities involve instruction in skills and knowledge of boating, sailing and other forms of seafaring and related activities. The principle of safety is conscientiously observed. Activities are largely centred on sailing and boating in the summer, and maintenance of equipment in the winter.

The programme for the Rangers and Rovers aims to achieve and realize the educational goals of Guiding and Scouting: to help Members to develop as human beings capable of living in harmony and peace with themselves, other people and the environment.

The Association runs Radio Guiding and Scouting which is centred on such communication activities as walkie-talkies, amateur radio and orienteering. Many Radio Guides and Scouts participate in voluntary rescue service teams.

Members with special needs are integrated into existing units if possible, and there are also special units with activities adapted to individual needs.

Working with the Community
Members participate in rescue service teams, and they have raised money for disabled war veterans. In line with its emphasis on service, the Association has helped establish workshops for the people with special needs.

In 1992-1993 The Guides and Scouts of Finland have worked together with World Wide Fund for Nature WWF Finland. A training package (books, equipment) has been sent to the troops. Finnish Guides and Scouts have also raised funds for nature protection and organized voluntary work camps with WWF.

Outdoor and Environmental Activities

Camping, including pioneering, games and cross-country competitions, has always been considered the highlight of Guiding and Scouting activities in Finland. An annual camp under canvas lasting from 7 to 10 days is usually included in the activities for each company. Camps are held in the woods near a lake or the sea. Members also go for weekend outings during school terms and for overnight hikes during holidays. Guides with special needs take part in national camps. In 1979 the Association organized its first international camp, Karelia-79. The second international camp, Miilu-85, was held in 1985, and the third, Tervas 90 in 1990. Planning of the fourth international camp has begun. It will take place in 1996.

In 1988 and 1989 the Association encouraged the involvement of all units in environmental activities by circulating an environmental education kit nationally in co-operation with the Finnish Association for Nature Conservation and the Circulation Movement.

Training

Trainings are held on all levels, arranged by the districts or by the National Organization. Special trainings for patrol leaders include various Guide and Scout skills, outdoor life, administration, psychology of leadership, citizenship and cultural education. There are joint gatherings at national level for Guides and Scouts, patrol leaders, Rangers and Rovers, and leaders.

Training has been sub-divided into leader training and skill training. Every year around 8,500 leaders are trained to various tasks. Leader training consists of a number of Basic Leader Courses organized by Districts. At the national level The Guides and Scouts of Finland organize Extensive Training Courses for leaders, in which Gilwell training has been combined with Nordic Trefoil training.

Communication and Co-operation

The Guides and Scouts of Finland promote international understanding and all members are encouraged to identify themselves as Finnish citizens as well as members of a major worldwide organization. International education is an important aspect of the programme, promoting international understanding, co-operation and peace. The Peace Education Programme of the Association was officially ratified in August 1982.

In 1989-1993 The Guides and Scouts of Finland have built a health care centre in Senegal together with Eclaireurs et Eclaireuses du Senegal. Finnish Guides and Scouts have participated in this project by attending work camps, by raising funds, and in troops by carrying out international education activities connected with the project.

The Association has embarked upon several major projects in co-operation with other countries. In 1986 a three-year vaccination project was initiated in Nepal in co-operation with UNICEF in order to improve the situation of Nepalese children and their mothers. This project was followed by a re-afforestation project with Nepal from 1989. In 1989 the Association began a project named Uniscout/Wergujaram which aimed to build a health centre in Senegal.
The Guides and Scouts of Finland co-operate closely with other Finnish youth organizations and with UNICEF.

The Guides and Scouts of Finland try to use all available channels to promote Guiding and Scouting. Publicity helps to secure the finance necessary for the organization of their various activities.

The magazine for all members is *Partio* and there is also a magazine especially for leaders, *Partiojohtaja*. The Swedish-speaking members receive a magazine in their own language, *Scoutposten*. There is also an audio-taped magazine for special members.

Assembly for a major undertaking in Finland.

France

Scoutisme Féminin Français

Component Associations:
L'Association des Eclaireuses et Eclaireurs de France (EEDF)
L'Association des Eclaireuses et Eclaireurs Israélites de France (EEIF)
Fédération des Eclaireuses et Eclaireurs Unionistes de France (FEEUF)
Les Guides de France (GDF)
Scouts Muselmans de France

Founder Member of WAGGGS	
Girl Guiding/Girl Scouting introduced:	**1921**
Membership 1992†:	**49,765**
Membership as % of female population:	**0.17%**
WAGGGS Region:	**Europe**

EEDF Girl Scout

EEDF Brownie

L'Association des Eclaireuses et Eclaireurs de France (EEDF)

Promesse

L'une des deux formules est à choisir selon les convictions personnelles:
Je promets sur mon honneur de faire tous mes efforts pour:
servir mon pays et l'amitié entre les hommes, rendre service en toute occasion, vivre notre Loi.
ou
Je promets sur mon honneur, avec l'aide de Dieu, de faire tous mes efforts pour:
servir mon pays et l'amitié entre les hommes, rendre service en toute occasion, vivre notre Loi.

Loi

L'Eclaireuse
1 est loyale.
2 est propre, maîtrise ses paroles et ses actes.
3 sourit, même dans les difficultés.
4 aime le travail et l'effort, ne fait rien à moitié.
5 se rend utile.
6 sait obéir, et agit en équipe.
7 respecte le travail et le bien de tous.
8 écoute les autres et respecte leurs convictions.
9 pratique la fraternité scoute.
10 aime et protège la nature et la vie.

Devise

Toujours prête
A rendre joyeusement le service qui t'est demandé,
A prendre une décision,
A découvrir et à agir.

Promesse des Louveteaux

Selon ses croyances et le désir de ses parents, le louveteau choisit l'une des deux formules suivantes:
Je promets de faire de mon mieux pour obéir à la Loi des Louveteaux.
ou
Je promets, avec l'aide de Dieu, de faire de mon mieux pour obéir à la Loi des Louveteaux.

Loi des Louveteaux

Un louveteau dit vrai.
Un louveteau obéit aux maîtres-mots de l'unité.
Un louveteau cherche à faire plaisir aux autres.

Devise des Louveteaux

De notre mieux

Promise

One of these two versions is to be chosen, according to personal conviction:
I promise on my honour to make every effort to:
serve my country and encourage friendship between people, help others at all times and to live by our Law.
or
I promise on my honour, with God's help, to make every effort to:
serve my country and encourage friendship between people; help others on every occasion and to live by our law

Law

A Girl Scout
1. is loyal.
2. is clean and controls her words and deeds.
3. smiles even under difficulties.
4. enjoys work and endeavour and does nothing by halves.
5. makes herself useful.
6. knows how to obey and is a good team member.
7. respects the work and belongings of all.
8. listens to others and respects their beliefs.
9. practices Girl Scout fellowship.
10. loves and protects nature and life.

Motto

Always prepared
to give cheerfully the help
you are asked for,
to take a decision,
to learn and to act.

Brownie Promise

According to her own convictions and her parents' wishes, the Brownie chooses one of the two Promises:
I promise to do my best to obey the Brownie Law.
or
I promise, with God's help, to do my best to obey the Brownie Law.

Brownie Law

A Brownie tells the truth.
A Brownie obeys the Pack passwords.
A Brownie seeks to give happiness to others.

Brownie Motto

The best we can

Age Groups

Aînée	Ranger	15/16-21
Eclaireuse	Girl Scout	11-15/16
Louveteau	Brownie	8-11

L'Association des Eclaireuses et Eclaireurs Israélites de France (EEIF)

Promesse

Je m'engage à vivre la Loi des EEIF.

Loi

L'E.I. participe à la vie de son groupe, des communautés dans lesquelles elle vit en assumant sa part de responsabilités.
L'E.I. apprend à comprendre son prochain et le respecte.
L'E.I. fait face aux difficultés.
L'E.I. développe ses qualités morales et physiques.
L'E.I. découvre, aime et protège la nature.
L'E.I. s'efforce d'acquérir des connaissances nouvelles, d'étudier la Thora.

Promesse des Bâtisseurs

Je m'efforce de suivre la Loi des Bâtisseurs et celle de ma Hévra (équipe).

Loi des Bâtisseurs

Avec Noë et les Animaux de l'Arche
- Je suis actif et de bonne humeur
- Je découvre et protège la nature
- Je participe à l'aventure de ma Hévra
- Je découvre la vie et l'histoire du Peuple Juif.

Promise

I undertake to live by the EEIF Law.

Law

The EI takes part in her group, and in the community in which she lives by taking her share of responsibility.
The EI learns to understand and respect others.
The EI faces up to difficulties.
The EI develops her moral qualities and physical abilities.
The EI learns about, loves and protects nature.
The EI tries to acquire new knowledge and to study the Torah.

Brownie Promise

I try to keep the Brownie Law and that of my Hevra (team).

Brownie Law

With Noah and the animals in the Ark
- I am active and good-tempered
- I learn about and protect nature
- I join in my Hevra's adventure
- I find out about the life and history of the Jewish people.

EEIF Girl Scout

EEIF Brownie

Age Groups

Perspective	Perspective Girl Scout	15 - 17
Eclaireuse	Girl Scout	12 - 15
Bétissette	Brownie	8 - 11

Fédération des Eclaireuses et Eclaireurs Unionistes de France (FEEUF)

FEEUF Girl Scout

Promesse
Je promets de faire tout mon possible pour:
- écouter la Parole de Dieu
- me mettre au service des autres
- vivre la loi

Loi
Une éclaireuse, un éclaireur:
- tient parole et ne fait rien à moitié, on peut lui faire confiance,
- réfléchit avant d'agir, est responsable de ses actes,
- vit en équipe, apprend à écouter et à partager,
- développe ses compétences et les met au service des autres,
- respecte, connaît et protège la nature,
- prend soin de son corps et de sa santé,
- conserve bonne humeur et maîtrise de soi, même dans les difficultés.

Devise
Sois prête

FEEUF Brownie

Promesse des Louveteaux - Louvettes
Avec l'aide de toute la meute, je promets, de faire de mon mieux pour respecter la Loi et la Charte de la meute, connaître Jésus, aider les autres, et...

Loi des Louveteaux - Louvettes
Chaque Louveteau, chaque Louvette
dans la bonne humeur,
fait de son mieux,
respecte les autres,
et vit l'Aventure de la Meute.

Devise
De notre mieux

Promise
I promise to do everything possible to:
- Listen to God's word
- Help others
- Live in accordance with the Guide Law

Law
A Girl Scout, a Scout:
- Keeps her/his word and does not do things by halves, she/he can be trusted,
- Thinks before she/he acts, takes responsibility for her/his actions,
- Lives in a team, learns to listen and share,
- Develops her/his skills and puts them at the service of others,
- Respects, gets to know and protects nature,
- Takes care of her/his body and health,
- Is cheerful and self-controlled, even in difficulties.

Motto
Be Prepared

Brownie/Cub Promise
With the help of the Pack, I promise to do my best to obey the Law and the Charter of the Pack, to get to know Jesus, to help others, and...

Brownie/Cub Law
Each Cub, each Brownie,
Is cheerful,
Tries his/her best,
Respects others,
And lives the adventure of the Pack.

Motto
Be Prepared

Age Groups

Aînée	Ranger	15 - 18
Eclaireuse	Girl Scout	12 - 15
Louvette	Brownie	8 - 11

Les Guides de France

Un engagement : la Promesse
Sur mon honneur, avec la grâce de Dieu, je m'engage a servir de mon mieux, Dieu, l'Eglise et la patrie; à aider mon prochain en toutes circonstances, à observer la Loi des Guides.

Des exigences : la loi
1 La guide est loyale.
2 La guide pense d'abord aux autres.
3 La guide est généreuse ; elle est prête à servir.
4 La guide est accueillante ; elle a l'esprit d'équipe.

5. La guide, soeur de toute autre guide, est présente à tous.
6. La guide découvre la nature ; elle y voit l'oeuvre de Dieu.
7. La guide sait obéir.
8. La guide ne craint pas l'effort ; elle ne fait rien à moitié.
9. La guide aime son travail et respecte celui des autres.
10. La guide est maîtresse de soi ; elle est pure et joyeuse.

Devise
Toujours prête

Promesse des Jeunes en marche
Adhérant à la Charte des 'Jeunes en marche'. Pour conduire ma vie sur le chemin des Béatitudes. Pour participer à un développement communautaire.
En lien avec les autres guides du monde entier. Je décide d'être 'Jeune en marche'.

La Charte des Jeunes en marche
Jeune en marche,
tu as la terre en partage, construis-la de tes mains.
Jeune en marche,
tu as un corps, ne l'abîme pas, mais qu'il manifeste ton désir de vivre.
Jeune en marche,
tu as la liberté, risque-la dans ta parole et dans tes actes.
Jeune en marche,
tu as la place parmi les hommes, participe avec eux au développement du monde.
Jeune en marche,
tu as la vie, ne l'enterre pas, mets-toi en marche sur le chemin des Béatitudes.

Devise des Jeunes en marche
LA MARCHE
En marche vers la vie adulte.
Agir, c'est s'engager.
Les JEM proposent aux jeunes d'agir pour le développement.
Pour cela 6 pistes d'actions sont ouvertes
- Vivre une solidarité internationale.
- Agir dans l'Eglise.
- Créer pour communiquer.
- Favoriser une vie plus humaine.
- S'engager dans le monde des jeunes.
- Partager avec les plus pauvres.

Promesse des Caravelles
Adhérant à l'appel que me lance la caravelle, en réponse à l'amour de Dieu, pour prendre part à la construction d'un monde plus juste, plus vrai, plus fraternel, solidaire de toutes les autres guides, aujourd'hui je m'engage à être caravelle.

GDF
Jeunes en marche

Les appels des Caravelles
Si tu veux être solidaire, combats l'indifférence et agis avec d'autres.
Si tu veux devenir toi-même, ose te confronter à d'autres et donne le meilleur de toi-même.
Si tu veux aller plus loin, fais le point et sors de tes frontières.
Si tu veux respecter la vie, découvre la nature et lutte pour un environnement plus humain.
Si tu veux construire le monde, prends ta part de responsabilité et mets tes compétences au service des autres.
Si tu veux bâtir l'avenir, fais équipe avec d'autres et garde confiance.
Alors, tu es sur le chemin de la liberté et de l'amour : tu réponds à l'Appel de Jésus-Christ.

GDF
Caravelles

Devise des Caravelles
L'EMBARQUEMENT
L'Embarquement vers des choix de vie, des formations, des relations.
Entreprendre, c'est vivre à fond. Les caravelles mènent les entreprises qu'elles choisissent (chantiers, spectacles, actions de service, exploits sportifs...) comme autant de moyens de découvrir et multiplier leurs potentialités.

Promesse des Guides
Avec vous toutes, confiante en Dieu qui m'aime, je promets de faire tout mon possible : pour rendre les autres heureux, pour être utile à mon pays et vivre selon la loi de toutes les guides du monde.

GDF Guide

Loi Guide
La guide se connaît. Elle manifeste sa joie de vivre.
La guide est responsable de ses choix. On peut lui faire confiance.
La guide prend sa place dans l'équipe. Elle agit avec les autres partout où elle vit.
La guide accueille l'autre. Elle apprend à le comprendre et à l'aimer.
La guide développe ses compétences pour elle-même et pour le service des autres.
La guide respecte la vie, la nature et le travail des hommes.
La guide vit l'Aventure de Dieu.

Devise des Guides
L'AVENTURE
L'Aventure d'un avenir à construire, d'une personnalité à enrichir.

GDF Jeannette

Partir à l'aventure, c'est choisir avec d'autres de réussir un projet et pour cela apprendre des techniques, vivre en équipe, se dépasser.

Promesse des Jeannettes
Je promets de faire de mon mieux pour aimer Dieu, connaître mon pays, dire oui à la loi de la ronde ; pour faire chaque jour un plaisir à quelqu'un et apporter la joie à la maison.

Loi jeannette
Une jeannette est propre.
Une jeannette est active.
Une jeannette est gaie.
Une jeannette dit toujours vrai.
Une jeannette pense d'abord aux autres.
Une jeannette est amie de Jésus.

Devise des jeannettes
LA FORET
La forêt d'un monde à connaître, comprendre et habiter.
Jouer dans la forêt, c'est apprendre à se sentir à l'aise partout : développer un esprit curieux, rencontrer l'autre, se débrouiller, connaître la nature, prendre des initiatives.

A commitment: the Promise
On my honour, with the grace of God, I promise to do my best to serve God, the Church and my country; to help others at all times, to obey the Guide Law.

Demands: the Law
A Guide is loyal.
A Guide thinks of others before herself.
A Guide is generous; she is prepared to help.
A Guide is friendly; she has team spirit.
A Guide is a sister to every other Guide and is help to all.
A Guide learns about nature in which she sees the work of God.
A Guide is obedient.
A Guide is hard-working; she does nothing by halves.
A Guide likes her work and respects that of others.
A Guide is self-controlled; she is pure and cheerful.

Motto
Always prepared

Promise of the Jeunes en marche
Adhering to the Charter of the Jeunes en marche. To lead my life on the way to the Beatitudes. To take part in community development. Bound with the other guides throughout the world, I decide to be 'Jeune en marche'.

The Charter of the Jeunes en marche
Jeune en marche, you have the Earth to share,
Build it with your hands,
Jeune en marche,
You have a body, do not abuse it,
but let it express your desire to live,
Jeune en marche,
You have freedom,
Use it in what you say and what you do,
Jeune en marche,
You have a place among mankind,
participate with those men and women in the development of the world.
Jeune en marche,
You have life, do not bury it,
Go forward on the way of the Beatitudes.

Youth on the Move (Jeunes en marche) Motto
A MOVE
Towards adult life.
To act is to become involved.
The JEM ask young people to act for development.
6 ways for action:
- experience international solidarity
- act within the Church
- create to communicate
- promote a more humane life
- become committed to the world of youth
- share with the poorest.

Caravelle Promise
Answering the call of the Caravelle, in response to the love of God, to participate in a world with more justice, more truth, more friendship, in solidarity with all the other guides, I take the commitment today to live like a Caravelle.

The Calls of the Caravelle
If you want to help others, fight indifference and join with others in action.
If you want to become yourself, face up to others and give your best.
If you want to go further, reflect on what has passed and expand your horizons further.
If you want to respect life, discover nature and work for a more humane environment.
If you want to build the world, take your share of responsibility and put your skills

at the service of others.
If you want to build the future, team up with others and keep confident.
Then, you are on the way to freedom and love: you answer Jesus Christ's call.

Caravelle Motto

Embark on a journey
Towards life choices, training, relationships.
Undertake and live life to the full. The Caravelles choose their own ventures (workshops, shows, service, sporting adventure...) as means to discover and multiply their abilities.

Guide Promise

With you,
Trusting in God who loves me, I promise to do everything possible to make others happy, to serve my country and to live according to the Law of all Guides throughout the world.

Guide Law

A Guide knows herself. She expresses her joy for living.
A Guide is responsible for her choices.
A Guide is trustworthy.
A Guide takes her place in the team.
A Guide works with others everywhere she lives.
A Guide is friendly to others. She gets to know and understand them.
A Guide develops her skills for herself and for the service of others.
A Guide respects life, nature and the work of mankind.
A Guide lives God's adventure.

Guide Motto

ADVENTURE
Your adventure is a future to build, a personality to enrich.
To go on a venture is to choose with others to be successful in a project and for that to learn techniques, to live as a team, to better ourselves.

Brownie Promise

I promise to do my best,
To love God,
Know my country,
Accept the law of the pack,
To do a good turn to someone every day,
And bring joy into my home.

Brownie Law

A Brownie is always clean.
A Brownie is always active.
A Brownie is always cheerful.
A Brownie always tells the truth.
A Brownie thinks first of others.

Brownie Motto

THE FOREST
The world is a forest to discover, understand and inhabit.
Play in the forest: learn to be at ease everywhere: develop a curious spirit, meet others, fend for yourself, discover nature, take initiatives.

Age Groups

Youth on the Move	Jeunes en marche	17-20
Caravelle Guide	Caravelle	15-16
Guide	Guide	11-14
Brownie	Jeannette	8-11

Scouts Muselmans de France

At the time this publication is going to press, a new Component Association is being accepted into Scoutisme Féminin Français. The Promise, Law and badge for the Scouts Muselmans de France will appear in a subsequent edition, along with other details.

Development of the Movement in France

Guiding in France is carried out under the auspices of Scoutisme Féminin Français, composed of the female members of four Associations. Each Association has units throughout France, and is structured on a local level by department and by region. Scoutisme Féminin Français has a commission composed of the International Commissioners from the four Associations. The commission meets regularly to discuss general issues affecting Guiding in France, to further good relations by exchanging ideas on common problems and to promote international understanding. Scoutisme Féminin Français is headed in rotation by one of the International Commissioners for a period of two years.

L'Association des Eclaireuses et Eclaireurs de France

L'Association des Eclaireuses et Eclaireurs de France is a secular co-educational

Association which strives to meet the needs of young people.

The Association has carried out studies of its aims, which have been discussed by study groups at all levels, and has investigated group leadership training. The studies have led to the implementation of programmes on sex education, moral training, the environment and creativity.

The Association emphasizes the need for greater participation of young people in policy-making meetings. It focuses on welcoming young people outside the Movement to camps, developing an Extension Branch for retarded children, carrying out nature conservation, extending international relationships and increasing projects to aid developing countries.

The Association publishes several periodicals for all age groups and their leaders including *L'Equipe* and *Routes Nouvelles.*

L'Association des Eclaireuses et Eclaireurs Israélites de France

L'Association des Eclaireuses et Eclaireurs Israélites de France, operative since 1923, is a co-educational Association. It aims to train young Jews to be aware of both their Judaism and their role in the community. It offers them a dynamic Judaic programme which incorporates participation in games, outdoor activities, artistic and musical expression, sport, and the learning of spiritual values.

The Association publishes several periodicals: *Bulletin E.E.I.F., Yossi* and *E.I.F.*

Fédération des Eclaireuses et Eclaireurs Unionistes de France

In 1970 the Fédération Française des Eclaireuses Unionistes merged with the Eclaireurs Unionistes de France to become the Fédération des Eclaireuses et Eclaireurs Unionistes de France, a co-educational federation providing a Protestant education.

In the Junior Branch most of the packs are mixed, as are the patrols within them. In the Intermediate Branch and the Rangers, both mixed and single-sex units operate. Whenever there is a mixed unit, a balance between girls and boys must be maintained and the proportion cannot be higher than 60/40%. Mixed units are headed by a team of male and female leaders. The Federation integrates disabled and migrant members into open units.

The Federation emphasizes the need for thorough training, and has a three-tier training programme. The first tier involves leaders from the age of 17 who receive training under four headings: knowledge of the child and the teenager; essential elements of Girl Scouting; the role of the unit; and activities. Training in special skills such as sailing, pottery and gymnastics is also provided.

The second tier involves leaders from the age of 19, with some training experience, and aims to further their general training and teach them how to run a camp. Personal development plays a more important part at this level. The third tier is the training of trainers, which is organized at national level, includes educational theory and aims at developing relations with young people.

The Federation publicizes its events and activities through the local and national press and through television reports included in weekly Protestant programmes. The Federation also publishes various periodicals: *Le Lien,* for leaders; *Kotick,* for members of the Junior Branch; and *AEIOU,* for members of the Intermediate Branch.

Les Guides de France

Les Guides de France is a single-sex Association. It provides a Roman Catholic educational base for the Guide programme.

The Association carries out activities designed for each age group and has introduced a junior section, Les Farandoles, catering to girls ages six and seven years, on an experimental basis. Extension units address the particular problems faced by girls with special needs and a special publication is produced, *Pour toi, le journal de Dominique,* which aims to help adolescents with learning disabilities through the use of drawings. In 1989 the Association organized a gathering focusing on Human Rights which brought together 5,000 of its members.

Guides de France is concerned with community development and has adopted the general theme of *Search for Development* for its programme involving migrant and disabled girls. Special units, named Unités Soleil, have been formed to attract young immigrants and children from disadvantaged backgrounds, providing opportunities to form intercultural friendships and the chance to learn about other religions. A special publication is produced for these groups entitled *Cap Soleil.*

Camping is a widespread activity among members. In 1990 Eurocamp brought together 1,500 members of the Movement of all ages from 12 European countries for a 15-day camp.

Guides de France has an international training centre at Mélan which welcomes young people from all over the world. The Association also publishes a periodical for each age group: *Journal Jeannette, Journal Guide, Cap Levant* and *Demain.*

Finally, Guides de France co-operates with the Scouts de France on many projects, and celebrates the United Nations' International Years.

Singing – always part of the Movement – gives both joy and a chance to perform to these Caravelles of Guides de France.

The Gambia

The Gambia Girl Guides Association

Girl Guiding/Girl Scouting introduced:	**1923**
Became Associate Member of WAGGGS:	**1966**
Became Full Member of WAGGGS:	**1987**
Membership 1992:	**5,223**
Membership as % of female population:	**1.18%**
WAGGGS Region:	**Africa**

Guide

Promise

I promise on my honour that I will do my best:
To do my duty to God, and my country;
To help other people at all times;
and
To obey the Guide Law.

Law

1 A Guide's honour is to be trusted.
2 A Guide is loyal.
3 A Guide's duty is to be useful and to help others.
4 A Guide is a friend to all and a sister to every other Guide.
5 A Guide is courteous.
6 A Guide is a friend to animals.
7 A Guide obeys orders.
8 A Guide smiles and sings under all difficulties.
9 A Guide is thrifty.
10 A Guide is pure in thought, word and deed.

Motto

Be Prepared

Brownie Promise

I promise to do my best to do my duty to God and my country; to help other people every day, especially those at home.

Brownie Law

A Brownie gives in to the older folk.
A Brownie does not give in to herself.

Brownie Motto

Lend a Hand

Age Groups

Guide	12-18
Brownie	7-11

Development of the Movement in The Gambia

Guiding activities in The Gambia began with the organization of the first Guide company in 1923. By 1924 there were two Guide companies and one Brownie pack and in 1928 the first Ranger company was started.

Unfortunately, due to a lack of leaders, Guiding activities ceased in 1931 and were not restarted until 1943. In 1946 Guiding was officially re-established in The Gambia and a local Association was formed. Membership grew slowly until the early 1950s when a visit from Olave Baden-Powell helped to boost the Movement's development.

Guiding is now found in every accessible area of the country and has reached all sections of the population, including each ethnic group. Many units in The Gambia are attached to schools.

The Programme

The Guide and Brownie programmes are based on those used by The Girl Guides Association (United Kingdom), and have been adapted to meet the interests of Gambian girls.

The Association runs recruitment drives to attract potential leaders to meet the demand created by girls wishing to join companies and packs.

Working with the Community

The Gambia Girl Guides Association is very aware of community needs and tries to meet them, whenever possible, by giving aid to the poor and the sick, and by giving assistance on public occasions. Guides also help in hospitals and clinics and visit homes for the elderly.

The Association has established a vocational centre at its headquarters at Kanifiny. The centre, staffed by four full-time and two part-time teachers, had 109 students in 1990, all primary school drop-outs. Its aim is to provide pupils with skills that will enable them to become self-employed. The first set of students finished the course in 1990 and then went on to work independently and in co-operative groups.

Outdoor and Environmental Activities
The number of weekend camps held currently exceeds two. In a bid to decentralize, increase membership and improve quality, Regional Commissioners now organize a variety of trainings ranging from one day, weekend or one week in duration. Guides also participate in tree-planting projects and have helped to clean such public places as parks, markets, mosques, playing fields and churches.

Training
The Association has a full-time trainer and plans to employ more full-time staff. A training committee establishes the annual training programme which includes national training workshops each year. The Gambia hopes to introduce trainings in the major local languages used in rural areas – Mankinka, Fula and Wolof.

Communication and Co-operation
Members of the Association participate in ceremonies and parades for such national celebrations as Remembrance Day and Independence Day. Thinking Day is another occasion when the national and international profile of Guiding is heightened through participation in campfires, tree-planting ceremonies and church services. The Association promotes exchanges at local, national and international levels. Units in the rural areas are urged to twin with units in the urban areas and thereby share resources and expertise.

At international level the Association has hosted sub-regional meetings and international visits including Guides of Canada/Guides du Canada.

The Gambia co-operates with other Girl Guide and Girl Scout organizations through the WAGGGS Mutual Aid Scheme, which has provided funds towards the Association's vocational centre at Kanifiny. The Association is also twinned with the Girl Guides of Canada/ Guides du Canada's province of Ontario which is supporting a poultry farming project at the vocational centre.

The Gambia Girl Guides Association is a member of the National Youth Council. It co-operates with the Department of Education, Youth, Sports and Culture, and also with many national non-governmental organizations, including the Scout Association, the Red Cross, the Boys' Brigade and the Family Planning Association. Gambia Girl Guides takes an active part in all national activities for women.

A young woman in The Gambia takes her Promise.

Germany

Ring Deutscher Pfadfinderinnenverbaende
(Union of German Girl Guide Associations)

Component Associations:
Bund der Pfadfinderinnen und Pfadfinder (BdP)
(Association of Girl Guides and Boy Scouts)
Verband Christlicher Pfadfinderinnen und Pfadfinder (VCP)
(Christian Girl Guide and Boy Scout Association)
Pfadfinderinnenschaft Sankt Georg (PSG)
(Girl Guide Association of St. George)

Became Associate Member of WAGGGS:	**1950**
Became Full Member of WAGGGS:	**1954**
Membership 1992[†]:	**47,585**
Membership as % of female population:	**0.12%**
WAGGGS Region:	**Europe**

BdP Guide

BdP Cub/Brownie

Bund der Pfadfinderinnen und Pfadfinder (BdP)

Guide and Scout Promise
Ich will, im Vertrauen auf Gottes Hilfe, nach den Regeln der Pfadfinderinnen und Pfadfinder mit Euch leben. (Das Versprechen kann auch ohne religiöse Formel abgelegt werden.)

Guide and Scout Law
Ich will hilfsbereit und rücksichtsvoll sein.
Ich will den anderen achten.
Ich will zur Freundschaft aller Pfadfinder und Pfadfinderinnen beitragen.
Ich will aufrichtig und zuverlässig sein.
Ich will kritisch sein und Verantwortung übernehmen.
Ich will Schwierigkeiten nicht ausweichen.
Ich will die Natur kennenlernen und helfen, sie zu erhalten.
Ich will mich beherrschen.
Ich will dem Frieden dienen und mich für die Gemeinschaft einsetzen, in der ich lebe.

Cub Promise
Ich will ein guter Freund sein und unsere Regeln achten.

Cub Law
Ein Wölfling nimmt Rücksicht auf andere.
Ein Wölfling hilft wo es kann.

Guide and Scout Promise
With confidence in God's help, I promise to live with you in accordance with the Guide and Scout Law. (The Promise can be given without the religious formulation.)

Guide and Scout Law
I will be helpful and considerate.
I will be respectful.
I will be a friend to all Guides and Scouts.
I will be honest and trustworthy.
I will use my own judgement and assume responsibilities.
I will not avoid difficulties.
I will acquaint myself with nature and help to conserve it.
I will become master of myself.
I will serve peace and the community I live in.

Cub Promise
I will be a good friend and respect our rules.

Cub Law
A Cub is considerate.
A Cub helps wherever she can.

Age Groups

Ranger	Ranger	16+
Pfadfinderin	Guide	11-15
Wölfling	Cub/Brownie	7-11

Verband Christlicher Pfadfinderinnen und Pfadfinder (VCP)

The Association does not have one uniform Promise. On admission the individual declares her readiness for co-operation and acknowledges the common working group rules.

Age Groups

Erwachsene	Adults	18+
Ranger	Ranger	14-18
Pfadfinderinnen	Guide	12-14
Kinderstufe	Children's level	7-11

Pfadfinderinnenschaft Sankt Georg (PSG)

Versprechen

Ich verspreche, mein Bestes zu tun, um Gott in meinem Leben zu erkennen, in der Gemeinschaft, in der ich lebe, mitverantwortlich zu handeln und die Spielregeln der Pfadfinderinnen zu beachten.
Die Pfadfinderin kann den Inhalt des Versprechens auch mit ihren eigenen Worten ausdrücken.

Gesetz

1 Die Pfadfinderin ist aufrichtig, man kann ihr vertrauen.
2 Die Pfadfinderin lernt, sich zu beherrschen.
3 Die Pfadfinderin bemüht sich, aus dem Glauben zu leben und übernimmt Verantwortung in Kirche und Gesellschaft.
4 Die Pfadfinderin versucht, den anderen zu verstehen.
5 Die Pfadfinderin kann sich in eine Gemeinschaft einordnen und ist zur Zusammenarbeit bereit.
6 Die Pfadfinderin weicht Schwierigkeiten nicht aus.
7 Die Pfadfinderin hilft, wo sie kann und tritt Unrecht entgegen.
8 Die Pfadfinderin lernt teilen und dankbar zu sein.
9 Die Pfadfinderin entdeckt die Natur und schützt das Leben.

Brownie Promise

Ich will in meinem Völkchen und in der Gruppe wirklich mitmachen und mein Bestes tun, um anderen Freude zu bereiten.

Brownie Law

Das Wichtel öffnet Augen und Ohren.
Das Wichtel denkt auch an die andern.
Das Wichtel entdeckt Jesus als Freund.
Das Wichtel kann sich freuen und macht anderen Freude.
Das Wichtel sagt seine Ideen und macht mit.

Brownie Motto

Ich will mein Bestes tun

Promise

I promise to do my best, to recognize God in my life, to engage myself with responsibility in the community I live in, and to observe the rules of the Guides.

When she makes her promise, the Guide may also express its meaning in her own words.

Law

1 The Guide is sincere, she can be trusted.
2 The Guide learns to control herself.
3 The Guide strives to live by her faith and to accept responsibility within the Church and society.
4 The Guide tries to understand others.
5 The Guide is able to fit into a community and is prepared to co-operate.
6 The Guide does not avoid difficulties.
7 The Guide helps, where she can, and opposes injustice.
8 The Guide learns to share and to be grateful.
9 The Guide discovers nature and protects life.

Brownie Promise

I will really take part in my patrol and in our group and do my best, to bring joy to others.

Brownie Law

The Brownie opens eyes and ears.
The Brownie thinks also of others.
The Brownie discovers Jesus as a friend.
The Brownie is able to enjoy herself and brings joy to others.
The Brownie says her ideas and participates.

Brownie Motto

I will do my best

VCP Guide

PSG Guide

PSG Brownie

Age Groups

Ranger	Ranger	16+
Caravelle	Caravelle	14-16
Pfadfinderin	Guide	10-13
Wichtel	Brownie	7-10

Development of the Movement in Germany

Ring Deutscher Pfadfinderinnenverbände was formerly composed of four separate Girl Guide Associations: the Bund Deutscher Pfadfinderinnen, the Evangelischer Mädchenpfadfinderbund, the Bund Christlicher Pfadfinderinnen in Bavaria and the Pfadfinderinnenschaft St. Georg.

In 1973 the Evangelischer Mädchenpfadfinderbund, the Bund Christlicher Pfadfinderinnen and the Christliche Pfadfinderschaft Deutschlands (Protestant Boy Scouts) merged to form the Verband Christlicher Pfadfinderinnen und Pfadfiner. In 1976 the Bund Deutscher Pfadfinderinnen and the Bund der Pfadfinder (Scout Association) also merged to become the Bund der Pfadfinderinnen und Pfadfinder (BdP) (Association of Girl Guides and Boy Scouts).

This was the situation up until 1990 when the historic re-unification of Germany took place. This event had direct repercussions within all the German Associations. Guiding had existed throughout the entire State of Germany prior to its division following the Second World War and now the path lay open for its re-establishment in the former Democratic Republic of Germany once again.

Bund der Pfadfinderinnen und Pfadfinder (BdP)

The BdP is an interdenominational Merged Association, open to all boys and girls. The Association has teams of male and female leaders at all levels, and local groups have the right to decide whether they wish to work in mixed or separate groupings.

The press is informed about special projects at national and local level, and coverage of these items is usually good. The Association publishes two quarterly periodicals, *Logo* and *Neue Briefe*.

Verband Christlicher Pfadfinderinnen und Pfadfinder (VCP)

The VCP is a Protestant merged Association for girls and boys of all denominations. Most of the groups are mixed at all age levels, and leadership training is carried out on a co-educational basis. Through a special voting system, every member participates in decision-making at the annual general assembly of the Association.

Faith plays an important part in the programme of the VCP and members are involved in a broad range of activities, mainly organized at regional level. These include working with socially deprived groups, campaigning for the rights of children in society and aiding community development. The VCP publishes a periodical for members, *Children in Society*, aiding community development and protection of nature. The VCP publishes a periodical for members, *Auf neuem Pfad*.

The VCP is a member of the Arbeitsgemeinschaft Evangelischer Jugend aej (Association of Protestant Youth) and is represented in the Deutscher Bundesjugendring (National Organization of Youth).

The VCP is a member of the Conference on Christianity in Guiding and Scouting (CCGS).

Pfadfinderinnenschaft Sankt Georg (PSG)

The PSG was founded in 1947 as the Association of Catholic Guides in the Federal Republic of Germany. Now it is open to all young girls who agree with the aims of the Association and are willing to work within their groups towards this realization.

The basic foundation of work is the gospel of Jesus Christ, and the Association aims to give young people greater access to the doctrine. A major aim of the programme is to encourage equal participation of girls and women in society and church. The PSG is also concerned with the needs of immigrant and disabled children.

The Brownie programme is centred on a puzzle which encourages Brownies to develop as individuals rather than to compare themselves with others. The Guide programme, called Lokomobile, has similar general principles to the Brownie programme, but its form and content correspond to the interests of the age group.

The Association's training for leaders is organized at regional level and consists of a combination of seminars and supervised practice. The training programme is divided into a general part and a specialized part for specific branch problems. The training of trainers, a responsibility of the national board, is more extensive and includes a training camp.

The Association encourages community development projects, and has an annual campaign dedicated to support relevant projects in Germany and abroad.

The PSG co-operates with other European Girl Guide/Girl Scout Associations and the International Catholic Conference of Guiding (ICCG).

The Association receives good press coverage on important events and publishes three periodicals: '?', *Unterwegs* and *Bundesinfo*.

The PSG is a member of the Bund Deutscher Katholischer Jugend (Association of Catholic Youth) and is represented in the Deutscher Bundesjugendring (National Organization of Youth).

A VCP Guide at camp.

Ghana

The Ghana Girl Guides Association

Girl Guiding/Girl Scouting introduced:	**1921**
Became Associate Member of WAGGGS:	**1960**
Became Full Member of WAGGGS:	**1969**
Membership 1992:	**6,746**
Membership as % of female population:	**0.09%**
WAGGGS Region:	**Africa**

Girl Guide

Promise

I promise that I will do my best:
To do my duty to God;
To serve my country and help other people; and
To keep the Guide Law.

Law

A Guide is loyal and can be trusted.
A Guide is helpful.
A Guide is polite and considerate.
A Guide is friendly and a sister to all Guides.
A Guide is kind to animals and respects all living things.
A Guide is obedient.
A Guide has courage and is cheerful in all difficulties.
A Guide makes good use of her time.
A Guide takes care of her own possessions and those of other people.
A Guide is self-controlled in all she thinks, says and does.

Motto

Be Prepared

Ananse Guide

Ananse Guide Promise

I promise that I will do my best:
To do my duty to God;
To serve my country and help other people; and
To keep the Ananse Guide Law.

Ananse Guide Law

An Ananse Guide is truthful, obedient and cheerful.
And thinks of others before herself.

Ananse Guide Motto

Always ready to help

Age Groups

Cadet	Girls at Training College
Ranger Guide	15-21
Junior Guide	12-15
Girl Guide	10-12
Ananse Guide	7-10
Pre-Ananse Guide	6-7

Development of the Movement in Ghana

Guiding in Ghana was launched in Accra in 1921 and spread to towns and villages all over the country during the next 20 years. In 1930 the Association's headquarters were built in Accra, and since 1945 cadet companies have been established in most of the women's training colleges.

The Programme

The programme is based on an eight point system and incorporates keeping fit; becoming a homemaker; giving service; keeping the Guide Law; getting to know people; enjoying the outdoors; thinking for yourself and exploring the arts. In 1987, the Junior Guides were created in line with the age groupings in the new national education system and the first group of the Pre-Ananse Guides also came into being.

Working with the Community

The Ghana Girl Guides Association supports national activities such as planting and harvesting; training 'returnees' to help them to become self-supporting, and assisting at immunization centres. Guides also help to identify, and respond to, the needs of the elderly.

The Association has launched a community development project in two villages near Achimota, involving 70 women. The participants work in five groups to produce palm kernel and palm oil, process Gari, and make bread and kenkey. A day care centre has been established to cater for children while their mothers work.

Outdoor and Environmental Activities

Members in Ghana camp both under canvas and in schools and colleges. The Association owns a training centre with camping facilities at Achimota, north of the capital, Accra.

Guides are involved in tree-planting projects, either at unit level or with the community. Many also receive training in fire fighting so that they are equipped to protect environmental resources.

Training

Trainings are organized at national, regional, district and local levels for all leaders.

Communication and Co-operation

The Ghana Girl Guides Association works in co-operation with the Ministry of Youth and Sports, the National Youth Organising Commission, Ghana National Trust Fund and National Council on Women and Development.

The community development projects centred near Achimota are the product of a twinning project between Ghana and the State of Nova Scotia, Girl Guides of Canada/Guides du Canada and are supported by The Canadian International Development Agency (CIDA).

The Association informs the general public about its activities through the mass media and personal contacts.

Guides attend memorial service for Mrs Dorothy Wilkinson.

Greece

Soma Hellinidon Odigon
(The Greek Girl Guides Association)

Girl Guiding/Girl Scouting introduced:	**1932**
Became Associate Member of WAGGGS:	**1933**
Became Full Member of WAGGGS:	**1948**
Membership 1992:	**17,882**
Membership as % of female population:	**0.33%**
WAGGGS Region:	**Europe**

Guide

Bird

I Ipóshesi
Ipóshome stin timi mou na prospathisso:
Ná káno to kathikon mou pros ton Theó ke tin Patrida
Ná voïthó ólous pantoú ke pántote.
Ná ipakoúo ston Nómo tis Odigoú.

O Nomos
1 I Odigós léi ké sévete tin alíthia.
2 Tirí toós nómous ke xéri na pitharchí.
3 Ine ikani ke próthymi na phani chríssimi.
4 Ine kali phíli ke íne evgeniki mé ólous.
5 Ine aessiódoxi ke próschari.
6 Aghapá ti physsi ke prostetévi ta zóa ke ta phytá.
7 Ergházete efsynídita ke íne synepís.
8 Echi thárros ke psychraemia.
9 Ine kalí nicokyrá ke sévete tin idioktyssía ton állon.
10 Ine axioprepís ke elénchi tis sképsis, ta lógia ke tis praxis tis.

Motto
Ésso Étimi

Bird Promise
Ipóshome na prospathísso m'óli mou ti dynami:
Na ime pistó sto Theó ke stin Partída.
Na voithó tous álous pántote ke na férno ti khará sto spiti mou.

Bird Law
To Pouli ipakoúhi próthyma.
Den Sképtere móno ton eaftó tou ke.
Aghapá tous álous.

Bird Motto
Dosse cheri

Star Promise
Ime astéri próthymo tous állous na voithó ke to chamogeló mou poté den to zechno.
Agápi echo ke agaliá gia óllous anichtí, filous na écho s'óli ti gi.

Star Motto
Panda Fili

Promise
I promise on my honour to try:
To do my duty to God and to my Country.
To help everybody always and everywhere.
To obey the Law of the Guides.

Law
1 A Guide is truthful. She respects Truth.
2 She is law-abiding and disciplined.
3 She is able and willing to be useful.
4 She is a good friend and courteous to all.
5 She is cheerful and optimistic.
6 She loves nature and protects animals and plants.
7 She is conscientious in her work and reliable.
8 She has courage and does not panic.
9 She is a good housekeeper and respects the property of others.
10 She has dignity and controls her thoughts, words and deeds.

Motto
Be Prepared

Bird Promise
I promise to try as best I can:
To do my duty to God and my Country.
To help other people every day and bring cheerfulness to my home.

Bird Law
A Bird: Obeys willingly.
Does not think only of herself.
Loves those around her.

Bird Motto
Lend a Hand

Star Promise
I am a star eager to help the others and never forget my smile.
I have love and my arms are open to all, and friends I have around the world (song).

Star Motto
Always Friends

Age Groups

Megali Odigos,	Ranger,	
Naftodigos	Sea Ranger	15 - 18
Odigos	Guide	11 - 15
Pouli	Bird	7 - 11
Asteri	Star	4 - 6

Development of the Movement in Greece

Guiding was established in Greece in 1932 and was revived in 1945 after a period of inactivity during the Second World War. The Movement has since spread throughout the country and Soma Hellinidon Odigon (The Greek Girl Guides Association) is now the largest youth organization for girls and young women in Greece.

The Programme
The programme places emphasis on individual development, life in nature and service to the community. It aims at forming individuals who are aware of their talents and potential. Self-awareness is stressed through various activities such as community development, outdoor pursuits, games and sports, the arts, handicrafts, education in career orientation, conservation, environmental protection, research of national traditions and cultural events.

Recently an ad hoc committee in co-operation with the Branches formulated and proposed a new educational programme - always based on individual development, life in nature and service to the community. All Guiding activities are organized according to an integrated and co-ordinated programme, which meets the needs of each age group and ensures the gradual development of children through all age groups. In 1990 a new Branch was formed for pre-school-age children, which very quickly became popular.

In 1951 the Association started to welcome members with disabilities as a means of furthering their development and helping their integration into society. Special Groups follow the Guiding programme and are fully integrated in their respective Local Departments. A handbook has been produced and Special Groups have their own house on one of the Association's campsites near Athens. In the summer of 1993, for the first time in Greece, the Special Branch of the Association organized in the north of Greece (in Halkidiki) a European camp for Guides with special needs. Two hundred Guides from five European countries participated in the camp.

Working with the Community
Soma Hellinidon Odigon has a long tradition of service to the community and most girls participate in community development projects. Service camps have been held for Rangers since 1951 with the aim of helping remote communities and giving them new life. Over the years many Girl Guides and Girl Scouts from abroad have participated in these special camps.

The three most senior age groups have also carried out projects with other children and young people including environmental work, the revival of cultural traditions and the creation of libraries.

The Association has worked closely with Greek authorities in organizing welcoming stations for Greek refugees from Russia (in particular the Black Sea) and Albania. Aid missions have been organized for the Greek communities in Albania.

In 1988 the Ranger Group of the island of Rhodes won the Olave Award for replanting a forest that had been razed by fire, while at the same time enlisting the help of Rangers from all over Greece and mobilizing local authorities.

Outdoor and Environmental Activities
Outdoor activities are popular among members and every year all over Greece most Groups hold camps. There are two permanent campsites near Athens that belong to the Association and Brownies have their own "home" at Vari, in the Training Centre.

In 1988 an experimental survival camp addressing mainly Guide Branch Guiders functioned on a small uninhabited island in the Aegean Sea with great success, while Rangers camping on the island of Myconos made use of aeolic and solar energy to provide them with electric light for the camp and heat for cooking.

Training

Guides are educated from the very beginning (Brownies) by practising self-government in their Groups and Patrols. As a result, leadership training is promoted until they are adults and have an opportunity to become Group Leaders.

The leadership training system in Greece changed recently to meet the needs of young people of the '90s. It is now more flexible and consists of five training "cycles". Each cycle deals with a specific subject which is discussed in the course of a weekend. Training cycles are often held in various parts of the country on the following subjects: Guiding, self-government, Guiding programme, communication, nature. Once training is complete, a Leader may attend a special training camp to focus on leadership and other issues of interest. Several seminars (catering to particular preferences such as music, theatre, etc.) are available to Leaders during the year.

Camp Leaders also receive special training through a weekend workshop on camping techniques plus training at a camp of the age group they belong to. Those who want to become Leader Trainers attend a special training seminar. All Trainers can go through a "Trainer's Training" weekend once every two years (this alternates with the Trainers' Conference) to update their knowledge and acquire new training techniques. There are two national training centres: Irini Tsimbouki at Vari, near Athens, and Popi Zaharopoulou at Panorama, near Thessaloniki.

The Training Scheme of Soma Hellinidon Odigon was approved by the World Committee under the Accreditation Scheme of WAGGGS in 1992.

Communication and Co-operation

Soma Hellinidon Odigon regularly participates in international events and disseminates information on world and regional activities. International education is included in the programme of each age group and in leadership training. Groups are encouraged to travel abroad and the International Department assists them to participate in camps organized by other National Organizations. Recently a Scholarship Fund was established by the International Department to enable Guides from areas close to the border (as a rule less privileged than the rest of the country) to participate in camps abroad and experience international Guiding. Under this scheme Guides are selected following an appropriate test.

In addition the Association promotes international understanding through its periodicals, by assisting Guides from abroad to plan their visit to Greece, and through the Post Box Scheme. The Association has hosted international camps, regional seminars, and events such as the 1991 European International Commissioners' forum for WAGGGS and WOSM.

Guiding in Greece has always been supported and encouraged by the Greek community, which appreciates the contribution of Guiding to the development of girls and women in particular and the country in general. Every effort is made to keep the public informed of Guiding activities through such means as local media (newspapers, TV channels and radio stations), films and slide projections, exhibitions, round tables and lectures.

In 1990 the Association launched a dynamic communication campaign, which proved very successful, as it involved all mass media. Local Departments were provided with promotion material, such as posters and a video tape, and were mobilized on the local level. Within the framework of the Association's Action Plan for Development, a competition addressed to children aged 8-14 was announced and supported by the media in 1993. The competition theme was *Earth is beautiful as a picture - let's keep it this way*! Its main aim was to create awareness about environmental issues and to suggest that small steps taken by children every day can contribute to the solving of environmental problems. Response to the competition was tremendous: the Association received 32,000 answers.

Some Hellinidon Odigon publishes four periodicals: *Asteri*, for Stars; *Gorgohelidono*, for Brownies; *Parea*, for Guides and Rangers; and *Minimata*, for Leaders and adult members in general. The Association is a founding member of the Greek National Council of Youth Organizations.

Grenada

The Girl Guides Association of Grenada

Girl Guiding/Girl Scouting introduced: 1925
Became Associate Member of WAGGGS: 1990
Membership 1992: 830
Membership as % of female population: 1.9%
WAGGGS Region: Western Hemisphere

Promise

I Promise that I will do my best:
to do my duty to God
to serve the Queen and my country and help other people and
to keep the Guide Law.

Law

A Guide is loyal and can be trusted
A Guide is helpful
A Guide is polite and considerate
A Guide is friendly and a sister to all Guides
A Guide is kind to animals and respects all living things
A Guide is obedient
A Guide has courage and is cheerful in all difficulties
A Guide makes good use of her time
A Guide takes care of her own possessions and those of other people
A Guide is self-controlled in all she thinks, says and does.

Development of the Movement in Grenada

The first Guide company in Grenada was set up at the Church of England High School in 1925. Other Guide companies were soon formed and the first Brownie packs were introduced in 1927 and the first Ranger Company in 1928. In 1936 the government gave the Association a piece of land as the site for its headquarters.

Guiding had started well in Grenada but political problems in the following years slowed down the development of the Movement.

Until 1983 Grenada was a Branch Association of The Girl Guides Association (United Kingdom), but that year the United Kingdom granted Grenada self-government in all areas of work.

Guide

In 1985 the Association held its first international camp, attended by neighbouring Caribbean Associations. During the next few years trainers and advisors from WAGGGS and the United Kingdom visited Grenada to help the Association to develop its programme and a firm structure. Guiding is now active in most parishes with the majority of units attached to schools and a few to churches and communities.

In 1989 the first Rainbow unit was started in a small village called Binchgrove in the largest parish, St. Andrew.

The Programme

There are four sections within the Girl Guides Association of Grenada: Rainbows, Brownies, Guides and Rangers. The programme is based on an eight-point system incorporating physical fitness, the mind, outdoors enjoyment, homecraft skills, service to others, human relations, creativity and character.

Brownie

Working with the Community

The Association is involved in various service projects and intends to extend its involvement in community development. It is working on a drug prevention project and is involved in the distribution of information on AIDS.

Service projects include the collection of clothing, feeding bottles and other necessities for the children's ward at a local hospital. Guides also recently assisted at a special olympics for children with disabilities.

Outdoor and Environmental Activities
Camping is much enjoyed by members of the Association and both company and patrol leaders' camps take place regularly. In 1989 the Association participated in an environmental project 'River Source' in conjunction with the Scout Association in Grenada. In 1989 a fruit tree-planting project was also completed on the grounds of an old people's home.

Training
The Association has a training, camping and badge sub-committee, composed of two certified trainers and four prospective trainers which is responsible for preparing the annual training programme. Training sessions on special topics are held every month. Members of the training team visit companies and packs regularly to ensure that leaders are working effectively.

Communication and Co-operation
Grenada belongs to the Caribbean Link set up for the purpose of mutual aid and consultation among Guide Associations in the Commonwealth countries and islands of the Caribbean. The Association enjoys the respect and support of Government agencies as well as private sector companies and religious bodies. Guides participate in many national events and celebrations. The police and fire services help with training and many activities are organized jointly with the Scouts.
Grenada has set up a public relations sub-committee to promote Guiding activities to the general public.

Guatemala

Asociación Nacional de Muchachas Guías Scouts de Guatemala

Girl Guiding/Girl Scouting introduced: 1934
Became Associate Member of WAGGGS: 1957
Became Full Member of WAGGGS: 1969
Membership 1992: 750
Membership as % of female population: 0.02%
WAGGGS Region: Western Hemisphere

Promesa
Por mi honor, yo prometo hacer cuanto de mí dependa para cumplir mis deberes hacia Dios y mi país, ayudar a mis semejantes en cualquier momento y cumplir las leyes de las Muchachas Guías.

Ley
1 La guía tiene honor.
2 La guía es leal.
3 La guía es útil y ayuda a los demás.
4 La guía es amiga de todas y una hermana para las demás guías.
5 La guía es cortés.
6 La guía ama a los animales y plantas.
7 La guía es obediente.
8 La guía sonríe y canta ante las dificultades.
9 La guía es económica.
10 La guía es pura.

Lema
Siempre lista

Promesa de la caperucita
Yo prometo hacer todo lo mejor que me sea posible para cumplir mis deberes hacia Dios y mi Patria, ayudar a todos, todos los días, especialmente a los de mi casa.

Ley de la caperucita
Una caperucita se deja guiar de sus mayores.
Una caperucita no se guía a sí misma.

Lema de la caperucita
Dar Ayuda

Promise
On my honour, I promise to do my best to fulfil my duties to God and my country, to help other people at all times and to comply with the laws of the Girl Guides.

Guide

Law
1 A Guide is honourable.
2 A Guide is loyal.
3 A Guide is useful and helps others.
4 A Guide is a friend to all and a sister to every other Guide.
5 A Guide is courteous.
6 A Guide loves animals and plants.
7 A Guide is obedient.
8 A Guide smiles and sings under all difficulties.
9 A Guide is thrifty.
10 A Guide is pure.

Motto
Be Prepared

Little Riding Hood Promise
I promise to do the best I can to do my duty to God and my country and to help everyone every day, especially those at home.

Little Riding Hood

Little Riding Hood Law
A Little Riding Hood allows herself to be guided by her elders.
A Little Riding Hood is not guided by herself.

Little Riding Hood Motto
Lend a Hand

Age Groups

Guía Mayor	Ranger	16+
Guía Intermedia	Guide	11-15
Caperucita	Little Riding Hood	7-10

Development of the Movement in Guatemala

The Movement began in Guatemala in 1934 and the Association was officially formed in the following year. The Association received a plot of land following its service to the country during the revolution in 1944, and, due to the fundraising efforts of Movement members, a meeting house and swimming pool were constructed. In 1984, when the Association celebrated its 50th Anniversary, special efforts were made to increase membership. The government gave the Association the highest award in recognition of 50 years of service to the community, and the capital city honoured the Association with a gold medal diploma and ribbon.

The Programme

Companies exist in the capital city and the provinces, including the north of the country, where there are Indian groups. These girls make their Promise and Law in Kekchi, their native dialect.

Working with the Community

Service has always been a major concern of the Association and Guides have played an important part in relief work following natural disasters.

In Bethania and Lavarreda, two suburbs of Guatemala City, the Association has established women's clubs and holiday classes as part of a community development programme aimed at increasing the knowledge and experience of the women to the advantage of the community as a whole. The subjects offered at the women's clubs include hygiene, nutrition, home economics, handicrafts and family life education, and have been chosen with a view to raising living standards and their chances of self-sufficiency. The holiday classes, for girls aged 4-13, provide cultural and educational activities. Guides also baby-sit during meetings of the women's clubs, and are active in a school for blind children.

Outdoor Activities

Guides in Guatemala spend weekends at camp throughout the year, and longer periods during the school holidays in November and December. In past years, the Association has organized regional camps with the assistance of Guides and Rangers from Central America and Colombia.

Communication and Co-operation

The Association was involved in a twinning project with Norway between 1985 and 1987 which successfully supported a Guatemalan widows' and orphans' village.

The Association publishes a twice-yearly magazine called *Faro Guía,* which includes information on Guide activities, training hints and articles sent in by girls. It is distributed free to all members of the Association in Guatemala and is also sent to other Girl Guide/Girl Scout Associations abroad. Printing costs are covered by revenue from advertisements. The general public is informed about Guiding activities through talks, the newspapers and radio.

Guyana

Guyana Girl Guides Association

Girl Guiding/Girl Scouting introduced:	**1922**
Became Associate Member of WAGGGS:	**1969**
Became Full Member of WAGGGS:	**1975**
Membership 1992:	**625**
Membership as % of female population:	**0.16%**
WAGGGS Region:	**Western Hemisphere**

Promise
I promise that I will do my best:
To do my duty to God;
To serve my country and help other people; and
To keep the Guide Law.

Brownie Guide Promise
I promise that I will do my best:
To do my duty to God;
To serve my country and help other people; and
To keep the Brownie Guide Law.

Law
1 A Guide is loyal and can be trusted.
2 A Guide is helpful.
3 A Guide is polite and considerate.
4 A Guide is friendly and a sister to all Guides.
5 A Guide is kind to animals and respects all living things.
6 A Guide is obedient.
7 A Guide has courage and is cheerful in all difficulties.
8 A Guide makes good use of her time.
9 A Guide takes care of her own possessions and those of other people.
10 A Guide is self-controlled in all she thinks, says and does.

Brownie Guide Law
A Brownie Guide thinks of others before herself and does a good turn every day.

Motto
Be Prepared

Brownie Guide Motto
Lend a Hand

Age Groups

Ranger Guide	14 - 18 or 20
Guide	10 - 16
Brownie Guide	7 - 11

Development of the Movement in Guyana

Guiding began in Guyana in 1922 and the Movement was officially registered as a Branch Association of the Girl Guides Association (United Kingdom) in 1924. By 1927 the Association had its own headquarters in Georgetown and by 1932 two Ranger companies were in operation.

In the years that followed, much intensive training was undertaken throughout Guyana with the help of trainers from other countries.

The Programme
Guyana's programme is based on eight points: keeping fit, becoming a homemaker, giving service, keeping the Guide Law, getting to know people, enjoying the outdoors, thinking for yourself and exploring the arts.

Working with the Community
Working for the community is an important aspect of the work of Guyana Girl Guides Association. The Association has joined the government campaign called Advance Guyana, which includes community service projects, and Guides participate in national agricultural projects as part of this initiative. Guides are involved in campaigns for AIDS awareness and against drug abuse, as well as campaigns to grow more food including the promotion of fish-farming,

Guide

Brownie Guide

bee-keeping, poultry-farming and food preservation. Service projects include working with the disabled and visiting hospitals, orphanages and homes for the elderly.

Outdoor and Environmental Activities

Camping activities are regularly featured in the Guide programme. Guides take part in environmental activities as part of the national project Advance Guyana.

Training

The Association provides training for leaders working with each age group and has a national training team of six members.

Communication and Co-operation

Guyana is a member of the Caribbean Link, set up for the purpose of consultation and mutual aid among Guide Associations in the Commonwealth countries and islands of the Caribbean. It encourages international contacts whenever possible through participation in overseas events.

Haiti

Association Nationale des Guides d'Haiti

Girl Guiding/Girl Scouting introduced: 1942
Became Associate Member of WAGGGS: 1946
Became Full Member of WAGGGS: 1950
Membership 1992[†]: 2,505
Membership as a % of female population: 0.07%
WAGGGS Region: Western Hemisphere

Promesse
Sur mon honneur et avec la grâce de Dieu, je m'engage à servir de mon mieux, Dieu, l'Eglise, la Patrie, à aider mon prochain en toutes circonstances et à observer la Loi Guide.

Loi
1 La guide est loyale.
2 La guide pense d'abord aux autres.
3 La guide est généreuse, elle est prête à servir.
4 La guide est accueillante, elle a l'esprit d'équipe.
5 La guide, soeur de toute autre guide, est présente à tous.
6 La guide découvre la nature, elle y voit l'oeuvre de Dieu.
7 La guide sait obéir.
8 La guide ne craint pas l'effort, elle ne fait rien à moitié.
9 La guide aime son travail et respecte celui des autres.
10 La guide est maîtresse de soi; elle est pure et joyeuse.

Devise
Etre prête

Promesse des jeannettes
Je promets de faire de mon mieux pour être fidèle à Dieu, à mon pays, à mes parents, à la loi de la ronde et pour faire chaque jour un plaisir à quelqu'un.

Loi des jeannettes
Une jeannette est toujours propre.
Une jeannette est toujours active.
Une jeannette est toujours gaie.
Une jeannette dit toujours vrai.
Une jeannette pense d'abord aux autres.

Devise des jeannettes
De notre mieux

Promise
On my honour and with the grace of God, I undertake to do my best to serve God, the Church, my Country, to help other people in all circumstances and to observe the Guide Law.

Guide

Law
1 A Guide is loyal.
2 A Guide thinks first of others.
3 A Guide is generous, she is prepared to help.
4 A Guide is welcoming; she has team spirit.
5 A Guide, sister to every other Guide, is at the service of all.
6 A Guide learns about nature in which she sees God's work.
7 A Guide knows how to obey.
8 A Guide does not fear endeavour; she does nothing by halves.
9 A Guide likes her work and respects that of others.
10 A Guide is self-controlled; she is pure and cheerful.

Motto
Be Prepared

Brownie Promise
I promise to do my best to be faithful to God, my country, my parents, to the law of the pack and to do a good turn to someone every day.

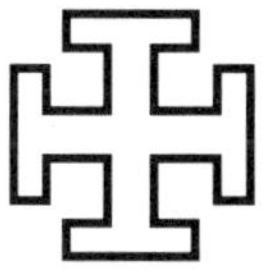
Brownie

Brownie Law
A Brownie is always clean.
A Brownie is always active.
A Brownie is always cheerful.
A Brownie always tells the truth.
A Brownie thinks first of others.

Brownie Motto
The best we can

Age Groups

Guide Aînée	Ranger	18-25
Guide Relais		15+
Guide	Guide	12+
Jeannette	Brownie	7-12

Development of the Movement in Haiti

Guiding began in Haiti when it was introduced along with other activities to a 'club' in a girls' school. At the same time another group of girls in the Pensionnat Sainte Rose de Lima formed a youth organization called Guides de Sainte Rose. These two groups formed the first Guide company in 1942. Guiding spread throughout the country and now reaches girls in all provinces.

In 1990, an intermediate branch between the Guides and the Guides Aînées was introduced on a trial basis as the Guides Relais.

Unit heads gather in Port-au-Prince to discuss the programme.

The Programme

The Association chooses a different theme as a basis for its programme of activities each year. This theme is adopted by all age groups.

Working with the Community

The Association places great emphasis on community service and Guides help in hospitals and canteens in many parts of the country. A major community project undertaken by Guides in Haiti is the running of a day care centre in the Port-au-Prince neighbourhood for factory workers' children. Two senior Guides oversee the centre where children aged 1-5 are looked after, stimulated, and receive a hot meal and a class of milk each weekday. Guides and Brownies throughout the Port-au-Prince district contribute to the success of this project.

Outdoor and Environmental Activities

Camping is an important part of the Association's programme and is a popular activity among members.

Guides in all areas of Haiti are involved in tree-planting projects, their contribution to the preservation of the environment.

Training

The official training programme includes courses on family life education, hygiene and social services.

Communication and Co-operation

Guides from Haiti attend international camps held by other Girl Guide/Girl Scout Associations.

The Association Nationale des Guides d'Haiti publicizes its activities through radio and television, and publishes *Fuse,* a magazine for Guides.

Guides work in co-operation with the Haitian Association of Voluntary Agencies (HAVA), the Red Cross and UNESCO. The Association maintains contact with the government, especially with the departments for agriculture, natural resources and rural development, education, social affairs, youth and sports, and social welfare.

Honduras

Asociación Nacional de Muchachas Guías de Honduras

Girl Guiding/Girl Scouting introduced: 1953
Became Associate Member of WAGGGS: 1981
Membership 1992†: 940
Membership as % of female population: 0.04%
WAGGGS Region: Western Hemisphere

Guide

Little Wing

Promesa
Yo prometo por mi honor, hacer cuanto de mí dependa para: cumplir con mi deber hacia Dios y mi Patria, ser útil al prójimo en todo momento y obedecer la ley Guía.

Ley
1 Una Guía es persona en cuyo honor se puede confiar.
2 Una Guía es leal.
3 El deber de una Guía es ser útil y ayudar a los demás.
4 Una Guía es amiga de todos y hermana de todas las Guías.
5 Una Guía es cortés.
6 Una Guía ve en la Naturaleza la obra de Dios, protege a los animales y las plantas.
7 Una Guía obedece órdenes.
8 Una Guía se enfrenta a las dificultades con entereza y optimismo.
9 Una Guía es económica.
10 Una Guía es pura en pensamientos, palabra y obras.

Promesa de la Alita
Yo prometo hacer todo lo posible para amar a Dios y a mi Patria, para ayudar a los demás, especialmente a los de mi casa.

Ley de la Alita
Una Alita es obediente y siempre está limpia y arreglada.
Una Alita es alegre y siempre dice la verdad.

Promise
I promise, on my honour, to do my best to do my duty to God and my country, to help other people at all times, and to obey the Guide Law.

Law
1 A Guide is a person whose honour is to be trusted.
2 A Guide is loyal.
3 A Guide's duty is to be useful and to help others.
4 A Guide is a friend to all and a sister to all Guides.
5 A Guide is courteous.
6 A Guide sees in nature the work of God; she protects animals and plants.
7 A Guide obeys orders.
8 A Guide faces difficulties with fortitude and optimism.
9 A Guide is thrifty.
10 A Guide is pure in thoughts, word and deed.

Little Wing Promise
I promise to do everything possible to love God and my country, to help others, especially those at home.

Little Wing Law
A Little Wing is obedient and always clean and tidy.
A Little Wing is cheerful and always tells the truth.

Age Groups

Guía Mayor	Senior Guide	15-18
Guía	Intermediate	
Intermedia	Guide	11-14
Alita	Little Wing	7-10

Development of the Movement in Honduras

Guiding in Honduras began in 1953 when the trainer/adviser for the Western Hemisphere gathered together a group of girls and women and told them about Girl Guiding/Girl Scouting and WAGGGS. She set up a committee which worked on the organization of the Asociación Nacional de Muchachas Guías de Honduras. The first National Executive Committee was established in 1958, at a time when a number of Brownie packs and Guide companies already existed.

In 1964 an office was obtained on the ground floor of the Archbishop's Palace in Tegucigalpa, which was used as a meeting place for members. By 1968, with the help of a member of the Peace Corps and periodic visits from the Western Hemisphere trainer/adviser, Guiding had spread to other towns both north and south of the capital.

The first National Assembly was held in 1972, and in the same year the Association obtained legal status.

The Programme

The programme, drawn up by the National Committee, has the needs of the Honduran girl in mind. With an emphasis on spiritual values, it aims to help girls take an active part in community life. Activities include handicrafts, nature study, health, community service, international education and citizenship training. Efforts are being made to increase the number of Senior Guides and to extend the Movement to girls who are unable to attend school.

Working with the Community

Intermediate and Senior Guides visit hospitals to read to the older patients, play with the children and make the surroundings more attractive by arranging flowers, cleaning and dusting. Since the appointment of a project co-ordinator for community development, projects have been organized in many regions of the country. The aim of these projects is to help communities become self-sufficient through training in literacy, handicrafts, citizenship, agriculture, health and hygiene.

The Association has launched a major project, Human Strength, to combat the use and effects of drugs, alcohol, tobacco and prostitution. Based in the capital city of Tegucigalpa and its twin town Comayaguela, the project incorporates a preventive campaign and a counselling and rehabilitation programme.

Outdoor and Environmental Activities

Camping is a popular activity among members of the Movement in Honduras. The Association runs an environmental awareness programme for rural inhabitants, who learn about the dangers of indiscriminate tree felling and proper techniques of reafforestation.

Training

A National Training Team is responsible for the preparation and implementation of the training programme, which is based on the Western Hemisphere Training Manual prepared in 1971 especially for National Organizations in the region. Training is carried out by means of regular training courses and seminars and through correspondence. The training programme is constantly evaluated and reviewed to keep it up to date.

Communication and Co-operation

Honduras participates in activities and events organized by the Western Hemisphere Region and encourages its members to attend events in neighbouring countries.

The Association informs the general public about Guiding through television, radio, newspapers, posters and exhibitions. A training bulletin, which provides such material as training programmes from other National Organizations and new methods and techniques, is circulated regularly to leaders. They also receive a regular bulletin on activities.

The Asociación Nacional de Muchachas Guías de Honduras maintains good relations with local authorities and with government departments, such as the Ministry for Education and the Ministry for Foreign Affairs. Guides also co-operate with the Church and the Scout Association. In 1983 the Association, together with the Lions Club, the National Ecology Association, Camara Junior and the Scout Association, was a founder member of the Committee for the Improvement and Conservation of the Environment, which in June of the same year organized the planting of some 30,000 trees.

Hong Kong

The Hong Kong Girl Guides Association

Girl Guiding/Girl Scouting introduced:	**1916**
Became Associate Member of WAGGGS:	**1978**
Became Full Member of WAGGGS:	**1981**
Membership 1986:	**33,570**
Membership as % of female population:	**1.18%**
WAGGGS Region:	**Asia Pacific**

Guide

Brownie Guide

Promise

As Hong Kong is a multi-national society a Guide upon enrolment may make her Promise in one of the following ways:

I promise that I will do my best,
To do my duty to God,
To serve the Queen and help other people, and
To keep the Guide Law.
or
I promise that I will do my best,
To do my duty to God,
To serve Hong Kong and help other people, and
To keep the Guide Law.
or
I promise that I will do my best,
To do my duty to God,
To serve my country .....,
To serve Hong Kong and help other people, and
To keep the Guide Law.

Law

A Guide is loyal and can be trusted.
A Guide is helpful.
A Guide is polite and considerate.
A Guide is friendly and a sister to all Guides.
A Guide is kind to animals and respects all living things.
A Guide is obedient.
A Guide has courage and is cheerful in all difficulties.
A Guide makes good use of her time.
A Guide takes care of her own possessions and those of other people.
A Guide is self-controlled in all she thinks, says and does.

Motto

Be Prepared

Brownie Guide Promise

As Hong Kong is a multi-national society a Brownie Guide upon enrolment may make her Promise in one of the following ways:

I promise that I will do my best,
To do my duty to God,
To serve the Queen and help other people, and
To keep the Brownie Guide Law.
or

I promise that I will do my best,
To do my duty to God,
To serve Hong Kong and help other people, and
To keep the Brownie Guide Law.
or
I promise that I will do my best,
To do my duty to God,
To serve my country ...,
To serve Hong Kong and help other people, and
To keep the Brownie Guide Law.

Brownie Guide Law

A Brownie thinks of others before herself and does a Good Turn every day.

Brownie Guide Motto

Lend a Hand

Age Groups

Ranger Guide	15-21
Guide	10-16
Brownie Guide	7-11

Development of the Movement in Hong Kong

Guiding began in Hong Kong in 1916 when a Girl Guide company was formed at the Victoria British School. An Association was organized and registered as a Branch Association of the Girl Guides Association (United Kingdom) in 1919.

Membership had increased steadily by that time, but suffered a major setback when Guiding activities were forbidden during the Second World War. Members continued to meet, however, and kept the spirit of Guiding alive. In 1948 a rally was held in the grounds of Government House and in the same year the Association was invited to join the newly formed Social Welfare Department. This marked the beginning of the Movement's involvement in social welfare in Hong Kong. In 1970 the Association adopted the Eight Point Programme. Handbooks and other reference material were produced in English and Chinese.

The Programme

The Promise, made by every enrolled member, is fundamental to the programme. Each girl, with the assistance of her Guider, is helped to a greater understanding and practice of the Promise through enjoyable and purposeful activities. An eight-point programme is presented with a different approach to all sections and helps each girl to mature by developing her mind, physical fitness, character, creative abilities, relationships with people, readiness and ability to serve others, homecraft skills and enjoyment of the outdoors.

Girl Guides work to raise funds during the Chief Commissioner Appeal Campaign.

Each girl is encouraged to set herself high standards and meet personal challenges. To educate the girls for a changing world, new badges on conservation, AP Environment and the AIDS Knowledge badge have been introduced. The Chief Commissioner's Guide badge is the highest award in Guide Section.

The Association's policy is to integrate girls with special needs into existing units.

A Ranger Unit has been established at the Tai Tam Correctional Institution where girls aged 14-21 are detained for minor criminal and drug-related offences. The Unit was started to encourage inmates to accept their responsibilities as members of society. However, there are Special Units established all over Hong Kong. Most of the activities are co-ordinated by a Special Unit Adviser, and include Badge Assessing Day, camps and service projects.

Working with the Community

All members are encouraged to participate in service projects, and a service badge is awarded to Guides who have given 40 hours of service. The Unit Involvement Scheme encourages members to help other people. Individual units implement community projects aimed in particular at the needs of the elderly, the disabled and underprivileged children in the locality. Guides also help in libraries and children's hospital wards, and participate in territory-wide projects such as Project Obris - the flying eye hospital, World Vision and Oxfam. Ranger Guides, Guides and Brownie Guides raise funds for medical use for the needy and for local hospitals. They also join in regular programmes on AIDS knowledge, anti-smoking and anti-drugs.

Outdoor and Environmental Activities

The Association has a number of residential campsites and one wilderness campsite, which provide excellent and safe environments for the girls to enjoy outdoor activities, including treasure hunts, wide games, orienteering, campfire, backwoods cooking, swimming and other camping skills. Guides participate in the Environmental Protection Day and take part in forestry work camps organized by the government during the summer holidays to learn and practise conservation.

Communication and Co-operation

The Association sends Commissioners, Trainers, Guiders, Rangers and Guides to participate in international activities whenever opportunities arise. On their return, delegates share their experiences at the annual Sharing Day. Many members from abroad visit and stay at Guide Headquarters every year and the Association has organized several international events/exchange programmes. The Association is also a member of the Hong Kong Council of Social Service and regularly meets with other uniformed groups.

The Association keeps the public informed of Guiding activities through the press, radio and television. It contributes regular columns for newspapers and magazines, and publishes a bi-monthly newsletter and parents' newsletter. The first Sunday in June every year has been designated "Guiders' Day" when girls show their appreciation.

Girl Guides participated in Jamboree on the Air, communicating by radio with their peers overseas.

Hungary

Magyar Cserkészleány Szövetség
(Association of Hungarian Girl Guides)

Founder Member of WAGGGS

Girl Guiding/Girl Scouting introduced:	**1919**
Girl Guiding/Girl Scouting banned:	**1948**
Re-admitted as Associate Member:	**1993**
Membership 1992:	**428**
Membership as % of female population:	**0.01%**
WAGGGS Region:	**Europe**

Guide

Brownie

Promise

Fogadom, hogy hiven teljesitem kötelességeimet, amelyekkel Istennek, hazámnak és embertársaimnak tartozom. Minden tölem telhetöt megteszek, hog másoknak segitsek. Ismerem a cserkésztörvényt, és azt mindenkor megtartom.

Law

1 A cserkészlány egyeneslelkü, és feltétlenül igazat mond
2 A cserkészlány hiven teljesíti kötelességeit
3 A cserkészlány ahol tud, segit
4 A cserkészlány minden cserkészt testvérének tekint
5 A cserkészlány gyöngéd másokkal, szigoru önmagával szemben
6 A cserkészlány szereti a természetet, jó az állatokhoz, kiméli a növényeket
7 A cserkészlány vezetöivel tevékenyen és készségesen müködik együtt
8 A cserkészlány vidám és meggondolt
9 A cserkészlány takarékos
10 A cserkészlány testben és lélekben tiszta.

Promise

I promise ...
to fulfil my duties faithfully which I owe to God, my country and other human beings
to do my best to help others
to know the Guide Law and keep it at all times.

Law

A Girl Guide is straightforward and tells the truth
A Girl Guide carries out her duties
A Girl Guide helps others whenever she can
A Girl Guide is a friend to all and a sister to every other guide
A Girl Guide is courteous to others and controls herself
A Girl Guide loves nature, is a friend to animals and cares for plants
A Girl Guide is ready to co-operate with her leaders actively
A Girl Guide is always happy and circumspect
A Girl Guide is thrifty
A Girl Guide is pure in body and soul

Age Groups

Girl Guides	11-16
Brownies	7-11

Development of the Movement in Hungary

The first Guide group in Hungary was set up in 1919. The National Association of Hungarian Girl Guides was founded in 1921 and recognized as a member of the International Council, the forerunner of WAGGGS, in 1922. In 1928 the Hungarian Girl Guides Association acted as hostess to the Fifth International Conference of Guiding when the World Association of Girl Guides and Girl Scouts was founded. In 1939 the first Girl Guide/Girl Scout World Camp, Pax Ting, was held in Hungary and attended by some 4,000 Guides from around the world.

During the war years of 1939 to 1945 the Movement was involved in relief work in hospitals and helping refugees. With the siege of the capital, the Association's activities were suspended. Guiding activities resumed after the war but in 1948 the government banned all youth organizations and the Association was forced to cease functioning for the next 40 years.

The first attempts to reorganize the Movement started in 1988, a response to political change in Hungary. In 1989 Magyar Cserkészlány Szövetség (The Association of Hungarian Girl Guides) was re-launched. A Central Committee concentrated on training potential leaders. By the end of 1991 Guide numbers had increased to include 24 groups, and the production of posters and promotional leaflets had helped to make the activities of the Association known to the public.

The Programme

The aim of the programme is to educate girls and young women to meet the needs of the country and their community. The programme keeps within national traditions and the basic values of the Movement. It aims to help girls to be aware and to prepare them for their roles in society and within the family. Topics covered are self-confidence, nutrition, environment and home economics, which includes budgeting, first aid, nursing of the sick, child care. The Association has plans to update the programme and hopes that young leaders will asssist it in this task.

Working with the Community

The Association has introduced a special programme for disadvantaged children aged five and six who are unable to attend nursery school.

Training

The Association has a training team which organizes a two-week camp each year to give training on the basics of Girl Guiding with sessions on topics of special interest. Training is included in regular leaders' meetings and the Association has participated in trainings organized by the Girl Guides of Austria and Germany.

Communication and Co-operation

The Association makes every effort to ensure that Guiding is better known within society, schools and churches. Posters and leaflets are published to inform potential members of the existence of the Association and its activities. Contact is maintained with the National Council of Youth Organizations in Hungary.

The Association publishes newsletters for Brownies and Girl Guides. Books have been published on character development and games. The WAGGGS Programme Pack has been translated into Hungarian and is used extensively.

Brownies say their Promises, pledging to become part of a Movement with a long tradition, recently renewed in Hungary.

Iceland

Bandalag Íslenskra Skáta
(The Icelandic Boy and Girl Scout Association)

Founder Member of WAGGGS

Girl Guiding/Girl Scouting introduced:	**1922**
Membership 1992:	**1,724**
Membership as % of female population:	**1.65%**
WAGGGS Region:	**Europe**

Girl Scout

Promise
Ég lofa að gera það sem í mínu valdi stendur til þess:
Að gera skyldu mína við guð og ættjörðina.
Að hjálpa öðrum og halda skátalögin.

Skátalögin
1 Skáti segir satt og stendur við orð sín.
2 Skáti er traustur félagi og vinur.
3 Skáti er hæverskur í hugsunum, orðum og verkum.
4 Skáti er hlýðinn
5 Skáti er glaðvær.
6 Skáti er öllum hjálpsamur.
7 Skáti er tillitssamur.
8 Skáti er nýtinn
9 Skáti er snyrtilegur í umgengni og ber virðingu fyrir eigum annarra.
10 Allir skátar eru náttúruvinir.

Motto
Ávallt viðbúin(n).

Brownie

Promise
On my honour I will do my best:
To do my duty to God and my Country,
To help others, and obey the Girl Scout Law.

Law
1 A Girl Scout tells the truth and keeps her word.
2 A Girl Scout is a loyal companion and friend.
3 A Girl Scout is modest in thought, word and deed.
4 A Girl Scout is obedient.
5 A Girl Scout is cheerful.
6 A Girl Scout is helpful to others.
7 A Girl Scout is considerate.
8 A Girl Scout is thrifty.
9 A Girl Scout is well-mannered and respects the possessions of others.
10 All Girl Scouts are friends of nature.

Motto
Always prepared

Age Groups

Svannar	Ranger	18+
Dróttskátar	Seniors	15-18
Skátar	Girl Scouts	11-15
Ylfingar	Cubs	10-11
Ljósálfar	Brownies	9-10

Development of the Movement in Iceland

The first troop for girls in Iceland was formed in the capital, Reykjavík, on July 7th 1922 under the direction of the YWCA. The connection between the YWCA and Girl Scouting only lasted a short while, but the Movement spread independently throughout most of the country. Within a few years many new troops for girls started.

Icelandic Girl Scouts became members of WAGGGS in 1928, and in 1939 the Icelandic Girl Scout Association was formed. In 1944 the two national Girl and Boy Scout Associations merged and became Bandalag íslenskra skáta (The Icelandic Boy and Girl Scout Association). The Association is believed to be the first merged Association in the world.

The Programme
The Constitution of Bandalag íslenskra skáta states that the main purpose of the Association is to aid children and young people into becoming independent, active and responsible individuals in society. The Association aims to fulfill that purpose through working in small groups, with outdoor experiences, projects

teaching various useful skills and with international co-operation.

Every county's Boy and Girl Scout groups are members of Bandalag íslenskra skáta. Each group has both boys and girls as members. The groups are divided into patrols with about six members, and about five patrols form a troop. In larger areas, troops join to form the county. Each county works mostly independently but organizes its programme according to the policies of Bandalag íslenskra skáta.

It is the responsibility of the Association to develop the programme for all age levels, and to co-ordinate leader training. The Association also handles the contact with Boy and Girl Scouts, as well as Associations from other countries.

In addition to the National Executive Board, three permanent committees are elected to handle the overall responsibilities of the work of the Association: the Programme Committee, the Training Committee and the International Committee.

Working with the Community

Working widely around Iceland are Rescue Squads. The members are Boy and Girl Scouts older than 18 years of age. The services they provide are, among other things, locating and rescuing lost people, for example the wilderness; giving aid and assistance on the occasion of natural disasters such as earthquakes; volcanic eruptions or bad weather; and providing first-aid at large outdoor gatherings. In many parts of the country the Rescue Squads are a part of the county's Boy and Girl Scout group, but in other places they work independently. The Rescue Squads are a recognised part of the country's public emergency system.

Various temporary community projects have also been a part of the Association's programme. Among them is the "Látum ljós okkar skína" campaign, where the Association distributes cat glitters to all six-year-old schoolchildren in the country, along with information about how to behave in the traffic. As the day is very short in Iceland during the height of winter, this message is very important. Along with cat glitters the children also receive an issue of the *Scoutmagasine*, where the Movement is introduced.

Outdoor and Environmental Activities

The programme for Icelandic Boy and Girl Scouts includes as many outdoor activities as possible, taking into consideration the landscape and the weather. During the winter the many huts owned by the various groups around the country are in constant use, and during the summer the patrols and troops attend the many organized camps or arrange their own camping expeditions. Every third year a national jamboree is organized. At Úlfjótsvatn, situated 70km from Reykjavík, the Association owns a campground.

Training

A training centre is operated at Úlfjótsvatn, and it is the central point of leader training in the country. The trainings organized range from skills training, to patrol leader training, to Gillwell courses.

Communication and Co-operation

In December 1993 a *Skátahandbók* (The Scout Manual) was published. It is an overall manual dealing with everything that has to do with the Movement and the indoor and outdoor programme. The Association publishes two to three issues of *Skátablaðið* (The Scout Magazine) a year, where various articles on related Association issues are published. *Skátamál* (Scout Issues) is published in eight issues a year and serves first and foremost as a newsletter. *Skátamál* is distributed to all Girl and Boy Scouts in Iceland.

Modern fundraising in Iceland uses computers and telephones to send telegraph messages at a profit!

India

The Bharat Scouts and Guides: The Girl Guide Section

Founder Member of WAGGGS (in conjunction with present day Pakistan and Bangladesh under the name of India)

Girl Guiding/Girl Scouting introduced:	**1911**
Became Full Member of WAGGGS (under the name India):	**1948**
Membership 1992:	**758,575**
Membership as % of female population:	**0.18%**
WAGGGS Region:	**Asia Pacific**

Guide

Promise

On my honour, I promise that I will do my best
to do my duty to God‡ and my country,
to help other people and
to obey the Guide Law.

Law

1 A Guide is trustworthy.
2 A Guide is loyal.
3 A Guide is a friend to all and a sister to every other Guide.
4 A Guide is courteous.
5 A Guide is a friend to animals and loves nature.
6 A Guide is disciplined and helps protect public property.
7 A Guide is courageous.
8 A Guide is thrifty.
9 A Guide is pure in thought, and word and deed.

Motto

Be Prepared

Bulbul

Bulbul Promise

I promise to do my best:
to do my duty to God‡ and my country,
To keep the Law of the Bulbul flock and
To do a good turn every day.

Bulbul Law

The Bulbul gives in to the elders,
The Bulbul is clean and courteous.

‡The world 'Dharma' may be substituted for 'God' if so desired.

Bulbul Motto

Do your best

Age Groups

Ranger	16-25
Guide	10-18
Bulbul	6-10

Development of the Movement in India

In 1948 India was welcomed as a separate member of WAGGGS, having been a Founder Member of the World Association, together with present day Pakistan and Bangladesh, in the name of India in 1928.

The Girl Guides Association (India) joined together with the nationally recognized Joint Movement in 1951, shortly after India became a Republic, to form the Bharat Scouts and Guides (Bharat being the ancient name for India). Guides and Scouts take part in jamborees, camp fires and other special events together, but carry out their training and camping programmes separately.

The Programme

Guiding exists in all of the administrative states in India, in both rural and urban areas. It is chiefly associated with schools, and in some schools it forms part of the curriculum of optional extra activities. The programme is based on community service and development.

The programme is updated periodically to suit the changing needs of girls in India. Although the Association has some special groups for disabled girls it encourages their integration into standard existing units where possible. Air Guiding is increasing in popularity and plans are underway to offer Guides water-based activities. In a few states Bunny groups have been introduced on an experimental basis for girls aged 3-6.

Working with the Community

The Bharat Scouts and Guides runs several national schemes to encourage community service and development. The Prime Minister's Shield Competition is open to groups of Guides and Rangers and involves organizing and carrying out projects in such areas as conservation of plants and animals, health and hygiene and adult education. The Rashtrapati Guide and Rashtrapati Ranger programmes are for individual Guides and Rangers working on projects in the same subjects.

Recently community development has been integrated into unit activities. Several community-oriented activities are also undertaken on a national scale such as national integration, community singing, leprosy awareness, sanitation promotion, child health and adult literacy.

Outdoor and Environmental Activities

The Association organizes frequent national and regional Integration Camps where members of the Movement are drawn together, regardless of caste, creed, nationality or faith, in order to create a feeling of national integration and unity.

Guides undertake environmental projects as part of the Prime Minister's Shield Competition and the President's Guide and Ranger programmes.

In 1989 Guides undertook tree-planting campaigns throughout India. A seminar at the Association's national headquarters in 1991 on Literacy and Environmental Awareness gave participants from every Indian state the opportunity to prepare environmental action plans for their areas.

Training

The Guide Wing has its own training scheme for adult leaders, organized by the National and the State Training Commissioners for Guides. The scheme involves basic and advanced training. Training camps, day courses and weekend trainings are frequently held, and there are separate training camps for each section.

Communication and Co-operation

The Bharat Scouts and Guides has always participated actively in international events. As Sangam, one of the four World Centres, is in India, many girls have had the opportunity to meet members of the Movement from abroad.

The Bharat Scouts and Guides informs the general public about Guiding through the press, radio and television. The Association receives much support from the central and state governments and this has resulted in the doubling of membership over a four-year period. The Guide Wing co-operates with all other major voluntary youth organizations working for the development of girls and young women in India.

Guides work on the national project to eliminate leprosy by the year 2000. The project screens school children, establishing "leprosy-free" schools.

Indonesia

Gerakan Pramuka Indonesia
(Indonesian Scout Movement)

Girl Guiding/Girl Scouting introduced:	**1912**
Became an Associate Member of WAGGGS:	**1975**
Became a Full Member of WAGGGS:	**1987**
Membership 1992†:	**98,656**
Membership as % of female population:	**0.10%**
WAGGGS Region:	**Asia Pacific**

Girl Scout

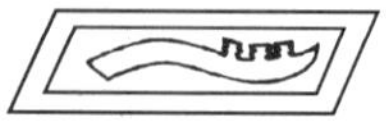

Brownie

Tri Satya
Demi kehormatanku aku berjanji akan bersungguh-sungguh
- menjalankan kewajibanku terhadap Tuhan dan Negara Kesatuan Republik Indonesia, dan menjalankan Pancasila;
- menolong sesama hidup dan mempersiapkan diri membangun masyarakat;
- menepati Dasa Darma.

Dasa Darma
Pramuka itu
1 Takwa kepada Tuhan Yang Maha Esa
2 Cinta alam dan kasih sayang sesama manusia
3 Patriot yang sopan dan kesatria
4 Patuh dan suka bermusyawarah
5 Rela menolong dan tabah
6 Rajin terampil dan gembira
7 Hemat, cermat dan bersahaja
8 Disiplin, berani dan setia
9 Bertanggungjawab dan dapat dipercaya
10 Suci dalam pikiran, perkataan dan perbuatan.

Brownie Promise
Aku berjanji akan bersungguh-sungguh
- menjalankan kewajibanku terhadap Tuhan dan Negara Kesatuan Republik Indonesia dan menurut aturan keluarga;
- setiap hari berbuat kebaikan.

Brownie Law
Siaga itu menurut Ayah-Ibunda-nya.
Siaga itu berani dan tidak putus asa.

Promise
On my honour I promise that I will do my best:
To do my duty to God, and to the Republic of Indonesia and to carry out Pancasila,
To help all living beings and be ready to build up the nation,
To obey the Dasa Darma.

Law
A Girl Scout is:
1 Reverent towards God.
2 Loving and cares for nature and her fellowman.
3 Courteous and chivalrous.
4 Obedient and ready to consult.
5 Steadfast and willing to help.
6 Diligent, skilful and cheerful.
7 Thrifty, accurate and simple.
8 Disciplined, brave and faithful.
9 Responsible and trustworthy.
10 Clean in thought, word and action.

Brownie Promise
On my honour I promise that I will do my best:
To do my duty to God, and the Republic of Indonesia, and to obey the Dwi Darma‡,
To do a good turn every day.

‡Dwi Darma to be changed by family norms.

Brownie Law
The Brownie obeys her parents.
The Brownie is valiant and never despairs.

Age Groups

Senior Ranger	21-25
Ranger	16-20
Girl Scout	11-15
Brownie	7-10

Development of the Movement in Indonesia

Guiding began in Indonesia in 1912 and, in the early years, there were more than 60 separate Scout and Girl Scout associations. In 1960, all the Associations agreed to form a new single National Association for girls and boys, and in 1961 the Gerakan Pandidikan Kepanduan Pradja Muda Karana (the Scouting Education Movement to Serve Young People), known as Gerakan Pramuka, Indonesia, was established. Members of the Association are known as Pramukas.

Within Gerakan Pramuka girls and boys belong to separate units although they join together for some activities. Girl Scouting takes place within schools and extends to communities and large industrial complexes.

The Programme

The broad outline for the programme is drawn up at national level. It is essentially an educational programme developed to suit the country's needs and intended to be a bridge between school and the educational opportunities outside. The programme is flexible so that it can be adapted to meet the varying needs within each of Indonesia's 26 provinces. This approach has proved very successful and has attracted many young people to the Movement.

The Gerakan Pramuka aims to equip girls for adulthood and a career, and programmes are carried out through a method of self-education: doing to learn, learning to earn and earning to live.

Learning by teaching is also effectively carried out by the Rangers, who are encouraged to acquire a knowledge of such subjects as home economics, first aid and dressmaking. Special units of Rangers/Rovers are formed so that members may pursue specific interests. These include air, sea, forest, agriculture, and law and order. Girls with special needs are encouraged to join the Movement, becoming members of either standard units or special extension units. Units have been set up in training institutions for children with special needs, especially in Jakarta.

Guides work on paper creations.

Working with the Community

A high priority is given to community development. The Gerakan Pramuka has a training centre at Cibibur, which is used as a national training centre and for training in community development. Cibibur has a health centre, recreational and sports facilities, and bee-keeping and horticultural projects.

Guides are involved in the planning, implementation and evaluation of projects, which include improving health and nutrition and providing family life education. Members of the Association won a UNESCO award for their literacy campaign in Malang Regency.

The Rangers and Rovers help on such projects as building rural roads, bridges, mosques, churches, dams and public toilets. They also help to provide supplies of drinking water and give support in times of national disaster.

Outdoor and Environmental Activities

Camping is an important part of the programme of the Gerakan Pramuka. A national camp is organized every two years, and provincial and regional camps are held during the dry season.

The Gerakan Pramuka organizes nature conservation activities, such as conducting surveys on endangered species and working to prevent their extinction. Rangers and Rovers also implement reafforestation schemes.

Training

A National Training Team, made up of six leaders (two from each branch), is appointed by the National Conference. It is responsible for all Guide training in Indonesia, and supervises provincial training teams. The training programme provides general training, specialized training in subjects which particularly interest the trainees, and training in leadership. Special instructors give training in crafts and skills.

Communication and Co-operation

Members of the Association take an active part in all events organized by the Asia Pacific Region. Visits from international guests are encouraged, as this is seen as a method of bringing international Girl Guiding/Girl Scouting closer to home. The Gerakan Pramuka regularly holds international camps for Rangers and Rovers from Indonesia and hosts visitors from neighbouring countries.

The Movement is well respected in Indonesia and receives much support from the public in the form of technical advice and training in specialized skills. The Association publishes two monthly magazines, *Pramuka* and *Warta Berkala,* and a weekly magazine called *Data Dan Peristiwa.* A national rally is held on 14 August each year, 'Pramuka Day'.

The Gerakan Pramuka works with UNESCO and takes part in United Nations International Years.

Camping and outdoor skills are an important part of the programme in Indonesia.

Ireland

Comhairle Bantreoraithe na hEireann
(The Council of Irish Guiding Associations)

Component Associations:
The Irish Girl Guides
Catholic Guides of Ireland

Girl Guiding/Girl Scouting introduced:	**1911**
Became Full Member of WAGGGS:	**1932**
Membership 1992:	**22,004**
Membership as % of female population:	**1.24%**
WAGGGS Region:	**Europe**

The Irish Girl Guides

Guide

Bantreoraithe na h-Éireann
An Gealltanas
Geallaim faoi bhri m'onóra, chomh fada agus is féidir liom, mo dhualgas do Dhia agus don tír a dhéanamh, teacht i gcabhair ar dhaoine eile i gcónaí, agus bheith umhal do dhlí na mBantreoruithe.

An Dlí
1 Is iontaofa onóir an bhantreoraí.
2 Tá an bantreoraí dílis.
3 Tá se de dhualgas ar an mbantreoraí teacht i gcabhair ar dhaoine eile.
4 Is cara do chach an bantreoraí agus is deirfíur do ghach bantreoraí eile i.
5 Tá an bantreoraí béasach.
6 Tá an bantreoraí cineálta leis na hainmhithe.
7 Tá an bantreoraí umhal dá cinnirí.
8 Tá an bantreoraí gealgháireach i ngach cruachás.
9 Tá an bantreoraí barainneach.
10 Tá an bantreoraí geanmnaí ina smaointe, ina briathar, agus ina gníomh.

Motto
Bí ullamh

Brownie Promise
Geallaim mo dhícheall a dhéanamh mo dhualgas do Dhia agus do mo thír a chomhlíonadh, cabhrú le mo theaghlach féin gach lá, agus bheith umhal do dhlí no Suaircíní.

Brownie Law
Déanann Suaircín cúram de dhaoine eile roimpi féin agus
déanann sí soilios gach aon lá.

Brownie Motto
Cuidign le daoine

Promise
I promise on my honour to do my best to do my duty to God and my country, to help other people at all times, and to obey the Guide Law.

Law
1 A Guide's honour is to be trusted.
2 A Guide is loyal.
3 A Guide's duty is to be useful and to help others.
4 A Guide is a friend to all, and a sister to every other Guide.
5 A Guide is courteous.
6 A Guide is a friend to animals.
7 A Guide obeys orders.
8 A Guide smiles and sings under all difficulties.
9 A Guide is thrifty.
10 A Guide is pure in thought, word and deed.

Motto
Be Prepared

Brownie Promise
I promise to do my best
to do my duty to God and my country
To help those at home every day, And to
obey the Brownie Law.

Brownie

Brownie Law
A Brownie thinks of others before herself and does a good turn every day.

Brownie Motto
Lend a Hand

Age Groups

Young Leaders	15 - 19
Ranger	14 - 21
Guide	$10\frac{1}{2}$ - 16
Brownie	6 - 11
Ladybirds	5 - 7
Ranger	14 - 21

Catholic Guides of Ireland

Brigin Guide

The Brigin Guide Promise
On my honour with the help of God I ...promise to do my best to serve God and his Church, to help other people at all times and to keep the Brigin Law.

The Brigin Guide Law
1 A Brigin always speaks the truth.
2 A Brigin promptly obeys with a smile.
3 A Brigin is helpful and kind.
4 A Brigin is polite and friendly.
5 A Brigin is never afraid to do the right thing.
6 A Brigin does all things for the glory of God.

The Guide Promise
On my honour with the help of God I ...promise to do my best to serve God and his Church, to be a responsible member of the community, to help other people at all times and to keep the Guide Law.

Guide

The Guide Law
1 A Guide can be Trusted.
2 A Guide is loyal.
3 A Guide is Helpful.
4 A Guide is Friendly.
5 A Guide is always Polite and Considerate
6 A Guide is Kind to everyone and respects all living things.
7 A Guide is Obedient.
8 A Guide is Cheerful.
9 A Guide has Courage - She is never afraid to do the right thing.
10 A Guide is Tidy - She takes care of her belongings and those of other people.
11 A Guide is Self Controlled in thought, word and deed.
12 A Guide does all things for the Glory of God.

The Ranger Guide Promise
On my honour, with the Grace of God, I ... promise to do my best to serve God and Holy Church, to help other people at all times and to keep the Guide Law.
I further promise as a Ranger Guide to be of service to the Community.

Structure of Organization
The administration of the Association is based on a principle of decentralization and operates at three levels, National, Diocesan/Regional and Local.

National Level
National Council is the governing body of the Association. It exercises all legislative, executive and administrative powers within the Constitution. It delegates the management of business of the Association to the National Executive Board.

Diocesan Level
The Diocesan or Regional Council or Committee administers Guiding within its territory according to the terms of its own Bye-Laws and subject to the limits of the Constitution and Rules of the Catholic Guides of Ireland.

Age Groups

Ranger Guide Section	15 - 19
Guide Section	$10\frac{1}{2}$ - 17
Brigin Guide Section	6 - 11

Development of the Movement in Ireland

Guiding started in Ireland in 1911 with the opening of the first company in southern Ireland. It was open to girls of all denominations. At this time there was no border between north and south, so Guiding was run as one organization for all Ireland as part of the Girl Guides Association (United Kingdom). In 1929 the Movement became The Irish Free State Girl Guides with its own Constitution and Council and operated in the Irish Free State (26 counties) and in 1938 the name was changed again to The Irish Girl Guides.

In 1932 Ireland became a full member of the World Association of Girl Guides and Girl Scouts with The Irish Girl Guides holding the membership.

In 1928 an organization called Clanna Brighde was formed to cater to the needs of Catholic girls in the 32 counties of Ireland. The activities of Clanna Brighde were based on the Girl Guide Movement. Clanna Brighde changed its name in 1932 to Catholic Girl Guides of Ireland. In 1935 it was decided that each diocese would be responsible for Catholic Guiding in its own area and this system continued until 1972 when the existing Diocesan membership came together again and formed the Federation of Catholic Girl Guides of Ireland. In 1977 the Federation became the Catholic Guides of Ireland.

In December 1992 it was agreed to establish the Council of Irish Guiding Associations which was ratified as a Full Member of WAGGGS at the 28th World conference in Denmark in 1993.

Irish Girl Guides

The Programme

The patrol system forms the basis of almost all Guide activities in Ireland, challenging members to develop to their full potential and encouraging team spirit and leadership qualities. A system incorporating tests and proficiency badges is used to measure personal progress.

Branch programmes are updated regularly to keep pace with the changing school syllabus and to ensure that the individual needs of the girls are met. Special emphasis is put on conservation and environmental projects as well as traditional crafts and skills.

The Senior Branch is composed of the Ranger section and Young Leader section, providing mutual training and social venues for the shared interest of this age group.

Where possible girls with disabilities are integrated into ordinary units and encouraged to take an active part in as much of the programme as possible. A committee has been formed to cater for the requirements of girls and leaders with special needs e.g. disability, underprivilege.

Working with the Community

In recent years several community projects were undertaken. A fundraising project resulted in the planting of 250,000 trees in Tanzania. To celebrate 80 years of Guiding in Ireland in 1991, members packed groceries in supermarkets to raise money to purchase 28 motorized wheelchairs which gave mobility to young people throughout Ireland.

Outdoor and Environmental Activities

Guides are involved in conservation

The environment is of special concern to all Guides in Ireland.

projects and have been fundraising to supply 250,000 trees to be planted in Tanzania in co-operation with Concern. This project finished in July 1991 at a national camp celebrating 80 years of Guiding in Ireland.

Communication and Co-operation

As a member of WAGGGS, The Irish Girl Guides has always played a very active part in the international field, sending delegates to camps, conferences, seminars and training events in many parts of the world.

The Irish Girl Guides is a founder member of the National Youth Council of Ireland, and members are encouraged to take a leading role in a number of the committees.

Catholic Guides of Ireland

The aim of the Catholic Guides of Ireland is to promote and foster the spiritual, moral, cultural, intellectual, social and physical development of its members in accordance with the ideals of the Guide Movement, so that Guides become mature people prepared for leadership and service in the home and community.

Outdoor and Environmental Activities

An appreciation of the outdoors and a concern for the environment are important aspects of the Guide Programme. In 1993, the Association launched its first national environmental campaign, encouraging Guides everywhere to take a fresh look at their local area and decide on a practical project to improve some aspect of it for the community at large. This campaign will culminate in the production of an environmental diary and the award of a special environmental badge to all participants.

Training

The National Youth Council of Ireland together with Trocaire (a national third world organization) has been instrumental in organizing a very innovative approach to development education. It enables leaders and young people to meet and work within two different cultures: it is hoped that active participation in this exchange of cultures will enhance this aspect of the Guide programme.

Communication and Co-operation

Guiding has something valuable to offer everyone. Through participation in a recent national television programme reaching almost 100,000 people, CGI has been able to involve its young people and leaders directly in presenting the real image of Guiding for today. This has also been an opportunity for the Association to take a new look at uniform.

In addition, in 1993, the Association has also been involved in its first countrywide leadership recruitment week, providing leadership opportunities for women everywhere.

In 1990 and 1991, The Irish Girl Guides and the Catholic Guides of Ireland, together with the two Irish Scouting associations hosted a party of children from Chernobyl. In 1992 a joint Guide and Scout appeal created awareness among the Associations' members of the plight of the people of Somalia and raised over £8,000 for Somalia famine relief.

Israel

Hitachdut Hatsofim Ve Hatsofot Be Israel

(Girl Scout Section – Israel Boy and Girl Scouts Federation)

Girl Guiding/Girl Scouting introduced:	**1919**
Became Associate Member of WAGGGS:	**1957**
Became Full Member of WAGGGS:	**1963**
Membership 1992:	**33,520**
Membership as % of female population:	**1.34%**
WAGGGS Region:	**Europe**

Girl Scout

Midot

1 Hatsofe devaro emeth.
2 Hatsofe neman lemdinato.
3 Hatsofe Chaver moil bachevra, ohev avoda veozer lezolato.
4 Hatsofe rea lechol adam veach lecol tsofe.
5 Hatsofe adeev.
6 Hatsofe chovev et hachaie vehazomech uemagen aleahem.
7 Hatsofe ish mishmaat.
8 Hatsofe aeno nofel berucho.
9 Hatsofe chaschan.
10 Hatsofe tahor bedibure ubamaasaw.

Motto

Heye nachon

The Girl Scout Promise

I will live my life correctly and do my duty
I will serve my people and my country
I will help all those in need
The Girl Scout Law, I protect and will protect
Be correct, correct forever
Be correct, correct forever

The Girl Scout Law

1 Girl Scouts tell the truth.
2 Girl Scouts are true to their country, their people and their language.
3 Girl Scouts are good citizens and love to work and help the needy.
4 Girl Scouts are a friend to all and a sister to all scouts.
5 Girl Scouts are polite and courteous.
6 Girl Scouts protect the countryside and animals.
7 Girl Scouts are disciplined.
8 Girl Scouts are always in good spirits.
9 Girl Scouts are frugal.
10 Girl Scouts are pure in thoughts and deeds.

Motto

Be Prepared

Brownie Promise

Hineni nachon lemaleh et hukat eidat haofarim, leasot maaseh tov bchol yom veyom, uloazor bemyuchad bevet horai.

Pack Law

Haofer metsayet latzvi.
Haofer kovesh yetsiro.

Brownie Motto

Nishma venaaseh

Brownie Promise

I am ready to keep the pack law, to do a good turn every day, and to help my parents especially at home.

Pack Law

The 'ofer' (Brownie) obeys the 'big deer'.
The 'ofer' does not give in to herself.

Brownie Motto

We'll listen and obey

Brownie

Age Groups

Tsofe	Ranger	15-18
Nachshon	Girl Scout	11-14
Ofer	Brownie	9-10

Development of the Movement in Israel

The Israel Boy and Girl Scout Federation is composed of six Component Associations: the Hebrew Boy and Girl Scout Association, the Arab Schools Boy and Girl Scouts, the Israel Arab Boy and Girl Scouts, the Israel Greek Orthodox Boy and Girl Scouts, the Israel Catholic Boy and Girl Scouts and the Israel Druze Boy and Girl Scout Association.

Scouting in Israel is much older than the State of Israel itself. It dates back to 1919 when men who happened to be Scouts went to Palestine and aroused the interest of others in the formation of a Scout Association.

The Programme

Girl Scouting plays a special role in the life of the country, and the programme emphasises training in the service of the state and its people. The Federation has worked at developing national and political awareness, fuller involvement in community life, closer co-operation between minority groups in the different associations, more self-government and a wider age range in the older age group. Much attention has also been paid to developing programmes for the Ranger/ Rover age group, the result of which has been an increase in Ranger/Rover membership. Girl Scouting among underprivileged children has increased, and over 30% of the membership comes from low-income communities. Girl Scouting among the disabled in all the Component Associations has also increased.

Working with the Community

Community activities for the Ranger/ Rover age group include the establishment of small groups which spend a year (between leaving school and undertaking national service) in development towns, giving service to the community and helping with Girl Scouting and Scouting activities in youth clubs, kindergartens and schools. Many groups of Rangers/Rovers go to kibbutzim as part of their national service.

Outdoor and Environmental Activities

All the Associations incorporate regional camps and cross-country hikes as important parts of the programme. Members are encouraged to participate in tree-planting campaigns whenever possible.

Communication and Co-operation

Members of the Associations are encouraged to form their own international contacts by corresponding with other Girl Guides/Girl Scouts throughout the world.

The Federation publishes an illustrated magazine, *Heye Nachon* (Be Prepared), which contains news and information about Girl Scouting in Israel.

Italy

Federazione Italiana dello Scautismo (FIS)
(National Organization of Italian Girl Guides and Girl Scouts)

Component Associations:
Associazione Guide e Scouts Cattolici Italiani (AGESCI, Italian Catholic Guides and Scouts Association)
Corpo Nazionale Giovani Esploratori ed Esploratrici Italiani (CNGEI, National Organization of Italian Scouts and Girl Scouts)

Girl Guiding/Girl Scouting introduced:	**1912**
Became Associate Member of WAGGGS:	**1946**
Became Full Member of WAGGGS:	**1948**
Membership 1992:	**81,651**
Membership as % of female population:	**0.28%**
WAGGGS Region:	**Europe**

Associazione Guide e Scouts Cattolici Italiani (AGESCI)

AGESCI Guide

Promessa
Con l'aiuto di Dio prometto sul mio onore di fare del mio meglio: per compiere il mio dovere verso Dio e verso il mio Paese; per aiutare gli altri in ogni circostanza; per osservare la Legge scout.

Legge
La Guida e lo Scout:
1 pongono il loro onore nel meritare fiducia;
2 sono leali;
3 si rendono utili ed aiutano gli altri;
4 sono amici di tutti e fratelli di ogni altra Guida e Scout;
5 sono cortesi;
6 amano e rispettano la natura;
7 sanno obbedire;
8 sorridono e cantano anche nelle difficoltà;
9 sono laboriosi ed economi;
10 sono puri di pensieri, parole ed azioni.

Motto
Sii preparata

Promessa della Coccinella
Prometto con l'aiuto e l'esempio di Gesù, di fare del mio meglio nel migliorare me stessa, nell'aiutare gli altri, nell'osservare la Legge del Cerchio.

Legge della Coccinella
La Coccinella pensa agli altri come a se stessa.
La Coccinella vive con gioia e lealtà insieme al Cerchio.

Promise
With God's help I promise on my honour that I will do my best: to do my duty to God and my country; to help other people at all times; to obey the Guide Scout Law.

Law
A Guide and a Scout:
1 consider their honour to be trusted;
2 are loyal;
3 want to be useful and help others;
4 are friends to all and brothers/sisters to every other Guide and Scout;

Ladybird

5 are courteous;
6 love and respect nature;
7 know how to obey;
8 smile and sing under all difficulties;
9 are hardworking and thrifty;
10 are pure in thought, word and deed.

Motto
Be prepared

Ladybird Promise
I promise with the help and example of Jesus that I will do my best: to help other people; to obey the Round Law.

Ladybird Law
The Ladybird takes care of the other people as of herself.
The Ladybird lives joyfully and loyally with her Pack.

Age Groups

Scolta	Ranger	16-19/21
Guida	Guide	11/12-16
Coccinella	Ladybird	7/8-11/12

Corpo Nazionale Giovani Esploratori ed Esploratrici Italiani (CNGEI)

CNGEI
Girl Scout

Promessa
Prometto sul mio onore di fare del mio meglio per:
- compiere il mio dovere verso Dio, la patria e la famiglia;
- agire sempre con disinteresse e lealtà;
- osservare la Legge Scout.

Legge
1 La parola dell'Esploratrice è sacra.
2 L'Esploratrice è leale, forte e coraggiosa.
3 L'Esploratrice è buona e generosa.
4 L'Esploratrice è amica di tutti e sorella di ogni altra Esploratrice.
5 L'Esploratrice è cortese e tollerante.
6 L'Esploratrice rispetta e protegge i luoghi, gli animali, le piante.
7 L'Esploratrice è coscientemente disciplinata.
8 L'Esploratrice è sempre serena, anche nelle difficoltà.
9 L'Esploratrice è sobria, economa, laboriosa, perseverante.
10 L'Esploratrice è pura di pensiero, corretta nelle parole e negli atti.

CNGEI
Wolf Cub
(Brownie)

Motto
Sii preparata

Promessa del lupetto
Prometto di fare del mio meglio per amare Dio, la patria e la famiglia, osservare la legge del Branco e compiere ogni giorno una buona azione.

Legge del lupetto
Il lupetto ascolta il vecchio lupo.
Il lupetto non cede mai a se stesso.

Motto del lupetto
Del nostro meglio

Promise
I promise on my honour to do my best to:
do my duty to God, my country and my family:
always act impartially and with loyalty:
obey the Girl Scout Law.

Law
1 A Girl Scout's word is to be trusted.
2 A Girl Scout is loyal, strong and brave.
3 A Girl Scout is good and generous.
4 A Girl Scout is a friend to all and a sister to every other Girl Scout.
5 A Girl Scout is courteous and tolerant.
6 A Girl Scout respects and protects places, animals and plants.
7 A Girl Scout is self-disciplined.
8 Girl Scout is always calm, even in difficulties.
9 A Girl Scout is moderate, thrifty, hard-working, persevering.
10 A Girl Scout is pure in thought and correct in word and deed.

Motto
Be Prepared

Wolf Cub Promise
I promise to do my best to love God, my country and my family, to obey the Law of the Pack and to do a Good Turn every day.

Wolf Cub Law
The Wolf Cub listens to the old wolf.
The Wolf Cub never gives in to herself.

Wolf Cub Motto
The best we can

Age Groups

Rover	Ranger	15/16-18/19
Esploratrice	Girl Scout	11/12-15/16
Lupetto	Wolf Cub (Brownie)	8-11/12

Development of the Movement in Italy

Girl Guiding/Girl Scouting activities began in Italy as early as 1912, but were suppressed during the 1920s and did not start again until 1944.
The Federazione Italiana Guide Esploratrici was formed in 1945 to link the two existing Associations of Girl Guides and Girl Scouts: Unione Nazionale Giovani Esploratrici Italiane and the Associazione Guide Italiane. In 1974 the latter merged with the Associazione Scouts Cattolici Italiani to form Associazione Guide e Scouts Cattolici Italiani (AGESCI). In 1976 the Unione Nazionale Giovani Esploratrici Italiane became the Corpo Nazionale Giovani Esploratori ed Esploratrici Italiani (CNGEI).

Associazione Guide e Scouts Cattolici Italiani (AGESCI)

The Programme

AGESCI emphasizes a clear Christian commitment. The shared programme for girls and boys focuses on co-education, religious education, good citizenship and peace education. Responsibility is shared at all levels between male and female members. Many Ranger, Rover, and Brownie/Cub units are mixed. Guide branch activities are carried out either in parallel units, with leaders working together to organize suitable joint activities periodically, or in mixed units. Patrols are always single-sex. AGESCI is studying all aspects of co-education and organizes study groups on this subject. Members with special needs are integrated into standard units, and a national working group studies difficulties which arise in order to give support and information to leaders.

Working with the Community

Community service is an important aspect of the Association's activities and a national programme has been developed to ensure that all members are trained and ready to help out in case of emergency. AGESCI also supports a programme for adults who wish to devote a year to voluntary service. In 1993 over 1,000 members volunteered to help refugees and hospitals in Albania, repairing and rebuilding in projects as requested.

Outdoor and Environmental Activities

Every year, regional and district camps are held for the different branches. The Association runs permanent summer campsites (Colico, Spettine and Costigiola in northern Italy and Marineo in Sicily) where Guides and Rangers learn skills on pioneering, nature and new communication techniques. In addition AGESCI has a work group which studies conservation projects suitable for support from its members.

Training

The Association runs three training programmes: one at regional level for Rangers and Rovers, offering vocational guidance for service; another at regional level for leaders of each age group; and a third at national level, for more advanced training in educational methods and service.

AGESCI Guides help paint a fence as part of a week-long volunteer activity in Albania. Over 1,000 Guides and Scouts rotated service of week-long intervals in 1993.

Communication and Co-operation
AGESCI has improved its methods of informing the general public about its activities, and has enhanced the image of Guiding and Scouting in Italy. It is well-received by the media and the public. The Association co-operates with Les Guides du Burkina Faso and with Scouts du Burkina Faso on projects chosen in accordance with the twin Associations.

Agreements on training co-operation for leaders were set up with Scout and Guide Associations in Slovenia, Albania and Romania.

The Association publishes four monthly magazines: *Scout-Giochiamo* for Brownies and Cubs; *Scout-Avventura* for Guides and Scouts; *Scout-Camminiamo Insieme* for Rangers and Rovers; and *Scout-Proposta Educativa* for leaders. It also publishes *Agescout*, a fortnightly newsletter distributed to leaders and interested parties outside the Association.

AGESCI co-operates with several Italian organizations focusing on current youth issues such as drug addiction and preventing youth hardship.

Corpo Nazionale Giovani Esploratori ed Esploratrici Italiani (CNGEI)

CNGEI emphasizes that it is open to young people of both sexes and all religious beliefs. The Association functions under the patronage of the President of the Italian Republic.

The Programme
The Programme for girls and boys is the same, focusing on co-education, good citizenship, as well as both peace and spiritual education which encourages members to ascertain their own beliefs. All units are mixed with separate male and female patrols in the Girl Scout and Boy Scout age group. Leadership responsibility at all levels is shared equally between men and women. CNGEI embarked on a co-educational programme after much study and has published a book on the principles of co-education. Members with special needs, are integrated into existing units within CNGEI.

Working with the Community
CNGEI takes part in community service projects and has worked with AGESCI to help victims of natural disasters, helping to rescue inhabitants, salvage crops, co-ordinate groups of volunteers and operate field telephones. Community service is an important aspect of the Ranger programme and each year a special national programme is implemented, for example the integration of immigrants in 1989/90.

Outdoor Activities
Regular national camps are held such as a meeting for elder Wolf Cubs in Liguria in 1988 and a Wolf Cub Olympic Games in Trentino in 1990. The Association holds a 'Tecnicamp' every year which gives participants the opportunity to learn a skill such as pioneering, hiking or sailing.

Training
The Association runs three leadership training programmes. The basic course, at district level, offers information on Girl and Boy Scouting. The preliminary course, organized at national level, is compulsory for leaders of all units and the third, the master course is targeted at leaders of each age group and involves participants in a short research project.

Communication and Co-operation
The Association encourages units to attend international camps abroad and sends qualified leaders to international seminars.

CNGEI informs the general public about its activities through the press and publishes a monthly magazine for members, *Scoutismo* with *Notiziario* included as an insert for leaders.
In addition, CNGEI has co-operated with the Ministry of the Interior in recent years, attending a consultation group on youth problems with AGESCI and other youth organizations.

Ivory Coast

Scoutisme Féminin de Côte d'Ivoire

Component Associations:
Guides de Côte d'Ivoire
Eclaireuses Unionistes de Côte d'Ivoire
Eclaireuses Laïques de Côte d'Ivoire

Became Associate Member of WAGGGS:	**1963**
Membership 1992:	**3,850**
Membership as % of female population:	**0.06%**
WAGGGS Region:	**Africa**

Guides de Côte d'Ivoire

Promesse

Sur mon honneur, avec la grâce de Dieu, je m'engage
à servir de mon mieux Dieu, l'Eglise et la patrie;
à aider mon prochain en toute circonstance;
à observer la loi des guides.

Loi

1 La Guide est loyale.
2 La Guide pense d'abord aux autres.
3 La Guide est généreuse; elle est prête à servir.
4 La Guide est accueillante; elle a l'esprit d'équipe.
5 La Guide, soeur de toute autre guide, est présente à tous.
6 La Guide découvre la nature; elle y voit l'oeuvre de Dieu.
7 La Guide sait obéir.
8 La Guide ne craint pas l'effort; elle ne fait rien à moitié.
9 La Guide aime son travail et respecte celui des autres.
10 La Guide est maîtresse de soi; elle est pure et joyeuse.

Devise

Toujours prête

Promesse des Jeannettes

Je promets de faire de mon mieux
pour être fidèle à Dieu, à la patrie, à mes parents, à la loi de la ronde, et pour faire chaque jour un plaisir à quelqu'un.

Loi des Jeannettes

Une jeannette est toujours propre.
Une jeannette est toujours active.
Une jeannette est toujours gaie.
Une jeannette dit toujours vrai.
Une jeannette pense d'abord aux autres.

Devise des Jeannettes

De notre mieux

Promise

On my honour, with the grace of God, I undertake
to do my best to serve God, the Church and my country;
to help others in all circumstances;
and to obey the Guide Law.

Law

1 A Guide is loyal.
2 A Guide thinks first of others.
3 A Guide is generous; she is prepared to help.
4 A Guide is welcoming; she has team spirit.
5 A Guide, sister to every Guide, is at the service of all.
6 A Guide learns about nature in which she see God's work.
7 A Guide knows how to obey.
8 A Guide does not fear endeavour; she does nothing by halves.
9 A Guide likes her work and respects that of other people.
10 A Guide is self-controlled; she is pure and cheerful.

GCI Guide

GCI Brownie

Motto
Always prepared

Brownie Promise
I promise to do my best
to be faithful to God, my country, my parents, the Law of the Pack and to do a good turn to someone every day.

Brownie Law
A Brownie is always clean.
A Brownie is always active.
A Brownie is always cheerful.
A Brownie is always truthful.
A Brownie thinks first of others.

Brownie Motto
The best we can

Age Groups

Aînée	Ranger	18-25
Guide	Guide	12-17
Jeannette	Brownie	8-12

Eclaireuses Unionistes Girl Scout

Eclaireuses Unionistes Lark

Eclaireuses Unionistes de Côte d'Ivoire

Promesse
Avec l'aide de Dieu, je promets sur mon honneur de faire mon possible pour servir Dieu, ma patrie, et ma famille, aider les autres en tout temps, obéir à la loi des éclaireuses.

Loi
1 Une éclaireuse est loyale on peut compter sur elle, elle ne ment jamais.
2 Une éclaireuse est disciplinée, elle obéit joyeusement, elle est exacte et ordonnée.
3 Une éclaireuse est calme, elle sait se dominer.
4 Une éclaireuse est énergique et travailleuse. Elle ne craint pas les difficultés.
5 Une éclaireuse est bonne. Elle est obligeante et polie.
6 Une éclaireuse est l'amie de tous et la soeur de toutes les autres éclaireuses.
7 Une éclaireuse est sobre dans ses goûts et sa parure.
8 Une éclaireuse est l'amie des animaux et des plantes.
9 Une éclaireuse est toujours de bonne humeur, elle s'efforce de faire règner la joie autour d'elle.
10 Une éclaireuse est pure dans ses pensées, ses paroles et ses actes.

Devise
Soit prête

Promesse des Alouettes
Je promets de faire de mon mieux
pour servir Dieu, ma famille, obéir à la loi des alouettes et faire chaque jour un plaisir à quelqu'un.

Loi des Alouettes
Alouette, écoute ta cheftaine.
Alouette, aide sans te fatiguer.
Alouette, aide joyeusement.

Devise des Alouettes
De notre mieux

Promise
With God's help I promise on my honour to do everything possible to serve God, my country and my family; to help others at all times and to obey the Girl Scout Law.

Law
1 A Girl Scout keeps her word.
2 A Girl Scout knows how to obey and control her feelings.
3 A Girl Scout is energetic and prepared to help.
4 A Girl Scout is welcoming.
5 A Girl Scout is a sister to everyone.
6 A Girl Scout respects and protects nature.
7 A Girl Scout is thrifty.
8 A Girl Scout is always good-tempered.
9 A Girl Scout does nothing by halves.
10 A Girl Scout is pure in her thoughts, her words and her deeds.

Motto
Always prepared

Lark Promise
I promise to do my best
to serve God and my family, obey the Law of the Larks and do a good turn to someone every day.

Lark Law
Lark, listen to your leader.
Lark, help others without getting tired.
Lark, help cheerfully.

Lark Motto
The best we can

Age Groups

Eclaireuse	Girl Scout	11-16
Alouette	Lark	7-10
Aînée ou Branche Rouge		20+

Eclaireuses Laïques de Côte d'Ivoire

Promesse

Je promets sur mon honneur et devant Dieu de faire tous mes efforts pour: Servir mon pays, rendre service en toute occasion, obéir à la loi de l'éclaireuse.

Loi

1 l'éclaireuse n'a qu'une parole,
2 l'éclaireuse est loyale et chevaleresque,
3 l'éclaireuse se rend utile et fait chaque jour une bonne action,
4 l'éclaireuse est l'amie de tous et la soeur de toutes les Eclaireuses,
5 l'éclaireuse est courtoise et respectueuse des convictions des autres,
6 l'éclaireuse est bonne pour les animaux et les plantes,
7 l'éclaireuse sait obéir,
8 l'éclaireuse est toujours de bonne humeur,
9 l'éclaireuse est travailleuse, économe et respectueuse du bien d'autrui,
10 l'éclaireuse est propre dans son corps, ses paroles, ses pensées et ses actes.

Loi des aînées

L'éclaireuse aînée est une femme d'honneur.
L'éclaireuse aînée est une femme de caractère.
L'éclaireuse aînée a le sens de responsabilité.
L'éclaireuse aînée place l'intérêt général avant l'intérêt personnel.
L'éclaireuse aînée s'informe et lutte pour un monde plus humain.

Devise

Prête à servir

Promesse des Louvettes

Je promets de faire de mon mieux et avec l'aide de Dieu, pour obéir à la loi des Louvettes et faire chaque jour une bonne action.

Loi des Louvettes

Une louvette dit toujours vrai.
Une louvette cherche à faire plaisir aux autres.
Une louvette obéit au maître mot de la meute.

Devise des Louvettes

De notre mieux

Motto

Prepared to help

Brownie Promise

I promise to do my best to obey the Brownie Law and to do a good turn every day.

Brownie Law

A Brownie always tells the truth.
A Brownie seeks to give happiness to others.
A Brownie obeys the Pack password.

Brownie Motto

The best we can

Age Groups

Eclaireuse aînée		17-21
Eclaireuse	Girl Scout	12-16
Louvette	Lark/Brownie	6-11

Development of the Movement in the Ivory Coast

Girl Guiding and Girl Scouting in the Ivory Coast is carried out under the auspices of Scoutisme Féminin de Côte d'Ivoire, which co-ordinates the activities of the three Component Associations: the Association des Guides de Côte d'Ivoire, formed in 1955; the Association des Eclaireuses Unionistes, formed in 1958, and the Association des Eclaireuses Laïques, (formerly Les Eclaireurs et Eclaireuses de Côte d'Ivoire) formed in 1937. Girl Guides and Girl Scouts are now active throughout the entire country.

The Programme

The programme includes a wide range of activities designed to assist girls in development of character, civic responsibility and community service.

Working with the Community

Involvement in the community is central to the activities of Girl Guides and Girl Scouts in the Ivory Coast. Members regularly help out at a home for abandoned children. To help alleviate unemployment since 1981 the Associations have aimed their programme of activities at developing projects to provide employment for members.

Eclaireuse Laïque

In urban areas these have included establishing a handicraft workshop, and in rural areas setting up agricultural and livestock projects. These projects aim to make participants aware of their responsibilities to themselves and their families, by keeping them constructively occupied and encouraging them to remain in villages rather than joining the large number of unemployed people living in urban centres.

Outdoor and Environmental Activities

Camping is a regular activity for Girl Guides and Girl Scouts in the Ivory Coast and training camps and inter-company camps are held, as well as national and international camps.

Training

Each Association emphasizes the need for training, and trainers and leaders are in great demand. The Association des Guides de Côte d'Ivoire has produced a training progress chart to show the different stages to be covered by Girl Guides/Girl Scouts. Regular national and international leadership training camps are held and a book of technical notes on leadership training has been published.

Communication and Co-operation

Members are encouraged to become involved in the international aspect of Girl Guiding and Girl Scouting whenever possible by attending gatherings and training camps abroad.

Scoutisme Féminin de Côte d'Ivoire informs the public about its special events through the radio and television.
The Association has also developed a good working relationship with the churches. It works closely with other national organizations which are under the care of the Ministry for Sport and Youth, and is a member of the Fédération Ivoirienne du Scoutisme.

Jamaica

The Girl Guides Association of Jamaica

Girl Guiding/Girl Scouting introduced:	**1915**
Became Associate Member of WAGGGS:	**1963**
Became Full Member of WAGGGS:	**1966**
Membership 1992:	**2,484**
Membership as % of female population:	**0.2%**
WAGGGS Region:	**Western Hemisphere**

Promise
I promise that I will do my best:
To do my duty to God;
To serve the Queen and my country,
and help other people;
And to keep the Guide Law.

Law
1 A Guide is loyal and can be trusted.
2 A Guide is helpful.
3 A Guide is polite and considerate.
4 A Guide is friendly and a sister to all Guides.
5 A Guide is kind to animals and respects all living things.
6 A Guide is obedient.
7 A Guide has courage and is cheerful in all difficulties.
8 A Guide makes good use of her time.
9 A Guide takes care of her own possessions and those of other people.
10 A Guide is self-controlled in all she thinks, says and does.

Motto
Be Prepared

Brownie Promise
I promise that I will do my best:
To do my duty to God,
To serve the Queen and my country,
and help other people,
And to keep the Brownie Guide Law.

Brownie Law
A Brownie thinks of others before herself, and does a good turn every day.

Brownie Motto
Lend a Hand

Age Groups

Senior Branch	14-20
Guide	11-16
Brownie	7-11

Guide

Development of the Movement in Jamaica

The first Guide company in Jamaica was formed in Spanish Town, in 1915. A year later the first camp was held, and by 1919 a Ranger unit had been started. In 1967 the Girl Guides Association of Jamaica was registered as a non-profit company limited by guarantee.

In 1983 the Association launched an expansion programme with the aim of extending Guiding in rural areas. Financed by the commercial sector on the island, the programme was aided by the addition of staff both at headquarters and in the field.

In 1989 the Association embarked on a major fundraising programme for a new headquarters complex to replace one building destroyed by fire in 1982 and another severely damaged by hurricane in 1988. Thanks to generous contributions from individuals and organizations both in Jamaica and overseas, this project was completed, and the official opening was held in November 1992. A skills training project is due to start in late 1993, and the Headquarters is being used extensively for Pack Holidays and camps.

Brownie

The Programme
The programme in Jamaica places emphasis on giving service, keeping fit and enjoying the outdoors, family life education, nutrition, exploring the arts, thinking for yourself and decision making. Girls with special needs are integrated into companies and packs if possible, although the Association also has some special units.

Working with the Community
Rangers, Guides and Brownies participate in community projects. They contribute to anti-litter campaigns, organize activities for people with disabilities, and give service to the elderly and the sick in hospitals and to children in children's homes. Rangers and Guides have also been involved in child health projects including immunization campaigns, and in peer counselling projects such as the YES project (Youth for Education in Sexuality) sponsored by the IPPF.

Outdoor and Environmental Activities
The Association has its own campsite, Pax Acres. In 1989 the Association introduced a national tree-planting project and Guides designed posters as part of the Western Hemisphere environmental project. Members are also involved in a water project.

Training
One full-time Travelling Trainer maintains a regular training programme in Eastern Jamaica. Members of the training team give training on a regular basis at National Headquarters, and hold Annual Residential Training in the summer holidays.

Communication and Co-operation
As a member of the Caribbean Link, set up for the purpose of consultation and mutual aid among Guide Associations in the Commonwealth countries and islands of the Caribbean, Jamaica co-operates extensively with neighbouring countries and shares its training knowledge with other National Organizations.

The Guide and Scout Associations hold joint bi-monthly luncheons for leaders of both Associations.

Japan

Girl Scouts of Japan

Founder Member of WAGGGS
Girl Guiding/Girl Scouting introduced: 1919
Re-admitted as Associate Member of WAGGGS: 1952
Re-admitted as Full Member of WAGGGS: 1960
Membership 1992: 88,331
Membership as % of female population: 0.14%
WAGGGS Region: Asia Pacific

Yakusoku
Watakushi wa meiyo ni kakete:
Kami to kuni to ni taisuru tsutome o okonai;
Itsumo tano hitobito a tasuke;
Gaaru Sukauto no okite o mamoru yoni itashimasu.

Okite
1 Gaaru Sukauto no meiyo wa shinrai sareru koto de arimasu.
2 Gaaru Sukauto wa chujitsu de arimasu.
3 Gaaru Sukauto no tsutome wa, hito o tasuke hito ni yakudatsu koto de arimasu.
4 Gaaru Sukauto wa subeteno hitobito no tomodachi de ari, tano Gaaru Sukauto towa tagaini shimai de arimasu.
5 Gaaru Sukauto wa reigi o tadashiku shimasu.
6 Gaaru Sukauto wa ikimono o kawaigari masu.
7 Gaaru Sukauto wa kiritsu ni shitagai masu.
8 Gaaru Sukauto wa kaikatsu de arimasu.
9 Gaaru Sukauto wa kenyaku shimasu.
10 Gaaru Sukauto wa omoi nimo, kotoba nimo, okonai nimo junketsu de arimasu.

Motto
Sonaeyo tsune ni

Brownie Promise
Watakushi wa kami to kuni o aishi, mainichi hitobito o tasuke tokuni uchino otetsudai o shimasu.

Brownie Motto
Te o kase

Girl Scout

Promise
On my honour, I will try:
To do my duty to God and my country;
To help other people at all times;
To obey the Girl Scout Law.

Law
1 A Girl Scout's honour is to be trusted.
2 A Girl Scout is loyal.
3 A Girl Scout's duty is to be useful and to help others.
4 A Girl Scout is a friend to all and a sister to every other Girl Scout.
5 A Girl Scout is courteous.
6 A Girl Scout is a friend to animals.
7 A Girl Scout obeys orders.
8 A Girl Scout is cheerful.
9 A Girl Scout is thrifty.
10 A Girl Scout is clean in thought, word and deed.

Motto
Be Prepared

Brownie

Brownie Promise
I promise to do my best to love God and my country;
To help other people every day especially those at home.

Brownie Motto
Lend a Hand

Age Groups

Ranger	15-17
Senior	12-15
Junior	9-12
Brownie	6-9

Development of the Movement in Japan

Girl Scouting was first introduced to Japan by a British missionary teacher in 1919. The Movement gradually spread and in 1920 took the name Nippon Joshi Hododan (Girl Guides of Japan). Unfortunately Girl Scouting was banned by the government during World War II, but its spirit remained. The Movement was restarted in 1947 and officially recognized as Girl Scouts of Japan in 1949. During the past 70 years, Girl Scouts of Japan has been offering various programmes to foster self-reliance and the development of women in Japan.

Girl Scouts in Japan learn to care for young children.

The Programme

In order to keep pace with drastic changes occuring in the economy and within society in Japan, the Association has put together a programme to meet the needs of girls and young women. The programme is divided into three areas: self-development, relationships with people and enjoyment of the out -of-doors. Each area is adapted for the various age groups. In order to reflect what girls and young leaders really want in the programmes, the Association has organized gatherings at national and local level, as well as a Young Leaders' Symposium. Mindful that education is a life-long process, an Adult Scouts branch helps Leaders and offers help in general.

Working with the Community

To commemorate the 70th anniversary of the Movement, the Association has launched a full community development programme called 'Do Girl Scouting with community people' all over Japan. This programme includes projects for disabled and elderly people. A development education project has been launched, and the Association has sent young leaders to three Asian countries in 1989. This exercise was repeated with Rangers in 1990 in co-operation with Japanese and local NGOs dealing with community development.

Outdoor and Environmental Activities

Senior and Ranger camps are held every year at the national camp centre. Local councils have now started international camps, and the Association has been investigating camp programmes which meet the current changes in our lifestyles.

The Association has been active in recycling, cleanups of rivers and lakes and planting of trees in co-operation with other organizations. Environmental awareness activities for the general public are also stressed and, in 1991 the Asia Pacific Environmentalist badge was introduced.

Communication and Co-operation

It is important to deepen international understanding for girls in Japan, therefore more than 200 Girl Scouts participate in various overseas programmes every year, and international exchange programmes have been flourishing on troop and council level. In 1992 the Association invited young leaders from the Asia Pacific region to its Young Leaders' Symposium.

Girl Scouts of Japan produces several periodicals: *Leaders Magazine*, published eight times a year; a newsletter, issued six times a year; *Trainer News* and *Girl Scouts Magazine*, produced quarterly. The Association produces many publicity pamphlets and posters and informs the general public about its activities through major newspapers and television.

Girl Scouts of Japan is an active member of the National Council of Youth Organizations in Japan and the National Assembly for Youth Development. The Association also co-operates with UNICEF, UNESCO and other international NGOs.

Jordan

The Jordanian Association for Boy Scouts and Girl Guides

Girl Guiding/Girl Scouting introduced:	**1938**
Became Associate Member of WAGGGS:	**1963**
Became Full Member of WAGGGS:	**1978**
Membership 1992:	**8,200**
Membership as % of female population:	**0.41%**
Member:	**Arab Regional Group**

Promise
I promise on my honour to fulfil my duty towards God, my country and the Sultan.
To help people.
And to keep Guides law.

Law
1 The Guide honour is to be trusted. (Honourable)
2 The Guide is faithful to God, to her country, to her parents and to her superiors, and subordinates (Faithful)
3 The Guide is useful and helps others. (Useful)
4 The Guide is a friend to all, and a sister of other Guides. (Friendly)
5 The Guide is a girl of a good character. (Ethical)
6 The Guide is kind to animals. (Kind)
7 The Guide obeys her parents, the head of the patrol division, and the leader of the group. (Obedient)
8 The Guide faces hardship patiently smiling. (Smiling)
9 The Guide is not extravagant. (Saving)
10 The Guide should be clean, have clean mind and thoughts. (Clean)

Motto
Be Prepared

Brownie Promise
I promise to do my best:
To do my duty to God, my country, and the King;
To obey the Brownie's Law, and to carry out a good deed every day.

Brownie Motto
Do my best

Age Groups

Ranger	18-23
Girl Guide	11-18
Brownie	7-11

Development of the Movement in Jordan

Guiding in Jordan began in 1938, although it was only in 1953 that the first Guide company was officially recognized. Girls in schools were then encouraged to become Guides, and courses were held for teachers wishing to become leaders.

In 1954 the first Brownie pack was started, and by 1955 membership had increased to about 2,000. In 1962 the Girl Guide Association of Jordan was set up and Her Majesty Queen Zein Al Sharaf appointed as its first Honorary President. The following year His Majesty King Hussein issued a decree placing the Association under royal patronage.

In 1975 the first conference of Scout and Guide leaders was held at Ajlun, the national campsite, where it was decided that the Girl Guide Association of Jordan would merge with the Boy Scouts Association. In 1976 the Boy Scouts and Girl Guides of Jordan was formed.

In 1985 the second conference of Scout and Guide leaders was held in Amman.

In 1988 Princess Basma Bint Talal became the President of The Jordanian Association of Boy Scouts and Girl Guides of Jordan.

Girl Guide

Brownie

The Programme
Great emphasis is placed on the Promise and Law. In 1967 a national camp was held where girls and leaders met to discuss the adaptation of the programme to the needs of the Jordanian girl. Ten divisions were set up and each one was responsible for implementing its own programme and carrying out trainings.

Working with the Community
Guides in towns and villages throughout Jordan play their part in national service and community development projects. Guides regularly visit hospitals, orphanages, homes for the disabled and the elderly, entertaining the residents and distributing gifts. The Association organizes lectures on hygiene and sanitation and responds to appeals for blood donors.

Outdoor and Environmental Activities
Camping is a popular activity among members of the Association in Jordan and the national campsite, at Ajlun, is widely used by members.

Guides are involved in environmental initiatives including tree-planting to combat soil erosion and the tidying up of the countryside.

Training
The importance of training is stressed at all levels. Summer training camps, short-term trainings and refresher courses are held throughout the year according to the needs of the districts.

Communication and Co-operation
The Association takes part in important national and international ceremonies and also publicizes its activities through exhibitions.

Many Guides and leaders are trained in community service, life saving and fire fighting by officers from the Jordanian Civil Defence Department.

Guiding as a whole receives the full support of those concerned with youth education and community development

Training is at the heart of an excellent Girl Guide/Girl Scout programme.

Kenya

Kenya Girl Guides Association

Girl Guiding/Girl Scouting introduced:	**1920**
Became Associate Member of WAGGGS:	**1963**
Became Full Member of WAGGGS:	**1975**
Membership 1992:	**52,320**
Membership as % of female population:	**0.39%**
WAGGGS Region:	**Africa**

Promise

I promise on my honour that I will do my best:
To do my duty to God and my Country,
To help other people at all times,
and
To obey the Guide Law.

Law

1 A Guide's honour is to be trusted.
2 A Guide is loyal.
3 A Guide's duty is to be useful and to help others.
4 A Guide is a friend to all and a sister to every other Guide.
5 A Guide is polite and considerate.
6 A Guide preserves and loves nature.
7 A Guide is obedient and has respect for others.
8 A Guide is courageous and should be cheerful under all circumstances.
9 A Guide is careful and avoids wastefulness.
10 A Guide is pure in thought, word and deed.

Motto

Be Prepared

Brownie Promise

I promise to do my best:
To do my duty to God and my Country,
To help other people every day,
And to keep the Brownie Law.

Brownie Law

A Brownie is truthful, obedient and cheerful;
A Brownie thinks of others before herself.

Brownie Motto

Lend a Hand

Age Groups

Ranger Cadets	18-24
Ranger	14-18
Guide	10-13
Brownie	6-9

Guide

Development of the Movement in Kenya

Guiding began in Kenya in 1920, when the first Guide company held its meeting in the grounds of Government House in Nairobi. A Brownie pack was started in the same year in a primary school, and in 1923 a Cadet company was opened in Nairobi. In 1922 the Association was registered as a Branch Association of the Girl Guides Association (United Kingdom).

During the early years Guiding was confined to schools attended only by European girls, but in 1935 the first Indian Guide company and Brownie pack were opened in Nairobi. The following year saw the introduction of the first Guide company for African girls. Guiding spread rapidly, except during the Second World War, and in 1943 the first rally for African Guides was held. In 1949 the fairy lore imagery used in Brownie activities was replaced by bird lore, which had more relevance to the Kenyan girl.

Brownie

The Programme

Kenya's programme is based on the Promise and Law and has five distinct yet correlated sections for Brownies, Guides, Rangers, Ranger Cadets and Adult Leaders. Each section provides a wide range of challenges that encompass all modes of life relevant to the particular age group.

All four branches of the Movement have extension units for girls with special needs. Most of these units are attached to schools, although girls with disabilities are integrated into other units if possible.

Working with the Community

Members from all branches of the Association undertake Community Service. Immunization - Child Survival Project is a joint venture by Kenya Girl Guides Association/Kenya Scouts Association/Kenya Expanded Programme on Immunization (KEPI) funded by UNICEF, to educate mothers in the rural districts of South Nyanza, Siaya and Kitui. It was started in 1991 with very encouraging responses from mothers who had their children immunized against child killer diseases.

Guides have been involved in Adult Literacy for more than ten years. This includes instruction on basic formal education, reading and writing, simple accounts for vegetable vendors and establishing kitchen gardens to provide families with vegetables.

In Nairobi, Guides and Rangers adopted children from Kibera slums. Every week they take them food, and instruct them on simple hygiene. Rangers in Nyeri maintain vegetable gardens in Mahiga Children's Home for the destitute.

Kenya Girl Guides Association has over the last two decades established community projects. Mitaboni and Mathare Projects for school leavers and women from the slum villages were handed over to the communities for further development. Trees for food projects at Emali and Ainabkoi are progressing.

In 1992 Transitional Training Centre, Shanzu-Mombassa was started to train disabled girls in dressmaking, accounting and homecraft. Apart from training the girls – two years course for future employment – the project is geared to be an income generating one.

The Guides have joined other non-governmental organizations with support from the Government to survey practical measures to combat the street children problem.

The Kenya Girl Guides Association participates in the annual Freedom from Hunger Walk to raise money for projects initiated and maintained by Freedom from Hunger Council, a non-governmental organization. This NGO project's major objective is to combat hunger and malnutrition in rural areas through practical instruction.

Outdoor and Environmental Activities

National camps, which also cater for girls with special needs, are held regularly in Kenya, which has also marked important occasions, such as the Centenary of the Birth of the World Chief Guide, with international camps.

The Association has a campsite at its headquarters in Nairobi and another at Shanzu - Mombasa. An annual camp cup competition is held for the best patrol. Guides also enjoy such activities as mountaineering, canoeing and expeditions through participation in the President's Award Scheme.

Camping has become a favourite Guide activity in Kenya, with high demand for qualified personnel. The following camps are run:

- Training Camps
- Service Camps
- Test Camps
- Leisure Camps
- Celebration Camps.

A number of conservation activities are conducted, such as planting tree seedlings to cover the ground and prevent soil erosion. This is done by every unit in the Association. Also, clean up campaigns and anti-litter campaigns are conducted by every unit, and last year the Association held a cleanup Nairobi Campaign with Guides of Nairobi City, Scouts, UNEP, Nairobi City Council and many other Youth Organizations in the City and members of the community in each estate.

Training

The Kenya Girl Guides Association has six full-time trainers and several national and regional trainers. It regularly invites teachers and trainers from neighbouring countries to attend training sessions. Regional and national trainings are provided up to advanced levels.

The Guide population in Kenya has increased tremendously in the last decade. Area Training Teams were started in 1987 to train Guide Leaders in the provinces. A National Annual Trainers Workshop is held early each year for training teams to meet and plan the training programme for the year. This helps the six full-time trainers, seconded by the Teachers Service Commission, to concentrate on the provinces and Group leaders requiring their services. Full-time trainers back up the work of volunteers in addition to carrying out normal administrative duties.

The training scheme for all branches is constantly revised to keep in trend with the changes in society.

Communication and Co-operation

The Kenya Girl Guides Association has welcomed Girl Guides and Girl Scouts from around the world, and its members attend camps and seminars abroad. The Association hosted the WAGGGS' 26th World Conference in 1987 and a Sub-Regional Young Adults Seminar on Community Development in 1990.

The Association has special links with Girl Guides of Canada/Guides du Canada and the Trees for Food Project is a product of a twinning relationship between Kenya and the State of Ontario.

The Association is well known by other charitable organizations and the public for its service, and occasionally publicizes its training on television and local radio. The Association publishes a periodical, *The Kenya Guide magazine*, which is distributed outside the membership. It also produces newsletters to provide a means of communications between headquarters and rural members.

The Association takes part in the United Nations' Environmental Programme and works with other women's organizations with similar aims. It is a member of the National Youth Council of Kenya and takes part, with other youth organizations, in such projects as tree-planting, organized by the Department of Community Development, Harambee Youth Week and Universal Children's Day. The Kenya Girl Guides Association co-operates with the Kenya Scouts Association, and trainers from both associations participate in each other's training seminars, workshops and conferences.

Guides at Shanzu-Mombasa participate in the opening of the Transitional Training Centre for the disabled.

Kiribati

The Girl Guides Association of Kiribati

Girl Guiding/Girl Scouting introduced: 1926
Became Associate Member of WAGGGS: 1990
Membership 1989: 384
Membership as % of female population: 1.26%
WAGGGS Region: Asia Pacific

Guide

Brownie

Promise

I promise that I will do my best;
To do my duty to God
To serve my Country and help other people and
To keep the Guide Law.

Law

- A Guide is loyal and can be trusted
- A Guide is helpful
- A Guide is polite and considerate
- A Guide is friendly and a sister to all Guides
- A Guide is kind to animals and respects all living things
- A Guide is obedient
- A Guide has courage and is cheerful in all difficulties
- A Guide makes good use of her time
- A Guide takes care of her own possessions and those of other people
- A Guide is self controlled in all she thinks, says and does.

Development of the Movement in Kiribati

In 1926 a member of the London Missionary Society introduced Guiding to Kiribati, then known as the Gilbert Islands. The first Guide and Ranger companies were opened at the Training College for London Missionary Pastors in Rongorongo on the island of Beru. A few years later the Catholic church also started units around the country.

Guiding activities were interrupted during the Second World War when the islands were occupied by foreign troops and the missionaries who had supported the Movement left the area.

In 1957 Guiding was re-started in the three main centres of Tarawa: Bairiki, Betio and Bikenibeu, supported by both local and expatriate women. The Association grew and reached schools in the outer islands. Cadet troops were also started at the training college and in secondary schools.

The Department of Education gave the Association its full support in developing Guiding and seconded two teachers to the Association to travel to the outer islands to train leaders and assist in the recruitment of girls. The Association was also allowed to use the postal service free of charge.

In 1979 the Gilbert Islands became an independent republic under the name of Kiribati. In 1989 The Girl Guides Association of the United Kingdom signed a Deed of Transfer giving The Girl Guides Association of Kiribati self-government in all areas of work.

In 1989 the Association devised a five-year plan to extend the Movement to the outer islands, a development hampered by lack of funds.

The Programme

The programme used by the three branches, the Sunbeams, Guides and Rangers, was created by the Pacific Islands in 1969. It has been upgraded several times since its introduction to ensure its continued relevance. Its eight-points offers Guides opportunities to develop physical fitness, the mind, outdoor enjoyment, homecraft skills, service to others, human relations, creativity and character.

The Ranger Programme is currently under revision.

Working with the Community

Members are involved in several service projects such as cleaning public areas, graveyards, church compounds and market places. During the past two years ten-week sewing and cookery courses have been introduced at two centres.

Outdoor and Environmental Activities

Most Guide and Ranger units camp four to six times a year. The Association has leased a small islet which provides an excellent campsite with a permanent shelter.

Training

A sub-committee on training is responsible for drafting and implementing an annual training programme. Weekend residential trainings are held two or three times a year and the Association is now concentrating on training new leaders. Attempts have been made to hold national trainings in the past but, as these have proved expensive, training sessions are now organized on a regional basis which is more cost-effective. In addition, the Association owns a small house which it plans to turn into a training centre, offering accommodation.

Communication and Co-operation

Representatives of the Association have attended camps and trainings in neighbouring countries and in the United Kingdom and New Zealand.

Guiding in Kiribati is held in high esteem by the public, the government, the churches and other organizations in the community. Members are called upon to participate in national projects and civic ceremonies.

The Association also co-operates with the Scout Movement in Kiribati and joint activities are held periodically. The Association also benefits from involvement with the Red Cross Society, which helps to locate girls with disabilities who may benefit from Guiding, and offers training support.

Leaders learn a new activity at a training session.

Korea

Girl Scouts of Korea

Girl Guiding/Girl Scouting introduced: 1946
Became Associate Member of WAGGGS: 1957
Became Full Member of WAGGGS: 1963
Membership 1992: 184,993
Membership as % of female population: 0.85%
WAGGGS Region: Asia Pacific

Girl Scout

Brownie

Sun-Seo

Na-neun na-e myung-ei-rul geol-go-da-um-e jo-mo-geul gut-go-ji-ki-get sum-ni-da.

1 Ha-neu-nim-gwa na-ra-reul wi-ha-yo na-e him-eul da ha-get seum-ni-da.
2 Hang-sang da-run sa-ram-ul do-wa-joo-get sum-ni-da.
3 Girl Scout-ui geu-eu-rul jal ji-ki-get sum-ni-da.

Gen-eul

1	Girl Scout-nun	jin-sil ha-da
2	Girl Scout-nun	choi-sun-eul da-han-da
3	Girl Scout-nun	nam-eul dop-nun il-e ap-jang sun-da
4	Girl Scout-nun	mo-dun sa-ram-eul hyong-je-ro yeo-gin-da
5	Girl Scout-nun	ye-eu-ga ba-ru-go chin-jeol-ha-da
6	Girl Scout-nun	ja-yeon-eul sa-rang-ha-myo seng-myong-eul jeon-jung-han-da
7	Girl Scout-nun	gy-chik-eul jal ji-kin-da
8	Girl Scout-nun	o-ryo-um sok-ye-seo-do mi-so-rul ji-nin-da
9	Girl Scout-nun	shi-gan-gua mul-ja-rul a-ggin-da
10	Girl Scout-nun	mal-gua hyeng-dong-eul ba-ru-ke han-da

Motto

Junbi

Brownie Promise

Na-neun na-e myung-ei-rul geol-go-da-um-e jo-mo-geul gut-go-ji-ki-get sum-ni-da.

1 Ha-neu-nim-gwa na-ra-reul wi-ha-yo na-e him-eul da ha-get seum-ni-da.
2 Hang-sang da-run sa-ram-ul do-wa-joo-get sum-ni-da.
3 Girl Scout-ui geu-eu-rul jal ji-ki-get sum-ni-da.

Brownie Law

1 Na-nun son-oui sa-ram-eui teu-sul jal-bat-tum-ni-da.
2 Na-nun mom-gwa ma-um-ul dan-jung-hi hab-ni-da.
3 Na-nun nai-ga hal-il-eul jul-gul-gei hab-ni-da.

Brownie Motto

Do-ub-ja

Promise

On my honour, I will try:

1 To do my duty to God and my country;
2 To help other people at all times;
3 To keep the Girl Scout Law.

Law

1 A Girl Scout's honour is to be trusted.
2 A Girl Scout does her best.
3 A Girl Scout takes the initiative in helping others.
4 A Girl Scout is a sister to all.
5 A Girl Scout is courteous and kind.
7 A Girl Scout observes the rules.
8 A Girl Scout is cheerful under any difficulties.
9 A Girl Scout makes good use of her time and avoids wastefulness.
10 A Girl Scout is self-controlled in all she thinks, says and does.

Motto

Be prepared

Brownie Promise

On my honour, I will try:

1 To do my duty to God and my country;
2 To help other people at all times;
3 To keep the Girl Scout Law.

Brownie Law

1 I am obedient to the older folk.
2 I am pure in thought, body and deed.
3 I do my own work cheerfully.

Brownie Motto

Lend a Hand

Age Groups

Sung-in dai	Adult Member	over 22
Yeon-Ku dai	Cadet	19-22
Yeon-jan dai	Senior	16-18
So-nyo dai	Junior	13-15
Yu-nyo dai	Brownie	
Jindalrae		10-12
Kaenaree		7-9
Mindlrae dai	Pre-Brownie	5-6

Development of the Movement in Korea

Girl Scouting started in Korea in 1946, but its expansion was temporarily halted by war in 1950. The Movement was revived in 1955 when a WAGGGS trainer visited the country. Girl Scouting has since gained greatly in popularity as a result of leader enthusiasm and persistence.

The Programme

The programme of Girl Scouts of Korea is constantly under review so that it can continue to meet the needs of girls in a changing world. It has four main goals: developing an awareness of values; furthering human relationships; being well-adjusted in life; and contributing to the community, the nation and the world. Most of the troops are organized in schools, but efforts are being made to form troops outside the educational system and to meet the needs of a rapidly changing society.

In 1989 two new branches were established, Pre-Brownie and Adult Members. Extension troops have been operating in Korea since 1977 for girls with special needs and a Disabled Supporting Fund was also established in 1988.

Working with the Community

Girl Scouts are involved in service projects such as cleaning public places and knitting for people in need. The Association runs practical and leisure programmes at its headquarters for young people as a public service. It has also started leadership training for women outside the Movement with the aim of recruiting troop leaders and members of support groups. In 1990 Girl Scouts of Korea received the President's Award from the Korean government in recognition of its service.

In 1991 Korean Girl Scouts marked WAGGGS Peace Day by sending peace bags containing practical gifts to war-torn countries of the world.

Outdoor and Environmental Activities

A national camp has been held every five years since 1970 and invitations have been issued to Girl Guides and Girl Scouts from other National Organizations. An annual national camp is held for people with special needs and Girl Scouts participate in a variety of outdoor activities including orienteering, water activities and skiing.

Girl Scouts in Korea are involved in environmental activities such as clean-up and tree-planting campaigns.

Training

Girl Scouts of Korea have introduced leadership classes for adult leaders and hold many forums and symposiums.

Communication and Co-operation

Members of the Association take part in camps and seminars abroad and receive visitors from other National Organizations. Four provincial councils have established sisterhood relationships with foreign provincial councils.

An annual Girl Scout Week celebrates the founding of the Association and raises its public profile. Special activities are undertaken by all age groups to publicize the Movement through the campaign, 'Let's Smile, Greet Others, and Be Kind'. The Association publishes a monthly magazine called *Sonyodan*.

Girl Scouts of Korea works with the National Council of Youth Organizations and actively co-operates with the Boy Scouts Association of Korea, UNESCO and the YMCA. The Association co-operates with other non-governmental organizations and government agencies as a member of the National Council for Environmental Conservation and the Korea Publications Ethics Committee.

The Girl Scouts of Korea celebrate peace by making Peace Packs for refugees.

Kuwait

Kuwait Girl Guides Association

Girl Guiding/Girl Scouting introduced: 1957
Became Associate Member of WAGGGS: 1966
Became Full Member of WAGGGS: 1972
Membership 1992†: 7,778
Membership as % of female population: 0.86%
Member: Arab Regional Group

Girl Guide

Brownie

Promise
I promise upon my honour to do my best, in doing my duty towards God and my country;
in helping people under all circumstances;
in following the Law of the Girl Guides.

Law
1 The honour of the Girl Guides is faith and confidence.
2 The Girl Guide is sincere towards her country, her parents, her seniors and her juniors (sincere).
3 The Girl Guide should be useful to herself and to others (useful).
4 The Girl Guide is the friend to all and sister to every other Girl Guide (lovable).
5 The Girl Guide is of good character (polite).
6 The Girl Guide is kind to animals (kind).
7 The Girl Guide sincerely obeys her parents, the head of her division and the leaders of her group.
8 The Girl Guide smiles in the face of trouble and faces it with patience and steadfastness (smiling).
9 The Girl Guide is thrifty.
10 The Girl Guide is pure-hearted, decent in word and generous in deed (pure).

Brownies plant flowers to improve the community after the destruction of the Gulf War.

Brownie Promise
I promise to do my best in carrying out my duty towards God and my country, and in helping people under all circumstances, especially those at home.

Brownie Law
The Brownie must obey those who are older, must be resolute, must not yield to her whims, must take the Brownie Promise.

Age Groups

Senior Guide	17-23
Guide	12-16
Brownie	7-11

Development of the Movement in Kuwait

Guiding in Kuwait began in 1957 on a limited basis. By 1960, however, much improved programmes had helped to strengthen the Movement, and Guiding then spread to most schools throughout the country. The Association became established by 1965 and was licensed by the Ministry of Social Affairs and Labour. It became recognized in the country as an active educational force which offered young girls and women an opportunity for training in leadership.

The Programme

The programme is based on the principles of educational psychology and sociology, aiming to develop the girl's personality, making her self-sufficient, and encouraging her to contribute to the community. There are special programmes and activities for members with special needs.

Working with the Community

Service projects have included participation in public services, cleaning the city, collecting clothes and food for the poor, and helping with charity projects.

Outdoor and Environmental Activities

Camping has always been a popular activity among members of the Association in Kuwait. As well, conservation forms part of its community service programme.

Communication and Co-operation

Members have attended international Girl Guide/Girl Scout gatherings and camps whenever possible and the Association has hosted several international training camps and meetings in Kuwait.

Brownies paint a mural for the Guide Headquarters. The new headquarters, opened in 1992, replaced the original after it was destroyed in the Gulf War.

Latvia

Latvijas Skautu un Gaidu Centrāla Organizācija
(Latvian Scout and Guide Central Organization)

Founder Member of WAGGGS

Girl Guiding/Girl Scouting introduced:	**1921**
Girl Guiding/Girl Scouting banned:	**1940**
Re-admitted as Associate Member of WAGGGS:	**1993**
Membership 1992:	**900**
WAGGGS Region:	**Europe**

Guide

Gaidu solijums
Ar goda vārdu solos visiem spēkiem censties: būt uzticīga Dievam un Latvijai, palīdzēt tuvākajiem katrā brīdi, pildīt gaidu likumus.

Gaidu likumi
1 Gaida ir patiesa
2 Gaida ir uzticīga Tevijai
3 Gaida ir pašaizliedzīga un palīdzīga
4 Gaida ir draudzīga un iecietīga
5 Gaida ir pieklājīga
6 Gaida ir dzīvnieku draudzene
7 Gaida ir paklausīga
8 Gaida ir moža grūtībās
9 Gaida ir darbīga un taupīga
10 Gaida ir tīra domās, vārdos un darbos.

Motto
Arvien modra!

Little Fire Promise
Censties gribu guntina
Paklausīga, laba bút,
Lai mirdz mans tikuminš
Kā mirdz spoža uguntina

Little Fire Law
1 Guntina klausa vecāko
2 Guntina valda sevi

Little Fire Motto
Cenīšos!

Promise
On my honour, I promise to do my duty to God and Latvia;
to help my neighbour at all times,
and to obey the Guide Laws.

Law
1 A Guide is trustworthy
2 A Guide is loyal to fatherland
3 A Guide is self-denying and helpful
4 A Guide is friendly and tolerant
5 A Guide is courteous
6 A Guide is a friend to animals
7 A Guide is obedient
8 A Guide is alert in hardships
9 A Guide is active and thrifty
10 A Guide is clean in thought, words and deeds.

Motto
Be prepared

Little Fire Promise
I promise to do my best, to be obedient and to be in my virtue as bright fire.

Little Fire Law
1 Little Fire gives in to the wishes of her elders.
2 Little Fire is self-possessed.

Little Fire Motto
Do my best.

Age Groups

Lielgaida	Ranger	16 upwards
Gaida	Guide	11-16
Guntina	Little Fire	7-11

Development of the Movement in Latvia

Guiding was started in Latvia in 1921 under the umbrella of the Latvian Youth Organizations. In early 1922 the Latvijas Gaidu Centrālā Organizācija (The Girl Guides Central Organization of Latvia) was set up and Girl Guiding was permitted to operate as an independent organization. Latvia was a Founder Member of WAGGGS in 1928, enjoyed a visit from Olave Baden-Powell, World Chief Guide in 1933 and had a very active Guiding life until the Movement was banned in 1940.

Fifty years later, in 1990, Latvian Guiding and Scouting was officially re-started as Latvijas Skautu un Gaidu Centrālā Organizācija (LSGCO, The Latvian Scout and Guide Central Organization). WAGGGS appointed the Swedish Guide and Scout Council, which already had contacts with Latvia as the Western European 'Link' country for the organization, promoting a close working relationship between the two countries.

Guiding has now been successfully re-introduced to many areas of the country including some small villages.

The Programme

The aim of the programme is to assist young people in achieving their full physical, intellectual and spiritual potential and to help them become responsible members of their local, national and international communities. It is based on 'Duty to God', 'Duty to others', and 'Duty to oneself'. The majority of programmes are carried out separately, especially the weekly meetings where the girls do not meet together with the boys. Programme alternatives make the activities suitable for girls from the city or small rural villages.

Working with the Community

In keeping with the Promise, Latvian Guides help other people and serve their communities. They help elderly people, participate in tree-planting, and work on keep the environment clean campaigns. They help to keep in order historical and cultural monuments in Latvia.

Outdoor and Environmental Activities

Outdoor activities are popular in Latvian Guiding. Latvian Guides spend their time in weekend and week summer camps, and they have weekend hiking in other seasons. Unit camps and district camps are held every summer, and the first large international camp will be held in 1994.

Training

Training is carried out jointly with the Scouts. There are three types of training: for Patrol leaders, new leaders and experienced leaders. Much training is conducted by Swedish trainers with the assistance of a few former leaders.

Communication and Co-operation

Girl Guiding is well accepted by the public and by high officials in the Ministry of Education. The government is keen to support Guiding but unfortunately the present economic situation in the country does not permit this. Nevertheless groups are given free of charge the use of schools and rooms belonging to the local government. Contacts with churches are excellent.

A National Youth Council is to be set up and the Guides and Scouts will be important members, as they are considered to be the best organized Movement in the country.

The LSGCO publishes a magazine called *Ugunskurs* which includes news, ideas and reports and is geared towards the leader as well as young members.

Brownies and Guides play a game at camp in Latvia.

Lebanon

Organisation Nationale des Guides et des Eclaireuses du Liban

Component Associations:
Association des Guides du Liban
Association des Eclaireuses du Liban

Girl Guiding/Girl Scouting introduced:	**1939**
Became Associate Member of WAGGGS:	**1955**
Became Full Member of WAGGGS:	**1963**
Membership 1992:	**3,664**
Membership as % of female population:	**0.27%**
Member:	**Arab Regional Group**

Guide

Association des Guides du Liban

Promesse

Avec vous toutes, confiante en Dieu qui m'aime, je promets de faire tout mon possible: pour rendre les autres heureux, pour être utile à mon pays, et vivre selon la loi de toutes les guides du monde.

Loi

1 On peut compter sur une guide.
2 La guide est loyale.
3 Le devoir d'une guide est d'être utile et de servir les autres.
4 La guide est l'amie de tous.
5 La guide est généreuse.
6 La guide aime les plantes et les animaux.
7 La guide sait obéir, elle a l'esprit d'équipe.
8 La guide est maîtresse de soi; elle réagit dans les difficultés.
9 La guide a le respect des autres et de leurs biens.
10 La guide est pure et joyeuse.

Devise

Etre prête

Brownie

Promesse des Jeannettes

Je promets de faire de mon mieux pour être fidèle à Dieu, au Liban, à la loi de la Ronde, à mes parents, et pour faire chaque jour un plaisir à quelqu'un.

Loi des Jeannettes

Une jeannette est toujours propre.
Une jeannette est toujours active.
Une jeannette est toujours gaie.
Une jeannette dit toujours vrai.
Une jeannette pense d'abord aux autres.

Devise des Jeannettes

De notre mieux

Promise

With you all, trusting in God who loves me, I promise to do my best: to make other happy, to be useful to my country and to live according to the Law of all Guides of the world.

Law

A Guide is reliable.
A guide is loyal.
A Guide's duty is to be useful and help others.
A Guide is a friend to all.
A Guide is generous.
A Guide loves plants and animals.
A Guide knows how to obey, she has team spirit.
A Guide is self-controlled; she does not give in to difficulties.
A Guide has respect for others and their belongings.
A Guide is pure and cheerful.

Motto
Be Prepared

Brownie Promise
I promise to do my best to be faithful to god, Lebanon, the Pack Law and my parents, and to do a good turn to someone every day.

Brownie Law
A Brownie is always clean.
A Brownie is always active.
A Brownie is always cheerful.
A Brownie always tells the truth.
A Brownie thinks first of others.

Brownie Motto
The best we can

Age Groups

Jeunes en marche	Youth on the Move	17 - 21
Caravelle Guide	Caravelle	15 - 17
Guide Farandole	Farandole Guide	12 - 15
Jeannette	Brownie	7 - 12

Association des Eclaireuses du Liban

Promesse
Avec vous toutes, confiante en Dieu qui m'aime, je promets de faire tout mon possible: pour rendre les autres heureux, pour être utile à mon pays, et vivre selon la loi de toutes les éclaireuses du monde.

Loi
L'éclaireuse envers elle-même
- L'éclaireuse est courtoise et généreuse.
- L'éclaireuse obéit sans réplique et ne fait rien à moitié.
- L'éclaireuse est maîtresse d'elle-même, elle sourit et chante dans ses difficultés.
- L'éclaireuse est économe et prend soin du bien d'autrui.
- L'éclaireuse est pure dans ses pensées, ses actes et ses paroles.

L'éclaireuse envers la société
- L'éclaireuse met son honneur à mériter confiance.
- L'éclaireuse est faite pour servir et aider son prochain.
- L'éclaireuse est amie de tous et soeur de toute éclaireuse.

L'éclaireuse envers son pays
- L'éclaireuse est fidèle à son pays.
- L'éclaireuse participe au développement du Liban.

L'éclaireuse et la nature
- L'éclaireuse voit la beauté de la nature, elle aime les plantes et les animaux.

Motto
Etre prête

Little Wing Promise
Je promets de faire de mon mieux pour obéir à Dieu, aimer mon pays, prêter la main chaque jour.

Little Wing Law
La petite aile va à la découverte de son monde et propage l'amour et la gaieté.

Little Wing Motto
Fait de son mieux

Promise
With you all, trusting in God who loves me, I promise to do everything possible: to make others happy, be useful to my country and live according to the Law of all the Girl Scouts of the world.

Law
The Girl Scout towards herself
- A Girl Scout is courteous and generous.
- A Girl Scout obeys without question and does nothing by halves.
- A Girl Scout is self-controlled, she smiles and sings under difficulties.
- A Girl Scout is thrifty and takes care of other people's belongings.
- A Girl Scout is pure in her thoughts, her deeds and her words.

The Girl Scout towards society
- A Girl Scout's honour is to be trusted.
- A Girl Scout's purpose is to be of service and help others.
- A Girl Scout is a friend to all and a sister to every Girl Scout.

The Girl Scout towards her country
- A Girl Scout is loyal to her country.
- A Girl Scout participates in the development of Lebanon.

The Girl Scout and nature
- A Girl Scout sees the beauty of nature, she loves plants and animals.

Motto
Be Prepared

Girl Scout

Little Wing

Little Wing Promise
I promise to do my best to obey God, love my country and to lend a hand every day.

Little Wing Law
The Little Wing sets out to discover her world and spreads love and cheerfulness.

Little Wing Motto
Does her best

Age Groups

Eclaireuse aînée	Ranger	16-20
Eclaireuse	Girl Scout	13-16
Petite aile (Zahrat)	Little Wing	7-12

Development of the Movement in Lebanon

Girl Guiding/Girl Scouting started in Lebanon in 1939 with the establishment of the Association des Guides du Liban. In 1958 the Association des Eclaireuses du Liban was established and in 1961 the two main Associations combined as one National Organization, the Organisation Nationale des Guides et des Eclaireuses du Liban, which was recognized by the government.

The Programme
The Organisation Nationale des Guides et des Eclaireuses du Liban has suffered much in the political troubles and war, from 1975 to 1990. It has been impossible to plan regular activities. But in spite of the difficulties the Organisation continued to work and could raise enough money to replace its destroyed headquarters by buying new premises in Antelias in the neighbourhood of Beirut.

Improvement of the situation in the country gave a new start to the development of Girl Guiding/Girl Scouting, and membership increased all over Lebanon.

The Organisation Nationale des Guides et des Eclaireuses du Liban has contacts with unrecognized Lebanese Guide Associations, with a view to making a large federation to include them all.

Working with the Community
Service projects include carrying out relief work with refugees, disabled people and underprivileged children. New projects are being undertaken to take care of old people.

A special input on environment was the main motto for 1993. Round tables and conferences were organized to sensitize people on pollution problems in the country. Some Girl Guide/Girl Scout troops undertook to repair public gardens in Beirut and its neighbourhood while others were planting trees in rural areas.

Communication and Co-operation
The Organisation Nationale des Guides et des Eclaireuses du Liban participates in international events whenever possible, and has been represented in gatherings and trainings in other countries. Lebanese trainers take an active part in the Arab Regional Group, helping National Organizations in their preparation for membership in WAGGGS and serving on planning committees.

The two Associations organize shared activities with some Scout Associations with whom it has a good working relationship, as well as undertaking development projects with other youth and welfare organizations.

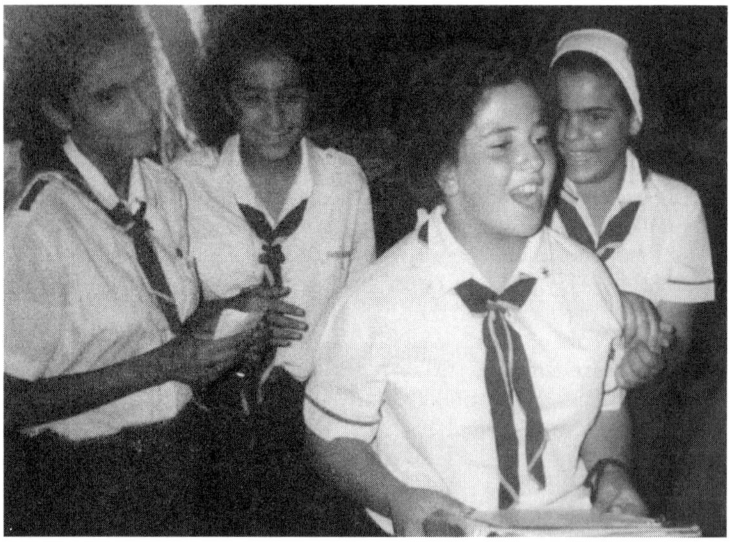

Singing around a campfire is universally known by all Girl Guides and Girl Scouts, including these Guides in Lebanon.

Lesotho

Lesotho Girl Guides Association

Girl Guiding/Girl Scouting introduced: 1925
Became Associate Member of WAGGGS: 1978
Became Full Member of WAGGGS: 1990
Membership 1992†: 2,425
Membership as % of female population: 0.26%
WAGGGS Region: Africa

Promise

I promise on my honour to do my best
To do my duty to God and my country
To help other people at all times
And to obey the Guide Law.

Law

1 A Guide is to be trusted.
2 A Guide is loyal.
3 A Guide is helpful.
4 A Guide is friendly and is a sister to all Guides.
5 A Guide considers other people.
6 A Guide is kind to animals and respects all living things.
7 A Guide is obedient.
8 A Guide is brave and cheerful in all difficulties.
9 A Guide is thrifty.
10 A Guide controls herself in all she thinks, say and does.

Brownie Promise

I promise to do my best
To do my duty to God and my country
To help other people every day
Especially those at home.

Brownie Law

A Sunbeam thinks of others before herself.

Age Groups

Cadet	17-21
Ranger	13-17
Guide	8-12
Brownie	6-8

Development of the Movement in Lesotho

Guiding in the Kingdom of Lesotho was introduced in 1925 by the Chief Commissioner of the Girl Guides Association of South Africa. Since the membership was small, activities were carried out under its auspices until 1961 when South Africa left the Commonwealth of Nations. The Association in Basutoland (now known as Lesotho) was then administered as a Branch Association of the Girl Guides Association (United Kingdom).

Following Lesotho's independence in 1966, a Chief Commissioner and a Deputy Chief Commissioner were appointed, and Guiding continued to spread to many areas of the country. The Association welcomed trainers from the Girl Guides Association (United Kingdom) on several occasions. In 1975 the Association was reorganized and in 1976 a WAGGGS trainer/adviser visited to assist Lesotho in its development.

In 1977 the Girl Guides Association (United Kingdom) approved a deed of transfer, making the Lesotho Girl Guides Association self-governing in all areas of work.

The Programme

The programme is designed to help girls become useful and loyal citizens of their country. Since Lesotho is an agricultural country, training in agricultural skills is an important part of the overall programme.

Working with the Community

Service also plays an important part in the Lesotho Girl Guides Association. Guides and Rangers assist the community in many ways: in Maseru they look after the elderly at a home and help to raise funds. They organize activities for pupils with special needs, clean children's wards, and help to teach them to read and write.
In the Butha-Buthe District, in the north,

Guide

Brownie

members have built a stone bridge to replace an old bridge swept away by floods. Another project has involved the construction of a well to provide clean water suitable for domestic use and human consumption. The Association also runs a successful Fish Pond project in Morifi.

Outdoor and Environmental Activities

District rallies are held annually and are attended by members of all age groups. The Association is committed to tree-planting projects and Guides celebrate Tree-Planting Day on March 21 each year, when they plant thousands of trees throughout the country. The trees lining one of the major highways have been planted by the Guides. Many groups also clean streets and public areas.

Training

The training team, which is responsible for both training and the overall programme, has ten members. A few trainings are held nationally such as training for trainers and young leaders, but most training sessions are organized on a regional basis due to transport difficulties.

Communication and Co-operation

The Association participates in Africa Region activities and, if finances permit, tries to send representatives to other international events as well.

The fish pond project in Morifi is a product of a twinning relationship with Guides in Alberta, Canada. The Association also carries out projects with the Lesotho Scouts Association including building a school with two classrooms and an office.

In addition, the Lesotho Girl Guides Association works with the Red Cross Society, the Work Camps Association, and also on the Prince Mohato Award Scheme, an award which encourages personal development and achievement.

The Guides are well received by members of the community, particularly due to their involvement in community life through service and development projects.

Liberia

The Liberian Girl Guides Association

Founder Member of WAGGGS	
Girl Guiding/Girl Scouting introduced:	**1920**
Contact with WAGGGS lost:	**1930**
Re-admitted as Associate Member of WAGGGS:	**1966**
Became Full Member of WAGGGS:	**1975**
Membership 1992:	**345**
Membership as % of female population:	**0.02%**
WAGGGS Region:	**Africa**

Promise
I promise on my honour that I will do my best:
To do my duty to God;
To serve my country and help other people;
And to keep the Guide Law.

Law
1 A Guide is loyal and can be trusted.
2 A Guide is helpful.
3 A Guide is polite and considerate.
4 A Guide is friendly to all and a sister to all Guides.
5 A Guide is kind to animals and respects all living things.
6 A Guide is obedient.
7 A Guide has courage and is cheerful in all difficulties.
8 A Guide makes good use of her time and talent.
9 A Guide takes care of her own possessions and those of other people.
10 A Guide controls herself and is clean in all she thinks, says and does.

Motto
Be Prepared

Brownie Guide Promise
I promise that I will do my best:
To do my duty to God;
To serve my country and help other people;
And to keep the Brownie Guide Law.

Brownie Guide Law
1 A Brownie Guide thinks of others before herself.
2 A Brownie Guide does a Good Turn every day.

Brownie Guide Motto
Be Helpful

Age Groups
Ranger	16-21
Guide	12-16
Brownie Guide	7-11

Development of the Movement in Liberia

Guiding in Liberia started in 1920, and in 1928 the Association became a Founder Member of WAGGGS. By 1930, however, all contact between WAGGGS and the Liberian National Organization had been lost and its membership was cancelled in 1931. From 1953 to 1955 efforts were made to revive Guiding and in 1955 a representative of WAGGGS visited Liberia and helped to bring together isolated groups of Guides to form the nucleus of a National Organization. Over the next 10 years Guiding spread to all areas of the country with the help of WAGGGS trainers and advisers.

During recent months Liberia has been partitioned after a period of civil war. Guiding activities were suspended for a period, but are being re-established.

Guide

Brownie Guide

The Programme
Girl Guiding in Liberia has been mainly confined to schools with open companies in a few areas. The programme is based on eight-points: keeping fit, becoming a homemaker, giving service, keeping the Guide Law, getting to know people, enjoying the outdoors, thinking for oneself and exploring the arts.

Working with the Community
Emphasis in the past has been placed on community service including visits to daycare centres, children's wards in hospitals, and schools for the blind and deaf, to entertain the children. From 1987-88 the Association added to that by undertaking a health and sanitation project involving the construction of a well and two toilets in a village of 100 huts. The village previously had had no such facilities.

Outdoor and Environmental Activities
Camping has played an important role in the Association by helping to retain membership. Camps have focused on such subjects as health, hygiene, childcare, cooking, agriculture and gardening, often with instruction by experts from the community. Other camp activities have included handicrafts, singing, hair plaiting and traditional dancing.

With respect to guarding the environment, Guides have been involved in clean-up campaigns and planting flowers. With the aid of an agriculturist, members also planted 125 coconut trees on the Association's campsite.

Communication and Co-operation
In the past the Association has been represented at international gatherings and seminars. Traditionally the National Organization has maintained good contact with the public through the press, radio and television and has co-operated with such non-governmental organizations as the YWCA, YMCA, the Red Cross, the Family Planning Association of Liberia, and the Boy Scouts of Liberia.

Girls at a day camp make their Promise.

Libya

Public Scout and Girl Guide Movement of Libya

Girl Guiding/Girl Scouting introduced: 1958
Became Associate Member of WAGGGS: 1966
Became Full Member of WAGGGS: 1981
Membership 1992†: 1,884
Membership as % of female population: 0.09%
Member: Arab Regional Group

Promise

I promise on my honour:

1 To endeavour to do my duty towards God, my Country and the People
2 To help people and other creatures at all times.
3 To obey the Scout Law.

Law

1 The honour of a Girl Guide is to be trusted and relied on.
2 A Girl Guide is faithful to the guardian thereof, her Country, and to each of the superiors and subordinates thereof.
3 A Girl Guide is useful and helpful to others.
4 A Girl Guide is a friend to all and is a sister to every other scout.
5 A Girl Guide is well mannered.
6 A Girl Guide is kind to animals.
7 A Girl Guide is obedient to her parents and superiors without hesitation in matters of righteousness.
8 A Girl Guide smiles at and disdains hardships.
9 A Girl Guide is frugal.
10 A Girl Guide is pure in thought, word and deed.

Motto

Be Prepared

Development of the Movement in Libya

Guiding began in Libya in 1958 when a Brownie pack was opened at a girls' primary school in Tripoli. The leader was Libyan, assisted by an experienced leader from Lebanon and an intensive leader training programme was organized for a selected group of Libyan girls. On completion of the course some of them established a Senior Guide unit, with the assistance of the Scout Association, and, soon afterwards, a Guide company was opened.

Initially Guiding did not extend beyond a small number of women teachers and students, but gradually more and more people joined the Movement. Additional units were formed in Tripoli and a commissioner was chosen for each section. In 1959 Guiding spread to Benghazi, and soon afterwards to other regions of the country.

Girl Guide

The Programme

The programme for each age group is based on religious, national, international and social aspects. Activities are varied according to the age section and include skills, community service, outdoor life, songs and music, crafts and visits to places of interest.

Working with the Community

The Association endeavours to foster a spirit of service and carries out a wide range of activities including literacy work and helping people with special needs. Members also help families in need and take part in national traffic weeks.

Brownie

Outdoor and Environmental Activities

There is great emphasis on camping, and the Association owns several well-equipped campsites.

Training
The Association has made great efforts to improve leadership training. A training committee prepares an annual training schedule which includes training sessions for leaders from all over the country and training camps for Guides and Senior Guides.

Communication and Co-operation
In 1966 the Association, then the Girl Guides of Libya, hosted the first Arab Girl Guides jamboree and the Arab Girl Guides Conference in Tripoli. An important aspect of the programme is the promotion of international understanding and participation in Arab and other international Girl Guiding/Girl Scouting activities.

The Association is well-known and has a high standing in the community. The principles of the Movement have won support and respect throughout the country. Leaders have very good relations with women in other fields of work. Guide and Scout programmes are broadcast several times a year on the radio or television.

A half-yearly periodical is published containing news and information of interest to all age groups.

Brownies create a Trefoil out of shells near the Guide headquarters in Joddaiem.

Liechtenstein

Pfadfinder und Pfadfinderinnen Liechtensteins
(Boy Scouts and Girl Guides of Liechtenstein)

Girl Guiding/Girl Scouting introduced:	**1932**
Became Associate Member of WAGGGS:	**1948**
Became Full Member of WAGGGS:	**1952**
Membership 1992:	**443**
Membership as % of female population:	**3%**
WAGGGS Region:	**Europe**

Versprechen
Ich verspreche, dass ich mit der Hilfe Gottes versuchen will, mein Bestes für meine Mitmenschen und unser Land zu tun, den Fürsten zu achten und nach dem Pfadfinder/Innen-Gesetz zu leben.

Gesetz
Als Pfadfinder/Pfadfinderin
suche ich meinen Weg zu Gott bin ich aufrichtig
helfe ich, wo ich kann
überwinde ich Schwierigkeiten
entscheide ich und setze mich ein
bin ich zuverlässig
schütze ich Natur und Umwelt
bereite ich Freude
verstehe und achte ich andere
bin ich ein guter Freund/eine gute Freundin.

In Uebereinstimmung mit diesem Gesetz ergänze ich für mich und meine Gruppe:

Motto
Allzeit bereit

Bienle Versprechen
Ich will mir Mühe geben, Gott und meine Familie gern zu haben, unser Gesetz zu befolgen und für alle ein guter Kamerad/eine gute Kameradin zu sein.

Bienle Gesetz
Ein Wold/Bienle hält seine Augen offen und hilft allen.
Ich bin ein Wolf/Bienle - Du bist ein Wolf/Bienle; auf uns ist Verlass.

Bienle Gesetz
Allzeit bereit

Promise
I promise that with God's help I will try and do my best for my fellow beings and our country, to respect the Prince and live according to the Scouts/Guides Law.

Law
As a Scout/Girl Guide
I seek my way to God
I am upright
help where I can
overcome difficulties
make decisions and take action
I am reliable
protect nature and the world around us
give pleasure
understand and respect others
I am a good friend

In conformity with this Law I amend as follows, for myself and my group:

Motto
Be Prepared

Brownies' Promise
To the best of my ability I will love God and my family, abide by our Law and be a good comrade to everyone.

Brownies' Law
A Cub Scout/Brownie is observant and helps everyone.
I am a Cub Scout/Brownie - you are a Cub Scout/Brownie; we are reliable.

Age Groups

Ranger	Ranger	18+
Pioniere	Pioneers	15-18
Pfadfinderin	Girl Guide	11-15
Bienle	Brownie	7-11

Girl Guide

Brownie

A Guide in uniform.

Development of the Movement in Liechtenstein

Scouting in Liechtenstein began in Schaan in 1931 and Guiding started in Vaduz in 1932. A first-aid group for Scouts and Guides was founded in 1973.

The Scouts and Guides have had their own shop since 1976 and in 1979 they started publishing a bi-monthly magazine for leaders, which is called *Knoten*.

Co-operation between the Scout and the Guide Associations has increased since 1981, when joint activities were organized to celebrate the 50th Anniversary of the Scout Movement in Liechtenstein. In 1989, the two Associations merged and its official name now is "Pfadfinder und Pfadfinderinnen Liechtensteins". HSH Prince Nikolaus of Liechtenstein and his sister, HSH Princess Nora are Honorary Members of the Movement.

Among the main events in the scouting year are the annual summer camps, winter camps and various activities for all branches at national level.

The Programme

Each division draws up its own programme. Leaders organize various activities for all branches at local and national level and these are adapted to meet the requirements of the individual and the community.

Working with the Community

Members of the Association are involved in many community service projects.

During Lent, Guides organize a Soup Day in most villages, together with the Liechtenstein Lent Charity.

In 1986 the Liechtenstein Scouts and Guides started a community development project in co-operation with the Egyptian Scout Federation. The aim of this 'Palm Tree Project' in El Arish/Egypt is to establish a palm tree factory (which can process all parts of a palm tree, including the dates) and therefore provide jobs for the inhabitants of the region. During this project, exchanges of Egyptian and Liechtenstein Boy Scouts and Girl Guides also took place.

Outdoor and Environmental Activities

Summer, autumn and winter camps are enjoyed by all members of the Association. Various outdoor activities also are organized during the annual programmes of all branches.

Training

Attendance at international gatherings is encouraged and the number of members participating in international camps, seminars and training sessions is increasing. During the last years members participated in Juliette Low Seminars, Eurofolk, World Jamborees, Rover Moots, several international training sessions, seminars and camps.

Communication and Co-operation

The Association informs its members and the general public about its activities through the national press as well as through its bi-monthly magazine *Knoten*.

The Association supports activities of the Liechtenstein Lent Charity and the Liechtenstein Missionary Society.

Luxembourg

Bureau de Liaison des Associations Guides du Luxembourg

Component Associations:
Association des Girl Guides Luxembourgeoises (AGGL)
Letzeburger Guiden (LG)

Founder Member of WAGGGS

Girl Guiding/Girl Scouting introduced	**1915**
Membership 1992:	**2,739**
Membership as % of female population:	**1.4%**
WAGGGS Region:	**Europe**

Association des Girl Guides Luxembourgeoises

Promesse

Ech verspriechen op méng Eéier, mei Bescht ze mân fir:
Trei zu Gott an zum Land ze stoen;
Allen de'an der Noet sin ze höllefen;
d'Guidegesetz ze befolejen.

Code

1 Eng Guide e Wuert.
2 Eng Guide stét trei ze hirer Pflicht.
3 Eng Guide ass ömmer berét ânere beizestoen.
4 All Guiden sin Schwestern.
5 Eng Guide ass offen an heiferlech geint jidderén.
6 Eng Guide ass gudd geint De'eren.
7 Eng Guide huet Disziplin.
8 Eng Guide ass ömmer frou.
9 Eng Guide huet energie, fleisseg a spursam.
10 Eng Guide ass propper u Kirper a Seil; si sét a möcht neischt Schlechtes.

Motto

Solidarité

Brownie Promise

Ech verspriechen mei Bescht ze man fir:
Wichtelchesgesetz ze befollegen;
All Dag eppes Gutts ze dun.

Brownie Law

Eng Wichtelchen ass fröndlech a frou.
Eng Wichtelchen ass urdentlech a propper.
Eng Wichtelchen sét t'Worecht a follegt gudd.

Motto

Solidarité

Promise

I promise on my honour to do my best:
To serve God and my Country;
To help all those in need;
To obey the Guide Law.

Law

1 A Guide's word is sacred.
2 A Guide is faithful to her duty.
3 A Guide is always ready to help her neighbours.
4 All Guides are sisters.
5 A Guide is frank and courteous.
6 A Guide is good to animals.
7 A Guide is disciplined.
8 A Guide is always cheerful.
9 A Guide is energetic, hard working and thrifty.
10 A Guide is clean in body and soul; she says and does nothing bad.

Motto

Solidarity

Brownie Promise

To obey the Law of the Brownies and to do a good thing every day.

Guide

Brownie

Brownie Law
A Brownie is friendly and happy at heart.
A Brownie is organized and cares for cleanliness.
A Brownie speaks the truth and listens to advice.

Brownie Motto
Solidarity

Age Groups

Ranger	Ranger	16-23
Caravelle	Guide (Senior)	14-16
Aventure	Guide (Junior)	11-14
Wichtelchen	Brownie	7-11

Letzeburger Guiden

Guide

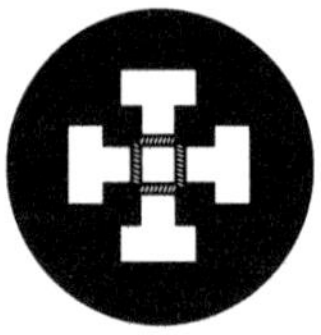
Brownie

D'Verspriéchen
Ech verspriéchen op meng E'er a mat der Höllef vum Härgott mei Bescht ze dun, fir dem Härgott, der Kirch an der Hémecht ze dengen, alle Leit ze hëllefen wé a wo kann an d'Guide-Gesetz ze befollechen.

D'Gesetz
1 Eng Guide, e Wuert.
2 Eng Guide ass trei dem Härgott, der Kirch an der Hémecht, och all dénen dé iwert an önnert hir stin.
3 Eng Guide mécht sech netzlech an hölleft jidverengem.
4 Eng Guide ass gudd gént all Mönsch an d'Schwester vun all âner Guide.
5 Eng Guide ass héflech.
6 Eng Guide geseit an der Natur d'Wierk vum Härgott a schont d'Planzen an d'Déeren.
7 Eng Guide follecht op d'Wuert a mecht neischt hallef.
8 Eng Guide lacht a sengt och wann et schwéer fällt.
9 Eng Guide ass spuersam.
10 Eng Guide ass reng a Gedanken, Wuert a Wierk.

Motto
Ëmmer bereet

Promise
I promise on my honour and with the help of God to do my best to serve God, the Church and my Country, to help everybody at all times and to follow the Guide Law.

Law
1 A Guide speaks the truth.
2 A Guide is faithful to God, the Church and her Country and to all people, whether above her or below her.
3 A Guide is kind to other people and a sister to all other Guides.
4 A Guide is polite.
5 A Guide serves and helps everybody.
6 A Guide sees in nature the work of God and respects plants and animals.
7 A Guide is obedient and does nothing by halves.
8 A Guide laughs and sings under all difficulties.
9 A Guide is thrifty.
10 A Guide is pure in thought, word and deed.

Motto
Be Prepared

Brownie Promise
Ech verspriéche mäi Bescht zu dun, fir dem Härgott, méngen Elteren an dem Wichtelchersgesetz ze follechen, an all Dag engem eng Freed ze man.

Brownie Law
1 De Wichtelchen denkt fir d'éischt un di aner.
2 Dem Wichtelchen entgeet näischt.
3 De Wichtelchen as ëmmer propper.
4 De Wichtelchen seet ëmmer d'Wouerécht.
5 De Wichtelchen as ëmmer frou.

Brownie Motto
Mir dun äist Bescht

Brownie Promise
I promise to do my best to be obedient to God, to my parents and to the Brownie Law and to give happiness to somebody every day.

Brownie Motto
We do our best

Age Groups

Guide aînée	Ranger	16+
Caravelle	Caravelle Guide	14-16
Aventure	Adventure Guide	11-14
Wichtelchen	Brownie	8-11

Development of the Movement in Luxembourg

Guiding started in Luxembourg in 1915 and the following year the many different troops in the country were united by the formation of an Association.

The Association des Girl Guides Luxembourgeoises was constituted in 1921 and The Letzeburger Guiden (Catholic Luxembourg Girl Guides) was founded in 1938 by the Director of the Action Catholique Féminine Luxembourgeoise.

In 1958 the two Associations were linked by the formation of The Bureau de Liaison des Associations Guides du Luxembourg. In 1960 the WAGGGS World Conference recognized the Bureau de Liaison des Associations Guides du Luxembourg as the National Organization of Luxembourg.

In 1990 HRH the Grand-Duchess Joséphine-Charlotte of Luxembourg was officially introduced as Chief Guide of the Bureau de Liaison.

Association des Girl Guides Luxembourgeoises

The Programme

In 1990 the Association started on elaborating new programmes for the Brownie, Guide and Ranger sections. The Brownie programme has been finished and was introduced at the beginning of 1993. The Guide programme will follow soon. The Guiders' training programme will also be revised.

Working with the Community

Since 1987, through the Mutual Aid programme, the Association helped the Girl Guides Association of Gambia to build their national headquarters including a vocational centre. This centre is open for admission to girls who wish to be trained for self-reliance. To the satisfaction of both partners the vocational centre is a great success. Several sets of students have completed this training and some of them are engaged in production work. With the Association's help a Congress Hall will now be added.

HRH the Grand-Duchess Joséphine-Charlotte, Chief Guide of Luxembourg, opens the Association's "biotope" and nature path at the training centre in Colpach.

Outdoor and Environmental Activities

The Association has three camping centres: an international centre in the country's capital city Luxembourg; a chalet in Esch-sur-Alzette near the French border; and a training centre at Colpach near the Belgian border. This centre is not in use for the moment as it was damaged by arson at the beginning of May 1993. Fundraising has started to help rebuild it.

The Association's concern for the environment was demonstrated by the implementation of a nature path for the 75th anniversary of the Association in 1990. This nature path starts from the training centre in Colpach. Trees and hedges have been planted for the last 3 years, the existing path has been embellished and wooden signs carved with the names of trees and hedges have been installed. In the middle of the nature path a marshy meadow has been hired and a "biotope" installed. On 23 May 1993 the Association officially inaugurated its biotope and nature walk.

Communication and Co-operation

The Association has always encouraged the furthering of international contacts. So whenever possible the Guides participate in international events and camps. On Thinking Day Guides always try to promote Thinking Day contributions and they are proud to have very good results.

The Association maintains good relations with the community, other youth movements, and many women's organizations. It is a member of the General Conference of the Youth of Luxembourg. The Association publishes a quarterly periodical: *Solidarité*.

Letzeburger Guiden

The Programme

The division of membership into four age groups has played a significant part in improving the standard of activities within the Association. The Adventure Guides celebrate Thinking Day each year, the Caravelle Guides celebrate the "Cara-Pio-Day", together with the Pioneer Scouts. The two age groups are equally responsible for the organization of a Guide fair on Ascension Day. The Route branch, encompassing Rangers and Rovers, has a diverse programme. Joint meetings are organized, and joint trainings of Guide and Scout leaders are encouraged.

Girls with special needs are active members of the Association.

Outdoor and Environmental Activities

The Association holds an annual rally for the Wichtelcher age group together with the Wëllefcher from the Lëtzebuerger Scouten, attended by members from all over the country. Wichtelcher camps are also held annually, lasting for several days.

Training

Training weekends and teaching sessions are organized for all leaders and each leader spends some time in a troop other than her own. Many leaders' days are held throughout the year.

Communication and Co-operation

The Letzeburger Guiden is eager to establish contacts with as many Girl Guides/Girl Scouts from other countries as possible. Guides participate in training camps and international gatherings and several troops have attended international camps and have welcomed foreign Girl Guide/Girl Scout troops visiting Luxembourg.

The Association maintains good relations with the community. It publishes a periodical, *En Route*, for Rangers and Rovers, a periodical *CCContact* for leaders from the Letzeburger Guiden and the Letzeburger Scouten, a periodical *C.P. News* for Caravelles and Pioneers, a periodical *Papperlapapp* for Adventures and Explorers, a periodical *Sputnik* for Wichtelcher and Wëllefcher.

The Letzeburger Guiden is regularly represented at meetings held by other Catholic and youth organizations in Luxembourg. These include the Service National de la Jeunesse, the Conférence Générale de la Jeunesse, the Conférence de Mouvements Catholiques Luxembourgeois, the Conseil de la Pastorale Familiale, the Justicia et Pax and the Association Natura.

Madagascar

Skotisma Zazavavy eto Madagasikara
(Fédération du Scoutisme Féminin de Madagascar)

Component Associations:
Fanilon'ny Madagasikara (Guides de Madagascar)
Mpanazava eto Madagasikara (Eclaireuses Unionistes de Madagascar)
Kiadin'ny Madagasikara (Female Branch of Eclaireurs et Eclaireuses de Madagascar)

Girl Guiding/Girl Scouting introduced:	**1941**
Became Associate Member of WAGGGS:	**1963**
Became Full Member of WAGGGS:	**1987**
Membership 1992:	**6,334**
Membership as % of female population:	**0.11%**
WAGGGS Region:	**Africa**

Fanilon'ny Madagasikara

Promesse

Sur mon honneur et avec la grâce de Dieu, je m'engage à servir de mon mieux: Dieu, l'Eglise et la Patrie, à aider mon prochain en toutes circonstances, à observer la loi des guides.

Loi

1 La guide est loyale.
2 La guide pense d'abord aux autres.
3 La guide est généreuse, elle est prête à servir.
4 La guide est accueillante, elle a l'esprit d'équipe.
5 La guide, soeur de toute autre guide, est présente à tous.
6 La guide découvre la nature, elle y voit l'oeuvre de Dieu.
7 La guide sait obéir.
8 La guide ne craint pas l'effort; elle ne fait rien à moitié.
9 La guide aime son travail et respecte celui des autres.
10 La guide est maîtresse de soi; elle est pure et joyeuse.

Devise

Toujours prête

Promesse des Jeannettes

Je promets de faire de mon mieux: pour être fidèle à Dieu, à mon pays, à mes parents, à la loi de la ronde, et pour faire chaque jour un plaisir à quelqu'un.

Loi des Jeannettes

Une jeannette est toujours propre.
Une jeannette est toujours active.
Une jeannette est toujours gaie.
Une jeannette dit toujours vrai.
Une jeannette pense d'abord aux autres.

Devise des Jeannettes

De notre mieux

Promise

On my honour and with the grace of God, I undertake to do my best to serve God, the Church and my country; to help others in all circumstances and to keep the Guide Law.

Law

1 A Guide is loyal.
2 A Guide thinks first of others.
3 A Guide is generous, she is prepared to help.
4 A Guide is welcoming; she has team spirit.

Girl Guide

Brownie

5 A Guide, sister to every other Guide, is at the service of all.
6 A Guide learns about nature in which she sees God's work.
7 A Guide knows how to obey.
8 A Guide does not fear endeavour; she does nothing by halves.
9 A Guide likes her work and respects that of other people.
10 A Guide is self-controlled; she is pure and cheerful.

Motto
Be prepared

Brownie Promise
I promise to do my best:
to be faithful to God, my Country, my parents and the law of the Pack, and to do a good turn to someone every day.

Brownie Law
A Brownie is always clean.
A Brownie is always active.
A Brownie is always cheerful.
A Brownie always tells the truth.
A Brownie thinks first of others.

Brownie Motto
The best we can

Age Groups

Eclaireuse aînée	Ranger	17-21
Guide	Guide	12-16
Jeannette	Brownie	7-11

Girl Scout

Mpanazava eto Madagasikara

Promesse
Je promets sur mon honneur de faire tout mon possible pour:
servir Dieu, la Patrie, la famille; aider les autres chaque jour; obéir à la loi des Mpanazava.
C'est avec l'aide de Dieu que je le promets.

Loi
1 Une Mpanazava est loyale.
2 Une Mpanazava est disciplinée, obéit avec joie, ponctuelle et ordonnée.
3 Une Mpanazava est calme, elle sait se maîtriser.
4 Une Mpanazava est courageuse, travailleuse, elle ne craint point les difficultés.
5 Une Mpanazava est bonne, polie, aide les autres.
6 Une Mpanazava est l'amie de tout le monde et la soeur des autres éclaireuses.
7 Une Mpanazava est simple, elle sait se modérer dans ses goûts et sa toilette.
8 Une Mpanazava est l'amie des animaux et des plantes.
9 Une Mpanazava est toujours de bonne humeur, elle fait tout son possible pour faire régner la paix autour d'elle.
10 Une Mpanazava est pure dans sa pensée, sa parole et sa conduite.

Devise
Prête

Promesse des Petites Ailes
Je promets de faire de mieux en mieux pour servir Dieu, aimer ma patrie, aider chaque jour.

Loi des Petites Ailes
Les Petites Ailes écoutent la Cheftaine. Les Petites Ailes s'aiment comme des soeurs.

Devise des Petites Ailes
Aider

Promise
I promise on my honour to do everything possible to:
serve God, my country and my family; to help others every day and to obey the Girl Scout Law.
It is with God's help that I promise this.

Law
1 A Girl Scout is loyal.
2 A Girl Scout is disciplined, obeys cheerfully, is punctual and tidy.
3 A Girl Scout is calm and self-controlled.
4 A Girl Scout is brave, hard-working and is not afraid of difficulties.
5 A Girl Scout is good, polite and helps others.
6 A Girl Scout is a friend to all and a sister to other Girl Scouts.
7 A Girl Scout is unaffected; she is moderate in her tastes and her dress.
8 A Girl Scout is a friend to animals and plants.
9 A Girl Scout is always good-tempered, she does all she can to create peace around her.
10 A Girl Scout is pure in her thoughts, her words and her deeds.

Motto
Prepared

Little Wing Promise
I promise to do my very best to serve God, love my Country, and be helpful every day.

Little Wing Law
Little Wings listen to their Leader.
Little Wings love each other like sisters.

Little Wing Motto
To help

Age Groups

Eclaireuse aînée	Ranger	17-21
Mpanazava	Guide	12-16
Petite Aile	Little Wing	7-11

Kiadin'ny Madagasikara

Promesse
Je promets sur mon honneur et devant Dieu de faire tous mes efforts pour:
ou (selon les convictions)
Je promets sur mon honneur de faire tous mes efforts pour:
Servir mon pays, rendre service en toute occasion, obéir à la loi de l'éclaireuse.

Loi
1 L'éclaireuse n'a qu'une parole.
2 L'éclaireuse est loyale et chevaleresque.
3 L'éclaireuse se rend utile et fait chaque jour une bonne action.
4 L'éclaireuse est l'amie de tous et la soeur de toutes les éclaireuses.
5 L'éclaireuse est courtoise et respectueuse des convictions des autres.
6 L'éclaireuse est bonne pour les animaux.
7 L'éclaireuse sait obéir.
8 L'éclaireuse est toujours de bonne humeur.
9 L'éclaireuse est travailleuse, économe et respectueuse du bien d'autrui.
10 L'éclaireuse est propre dans son corps, ses paroles, ses pensées et ses actes.

Devise
Tout droit

Promesse des Jeannettes
Je promets de faire de mon mieux et avec l'aide de Dieu, pour être fidèle à la loi des louvettes;
ou (selon ses croyances et le désir de ses parents)
Je promets de faire de mon mieux pour être fidèle à la loi des louvettes.

Little Wing

Loi des Jeannettes
Une louvette dit toujours vrai.
Une louvette cherche à faire plaisir aux autres.
Une louvette obéit aux maîtres-mots de la Meute.

Devise des Jeannettes
De notre mieux

Promise
I promise on my honour and before God to do everything possible to:
or (according to her beliefs)
I promise on my honour to do everything possible to:
Serve my country, be helpful on all occasions and obey the Girl Scout Law.

Girl Scout

Law
1 A Girl Scout keeps her word.
2 A Girl Scout is loyal and generous.
3 A Girl Scout makes herself useful and does a good turn every day.
4 A Girl Scout is a friend to all and a sister to all Girl Scouts.
5 A Girl Scout is courteous and considerate of other people's convictions.
6 A Girl Scout is kind to animals.
7 A Girl Scout knows how to obey.
8 A Girl Scout is always good-tempered.
9 A Girl Scout is hard-working, thrifty, and considerate of other people's belongings.
10 A Girl Scout is clean in her body, her words, her thoughts and her deeds.

Motto
On a straight path

Brownie Promise
I promise to do my best and with God's help, to be faithful to the Brownie Law;
or (according to her beliefs and the wish of her parents)
I promise to do my best to be faithful to the Brownie Law.

Brownie

Brownie Law
A Brownie always tells the truth.
A Brownie seeks to give happiness to others.
A Brownie obeys the pack passwords.

Brownie Motto
The best we can

Age Groups

Eclaireuse aînée	Ranger	17-21
Eclaireuse	Girl Scout	12-16
Louvette	Brownie	7-11

Development of the Movement in Madagascar

The Skotisma Zazavavy eto Madagasikara (Fédération du Scoutisme Féminin de Madagascar), composed of three Associations, works to expand Girl Guiding and Girl Scouting in the country, and to help with leadership training.

Fanilon'ny Madagasikara

Guiding which catered for the needs of the Catholic girl was introduced into Madagascar in 1941 by a commissioner from the Guides de France. The first companies and packs were started in 1942 and Guiding expanded rapidly. In 1961 the Association became self-governing in all aspects of its work, and became known as Fanilon'i Madagasikara.

The Programme

The Association is reviewing the programme with a view to introducing an intermediate Guide section for girls aged 15-17. The Association aims to train girls in citizenship and to involve them in the development of the Catholic Church and the country.

Working with the Community

The Association's activities have centred on development projects under the theme 'Woman, Malagasy Woman, Christian Woman: Involved'. Since 1980 the Association has run a centre, Sahafanilo, where plans for development activities are drawn up. The staff at the centre work with neighbouring communities and with young people from rural areas and from other youth organizations. The centre serves as a meeting place for groups.

Outdoor and Environmental Activities

Members have been involved in tree-planting and bee-keeping activities.

Training

One of the Association's priorities is adequate training for leaders. The training plan is subject to frequent revision to meet the needs and aims of young women. A special section, Amboara, is responsible for recruitment and initial training of adults.

Communication and Co-operation

The Association encourages members to take part in exchanges with Girl Guides/ Girl Scouts from abroad. On Thinking Day each year Guides take part in activities with members of other Girl Scout Associations in Madagascar.

Fanilon'i Madagasikara works with the Food and Agriculture Organization (FAO). The Association is a member of the International Catholic Conference of Guiding (ICCG), and takes an active part in the Conseil de la jeunesse de Madagascar and the Centrale Catholique de la jeunesse. It co-operates with several government departments, such as the Ministry for Agriculture, the Ministry for Youth, and the Ministry for Education.

Mpanazava eto Madagasikara

Mpanazava eto Madagasikara was set up in 1941 by missionary sisters and provides a Protestant education. In May 1941 the first training camp for Girl Scouts was organized, and three months later three Girl Scout companies and one Brownie pack were in existence. Membership spread to rural areas quickly and by 1946 a Ranger unit had been formed.

The Programme

The emphasis of the programme is on community and its objectives are to encourage members to develop their own personal beliefs, to participate in community development, and to increase health and hygiene projects carried out with UNICEF. Regional training camps are held each year.

Working with the Community

The Association carries out training seminars on family life education to help girls to become responsible adults. It also runs projects on health and hygiene for mothers and children.

Communication and Co-operation

The Association participates in international seminars and gatherings. On Thinking Day each year Girl Scouts take part in activities with members of other Girl Guide/Girl Scout Associations in Madagascar. The Association also works with UNICEF on mother and child health projects.

Kiadin'ny Madagasikara

Kiadin'i Madagasikara is the female branch of the Eclaireuses et Eclaireurs de Madagascar, and is non-denominational. The first Brownie pack was formed in 1952 under the auspices of the Eclaireuses et Eclaireurs de France. Girl Scouting is now established in all regions of the island.

The Programme

The Association practises coeducation in accordance with the needs of the girls and wishes of parents. The older age groups carry out community development projects, and are encouraged to specialize in a technical skill.

Working with the Community

Each unit of Girl Scouts takes part in local service projects: activities include clearing and maintaining roadways and public buildings, setting up handicraft workshops, looking after groups of small children and following courses at the national centre at Tananarive.

Outdoor and Environmental Activities

The Association runs camps for all members.

Training

The Association runs training camps at local and regional level for leaders of each age group and for commissioners.

Communication and Co-operation

The Association participates in exchanges with neighbouring Girl Guide/Girl Scout Associations. On Thinking Day each year Girl Scouts take part in activities with members of other Girl Guide/Girl Scout Associations in Madagascar.

The Association publishes a quarterly newsletter, *Vona*.

Kiadin'i Madagasikara co-operates with other non-governmental organizations, and with governmental departments such as the Ministry for Youth, Sports, and the Ministry for Education. Members carry out nature projects with the World Wildlife Fund.

Guides learn about keeping bees – and keeping safe!

Malaysia

Persatuan Pandu Puteri, Malaysia
(The Girl Guides Association, Malaysia)

Girl Guiding/Girl Scouting introduced:	**1916**
Became Associate Member of WAGGGS: (as Malaya)	**1960**
Became Full Member of WAGGGS:	**1966**
Membership 1992:	**92,539**
Membership as % of female population:	**1%**
WAGGGS Region:	**Asia Pacific**

Guide

Persetiaan
Bahawa dengan sesungguhnya saya berjanji dan bersetia dengan sedaya upaya.
Menunaikan kewajipan saya kepada Tuhan, Raja dan Negara saya Malaysia
Menolong orang setiap masa dan
Mematuhi undang-undang Pandu Puteri.

Undang-undang
1 Seorang Pandu Puteri boleh dipercayai.
2 Seorang Pandu Puteri sentiasa taat dan setia.
3 Seorang Pandu Puteri suka menolong orang lain.
4 Seorang Pandu Puteri bersahabat dengan semua orang dan bersaudara dengan Pandu Puteri yang lain.
5 Seorang Pandu Puteri sentiasa bersopan santun.
6 Seorang Pandu Puteri berbuat baik kepada haiwan dan menjaga benda-benda yamg hidup.
7 Seorang Pandu Puteri sentiasa menurut perintah.
8 Seorang Pandu Puteri bersemangat dan bergembira walaupun dalam kesulitan.
9 Seorang Pandu Puteri sentiasa berjimat cermat.
10 Seorang Pandu Puteri suci dalam fikiran, perkataan dan perbuatan.

Cogan
Selalu Sedia

Brownie

Brownie Promise
Dengan sesungguhnya saya berjanji dan bersetia.
Akan menjalankan kewajipan saya kepada Tuhan, Raja dan Negara saya Malaysia.
Menolong orang setiap hari terutama mereka dirumah.
Mematuhi Undang-Undang Tunas Puteri.

Brownie Law
1 Tunas Puteri selalu menurut ajaran orang yang tertua darinya.
2 Tunas Puteri tidak turut kehendak hatinya sahaja.

Brownie Motto
Tolong orang selalu

Promise
On my honour I promise that
I will do my best, to do my duty to God, King and my country Malaysia
to help other people at all times and
to obey the Guide Law.

Law
1 A Guide's honour is to be trusted.
2 A Guide is loyal.
3 A Guide's duty is to be useful and to help others.
4 A Guide is a friend to all and a sister to every other Guide.
5 A Guide is courteous.
6 A Guide is a friend to animals.
7 A Guide is obedient.
8 A Guide smiles and sings under all difficulties.
9 A Guide is thrifty.
10 A Guide is pure in thought, words and deed.

Motto
Be Prepared

Brownie Promise
I promise to do my best
To do my duty to God, the King and my country Malaysia.

To help other people every day especially those at home.
To obey the Brownie Laws.

Brownie Law
1 A Brownie gives in to older folks.
2 A Brownie does not give in to herself.

Brownie Motto
Lend a hand

Age Groups

Kadet Pandu Puteri	Cadet	20 and over
Renjer Puteri	Ranger	16-20
Pandu Puteri	Girl Guide	12-16
Tunas Puteri	Brownie	6-12

Development of the Movement in Malaysia

Guiding has gathered momentum and strength since it was introduced in Malaysia in 1916. Persatuan Pandu Puteri Malaysia (Girl Guides Association, Malaysia) has become one of the leading movements in the country and has gained particular recognition for its contribution towards unifying the various racial groups in Malaysia's multiracial society.

The Girl Guides Association of Malaya became an Associate Member of WAGGGS in 1960. In 1963 the new country of Malaysia was inaugurated and in December 1964 the Girl Guides Association of Sabah and Sarawak joined the Association.

The Programme
The programme used in Malaysia places particular emphasis on environmental and community development activities. It is based on eight points: keeping fit, becoming a homemaker, giving service, keeping the Guide Law, getting to know people, enjoying the outdoors, thinking for yourself and exploring the arts.

Working with the Community
Guides regularly help the elderly, visit local hospitals and collect clothes for the needy.

Outdoor and Environmental Activities
Camping activities are enjoyed by members of the Association and day camp activities include tent pitching, camp cooking and instruction in first aid.

Guides participate in national service projects organized by the Ministry of Youth and Sports during Youth Week. These projects generally take the form of clean-up campaigns and land clearance for recreation areas.

Training
Several states have their own headquarters and training halls. Emphasis is laid on stimulating interest in the Movement, promoting efficiency, and determining methods of work.

The Association has opened cadet companies in all 30 teacher training colleges, and provides training for cadet leaders.

Communication and Co-operation
Persatuan Pandu Puteri encourages participation in international trainings and gatherings whenever possible. In 1990 it hosted the Commonwealth Chief Commissioner's Conference.

The Malaysian Association has provided training on Family Life Education and Responsible living for senior leaders and trainers in co-operation with the International Planned Parenthood Federation. It also co-operates with the National Youth Council, the National Council of Women's Organizations, the Scout Association and the Young Men's Christian Association.

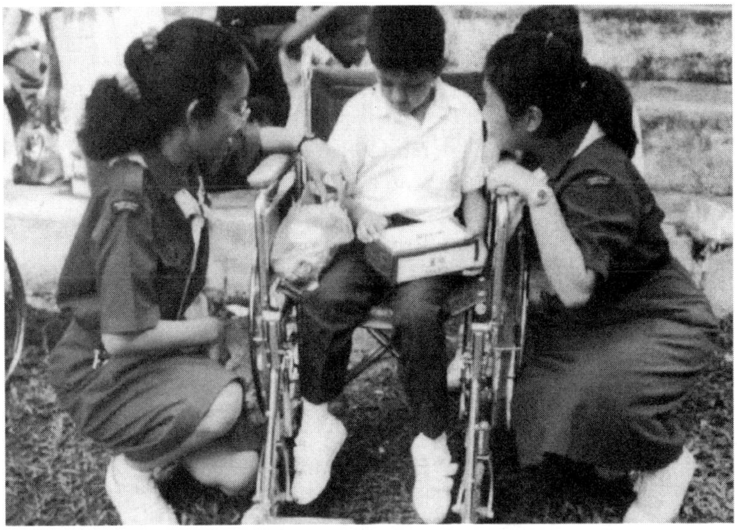

Guides help with a community service project assisting handicapped children.

Malta

The Malta Girl Guides Association

Girl Guiding/Girl Scouting introduced: 1918
Became Associate Member of WAGGGS: 1966
Became Full Member of WAGGGS: 1972
Membership 1992: 1,032
Membership as % of female population: 0.57%
WAGGGS Region: Europe

Guide

Brownie

Weghda
l-Inwieghed li naghmel mill-ahjar:
li naghmel id-dmir tieghi lejn Alla;
l-inservi lill Pajjizi, u nghin lill-proxmu tieghi;
li nzomm il-Ligi tal-Girl Guides.

Il-Ligi
1 Il-Girl Guide hija lejali u ta' min jafdha.
2 Il-Girl Guide tghin lil kulhadd.
3 Il-Girl Guide taf iggib ruha u tqis kulma taghmel.
4 Il-Girl Guide hija habiba u l-oht ta'kulhadd.
5 Il-Girl Guide hija hanina ma l-annimali u tirrispetta l-hlejjaq kollha.
6 Il-Girl Guide tobdi.
7 Il-Girl Guide hija kuragguza u tibqa ferhana f'kull saram.
8 Il-Girl Guide thaddem sewwa il-hin taghha.
9 Il-Girl Guide tiehu hsieb l-affarijiet taghha u ta haddiehor.
10 Il-Girl Guide taf tikkontrolla ruhha f'kull ma tahseb, tghid u taghmel.

Motto
Kun Lesta

Brownie Promise
Inwieghed li naghmel mill-ahjar:
li naghmel id-dmir tieghi lejn Alla;
l-inservi lill Pajjizi, u nghin lill-proxmu tieghi;
li nzomm il-Ligi tal-Brownies.

Brownie Motto
Midd Idejk

Promise
I promise that I will do my best:
To do my duty to God;
To serve my Country and help other people;
To keep the Guide Law.

Law
1 A Guide is loyal and can be trusted.
2 A Guide is helpful.
3 A Guide is polite and considerate.
4 A Guide is friendly and a sister to all Guides.
5 A Guide is kind to animals and respects all living things.
6 A Guide is obedient.
7 A Guide has courage and is cheerful in all difficulties.
8 A Guide makes good use of her time.
9 A Guide takes care of her possessions and those of other people.
10 A Guide is self-controlled in all she thinks, says or does.

Motto
Be Prepared

Brownie Promise
I promise that I will do my best:
To do my duty to God;
To serve my country and help other people;
To keep the Brownie Law.

Brownie Motto
Lend a Hand

Dolphin Motto
Friendly and helpful

Age Groups

Ranger	14-18
Guide	10-14
Brownie	7-10
Dolphin	5-7

Development of the Movement in Malta

Guiding was first introduced to Malta in 1918 when companies of British Guides were formed. In 1923 some Maltese girls became Guides and formed a separate division; the two divisions merged in 1938 to form a single body, The Malta Girl Guides Association, although there were still companies of British Guides. Malta gained independence in 1964 and Guiding activities continued to gain strength.

In 1974 Malta became a republic and four years later the British Guides companies left the island. The Association changed its name in 1984 to become the Girl Guides Association - Malta.

The Association is open to girls of every class, race, religion and nationality. It has a good relationship with the Scouts. Guides with special needs are encouraged to join local groups. In 1985 a pre-Brownie Programme known as the Dolphin Guide Programme was launched. The aim of the programme is "Socialisation through play".

The Programme

The eight-point programme gives the girls the opportunity to realise the aims of the Association; these are the development of character, self training and service for others, based on spiritual and moral values according to the principles embodied in the Promise and Law.

The programme fosters a love of country and promotes a full sense of citizenship by developing an interest in homecraft, health, social service, love of nature and the traditional arts and customs.

Guides attend regularly at church parades, the annual May Parade and on State occasions. The Association takes part in Thinking Day on the Air, and has its own official magazine, *The Guiding Light*.

Working with the Community

Service plays an important part in the programme. During the Second World War, the Association was awarded the Bronze Cross in recognition of the courage and endurance displayed by the Guides in Malta during the War, especially during the period of intense enemy activity. Members give service in children's homes and old people's homes. Guiders also donate blood to the Blood Bank.

Members participate in fundraising activities for charities and Badge Days, namely the Poppy Day Fund, Playing Field Association, Society for the Protection of Animals, Diabetics Cancer Fund and contributing towards the Charity Community Chest Fund under the auspices of the President of Malta and his wife, the latter being the Patron of the Association.

Guides are involved in projects such as "Make Malta Beautiful", "Clean up the World", "Peace .... one Day at Least", and "Guides for Refugees".

Outdoor and Environmental Activities

Guides often meet together at Island Rallies, camps and pack holidays. The focus at camps is frequently placed on nature study and respect for the countryside in order to encourage environmental awareness. The Association also organizes ecology courses and sea sports rallies for its members.

Training

To offer a better and effective service to the members a Training Panel was set up in 1968 to conduct leadership training, including camp training which is organized at district and national levels.

Communication and Co-operation

The international aspect of Girl Guiding is encouraged through international projects especially on Thinking Day, through penfriendship, exchange visits and attendance at international camps and seminars. A Twinning project with an American Council resulted in setting up an Island Library for members.

Brownies reaffirm their Promises after planting trees.

Mauritius

The Mauritius Girl Guides Association

Girl Guiding/Girl Scouting introduced: 1926
Became Associate Member of WAGGGS: 1975
Became Full Member of WAGGGS: 1981
Membership 1992: 1,184
Membership as % of female population: 0.2%
WAGGGS Region: Africa

Guide

Promise

I promise that I will do my best:
to do my duty to God,
To serve my country and help other people
and
To keep the Guide Law.

Law

1 A Guide is loyal and can be trusted.
2 A Guide is helpful.
3 A Guide is polite and considerate.
4 A Guide is friendly and a sister to all Guides.
5 A Guide is kind to animals and respects all living things.
6 A Guide is obedient.
7 A Guide has courage and is cheerful in all difficulties.
8 A Guide makes good use of her time.
9 A Guide takes care of her own possessions and those of other people.
10 A Guide is self-controlled in all she thinks, says and does.

Bluebird

Bluebird Promise

I promise I will do my best:
to do my duty to God,
To serve my country and help other people and
To keep the Bluebird Law.

Bluebird Law

A Bluebird thinks of others before herself and does a good turn every day.

Development of the Movement in Mauritius

Guiding began in Vacoas, Mauritius, in 1926 with the formation of a company for English-speaking girls. French-speaking girls later joined the company, and Guiding soon spread to other areas of the country, although membership was confined to girls of European descent.

In 1939 the Anglican community opened companies which admitted girls of all nationalities, and soon afterwards similar companies were opened by the Roman Catholic community.

In 1943 the first Island Council was formed and in 1946 the Mauritius Girl Guides Association's constitution was approved and it became a Branch Association of the Girl Guides Association (United Kingdom). Guiding in Mauritius continued to spread and, with the assistance of trainers from the United Kingdom, was established in five of the seven districts on the island. In 1980 a bill was passed by the Mauritius Legislative Assembly granting the Association legal status.

Guiding today has reached rural areas and schools and is open to all races and religions of the Island. In 1990 Guiding was extended to Rodrigues Island.

The Programme

The Mauritius Girl Guides Association programme is based on keeping fit, becoming a homemaker, giving service, keeping the Guide Law, getting to know people, enjoying the outdoors, thinking for yourself and exploring the arts. It encourages Rangers, Guides and Bluebirds to develop new and traditional skills enabling them to cope with the demands of modern society.

Working with the Community

Service projects have included kitchen-gardening (the products being sold to raise money for food parcels for the poor);

the distribution of clothing to the elderly; and church-cleaning. Cyclones have promoted Guides' involvement in disaster relief, both in organizing classes for children who have lost their homes and in joining other youth organizations in clearing the streets of debris.

A training project with the Girl Guides of Newfoundland, Canada, began in 1987. The project consisted of planting fruit trees and promoting the consumption of local fruit, which was encouraged through the sale of a recipe book produced by the Guides themselves, showing ways of using local fruit. Mauritius Girl Guides Association has now taken the project in hand and is developing it on the island and in Rodrigues, where Guides are planting and taking care of fruit trees.

Outdoor and Environmental Activities

During school holidays the Association organizes camps, usually held by the sea. Members enjoy other outdoor activities, including mountaineering and hiking.

Training

A training team consisting of five members meets monthly under the direction of the National Trainer to devise programmes for each branch. Leadership training is carried out at district and national level. In 1988 a seminar on Community and Development was held for Young Leaders of the Africa Region. Leadership training and training for trainers is carried out on national and district levels when needed.

Communication and Co-operation

The Guides raise their public profile by participating in parades and celebrations for Republic Remembrance Day.

The Association co-operates with the Mauritius Branch of the British Red Cross and works in close co-operation with the Ministry of Youth and Sports as well as with the Committee of the Council of Social Services. Mauritius Girl Guides Association is affiliated to the latter and also to the Mauritius Alliance of Women.

Learning crafts encourages girls to develop ways to work together in small groups.

Mexico

Guías de México, AC

Girl Guiding/Girl Scouting introduced: 1930
Became Associate Member of WAGGGS: 1948
Became Full Member of WAGGGS: 1957
Membership 1992: 2,487
Membership as % of female population: 0.01%
WAGGGS Region: Western Hemisphere

Guide

Promesa

Yo prometo por mi honor hacer cuanto de mí dependa para: cumplir con mi deber hacia Dios y México mi Patria; ser útil al prójimo en todas las circunstancias y obedecer la Ley Guía.

Ley

1 Una Guía es persona de honor.
2 Una Guía es leal.
3 El deber de una Guía es ser útil y ayudar a los demás.
4 Una Guía es amiga de todos y hermana de todas las Guías.
5 Una Guía es cortés.
6 Una Guía cuida a los animales y a las plantas y ve en la naturaleza la obra de Dios.
7 Una Guía obedece órdenes.
8 Una Guía se enfrenta a las dificultades con entereza y optimismo.
9 Una Guía es ahorrativa.
10 Una Guía se guarda pura en pensamientos, palabras y obras.

Motto

Bien preparadas

Fairy

Fairy Promise

Yo prometo hacer todo lo mejor que me sea posible para cumplir con mi deber hacia Dios y México mi Patria, ayudar a todos, todos los días, especialmente a los de mi casa.

Fairy Law

1 Una Hadita siempre dice la verdad.
2 Una Hadita es obediente y alegre.

Fairy Motto

Dar Ayuda

Promise

I promise on my honour
that I will do my best:
to do my duty to God and Mexico my country;
to help other people at all times
and to obey the Guide Law.

Law

1 A Guide's honour is to be trusted.
2 A Guide is loyal.
3 A Guide's duty is to be useful and to help others.
4 A Guide is a friend to all and a sister to every other Guide.
5 A Guide is courteous.
6 A Guide takes care of animals and plants and sees in nature the work of God.
7 A Guide obeys orders.
8 A Guide confronts difficulties wholeheartedly and with optimism.
9 A Guide is thrifty.
10 A Guide is pure in thought, in word and in deed.

Motto

Well prepared

Fairy Promise

I promise to do my best,
to do my duty to God and Mexico my country,
and to help everybody everyday,
particularly those at home.

Fairy Law

1 A Fairy always tells the truth.
2 A Fairy is obedient and cheerful.

Fairy Motto

Lend a Hand

Age Groups

Guía Mayor Guía	Ranger	15-18
Intermedia	Intermediate	13-15
Guía	Guide	9-13
Hadita	Fairy	6-9

Development of the Movement in Mexico

Girl Guiding began in Mexico in 1930 and in 1938 a National Association was formed with a programme adapted to the customs of Mexico, and the needs of Mexican girls. Guías de México AC now has Girl Guide companies throughout the country.

The Programme

The programmes are reviewed periodically in order to ensure that they are attractive and fulfil the changing needs of the girl. The present programme emphasises international education and ecology.

Working with the Community

Guides in Mexico are involved in many service projects including helping in orphanages and homes for the elderly.

Outdoor and Environmental Activities

National camps are held every year, one year for Guides and Intermediate Guides, and the next for Rangers and leaders. Brownies enjoy a national gathering every two years. Members are also involved in a national programme to combat environmental pollution.

Training

The Association places great importance on training and runs a full training programme, catering for all levels, at Ticalli, its headquarters in Mexico City. Regular regional trainings are also held. All training sessions are open to members of the Movement from other countries.

Communication and Co-operation

Mexican Girl Guides have many opportunities for international contacts as Mexico is the home of Our Cabaña, the WAGGGS World Centre, which welcomes members of the Movement from around the world throughout the year.

Guías de México organizes exchanges within the Republic to promote friendship and knowledge of folklore in different regions. Each year Guides aged 13 to 15 participate in a national exchange programme promoting good relations between Guide groups in different areas of the country.

Every year the Association celebrates national Guide week when members wear uniform and demonstrate the skills that they have learnt through the Guiding programme. This helps to raise the Association's public profile as does publicity received through press, radio and television.

The Association publishes three periodicals: *Cihuatl*, a magazine for all age groups; a monthly news bulletin and a quarterly magazine for leaders, *Nezaldi*.

Guides and Brownies plant bushes in Mexico City during the 1993 Guide Week.

Monaco

Association des Guides et Scouts de Monaco

Girl Guiding/Girl Scouting introduced:	**1929**
Became Associate Member of WAGGGS:	**1960**
Became Full Member of WAGGGS:	**1963**
Membership 1992:	**55**
Membership as % of female population:	**0.37%**
WAGGGS Region:	**Europe**

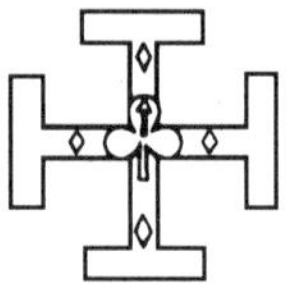

Guide

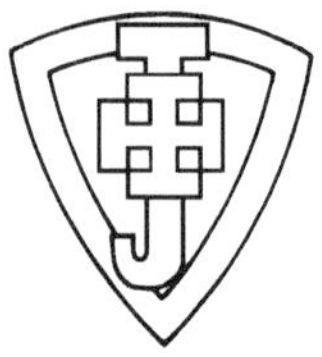

Brownie

Promesse
Sur mon honneur, avec la grâce de Dieu, je m'engage à servir de mon mieux Dieu, l'Eglise, le Prince, la Patrie; à aider mon prochain en toutes circonstances; à observer la Loi des guides.
ou
Sur mon honneur, je m'engage à servir de mon mieux Dieu, le Prince, la Patrie; à aider mon prochain en toutes circonstances; à observer la Loi des guides.

Loi
- La Guide se connaît, elle manifeste sa joie de vivre.
- La Guide est responsable de ses choix, on peut lui faire confiance.
- La Guide prend sa place dans l'équipe: elle agit avec les autres partout où elle vit.
- La Guide accueille l'autre: elle apprend à le comprendre et à l'aimer.
- La Guide développe ses compétences pour elle-même et pour le service des autres.
- La Guide respecte la vie, la nature et le travail des hommes.
- La Guide vit l'aventure de Dieu.

Devise
Toujours prête

Promesse des Jeannettes
Je promets de faire de mon mieux: pour être fidèle à Dieu, au Prince, à mon pays, à mes parents, à la loi de la ronde, et pour faire chaque jour un plaisir à quelqu'un.

Loi des Jeannettes
Une jeannette est toujours propre.
Une jeannette est toujours active.
Une jeannette est toujours gaie.
Une jeannette dit toujours vrai.
Une jeannette pense d'abord aux autres.
Une jeannette est amie de Jésus.

Devise des Jeannettes
De notre mieux

Promise
On my honour and with the grace of God, I undertake to do my best to serve God, the Church, the Prince and my country; to help others in all circumstances; to keep the Guide Law.
or
On my honour I undertake to do my best to serve God, the Prince, and my country; to help others in all circumstances; to keep the Guide Law.

Law
- A Guide knows herself. She expresses her joy for living.
- A Guide is responsible for her choices.
- A Guide is trustworthy.
- A Guide takes her place in the team.
- A Guide works with others everywhere she lives.
- A Guide is friendly to others. She gets to know and understand them.
- A Guide develops her skills for herself and for the service of others.
- A Guide respects life, nature and the work of mankind.
- A Guide lives God's adventure.

Motto
Always prepared

Brownie Promise
I promise to do my best: to be faithful to God, the Prince, my country, my parents, the law of the pack, and to do a good turn to someone every day.

Brownie Law
A Brownie is always clean.
A Brownie is always active.
A Brownie is always cheerful.
A Brownie always tells the truth.
A Brownie thinks first of others.
A Brownie is a friend of Jesus.

Brownie Motto
The best we can

Age Groups
Guide Aînée	Ranger	16-20+
Guide	Guide	12-16
Jeannette	Brownie	7-12

Development of the Movement in Monaco

The first Guide company in Monaco was formed in 1929, and Guiding developed under the auspices of the Guides de France. In 1953 work began on forming an independent Association which was achieved in 1956.

The Programme
The Association's programme has three main aims: to offer a wide range of interesting activities to girls and young women; to co-operate on important international projects; and to promote the Movement within the country through the media.

Working with the Community
The Association has opened a centre for children and adults with special needs.

Outdoor and Environmental Activities
Wide games are very popular in Monaco and give members a chance to use the skills they have acquired during training. In winter members participate in trips to the mountains to ski, and in summer all age groups are involved in camping activities.

Guides are involved in anti-pollution campaigns in rural and urban areas.

Communication and Co-operation
The Guides in Monaco encourage further development of international relations by means of international camps, training courses and joint celebrations of Thinking Day.

The Association des Guides de la Principaut de Monaco co-operates on projects organized by FAO, UNRWA, UNICEF and the Red Cross Society. The Association is especially anxious to commit itself to the cause of world peace. In addition, members have been involved in the Freedom from Hunger Campaign, National Leprosy Day, and campaigns against illiteracy.

Namibia

The Girl Guides Association of Namibia

Girl Guiding/Girl Scouting introduced: 1923
Became Associate Member of WAGGS: 1993
Membership 1992: 457
Membership as % of female population: 0.06%
WAGGGS Region: Africa

Guide

Brownie

Promise
I promise that I will do my best
To do my duty to God and to my Country;
To help other people at all times;
and to keep the Guide Law.

Law
1 A Guide is to be trusted.
2 A Guide is loyal.
3 A Guide is helpful.
4 A Guide is friendly.
5 A Guide is polite and thoughtful of others.
6 A Guide cares for the earth and living things.
7 A Guide is obedient.
8 A Guide is brave and cheerful.
9 A Guide is thrifty.
10 A Guide is pure in all that she thinks, says and does.

Age Groups

Guide	11-15
Brownie	7-10

Development of the Movement in Namibia

Guiding was established in the territory of South West Africa (known as Namibia since 1968) in 1923 as a Region of the Girl Guides Association of South Africa. During the years 1985 to 1990 when the independence of Namibia was being discussed, the Girl Guides Association of South Africa worked closely with this Region, assisting it in its preparations to become an independent organization. In 1990 when independence was declared in Namibia, the Girl Guides Association of Namibia was set up as an independent National Organization.

For administrative purposes the Association is divided into four Regions. The National Headquarters are located in Windhoek and are owned by the Association.

The Programme
As Girl Guiding in Namibia operated as a Region of the Girl Guides Association of South Africa until 1990, the programme used by this Association is very similar to that of South Africa. It aims to give girls the opportunity for self-training in the development of character and service for others, based on spiritual and moral values.

Compulsory clauses provide a good foundation, while a free choice enables girls to try out new ideas, extend themselves and take on challenges which will prepare them to be worthwhile members of the community.

Working with the Community
Units undertake service projects on a regular basis. Special activities are organized to celebrate occasions such as World Environment Day and Arbor Day, and these are often linked to a service project in the community. The Association is also interested in undertaking some community development work and has approached the YWCA and churches which are already carrying out projects in the areas of health, literacy and education.

Outdoor and Environmental Activities
Camping has not been a popular activity due to the political situation that has existed in the country. Now, however, leaders are being encouraged to organize camps.

Training
The Adviser for Training implements the Association's training programme in conjunction with a trainer from each of the four Regions.

Communication and Co-operation

The Association is recognized by the general public and is invited to assist at national functions. Guiding is well accepted in schools. The Association has maintained good contacts with several large organizations and corporations as well as with local municipalities which make annual grants to local associations.

Relationships with the Scouts are good and the Chief Commissioner of the Scout Association is a member of the National Council and vice versa. Relationships with all religious bodies are good and in some areas much assistance is received from churches.

The Association does not have any publications of its own as yet and, as its programme is so similar to that of the Girl Guides Association of South Africa, members use South African publications.

Brownies and Guides enjoy being part of the Association.

Nepal

Girl Scout Section of Nepal Scouts

Girl Guiding/Girl Scouting introduced:	**1952**
Became Associate Member of WAGGGS:	**1978**
Became Full Member of WAGGGS:	**1984**
Membership 1992:	**22,676**
Membership as % of female population:	**0.24%**
WAGGGS Region:	**Asia Pacific**

Girl Scout

Promise

On my honour I promise that I will do my best

1 to do my duty to God/Dharma, my Country and my King
2 to help other people at all times
3 to obey the Girl Scout law.

Law

1 A Girl Scout's honour is to be trusted.
2 A Girl Scout is loyal to her country, her King and her employers.
3 A Girl Scout's duty is to be useful and to help others.
4 A Girl Scout is a friend to all and a sister to every other Girl Scout no matter to what country, class or creed the other may belong.
5 A Girl Scout is courteous.
6 A Girl Scout is a friend to animals.
7 A Girl Scout obeys orders of her King, parents, Patrol Leaders, Scout Leaders, without question.
8 A Girl Scout smiles and sings under all difficulties.
9 A Girl Scout is thrifty.
10 A Girl Scout is clean in thought, word and deed.

Motto

Be Prepared

Brownie

Brownie Promise

I promise to do my best

1 to do my duty to God/Dharma, my Country and my King
2 to help other people at all times
3 to keep the laws of the Brownie pack.

Brownie Law

The Brownie gives in to her elders.
The Brownie is courteous and clean.
The Brownie utilizes her time properly.

Brownie Motto

Do your best

Age Groups

Ranger	17-25
Girl Scout	12-16
Brownie	7-11

Development of the Movement in Nepal

The late HM the King Tribhuvan Bir Bikram Shah Deva established the Nepal Scouts and Guides Association in 1952 and His Majesty the King became the first Chief Patron of the Association. In 1965, the name of the Association was changed to Nepal Boy and Girl Scouts Association. From then onwards the Girl Guides were known as Girl Scouts. In 1975 the name was further changed to the Nepal Scouts.

A five-year consolidation plan was introduced in 1975 which aimed to spread Scouting to all 75 districts of the kingdom and, at the same time, to consolidate and co-ordinate Scouting activities by the year 1980.

Currently, the Nepal Scouts, Girl Section has a separate Chief Commissioner, Training Commissioner, International Commissioner and other office personnel.

The Programme

Nepal Scouts is a Joint Association and some of its programme is common to both boys and girls. The programme emphasizes handicrafts, hiking, camping, nature conservation and Scout craft. Brownies, Girl Scout and Ranger activities are predominantly based in schools and at institutes of higher education.

Working with the Community

The Girl Scout Section is involved in numerous community projects associated with safe drinking water, literacy, kitchen garden production, drug abuse prevention and sanitation. The Association has participated in a national child survival project since 1988.

The Girl Scouts run a vocational training programme in sewing and knitting at the National Headquarters which aims to teach girls income generating skills and to improve the status of women in the community.

Girls are also involved in community services such as crowd control, traffic control, cleanliness, service camps, and natural disaster relief activities.

Outdoor and Environmental Activities

Girl Scouts are encouraged to take part in camping and outdoor activities and to protect their environment through afforestation programmes which have resulted in the planting of thousands of trees.

Training

The Girl Scouts' training is carried out separately from the Boy Scouts. There is a separate Training Committee run by a Professional Training Commissioner who is assisted by the Assistant Training Commissioner. There are four levels of training – Unit Leader's Course or Preliminary Training Course (PTC), Advanced, Certificate and Diploma. Training has been conducted in all the districts of the kingdom.

Communication and Co-operation

Girl Scouts of Nepal take part in international events whenever possible and welcome Girl Guide/Girl Scout visitors from other countries.

During the 1980s working relationships with other Girl Guide/Girl Scout Associations increased in number and resulted in the introduction of several joint projects. New Zealand supported the establishment of a rehabilitation centre for mentally retarded children in 1990 through the WAGGGS Mutual Aid Scheme. A twinning project focusing on tree-planting has been introduced in co-operation with Det Danske Spejderkorps (The Danish Guide and Scout Association) and Nepal is also twinned with Finland on an afforestation project.

Radio and television broadcast information about the Association's activities and a monthly Scout Bulletin is also published.

The Girl Scout Section of Nepal Scouts maintains excellent relations with other organizations. It has a reciprocal working relationship with organizations such as the Family Planning Association, Jaycees, Lions Club, Rotary Club, Red Cross, Women's Organization and also maintains cordial relations with the UNICEF and UNDP.

Netherlands

Scouting Nederland

Founder Member of WAGGGS

Girl Guiding/Girl Scouting introduced:	**1911**
WAGGGS Membership 1992:	**56,654**
Membership as % of female population:	**0.74%**
WAGGGS Region:	**Europe**

Guide

Brownie

Belofte

Ik beloof mijn best te doen (met hulp van God‡) een goede padvindster/gids to zijn, Iedereen te helpen waar ik kan, bewust het goede te zoeken en te bevorderen, en met te houden aan de padvindsters/ gidsen wet. Jullie kunnen op me rekenen!

Wet

Een padvindster/gids trekt er samen met anderen op uit om de wereld om zich heen te ontdekken en deze meer leefbaar te maken.
Zij is eerlijk, trouw en houdt vol.
Zij is spaarzaam en sober en heeft zorg voor de natuur.
Zij respecteert zichzelf en anderen.

Kabouter belofte

Ik beloof mijn best te doen (met de hulp van God‡) een goede kabouter/esta te zijn, iedereen te helpen waar ik kan, bewust het goede te zoeken en te bevorderen en me te houden aan de kabouter/esta wet. Jullie kunnen op met rekenen!

Kabouter/Esta wet

Een kabouter speelt samen met anderen in Bambilie
Een Esta speelt samen met de anderen in het land van Esta. Zij is eerlijk, vriendelijk, houdt vol en zorgt goed voor de natuur.

Promise

I promise to do my best (with the help of God‡) to be a good Guide, to help everyone wherever I can, to go consciously in search of the spiritual value in my life, and to live up to the Guide law. You can count on me!
(‡Members of Scouting Nederland may have permission to omit the words 'with the help of God'.)

Law

A Guide goes out with others to discover the world around her and to make it more worthwhile to live in.
She is honest, faithful and perseveres,
She is thrifty, and sober and takes good care of nature,
She respects herself and others.

Brownie promise

I promise to do my best (with the help of God‡)
to be a good Brownie/Esta,
to help everybody wherever possible, to go consciously in search of the spiritual value of my life, and to keep the Brownie law.
You can count on me!
‡Members of Scouting Nederland may have permission to omit the words 'with the help of God'.

Brownie/Esta law

A Brownie plays together with others in Bambiliё
An Esta plays together with others in the country of Esta.
She is honest, kind, perseveres and takes good care of nature.

Age Groups

Jongerentak/Loods	Sea Ranger/ Ranger	17-21
Sherpa, Matroos/Astronaut	Senior Guide, sea/air Senior	14-17
Padvindster Gids, Zeeverkenner/ Luchtverkenner	Guide, sea/air Guide	10-15
Kabouter/Esta	Brownie	7-11
Bever	Beaver	5-7

Development of the Movement in the Netherlands

The first Guide groups appeared in the Netherlands in 1911. In 1916 six of these groups formed Het Nederlandse Meisjes Gilde, which in 1928 was a Founder Member of WAGGGS. The Association changed its name to Het Nederlandse Padvindsters Gilde in 1933.

After the Second World War there were two Guide Associations active in the Netherlands: Het Nederlandse Padvindsters Gilde, which was partially sponsored by the Ecumenical Council of Youth and the Salvation Army; and De Nederlandse Gidsen, which catered to Roman Catholic girls. These two Associations were represented in WAGGGS by a joint council, the Nationale Padvindsters Raad.

In 1967 the Federation Scouting Nederland was formed as a result of the growing co-operation between the Nationale Padvindsters Raad and the Scouting Association for boys. Since 1973 there has been one organization for girls and boys, Scouting Nederland, which combines elements from all former associations and remains open to new developments. HRH Prince Claus is patron of this merged organization.

The Programme

Scouting Nederland offers a wide variety of programmes, some of which take part in single-sex units, whereas other programmes have been designed specifically for mixed units. Though a merged organization, groups themselves decide whether or not to have mixed units.

Given the abundance of water in the country, a large number of groups specialize in Guiding on the water; and recently an increasing number of girls have taken an interest in the challenges of aeronautics, joining airscout troops.

Beavers come together to enjoy free play in the house of "Hotsjietonia" where Tall-do-All lives. The characters in the programme provide a choice of activities.

The Brownies play together in the imaginary country of Bambilië, where almost everything is possible. The villages in the country suggest lots of attractive programmes. The Estas use a new programme specifically designed for mixed units, launched in 1991. Together with the children Jeroen, Hilde Rozemarijn and Deng there is a lot to experience in the town of Pals, where the statue of the Child with the Top Hat stands near the Volderia river.

The Guides, Sea-Guides and Air-Guides all use the "Scoutsprogramme", a renewed version of earlier programmes, presented in 1991. It is an attractive programme equally suited to the needs of single-sex and mixed units. It stimulates the initiative of the girls, and includes traditional Guide activities and a number of contemporary challenges.

Senior Guides, including the Senior Guides with an interest in nautics or aeronautics, have a joint programme with the venture scouts. In mixed or single-sex units they choose their own projects. Self-administration, with the assistance from the leader, is the most important feature of this programme.

The Ranger programme is based upon being completely self-supporting. Together with the Rover Scouts programmes are developed and executed.

Scouting Nederland has an Extension Branch for disabled Guides and Scouts, who may be in handicapped units, but can also be members of regular units.

Working with the Community

Scouting Nederland has undertaken projects that aim at supporting community life. In 1987-1989 a project aimed at reaching out towards the migrant community took place. At local level groups frequently take part in environmental action, contributing to the maintenance of nature and in line with our goal of service. Rangers, Rovers and leaders formed part of the back-up team for the World Games for the Handicapped held in the Netherlands in 1990.

Outdoor and Environmental Activities

At Easter and Whitsuntide Scouting Nederland goes camping. A number of regional camps are organized, and the National Patrol Competition takes place. At regular intervals a weekend camp for all the leaders in the Movement is organized, and a National Sea-Scout/ Guide camp also takes place regularly.

At local level groups take an active interest in nature conservation, taking part in actions to clean up nature areas and plant trees. On Scouting Nederland's own campsites, environment-friendly camping is promoted and information is provided to that end. In the European Jamboree (1994) and the World Jamboree (1995), to be organized by Scouting Nederland, the preservation of the environment will be one of the focal points.

Training

After an update, a new training scheme called "Tailor-made" was introduced in 1990-1992. The basic characteristics of the new training scheme are the easy accessibility of trainings given in the vicinity of the leaders. Another goal is continuous training. All leaders are expected to attend one training a year and a comprehensive range of trainings on a variety of issues, skills and techniques are being developed.

Communication and Co-operation

The Association promotes international education through publications, its leaders and at training courses. The European Jamboree and the World Jamboree are stimulating general interest in the international aspect of Guiding.

Scouting Nederland has worked on an education project for girls and women in co-operation with the Guides and Scouts of Yemen. At present the Association is co-operating with Cesky Junák - svazd skautu a śkautek (Czech Republic) and Slovensky Skauting (Slovakia). A particularly exciting element in the co-operation are the exchange visits, in which groups and districts take part.

Scouting Nederland informs the general public about its activities through press releases and promotion. Since 1985 a spokesperson has been appointed in every district to co-ordinate public relations activities. The Association publishes *Beverpost*, a magazine for the youngest age groups; *Scouty* for Brownies and Guides and *Scouting Magazine* for Rangers and leaders. Additionally the *Scouting Nederland Courant* is published for the volunteers at managerial level.

Girls learn to change a tyre as part of the programme.

Netherlands Antilles

Padvindstersvereniging van de Nederlandse Antillen
(Girl Scouts Association of Netherlands Antilles)

Girl Guiding/Girl Scouting introduced:	**1930**
Became Associate Member of WAGGGS:	**1978**
Became Full Member of WAGGGS:	**1981**
Membership 1992:	**564**
Membership as % of female population:	**0.58%**
WAGGGS Region:	**Western Hemisphere**

Girl Guide

Promesa
Mi ke trata seriamente di:
(1) Sirbi Dios i mi patria
(2) Yuda tur hende kaminda mi por
(3) Sigui reglanan di padvinderij.

Reglanan
1 Un padvindster ta honesto
2 Un padvindster ta fiel
3 Un padvindster ta kla pa yuda otro hende
4 Un padvindster ta un amigu i un ruman pa tur otro padvindster
5 Un padvindster ta kortes i atento
6 Un padvindster ta bon pa mata i pa animal
7 Un padvindster sa di obedesé
8 Un padvindster ta karga kontratiempo ku konformidat
9 Un padvindster sa di spar
10 Un padvindster ta desente den su pensamentu, su palabra i su echo.

Motto
Sea Prepará

Brownie Motto
Ban kompartí

Promise
I will earnestly try:
(1) To do my duty to God and my country
(2) To help all people where possible
(3) To obey the Guide Law.

Law
1 A Girl Guide is honest.
2 A Girl Guide is loyal.
3 A Girl Guide is willing to help.
4 A Girl Guide is a friend to all and a sister to all Guides.
5 A Girl Guide is courteous and attentive.
6 A Girl Guide cares for plants and animals.
7 A Girl Guide is obedient.
8 A Girl Guide accepts disappointments with cheerfulness.
9 A Girl Guide is thrifty.
10 A Girl Guide is pure in thought, in word, and in deed.

Motto
Be prepared

Brownie Motto
Let Us Share

Age Groups

Ranger	17+
Senior Guide	13-17
Junior Guide	10-13
Brownie	7-10

Development of the Movement in the Netherlands Antilles

Brownie

The first Guide company in the Netherlands Antilles was opened in Curaçao in May 1930 by one of the Component Associations of The Netherlands, Het Nederlandse Padvindsters Gilde. Soon afterwards the Association became the Nederlandse Padvindstergilde Curaçao, and in the following years Guiding continued to grow with assistance in programme and training developments from Het Nederlandse Padvindsters Gilde.
In 1967 Het Nederlandse Padvindsters Gilde requested WAGGGS and the

Western Hemisphere Committee to work directly with the Nederlandse Padvindstergilde Curaçao in order to forge links with National Organizations in the same geographical area. In 1972 the Nederlandse Padvindstergilde Curaçao became an independent Association.

Guiding has spread to all areas of the island of Curaçao and to all sectors of the community. The Association is working to expand Guiding to neighbouring islands. The name of the Association was changed to the Padvindstersvereniging van de Nederlandse Antillen in 1977.

The Programme

The programme for all age groups is planned to enable the girl to develop her character and mind, to attain a proficiency in her chosen activities and interests, to develop a willingness to help others and to gain a sense of fellowship. In 1984 the Association successfully launched the Ranger branch for girls aged 17 and over. Those who wish to continue Guiding after reaching 17 years of age are encouraged to become Rangers and take leadership training to become leaders.

Working with the Community

Community service plays an important part in the life of the Association, and each year a special programme is launched which involves all members. In 1990 the Association focused on supporting girls with drug-related problems and others who had left school prematurely.

Outdoor and Environmental Activities

Camping is a popular activity among all members and the Association also holds weekend camps for leaders.

In recent years the Association launched a tree-planting project with help from the government, and each member of the Association gave a tree to another child to plant. Much publicity resulted from this project and a series of eight films were made, with financial help of a government agency. For eight weeks the films were presented by local television during a programme sponsored by the Government Cultural Department. Copies of these films were presented to the public library for use in schools and by the public in general.

Training

Training is carried out by a team which includes the commissioner for training and trainers for Brownies and Guides. Meetings for leaders, which are usually held twice a month, also include training.

Communication and Co-operation

The Association has participated in events organized by National Organizations in neighbouring countries. It encourages members to attend international gatherings, and campaigns are planned to raise funds to cover the expenses.

The annual projects undertaken by the Association have helped to make Guiding known in the community. Relations with the government are good and the Association has been granted use of the land on which many of their troop houses stand. The Association holds occasional open houses to enable the public to learn more about the Movement.

The Association is a member of the Federation for Youth Care in the Netherlands Antilles and has good relations with the Scout Association.

Brownies in Curaçao enjoy taking part in a Guiding event.

New Zealand

The Girl Guides Association New Zealand (Inc.)

Founder Member of WAGGGS
Girl Guiding/Girl Scouting introduced: 1923
Membership 1992: 52,051
Membership as % of female population: 3.07%
WAGGGS Region: Asia Pacific

Promise
On my honour I promise to do my best
To serve my God, the Queen and my country,
And to live by the Guide Law.

Law
As a Guide -
- I can be trusted
- I am loyal
- I am helpful
- I am friendly and cheerful
- I am polite and considerate
- I care for the environment
- I use resources wisely
- I respect leadership
- I am a good team member
- I am self controlled and value myself.

Motto
Be Prepared

Brownie Promise
I promise to do my best:
To love God,
To serve the Queen and my country,
To help other people at all time s and to keep the Brownie Law.

Brownie Law
A Brownie is cheerful and friendly,
A Brownie cares for herself, her home and her community,
A Brownie does a Good Turn every day.

Brownie Motto
Lend a Hand

Age Groups

Ranger Guide	14-19
Guide	10-14
Brownie	7-10
Pippin	6

Development of the Movement in New Zealand

Guide

The Girl Guides Association of New Zealand was incorporated in 1923 from the Girl Peace Scouts, which started in 1908. The Association has members throughout the country and is also responsible for Girl Guiding in Western Samoa where the Movement was introduced in 1952. Although Girl Guiding has been popular in New Zealand since the 1920s, a great expansion has taken place since the early 1970s.

The Programme
The programme for Brownies and Guides emphasizes personal development and independence through the patrol system. A diverse programme of enjoyable activities and a progressive badge system combine individual options with opportunities to widen leisure interests and pursuits.

The Ranger programme expands the spectrum of opportunities, and members exercise individual choice and planning as well as assessing their own progress.

Brownie

Community service, joint activities and international opportunities play a major part, as do the challenge of the Duke of Edinburgh's Award Scheme and the opportunity to work for the highest Guide achievement, the Queen's Guide badge.

The Pippins, the Association's newest age group, have no Promise or set programme but, working closely with families and in a supervised atmosphere, the girls are encouraged to develop awareness of other people, themselves, and the world around them.

In isolated areas of the country, Guiding is carried out through correspondence in the form of a monthly letter or magazine. *The Lone Letter* is posted from one Girl Guide to another throughout a unit and members occasionally meet for camps or other special events. Members with special needs are also integrated into units if possible, and the Association also has a Special Needs Branch. In addition, the Guide handbook has been translated into Braille.

Working with the Community

Community service is an important part of the Girl Guide programme in New Zealand. Members have raised large sums of money to bring relief to disaster areas and to help countries in need of aid.

Outdoor and Environmental Activities

Outdoor activities, hiking, boating, and primitive camping, are still favourites among New Zealand Guides. Brownies have pack holidays in halls and holiday homes, Guides camp as units and attend large provincial or national jamborees and Rangers enjoy light-weight camping and hiking. Easy access to mountains, lakes and the sea-shore enable all to participate in exciting and challenging programmes which demand a high degree of skill and leadership. Ranger Guides and Scout Venturers have the opportunity to attend flying and gliding schools. The Association works with the Scout Association of New Zealand, and joint activities include holiday camps, conservation and anti-litter campaigns.

New Zealand's 1993 Thinking Day incorporated awareness of Women's suffrage and challenges for a new badge.

The Association was a Founder Member of the New Zealand Conservation Council and continues to play an active role. Regular projects are undertaken and each year specially organized national days are set apart for conservation.

Training

Trainings are provided for adult leaders on a local and national basis, and there are a number of residential training centres throughout the country. With increasing numbers of voluntary trainers (156 in 1993), efforts are made to keep pace with the needs of both new and experienced leaders. A three-stage training scheme for leaders is available, called Focus on Leadership, which includes both personal and Guiding skills.

Communication and Co-operation

International friendships and contacts with other countries are greatly encouraged, and increasing numbers of delegates from the Association attend gatherings, camps and conferences abroad. The Association also welcomes representatives from other Girl Guiding/ Girl Scouting organizations to major events and leadership trainings each year. WAGGGS Mutual Aid projects have received much support from the Association.

The Association has a national public relations adviser and a public relations committee. Posters, a videotape and other publicity material have been produced with the help of sponsorship from commercial firms. National press releases are sent out, and each of the 21 provinces has an adviser who prepares items for local press and radio. The Association publishes a bi-monthly periodical, *Te Rama*.

The Association is an active member of the Federation of New Zealand Youth Organizations and also co-operates closely with other national and international organizations working in the country. Combined training sessions with other youth organizations have become a common feature. Finally, the Association is in touch with the United Nations and its specialized agencies active in New Zealand. It receives regular UN publications and participates in special events.

Nicaragua

Federación Nacional de Muchachas Guías de Nicaragua

Girl Guiding/Girl Scouting introduced: 1940
Became Associate Member of WAGGGS: 1981
Membership 1992†: 75
Membership as % of female population: <1%
WAGGGS Region: Western Hemisphere

Promesa
Yo prometo, por mi honor, hacer cuanto de mí dependa para:
Cumplir mis deberes con Dios y mi Patria,
Servir al prójimo en toda circunstancia y
Obedecer la Ley Guía.

Ley
1 La Guía es una persona en cuyo honor se puede confiar.
2 La Guía es leal.
3 La Guía es útil y ayuda al prójimo.
4 La Guía es amiga de todos sin distinción de raza, clase social o religión.
5 La Guía es cortés.
6 La Guía ve la obra de Dios en la naturaleza.
7 La Guía es responsable, obediente y disciplinada.
8 La Guía es alegre y optimista en todas las dificultades.
9 La Guía es económica.
10 La Guía es pura de pensamiento, palabra y obra.

Lema
Siempre Activas

Promesa de las Haditas
Yo prometo hacer todo lo posible para cumplir con mis deberes para con Dios, mi Patria y mi familia;
Ayudar a otras personas cada día, especialmente a los de mi casa y mi colegio y obedecer la Ley de la Ronda.

Ley de las Haditas
1 La Hadita es alegre y obediente.
2 La Hadita es generosa y dice siempre la verdad.

Lema de las Haditas
Dar Ayuda

Promise
I promise, on my honour, to do my best
To fulfil my duties to God and my Country,
To serve other people in any circumstance and
To obey the Guide Law.

Law
1 A Guide is a person whose honour is to be trusted.
2 A Guide is loyal.
3 A Guide is useful and helps other people.
4 A Guide is a friend to all without distinction of race, social class or religion.
5 A Guide is courteous.
6 A Guide sees the work of God in nature.
7 A Guide is responsible, obedient and disciplined.
8 A Guide is cheerful and optimistic under all difficulties.
9 A Guide is thrifty.
10 A Guide is pure in thought, word and deed.

Motto
Always active

Fairy Promise
I promise to do everything possible to fulfil my duties to God, my Country and my family;
To help other people each day, especially those at home and at school and to obey the Pack Law.

Guide

Fairy Law
1 A Fairy is cheerful and obedient.
2 A Fairy is generous and always tells the truth.

Fairy Motto
Give help

Age Groups

Senior Guide	16-18
Guide	10-15
Fairy	7-9

Development of the Movement in Nicaragua

Guiding in Nicaragua began in 1940, when a well-known Nicaraguan educator opened a Guide company in a school in Managua. Progress was slow, but by 1972 the Movement had spread to four departments and the National Committee was considering applying for Associate Membership in WAGGGS. Unfortunately Guiding was brought to a standstill when an earthquake destroyed Managua.

In 1976, with the assistance of the trainer/adviser for the Western Hemisphere Region, the National Committee was re-established and Guide companies and Brownie packs re-opened. The Association received legal recognition in 1977, and despite civil disturbances in the country during 1978 and 1979, the National Council and leaders continued their work.

When the situation improved, vacancies on the council were filled and a full-time trainer was appointed with financial assistance from WAGGGS. Guiding is now established throughout the country.

The Programme
The programme is based on those used by the National Organizations of El Salvador and Mexico and the programmes of each branch are adapted for the age groups concerned. The Association has concentrated on the development of the Brownie branch, as it is felt that this group forms the foundation of the Association.

Working with the Community
Guides participate in a national literacy campaign in rural and mountain areas, and organize and train choirs which entertain children in nurseries, patients in psychiatric hospitals and the elderly. Senior Guides work with the disabled at the Zaragoza handicrafts centre, providing them with the materials needed for their work.

Training
The national trainer works closely with a training committee and a team of assistant trainers.

Communication and Co-operation
The Federación Nacional de Muchachas Guías de Nicaragua is very aware of the international aspect of Girl Guiding/Girl Scouting, as well as the significance of the World Association, and it participates in Western Hemisphere activities and events.

Guiding is well accepted by the private and public sectors and private enterprise is supportive of the Association's fundraising activities.

Nigeria

The Nigerian Girl Guides Association

Girl Guiding/Girl Scouting introduced:	**1919**
Became Associate Member of WAGGGS:	**1960**
Became Full Member of WAGGGS:	**1966**
Membership 1992:	**64,622**
Membership as % of female population:	**0.15%**
WAGGGS Region:	**Africa**

Promise
I promise, on my honour, to do my best
To do my duty to God and my Country;
To help other people at all times, and
To obey the Guide Law.

Law
1 A Guide's honour is to be trusted.
2 A Guide is loyal.
3 A Guide's duty is to be useful and to help others.
4 A Guide is a friend to all, and a sister to every other Guide.
5 A Guide is courteous.
6 A Guide is a friend to animals.
7 A Guide obeys orders.
8 A Guide smiles and sings under all difficulties.
9 A Guide is thrifty.
10 A Guide is pure in thought, word and deed.

Motto
Be Prepared

Brownie Promise
I promise to do my best
To do my duty to God and my Country;
To help other people every day, especially those at home.

Brownie Law
A Brownie is truthful, obedient and cheerful.
A Brownie thinks of others before herself.

Brownie Motto
Lend a Hand

Age Groups

Ranger	19-25
Guide	11-19
Brownie	7-11

Guide

Development of the Movement in Nigeria

The first Girl Guide company in Nigeria was formed in 1919 and before long companies were started in several schools in different parts of the country. Four years later, a committee of interested people was set up to encourage and direct the work of the rapidly spreading Movement. This committee, then known as the Central Nigeria Executive Committee, later became the Council of the Nigerian Girl Guides Association.

The first Brownie pack was registered in 1927, and in 1929 the first company was formed in a lepers' hospital. Ranger companies first appeared in Nigeria in 1934 and the further expansion of Girl Guiding led to the formation of Cadet companies. Girl Guiding quickly spread to all parts of the country and numbers increased rapidly.

Brownie

The Programme
The programme is based on eight points: keeping fit, becoming a homemaker, giving service, keeping the Guide Law, getting to know people, enjoying the out-of-doors, thinking for yourself and exploring the arts.

Working with the Community

The Association continually strives to involve members in community service work, especially with the elderly, the disabled and orphans.

Day Care Centres have been established in several states for children of working mothers together with a vocational training centre for girls with special needs, both mental and physical, with the aim of integrating them into society as active and productive members. The first section of the centre was opened in 1975, and in 1984 a sheltered workshop and physiotherapy unit were added. A number of the girls have learnt useful trades and have responded well to medical treatment.

Other projects have involved Guides in poultry-rearing and the cultivation of vegetables and flowers which are sold at special market days. Guides also help to care for motherless babies in homes.

Outdoor and Environmental Activities

Guides in most states have undertaken tree-planting projects in co-operation with the local community and other voluntary organizations. Rangers and Cadets have organized water purification projects in rural areas and have participated in general environmental hygiene campaigns.

Training

Trainings are organized at state level throughout the year for Guides and leaders. At national level there are two annual training camps, each lasting from 7 to 10 days, when new methods are introduced and ideas exchanged. One camp is attended by leaders and commissioners, and the other by Senior Guides and Rangers.

Communication and Co-operation

Guides and Brownies are encouraged to have friends in other countries and to learn about their cultures. Members of the Nigerian Girl Guides Association take an active part in international Girl Guiding/Girl Scouting and when possible attend international camps, trainings and conferences. In 1989 Nigeria hosted an Africa Region Sub-Regional Seminar on Community Development.

On the occasion of the Association's 70th anniversary in 1989 the Nigerian Government issued two Girl Guide stamps to commemorate the occasion in recognition of the Association's valuable contribution to the development of youth services.

The Nigerian Girl Guides Association often observes United Nations' Years.

Norway

Fellesråadet for Speiderpiker i Norge
(The Joint Committee of Girl Guides in Norway)

Component Associations:
Norges Speiderforbund
Norges KFUK-Speidere

Founder Member of WAGGGS

Girl Guiding/Girl Scouting introduced:	**1912**
Membership 1992:	**23,922**
Membership as % of female population:	**1.12%**
WAGGGS Region:	**Europe**

Norges Speiderforbund

Speiderløftet
Jeg lover etter beste evne:
Å tjene Gud,
hjelpe andre
og leve etter speiderloven.

Speiderloven
1 En speider er åpen for Gud og hans ord.
2 En speider kjenner ansvar for seg selv og andre.
3 En speider er hjelpsom og hensynsfull.
4 En speider er en god venn.
5 En speider er cerlig og pålitelig.
6 En speider kjenner naturen og verner om den.
7 En speider tenker og handler selvstendig og prøver å forstå andre.
8 En speider gjør sitt beste i motgang og vansker.
9 En speider er nøysom og prøver å klare seg selv.
10 En speider arbeider for fred og forståelse mellom mennesker.

Motto
Vaer beredt

Promise
I promise to the best of my ability:
to serve God,
to help others
and to live according to the Guide/Scout Law.

Law
1 A Guide is open to God and His word.
2 A Guide accepts responsibility for herself and others.
3 A Guide is helpful and considerate.
4 A Guide is a good friend.
5 A Guide is honest and trustworthy.
6 A Guide understands nature and protects it.
7 A Guide thinks and acts independently.
8 A Guide does her best in adversities and difficulties.
9 A Guide is thrifty and tries to manage on her own.
10 A Guide works for peace and understanding (between men/peoples).

Speiderforbund Guide

Speiderforbund Brownie

Motto
Be prepared

Norges KFUK-Speidere

Speiderløftet
I tro på Guds hjelp lover jeg:
Å tjene Gud og mitt land,
hjelpe andre
og leve etter speiderloven.

Speiderloven
1 En speider er åpen for Gud og hans ord.
2 En speider kjenner ansvar for seg selv og andre.

KFUK Guide

3 En speider er hjelpsom og hensynsfull.
4 En speider er en god venn.
5 En speider er aerlig og pålitelig.
6 En speider kjenner naturen og verner om den.
7 En speider tenker og handler selvstendig og prøver å forstå andre.
8 En speider gjør sitt beste i motgang og vansker.
9 En speider er nøysom og prøver å klare seg selv.
10 En speider arbeider for fred og forståelse mellom mennesker.

Motto
Vaer beredt

Brownie Promise
I tro på Guds hjelp lover jeg
å hjelpe andre
og alltid gjøre mitt beste.

Brownie Motto
Vaer beredt

KFUK Brownie

Promise
Believing in God's help I promise:
to serve God and my country,
to help others
and to live according to the Guide Law.

Law
1 A Guide is open to God and His word.
2 A Guide accepts responsibility for herself and others.
3 A Guide is helpful and considerate.
4 A Guide is a good friend.
5 A Guide is honest and trustworthy.
6 A Guide understands nature and protects it.
7 A Guide thinks and acts independently.
8 A Guide does her best in adversities and difficulties.
9 A Guide is thrifty and tries to manage on her own.
10 A Guide works for peace and understanding (between men/peoples).

Motto
Be prepared

Brownie Promise
Believing in God's help I promise
to help other people
and always do my best.

Brownie Motto
Be prepared

Age Groups

Rangere	Rangers	16-24
Vandrere	Guides	13-15
Stifinnere	Guides	10-12
Meiser	Brownies	7-9
Harer	Hares	6-7

Development of the Movement in Norway

Guides were active in Norway before the First World War and the oldest companies have records dating from 1912, although it was not until 1920 that the first national organization was formed, Norges KFUK-Speidere (YWCA Guides of Norway). A year later Norsk Speiderpikeforbund (Norwegian Girl Guides Association) was formed.

In 1978 Norsk Speiderpikeforbund merged with Norsk Speiderguttforbund for boys to become Norges Speiderforbund (the Norwegian Guide and Scout Association).

Members of Norges KFUK-Speidere, and all female members of Norges Speiderforbund, are represented in WAGGGS by Fellesrådet for Speiderpiker i Norge (the Joint Committee of Girl Guides in Norway).

The Programme
The programme for each Association contains the same basic elements, activities and methods of work. Each year members are expected to participate in the main elements of the programme: community service, active outdoor life, handicrafts and the ideals of Girl Guiding/Girl Scouting.

A feature of the Movement in Norway is the concept of the Group, which works at a local level. The Group usually consists of one unit from each age group, and may thus choose to have up to five units. The activities inspired by the programme are designed both for patrol participation, encouraging Guides to learn to take responsibility, and for individual action, allowing members to learn to work alone and thereby develop personal skills. Both Associations integrate disabled Guides into companies, and Norges Speiderforbund also has groups whose members are refugees.

Working with the Community

Guide companies and patrols undertake service projects in their own communities. Both Associations raise funds for such projects and one fundraising method is the annual Speiderjobben, when Guides undertake a wide variety of jobs to earn money.

Outdoor and Environmental Activities

Both Associations organize camps at local, regional and national level and invite Girl Guides/Girl Scouts from other countries to participate. Every four years each Association holds a special camp where thousands of members, including visitors from abroad, take part. The camping programme includes overnight hikes without tents. During the winter season, members participate in camps and overnight hikes in the snow.

The environment is a subject included in all national level trainings. The Association forms part of a joint committee working on environmental issues, financed by the government. Many patrols are involved in collecting waste paper for recycling.

Training

Both Associations arrange training for patrol leaders, unit leaders and trainers.

Communication and Co-operation

Norges Speiderforbund and Norges KFUK-Speidere recognize the importance of involvement in international activities. They encourage members to participate in seminars and conferences organized by the Europe Region and other bodies with mutual interests. They also take part in exchange projects with Girl Scouts of the USA and with Girl Guide/Girl Scout Associations of the other Nordic countries, and send groups and individuals to the World Centres.

The Associations co-operate with other organizations in the allocation and administration of funds for community projects. In addition, the Associations have an emergency relief fund to be used for particular relief operations.

The Associations are well known through their activities within the community. There are several periodicals published in Norway: *Speideren* and *Speiderbladet*, for Guides and Scouts; *Lederbladet* and *K-lederen* for leaders; *Peff*, for patrols; and *Flokken*, for Brownie and Cub leaders.

Both Associations participate in the National Council of Norwegian Youth Organizations, and encourage members to be involved in the international events organized by the Council.

Joining Guiding is both special and fun. It leads to a lifetime of involvement with others.

Oman

The National Organization for Scouts and Guides

Girl Guiding/Girl Scouting introduced: 1972
Became Associate Member of WAGGGS: 1987
Membership 1992: 5,148
Membership as % of female population: 0.64%
Member: Arab Regional Group

Guide

Brownie

Promise
1 I promise on my honour to fulfil my duty towards God, my country and the Sultan.
2 To help people;
3 And to keep Guides' Law.

Law
1 The honour of a Girl Guide is to be trusted.
2 A Girl Guide is faithful to God, her country, parents, and to both her seniors and juniors.
3 The Guide is useful and helps others.
4 The Guide is a friend to all, and sister of other Guides.
5 A Guide is a girl of good character.
6 A Guide is kind to animals.
7 A Guide obeys her parents, the head of the patrol division, and the leader of the group.
8 A Guide faces hardships patiently smiling.
9 A Guide is not extravagant
10 A Guide should be clean, have a clean mind and clean thoughts.

Brownie Promise
I promise upon my honour to:
1 Fulfil my duty towards God, my country and the Sultan.
2 Help all people, particularly those at home.
3 Abide to the Brownie Law.

Brownie Law
A Brownie obeys the elder.
A Brownie does not indulge herself.

Age Groups

Rangers	17-24
Guides	12-17
Zahras	7-12

Development of the Movement in Oman

The first Brownie packs and Guide companies were opened in elementary and intermediate schools in Muscat, the capital of Oman, in 1972. Guiding soon spread to other parts of the country, and the National Organization for Scouts and Guides was established by Royal Decree in 1975. The Omani Scout and Guide Organizations constitute the National Organization for Scouts and Guides. The two wings operate independently, but both have their headquarters in the same building in Muscat.

The Programme
The programme includes health education, character-building, handicraft, community service and international communication aspects. Each branch participates in these activities at a level appropriate to their age group. The Organization encourages disabled girls to participate in all Guiding activities.

Working with the Community
During municipal week the Guides and Brownies participate in many seminars, which train them in awareness of community services such as health and care of the environment. They are also trained in practical skills.

Outdoor and Environmental Activities
Apart from school camp activities, the National Organization for Scouts and Guides plays an important role in organizing national camping events. Camps are held twice a year and run for a week to ten days at a time. Girls are involved in community projects such as oral rehydration and vaccination programmes.

Training
One member of the National Committee is responsible for training in co-operation with a committee of six drawn from different areas of the country. The Committee reviews needs, sets priorities and plans activities. Annual training courses are held for leaders at both regional and national levels.

Communication and Co-operation
Oman participates in the WAGGGS conferences, and Arab Regional conferences, seminars and trainings.

The Guides are highly regarded by both the government and the public and are given much publicity and support by the media. The personal representative of His Majesty the Sultan is the president of the National Organization and the minister of education is vice president. Both are supportive of the Girl Guides.

The Organization has produced several publications, including a public relations booklet which documents Guiding in Oman, an information leaflet and a handbook.

Guides learn woodworking craft in Oman.

Pakistan

Pakistan Girl Guides Association

Founder Member of WAGGGS	
Girl Guiding/Girl Scouting introduced:	**1911**
Became Full Member of WAGGGS (under the name Pakistan):	**1948**
Membership 1992:	**101,634**
Membership as % of female population:	**0.18%**
WAGGGS Region:	**Asia Pacific**

Guide

Waada

Mein waada karti hun ke mein poori koshish karoongi ke, Khuda aur mulk ke ahkam per paband rahoon.
Baninau insaan ki madad aur tamir-e-Pakistan ke kamon mein hissa loon.
Guide ke qawanin ki pabandi karoon.

Qanoon

1 Guide qable aitemad hoti hai.
2 Guide wafadar hoti hai.
3 Guide milansaar aur tamam doosri Guides ki behan hoti hai.
4 Guide khosh akhlag aur doosrum ka khiyal rakhti hai.
5 Guide janwaron se acha selaouk karti hai aur har jandar chiz ka khiyal rakhti hai.
6 Guide hukam ki taamil karti hai aur apne naffas per qaboo rakhti hai.
7 Guide madadgar hoti hai aur woqt ka sehi istemal karti hai.
8 Guide mesaib aur mushkilat ka hosla mandi se mukabla karti hai.
9 Guide kifayat sauaar hoti hai, woh apni aur doosron ki chizon ki hifazat karti hai.
10 Guide apne qual-o-fail aur khiyalat mein pakiza hoti hai.

Motto

Teyar raho

Junior Guide Promise

Mein waada karti hun ke mein puri koshish karoongi ke, Khuda ke ahkam ki taamil karoon aur Pakistan se muhabat karoon Hamesha doosran ki madad karoon khas kar apne ghar walon ki, Chhotee Guide ke qanoon ki taamil karoon.

Junior Guide Law

Chhotee Guide baron ka kehna manti hai,
Chhotee Guide her rose eik achta kam karti hai,
Chhotee Guide apni mun mani nahein karti.

Motto

Hath batana

Promise

I promise that I will do my best, to do my duty to God*, and Pakistan.
To serve mankind and participate in nation building activities.
To obey the Guide Laws.

**For Buddhist Guides and Brownies, the words 'My religion' may be substituted for God in the first part of the Promise.*

Law

1 A Guide can be trusted.
2 A Guide is loyal.
3 A Guide is friendly and a sister to all other Guides.
4 A Guide is polite and considerate.
5 A Guide is kind to animals and respects all living things.
6 A Guide is obedient and self-disciplined.
7 A Guide is helpful and makes good use of her time.
8 A Guide is courageous and cheerful in all difficulties.
9 A Guide is thrifty and takes care of her own and other people's possessions.
10 A Guide is pure in thought, word and deed.

Motto

Be Prepared

Junior Guide Promise
I promise to do my best, to obey God, to love Pakistan, to help other people every day, especially those at home, and to keep the Junior Guide Law.

Junior Guide Law
A Junior Guide obeys her elders and tries to do a good turn every day.

Motto
Lend a Hand

Age Groups

Senior Guide	16-21
Guide	11-16
Junior Guide	7-11

Development of the Movement in Pakistan

Girl Guides have been active in the area which is now Pakistan since 1911. In 1928 this area, along with that of present-day India and Bangladesh, became a Founder Member of WAGGGS under the name of India.

In 1948 the Pakistan Girl Guides Association was welcomed as a separate member of WAGGGS.

The Association's national headquarters was opened in 1974. It provides residential facilities for trainings, camps and conferences at provincial, national and international level.

In 1983 Guiding was extended to Gilgit in the north of the country.

The Programme
The Association's programme meets the needs and aspirations of both rural and urban girls, and handbooks offer a wide selection of activities and new opportunities.

Working with the Community
Pakistan lays special emphasis on service to the disabled and on community projects in rural and urban slum areas. Service camps are organized on a regular basis, giving women the opportunity to learn about health and nutrition, sanitation, economic uplift, vegetable-growing, fruit-tree-planting, poultry farming and handicrafts.

Literacy centres and dispensaries have been opened and local leaders trained. The 'Each One Teach One' scheme for Guides and Senior Guides is a particularly important literacy project which has helped large numbers of adults to learn to read and write. The projects have been keenly supported by participants who, in addition to learning to read and write in Punjabi, Sindhi or Urdu, have also become literate in English.

Junior Guide

Students, both past and present, celebrate International Literacy Day on 8 September each year at their literacy centres, and hold exhibitions of their work. As part of the literacy campaign, Guide Companies have also set up small libraries in the Guide rooms of local schools. In 1989, Pakistan was awarded An Honourable Mention for the NOMA Literacy Prize given by UNESCO.

Pakistan also has successful vegetable-growing and health and sanitation projects which have involved many members of the Association in activities such as building wells, toilets and baths as well as improving drains.

Senior Guides work with disabled children and help out at mobile eye-clinics. To carry out these responsibilities effectively they are trained in first aid, home nursing, dispensing medicines and giving injections.

To honour Pakistan Guides who excel in community work the Pakistan Association's highest award, the President's Gold Medal, is awarded to Guides for outstanding service.

Pakistan has also won the WAGGGS Olave Award for community projects on two occasions.

Outdoor and Environmental Activities
Thousands of camps are held every year for all three branches at District/ Provincial and national level. Girls with special needs regularly attend camps, and are integrated with other Guides. Members of the Association participate in conservation projects, and have planted large numbers of trees of different varieties throughout the country.

Training
Training is important for the expansion of the Association and provincial branches hold basic and advanced training courses, which are well attended.

Communication and Co-operation
Every year members of the Association participate in trainings, seminars and camps held by National Organizations in other countries. The Association is much respected in Pakistan, and its activities, especially in the field of youth and women's welfare work, receive much public support.

The general public is informed about Guiding activities through newspapers, radio and television, and the Association publishes a magazine called *Guide Bulletin* and a yearly detailed report.

The Pakistan Girl Guides Association co-operates with local government, the Lions Club, social welfare agencies, educational institutions, UN agencies and other NGOs.

Guides scrub out a fountain to assist with community clean-up activities.

Republic of Panama

Asociación de Muchachas Guías de Panamá

Girl Guiding/Girl Scouting introduced: 1950
Became Associate Member of WAGGGS: 1952
Became Full Member of WAGGGS: 1966
Membership 1992: 982
Membership as % of female population: 0.08%
WAGGGS Region: Western Hemisphere

Promesa
Con la gracia de Dios, yo prometo por mi honor, hacer cuanto de mí dependa para:
Cumplir mis deberes para Dios y mi Patria,
Ser útil al prójimo en todas las circunstancias,
Obedecer la Ley Guía.

Ley
1 La Guía es persona de honor.
2 La Guía es leal.
3 La Guía es útil y ayuda al prójimo.
4 La Guía es amiga de todos, y hermana de las demás Guías.
5 La Guía es cortés.
6 La Guía ama las plantas y los animales y ve la obra de Dios en la Naturaleza.
7 La Guía es obediente y disciplinada.
8 La Guía afronta las dificultades con entereza y optimismo.
9 La Guía es económica.
10 La Guía es pura en sus pensamientos, palabras y obras.

Lema
Siempre listas

Promesa de la Alita
Prometo hacer todo lo mejor que me sea posible para cumplir con mis deberes hacia Dios y mi Patria.
Ayudar todos los días a los demás, especialmente a los de mi casa.

Ley de la Alita
La Alita siempre cede a los deseos de sus mayores.
La Alita nunca cede a sí misma.

Lema de la Alita
Ayudar

Promesa de la Chavelita
Prometo ser obediente y respetuosa con todas las personas.

Ley de la Chavelita
Portarme Bien.

Lema de la Chavelita
Sonreir.

Promise
With the grace of God I promise on my honour to do my best:
To fulfil my duties to God and my country,
To help other people in all circumstances,
To obey the Guide Law.

Law
1 A Guide is a person of honour.
2 A Guide is loyal.
3 A Guide is useful and helps other people.
4 A Guide is a friend to all and a sister to all other Guides.
5 A Guide is courteous.
6 A Guide loves plants and animals and sees in nature the work of God.
7 A Guide is obedient and disciplined.
8 A Guide smiles under all difficulties.
9 A Guide is thrifty.
10 A Guide is pure in her thoughts, words and deeds.

Motto
Be prepared

Little Wing promise
I promise to do my best to fulfil my duties to God and my country,

Guide

Little Wing

to help others every day, especially those at home.

Little Wing Law
A Little Wing always gives in to the wishes of her elders.
A Little Wing never gives in to herself.

Little Wing Motto
Give help

Chavelita

Chavelita Promise
I promise to be obedient and respectful to all people.

Chavelita Law
To behave well.

Chavelita Motto
Smile.

Age Groups

Cadete	Cadet	17-19
Guía Mayor	Ranger	15-17
Guía Intermedia B	Guide	12-14
Guía Intermedia A	Guide	10-12
Alita	Little Wing	7-9
Chavelita		$4\frac{1}{2}$-6

Development of the Movement in the Republic of Panama

Guiding in the Republic of Panama began in 1950 when an Association was formed.

The Programme
The programme is periodically reviewed by management committees, who determine changes and improvements. In order to help meet the shortage of leaders, the Association has groups of cadets, aged 17-19, who are in charge of Brownie packs while at the same time pursuing their own Guide programme.

Working with the Community
The Association is extremely active in several fields of service including literacy. The Asociación Nacional de Muchachas Guías de Panamá maintains a full-time study centre for children of school age, where two specialist teachers work under the guidance of adult leaders. The children are also looked after by Rangers, who help with recreational activities.

Members of the Association also visit hospitals and homes for those with mental disabilities and help out in nurseries. Guides in Panama help migrant Indian children to attend school by providing basic necessities such as shoes and clothing. They also raise funds to buy books for the children and to support literacy campaigns.

Outdoor and Environmental Activities
Guides in Panama are involved in environmental projects centred around ecology, anti-litter campaigns and tree-planting.

Training
Leadership training is given high priority and leaders' conferences have been held regularly since the first national conference of leaders in 1966.

Every two years the Association organizes a training session, which is occasionally attended by members from other Girl Guide/Girl Scout Associations. In addition, trainings are organized at regional level for leaders.

Communication and Co-operation
The Association participates in international meetings and gatherings and welcomes Girl Guides/Girl Scouts from other Associations who attend training and camping events in Panama. Members of the Association work with members of Girl Scouts of the USA in order to further international friendship and widen cultural awareness.

The Association is very conscious of the need for good public relations, and activities in this field have included exposure through the media, and visits to government officials, directors of companies and civic bodies. It has co-operated with the Soroptimist Club of Panama. The Association publishes a bulletin, *La Voz del Comité Nacional*.

Members of the Association hold an annual tea for the public at a large hotel in the capital with entertainment provided by Guides and Rangers.

Papua New Guinea

Girl Guides Association of Papua New Guinea

Girl Guiding/Girl Scouting introduced: 1927
Became Associate Member of WAGGGS: 1978
Membership 1992: 932
Membership as % of female population: 0.05%
WAGGGS Region: Asia Pacific

Promise

I promise that I will do my best,
To do my duty to God and my country,
To serve the Queen, To help people at all times, and,
To keep the Guide Law.

Law

1 A Guide is loyal and can be trusted.
2 A Guide is helpful.
3 A Guide is polite and considerate.
4 A Guide is friendly and a sister to all Guides.
5 A Guide is friendly to animals and respects all living things.
6 A Guide is obedient.
7 A Guide has courage and is cheerful in all difficulties.
8 A Guide makes good use of her time.
9 A Guide takes care of her own possessions and those of other people.
10 A Guide is self-controlled in all she thinks, says and does.

Motto

Be Prepared

Brownie Promise

I promise that I will do my best
To do my duty to God and my country
To serve the Queen, to help people at all times, and,
To keep the Brownie Law.

Brownie Law

A Brownie thinks of others before herself, does a good turn every day.

Brownie Motto

Lend a Hand

Age Groups

Rangers	16 - 22
Guides	$10\frac{1}{2}$/11 - 16
Brownies	7/$7\frac{1}{2}$ - $10\frac{1}{2}$/11
Sunbirds	$5\frac{1}{2}$-7/$7\frac{1}{2}$

Development of the Movement in Papua New Guinea

The first Guide company in Papua New Guinea was started in Papua near Port Moresby in 1927 by a missionary. Soon afterwards, other companies were established in the villages of Hula and Delena, and in 1933 the first Ranger company was opened.

The first Guide company in New Guinea was begun in 1939 when membership of the Movement totalled 120. Between 1942 and 1945 Guiding ceased to function but was restarted in 1946 with a Ranger company. Companies and packs then began to appear in several villages, organized by former Guides.

The Federal Council of the Girl Guides Association of Australia included the Girl Guides of Papua New Guinea as a division in 1948. A local Association was formed and a president appointed. The following year saw the appointment of a Territory Commissioner for the Association. In 1955 it was recognized as a state Association of the Girl Guides Association of Australia and in the following year a Constitution was prepared and accepted.

In 1976 the Papua New Guinea Association became independent of Australia and a new Constitution was introduced.

The Programme

Papua New Guinea uses the programme prepared by the South Pacific Guide Conference for use by countries in the South Pacific.

Guide

Brownie

An eight-point programme covers the essential elements of the Movement and caters to the special needs of girls and young women growing up in emerging nations of the South Pacific region. Members are recognized as being law-abiding, self-reliant citizens, playing a responsible part in the development of the nation at community as well as national levels. In 1988 the Sunbirds, a pilot group for younger girls, was introduced.

Working with the Community

Papua New Guinea is a diverse country and provinces are encouraged to develop community projects which answer their individual needs.

Community activities include hospital visits by members who also assist at health centres. Brownies have been involved in making warm knee rugs for blind children in a highlands centre.

In 1990, International Literacy Year, the Association issued a literacy challenge to its members to help overcome the low literacy levels in the country and introduced a literacy badge.

The Association runs a hostel, Friendship House, in the capital Port Moresby where some 60 working girls are accommodated in a secure and caring environment. Extensions to this much sought-after residence were opened in 1987 with financial assistance from Papua New Guinea's Guiding twin, the Province of British Columbia, Canada, and through the WAGGGS Mutual Aid Scheme.

Outdoor and Environmental Activities

An International Camp, Camp Aropa, held in 1988 to celebrate the Silver Jubilee of the establishment of Guiding on the island of Bougainville, was attended by participants from British Columbia (Canada), Australia, New Zealand, Solomon Islands and representatives from all over Papua New Guinea.

While it is not possible to camp outdoors in tents in Papua New Guinea, girls from Brownie age through to Rangers enjoy Pack Holidays and camping activities.

A tree-planting project has been one result of the twinning partnership with British Columbia, Canada.

Training

Training is considered to be very important in promoting quality Guiding and retaining leaders in Papua New Guinea. Training is conducted by a Training Team of experienced leaders and commissioners, and Regional Training Teams are planned for the future. The Association's first full time National Trainer was appointed in 1992 and already membership is growing.

Communication and Co-operation

All members of the Association are encouraged to 'think wide, think international' in an effort to establish better understanding and peace between nations. Visiting members from other countries are always warmly welcomed and Guides, Rangers and Leaders frequently participate in overseas camps, conferences and workshops.

In addition, the twinning relationship between Papua New Guinea and British Columbia, Canada greatly encourages international awareness as do relationships with other National Girl Guide/Girl Scout Organizations.

The Girl Guides Association is one of the major youth organizations in the country and maintains good relations with the government, churches and councils.

In local communities members co-operate with other organizations in such activities as walkathons, workshops, celebrations, and commemorations.

The Association publishes a monthly newsletter giving Girl Guiding/Girl Scouting news, programme ideas, and training to all members of the Association.

The Association co-operates with many non-governmental organizations including the Scout Association, the Red Cross Society, Boys' Brigade, St. Johns Ambulance Brigade and Association, and several United Nations agencies.

Paraguay

Asociación Guías Scouts del Paraguay

Girl Guiding/Girl Scouting introduced:	**1923**
Became Associate Member of WAGGGS:	**1966**
Became Full Member of WAGGGS:	**1978**
Membership 1992†:	**416**
Membership as % of femalc population:	**0.02%**
WAGGGS Region:	**Western Hemisphere**

Promesa
Por mi honor y con la gracia de Dios prometo hacer todo lo posible para cumplir mis deberes para con Dios, mi Patria y la Humanidad.
Servir al prójimo en todas las circunstancias y cumplir con las leyes Guías.

Ley
1 Una Guía es digna de toda confianza.
2 Una Guía es leal.
3 Una Guía es útil y ayuda a los demás.
4 Una Guía es amiga de todos y hermana de las demás Guías.
5 Una Guía es cortés.
6 Una Guía ve en la naturaleza la obra de Dios, por eso la admira y la respeta.
7 Una Guía acepta consejos y sugerencias.
8 Una Guía sonríe y canta en las dificultades.
9 Una Guía es económica.
10 Una Guía se conserva pura en pensamientos, palabras y obras.

Motto
Siempre Lista

Promesa de la Alita
Prometo hacer todo lo posible para cumplir mis deberes para con Dios y mi patria. Ayudar siempre a los demás, especialmente a los de mi casa y cumplir con Ley de la Ronda.

Ley de la Alita
Una Alita obedece a sus mayores.
Una Alita hace la buena acción diaria.

Lema de la Alita
Ayudar a todos

Promise
On my honour and with the grace of God I promise to do everything possible to fulfil my duties to God, my country and humanity;
to serve other people in all circumstances and to comply with the Girl Scout Laws.

Law
1 A Girl Scout is to be trusted.
2 A Girl Scout is loyal.
3 A Girl Scout is useful and helps others.
4 A Girl Scout is a friend to all and a sister to all other Guides.
5 A Girl Scout is courteous.
6 A Girl Scout admires and respects nature, for she sees in it the work of God.
7 A Girl Scout accepts advice and suggestions.
8 A Girl Scout smiles and sings under all difficulties.
9 A Girl Scout is thrifty.
10 A Girl Scout keeps herself pure in thoughts, words and deeds.

Motto
Be Prepared

Little Wing Promise
I promise to do everything possible to fulfil my duties to God and my country; to help others always, especially those at home; and to comply with the Law of the Pack.

Little Wing Law
A Little Wing obeys her elders.
A Little Wing does a daily good turn.

Little Wing Motto
Help everyone

Girl Scout

Little Wing

Age Groups

Mayor	Ranger	14-18
Guide Mediodía	Noon	12-13
Amanecer	Dawn	10-11
Alita	Little Wing	6-9

In 1962 the Association, renamed the Asociación Guías Scouts del Paraguay, received official recognition from the government.

Campus in Paraguay now have a new national camp headquarters, Nuestra Casita, which opened in 1991.

Development of the Movement in Paraguay

The first group of Girl Scouts in Paraguay, formed in 1923, was known as the Girl Scouts Brigade. The Association continued to develop well until 1938 when it was abolished.

Girl Scouting was reintroduced to Paraguay in 1959 when two separate initiatives were taken to establish activities. A group of Girl Scouts was started at the Escuela Normal Rural of San Lorenzo, and, at the same time, a training course for leaders was organized and participants later opened three Girl Scout companies.

After a visit to Paraguay by the Travelling Commissioner for the Western Hemisphere, a committee was set up, and in 1960 the Asociación de Niñas Guías Paraguayas was established.

The Programme

The Programme, created at national level, has the needs of the Paraguayan girl in mind. Activities include a range of crafts outdoor activities, homeskills training. They also focus on community service, international activities and training.

Training is carried out by volunteers and sessions for Leaders are held around three times per year for groups of ten to fifteen people. The organization is seeking more trainers and leaders in order to be able to expand its membership.

Working with the Community

The Paraguayan Girl Scouts Association places particular emphasis on community activities and encourages its members to participate in child health, sanitation, education and anti-drug addiction programmes. At present, the main programmes are directed to the "Preservation of the Environment", which includes albums about animals and plants on the verge of extinction.

Another project recently started is "Limpiemos Nuestra Ciudad" (Cleaning Our City), where each group looks after and cleans the public square in their neighbourhood or town. The work of these groups is supervised by the Girl Scouts, and at the National Camp, in January 1994, there will be prizes for the best team.

The Project "Nuestra Casita" (Our Little House), the headquarters of the Permanent Camp of the Asociación Guías Scouts del Paraguay, has been completed. The house, which is fully equipped, is ready for Girl Scout camps or recreational activities. The house has bedrooms, living room, kitchen, dining room, auditorium, bathrooms, changing room, swimming pool, hand ball and tennis courts, barbecue and a large open space.

In conjunction with the United Nations Department of Narcotics and the local Office of Drug Control the Association helps to combat drug addiction by organizing conferences in colleges, schools and among Girl Scouts.

Outdoor and Environmental Activities

The programme for each branch includes environmental preservation activities.

Training

The Asociación Guías Scouts del Paraguay holds regular training courses for leaders and patrol leaders, including one-day trainings.

Communication and Co-operation

Senior Girl Scouts, Young Adults and trainers participate in international trainings, camps and gatherings, in neighbouring countries.

The Asociación Guías Scouts del Paraguay informs the public about its activities, has good relations with the media, and publishes a monthly magazine on training and an annual newsletter.

It also co-operates with various organizations including the Ministry of Public Health, the Ministry of Agriculture, the National Council of Beneficial Entities, the national direction of Narcotics, the United Nations Narcotics Department and UNICEF.

Peru

Asociación Nacional de Guías Scouts del Perú

Girl Guiding/Girl Scouting introduced:	**1916**
Became Associate Member of WAGGGS:	**1960**
Became Full Member of WAGGGS:	**1963**
Membership 1992:	**2,349**
Membership as % of female population:	**0.02%**
WAGGGS Region:	**Western Hemisphere**

Guide

Promesa

Prometo por mi honor, hacer todo lo posible,
para cumplir mis deberes, para con Dios y mi Patria
Ayudar a mis semejantes en todo momento
y obedecer la Ley Guía.

Ley

1 Una Guía es responsable y digna de confianza.
2 Una Guía es leal.
3 Una Guía es útil.
4 Una Guía es amiga de todos y hermana de toda Guía.
5 Una Guía es cortés.
6 Una Guía protege a los animales y plantas y ve en la naturaleza la obra de Dios.
7 Una Guía es obediente.
8 Una Guía tiene valor y afronta con optimismo las dificultades.
9 Una Guía hace buen uso de su tiempo, es económica, cuida sus pertenencias y respeta las ajenas.
10 Una Guía es pura de pensamiento, palabra y obra.

Lema

Estar preparadas

Little Wing

Promesa de la Alita

Prometo hacer todo lo posible por cumplir mis deberes para con Dios y mi Patria.
Ayudar a otras personas, especialmente a los de mi casa.

Ley de la Alita

Una Alita es siempre activa, canta y sonríe ante las dificultades.
Una Alita piensa primero en los demás.

Lema de la Alita

Estar preparada

Promise

I promise on my honour, to do everything possible,
to fulfil my duties to God and my country;
to help other people at all times
and to obey the Guide Law.

Law

1 A Guide is responsible and is to be trusted.
2 A Guide is loyal.
3 A Guide is useful.
4 A Guide is a friend to all and a sister to all other Guides.
5 A Guide is courteous.
6 A Guide protects animals and plants and sees in nature the work of God.
7 A Guide is obedient.
8 A Guide is courageous and faces difficulties with optimism.
9 A Guide makes good use of her time and is thrifty; she takes care of her belongings and respects those of others.
10 A Guide is pure in thought, word and deed.

Motto

Be Prepared

Little Wing Promise

I promise to do everything possible to do my duty to God and my country;
to help other people especially those at home.

Little Wing Law

A Little Wing is always alert, she sings and smiles under difficulties.
A Little Wing thinks first of others.

Little Wing Motto

Give help

Age Groups

Guía de Servicio	Service Guide	18-25
Guía Mayor	Ranger	14-17
Guía Intermedia	Guide	10-13
Alita	Little Wing	7-9

Development of the Movement in Peru

Girl Guiding/Girl Scouting has existed in Peru since 1916, but it was not until 1945 that the National Association was set up under the sponsorship of the Ministry of Education. With the help of the WAGGGS Travelling Commissioner for the Western Hemisphere, activities were reorganized in 1953 and an autonomous Association was formed which was officially recognized by the Ministry of Education and chartered by Congress.

The Programme

Members of all four age groups have been instrumental in the planning of programmes in accordance with their needs and wishes. Service has been intensified, and trainings, round tables and discussions have been held on various aspects of Girl Guiding/Girl Scouting.

Working with the Community

The Asociación Nacional de Guías Scouts del Perú trains specialized teams to serve in national emergencies. The Association has an agreement of co-operation with the Government's Civil Defence Department which has led to this active participation in preparation for national disasters.

Other service teams are formed in the areas of health, nutrition, vaccination and recreation in poor areas. The Association has carried out programmes on nutrition, literacy, bio-gardens and local crafts in marginal areas. It also runs a child health project in nutrition and co-operates actively with CEDRO, the youth drug prevention institute.

The Castellana Guide Centre carries out numerous programmes including service projects and the Association co-operates with Ponle Corazón, a fundraising committee, to help pay expenses for poor children who have contracted cancer. The Association also organizes Health Promoter courses to teach members how to implement health projects within the community.

A four-year maternal and child health project was run with financial assistance from Danish Guides and Scouts which met its objectives and proved invaluable to community members. Proof of this is that it now subsists on an almost self-sufficient basis. Facilities include a programme for undernourished infants and a mothers' club which offers classes on nutrition and craftwork.

Outdoor and Environmental Activities

From 1987 to 1990 the Association focused on a tree-planting project and a campaign to improve the atmosphere, fight noise, eliminate rubbish heaps and conserve natural resources.

Collecting papers for a recycling project is part of a focused campaign to eliminate rubbish heaps.

Training

The Association organizes nationwide trainings at all levels.

Communication and Co-operation

Peru arranges programmes with other Member Organizations, welcomes Girl Guides/Girl Scouts from abroad and attends WAGGGS events.

The Asociación Nacional de Guías Scouts del Perú informs the general public about its activities through occasional television and radio interviews, and disseminates general information on special projects through the press.

The Association is regularly represented at meetings organized in the country by the United Nations' Development Programme and other United Nations agencies. Since the United Nations' resolution establishing the Decade for Women (1976-1985), the Association has participated in all related activities organized at national level. It has also carried out a training in leadership for women in co-ordination with the Commission of Women of the Organization of American States.

Philippines

Girl Scouts of the Philippines

Girl Guiding/Girl Scouting introduced: 1919
Became Associate Member of WAGGGS: 1946
Became Full Member of WAGGGS: 1948
Membership 1992: 1,250,928
Membership as % of female population: 4.16%
WAGGGS Region: Asia Pacific

Ang Pangako ng Girl Scout
Sa aking karangalan, gagampanan ko ang aking tungkulin sa Diyos at sa aking bayan; tutulong ako sa aking kapwa sa lahat ng pagkakataon at isasabuhay ko ang Batas ng Girl Scout.

Ang Batas ng Girl Scout
1 Ang Girl Scout ay mapagkakatiwalaan.
2 Ang Girl Scout ay matapat.
3 Ang Girl Scout ay matulungin.
4 Ang Girl Scout ay kaibigan ng lahat at kapatid ng bawa't Girl Scout.
5 Ang Girl Scout ay mapitagan.
6 Ang Girl Scout ay magalang sa lahat ng may buhay.
7 Ang Girl Scout ay disiplinado.
8 Ang Girl Scout ay may sariling paninindigan.
9 Ang Girl Scout ay matipid.
10 Ang Girl Scout ay malinis sa isip, sa salita at sa gawa.

Girl Scout

Motto
Laging Handa

Ang Pangako ng Star Scout
Ipinangangako ko na sisikapin kong:
Ibigin ang Diyos at ang aking bansa:
Tumulong sa ibang tao araw-araw,
lalung-lalo na sa mga kasama sa bahay.

Junior Scout

Ang Batas ng Star Scout
Ang Star Scout ay matapat.
Ang Star Scout ay masunurin.

Star Scout Motto
Maging matulungin

Star Scout Slogan
Magpaligaya ng kapwa araw-araw.

Star Scout

Promise
On my honour,
I will do my duty
to God and my country
to help other people at all times
and to live by the Girl Scout Law.

Law
1 A Girl Scout's honour is to be trusted
2 A Girl Scout is loyal.
3 A Girl Scout is helpful.
4 A Girl Scout is a friend to all and a sister to every other Girl Scout.
5 A Girl Scout is courteous.
6 A Girl Scout respects living things.
7 A Girl Scout is disciplined.
8 A Girl Scout is self-reliant.
9 A Girl Scout is thrifty.
10 A Girl Scout is clean in thought, word and deed.

Motto
Be Prepared

The Senior Girl Scout Pledge
(Recited after the Promise)
My special responsibility as a Senior Girl Scout is to render service by taking the Promise out into a wider world.

Star Scout Promise
I promise to do my best:
To help God and my country;
To help other people everyday; especially those at home.

Star Scout Law
A Star Scout is truthful.
A Star Scout is obedient.

Star Scout Motto
Lend a Hand

Star Scout Slogan
Make someone happy every day.

The Twinkler Promise

I love God, my country and people around me.
(Mahal ko ang Diyos, ang aking bayan at lahat ng tao sa aking paligid.)

The Twinkler Law

A Twinkler is cheerful, kind and helpful.
(Ang Twinkler ay masaya, mabait at matulungin.)

Age Groups

Cadet Scout	15-21
Senior Scout	12-15
Junior Scout	9-12
Star Scout	6-9
Twinkler Scout	4-6

Development of the Movement in the Philippines

Girl Scouting in the Philippines began as early as 1918, but it was not until 1939 that the Girl Scout Movement was formally launched. In 1940 Girl Scouts of the Philippines was chartered as a national organization.

The first national Girl Scouts' rally and the first leaders' training conference were held in 1941, and during the Second World War, although the Association suspended its activities, Girl Scout leaders committed themselves to service to victims and prisoners of war. After the war, the leaders set about rebuilding the Association and received much public support.

A National Council Convention, held every three years, is the Association's highest consultative and deliberative body which serves as a forum for guidelines, policies and directions. The 15th National Council Convention held in 1991 had the theme "Building Tomorrow on Today's Realities."

The Programme

The Association has created an outreach programme to integrate disabled members into units and to organize special committees to start Girl Scouting in small villages in depressed areas.
The Programme started with 11 programme fields in 1940, then was changed into the Nine Programme Emphases in 1968. Special projects on Six Golden Opportunities were added from 1988 to 1991 in observance of its 50th year.

A revised programme called the Eight-point Challenge took effect in July 1993. It focuses on well-being, family life, heritage and citizenship, world community, preparedness, economic self-sufficiency, arts and environment.

Working with the Community

The Girl Scouts of the Philippines' Chief Girl Scout Medal Scheme gives national recognition to girls who have completed year-long community development projects in the following areas: education, conservation, agriculture, preservation and promotion of Philippine culture, tourism and health.

Girl Scouts campaign to stop air pollution.

Girl Scouts of the Philippines undertakes a wide range of community projects including food production, health and sanitation, drug abuse prevention and anti-littering campaigns. The Association also gives service to disaster victims and low-income families.

Girl Scouts responded to the devastating earthquake which hit the Philippines in 1990 by raising funds for reconstruction projects in the Luzon Provinces, overseen by the Association. During the eruption of the Mount Pinatubo volcano in 1991, Girl Scouts of the Philippines undertook the Tulong-Bata service project to help child victims. The Project is in its third year operating in the lava-buried communities within a 20 km radius of the volcano and increases with every year's rainy season. The Department of Social Services recognized this as a significant contribution to the national rehabilitation programme.

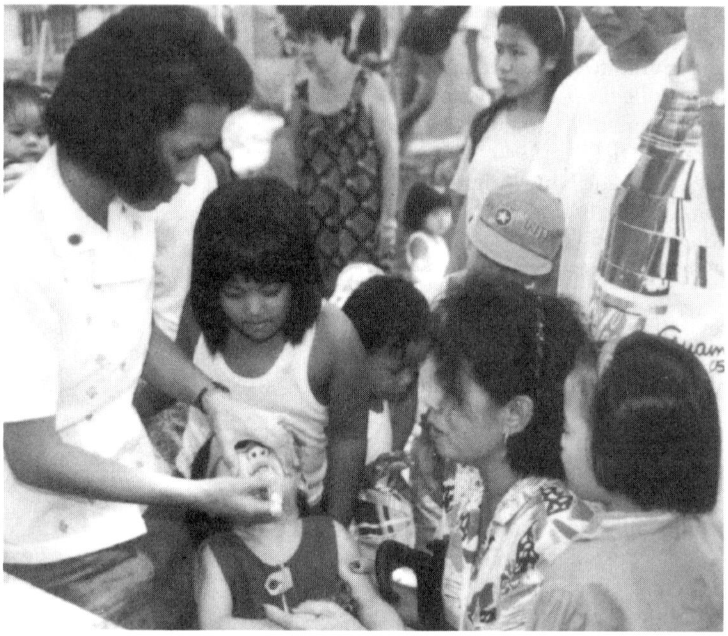

Girl Scouts work to immunize children during National Immunization Day.

The Tulong-Bata service project was extended to the Mount Mayon area after the 1993 eruption.

Outdoor and Environmental Activities

The Association runs six training and camping centres which are open all year round. Many councils have also established campsites, and a comprehensive camping programme is provided for girls at local, regional and national level. A national encampment is organized by the Association every triennium and Girl Guide/Girl Scout Associations from the Asia Pacific Region are invited.

Environmental preservation is a major concern and is integrated into almost all activities. Many Girl Scouts in the Philippines are involved in beautification and environmental activities such as tree-planting and information campaigns.

Training

The Association runs a continuous training programme at national, regional and council level. Courses are designed to meet the needs of girls, volunteers and professionals. National and regional training sessions are conducted annually on subjects such as administration, advanced amateur radio communications and camp management. The Association has sent trainers on exchange programmes to other Member Organizations within the Asia Pacific Region. A National Trainers' Conference Workshop is held annually to provide trainers with professional skills and to help them to cope effectively with the changing times.

Communication and Co-operation

The Association encourages international contacts whenever possible and Girl Scouts regularly participate in international events, visits to World Centres and post box exchanges.

From 1987 to 1990, a three-year scholarship programme, co-sponsored by the Girl Scouts of the USA, enabled 15 professional workers to train at Edith Macy Convention centre in the USA.

Girl Scouts of the Philippines publishes a quarterly magazine, *The Girl Scout*. The Association utilizes the media to inform the public about its activities and local councils publicize their activities through newsletters and radio programmes making use of the Junior Journalist Guild and Radio-Television Clubs.

Girl Scouts of the Philippines co-operates with UNICEF, Boy Scouts of the Philippines and other non-governmental organizations. It also has a working relationship with the Department of Social Services and Development, the Department of Environment and National Resources, the Department of Health and the Department of Education, Culture and Sports.

Portugal

Associação Guias de Portugal

Girl Guiding/Girl Scouting introduced: 1919
Became Associate Member of WAGGGS: 1963
Became Full Member of WAGGGS: 1975
Membership 1992: 7,483
Membership as % of female population: 0.14%
WAGGGS Region: Europe

Promessa
Prometo sob minha honra e com a ajuda de Deus, fazer o possível por:
- Cumprir os meus deveres para com Deus e a Pátria.
- Ajudar o próximo em todas as ocasiões e obedecer à Lei das Guias.

Lei
1 O sentimento de honra da Guia é sagrado, a sua palavra merece toda a confiança.
2 A Guia é leal.
3 A Guia é útil e pratica diàriamente uma Boa Acção.
4 A Guia é amiga de todos e irmã de todas Guías.
5 A Guia é atenciosa e delicada.
6 A Guia vê a obra de Deus na natureza e protege as plantas e os animais.
7 A Guia é obediente.
8 A Guia tem sempre boa disposição de espírito.
9 A Guia é económica, amiga do arranjo e da ordem e respeitadora do bem alheio.
10 A Guia é pura em pensamentos, palavras e acções.

Motto
Sempre Alerta

Promessa – Little Bird
Prometo fazer o possível por:
Cumprir os meus deveres para com Deus e a Pátria ajudar sempre o próximo, especialmente todos em minha casa.

Lei – Little Bird
A Avesinha é obediente.
A Avesinha anda sempre limpa e arranjada.
A Avesinha está sempre alegre.
A Avesinha diz sempre a verdade.

Motto – Little Bird
A Avesinha ajuda sempre

Promise
I promise, on my honour and with God's help:
To do my duty to God and Country.
To help other people at all times.
To obey the Guide Law.

Law
1 A Guide's honour is sacred .. and her word worthy of complete trust.
2 A Guide is loyal.
3 A Guide is useful and does a Good Deed every day.
4 A Guide is a friend to all and a sister to every other Guide.
5 A Guide is kind and courteous.
6 A Guide sees the hand of God in Nature and protects plants and animals.
7 A Guide is obedient.
8 A Guide is always cheerful.
9 A Guide is thrifty, likes good order and respects the property of others.
10 A Guide is pure in thought, word and deed.

Motto
Be Prepared

Little Bird Promise
I promise to do my best:
To do my duty to God and country and to help others, especially those at home.

Little Bird Law
A Little Bird is obedient.
A Little Bird is always clean and tidy.
A Little Bird is cheerful.
A Little Bird always tells the truth.

Guide

Little Bird

Little Bird Motto
A Little Bird always helps

Age Groups

Guia Moinho	Ranger	17+
Guia Caravela	Junior	14-17
Guia Aventura	Guide	10-14
Avesinha	Little Bird	6-10

Development of the Movement in Portugal

Guiding in Portugal began in 1919 when the first Guide companies were started in Oporto. The Movement later spread to Lisbon, and in 1930 Brownie packs and Guide companies were established on the island of Madeira. The Association became a recognized national Movement in 1934, but by 1938 all Guiding activities had been suspended because of political unrest. Only the Madeira Region was able to keep the flame alive, which helped the Association resume activities in 1952. In 1991 the Association celebrated its 60th anniversary as a single-sex organization open to all girls and young women.

The Programme
The programme is common to all age groups and is adapted to suit the level of the girls' development, and the needs of the different localities.

Working with the Community
The Associação Guías de Portugal has introduced projects to alleviate the problems of migrants including a resettlement and re-education programme for people returning home to Portugal to enable them to overcome illiteracy, drug abuse and problems caused by disabilities. Guides also give girls and women lessons in cooking, handicrafts, sewing and other basic skills.

In 1992 the Senior Patrol (Windmills) – Poney Patrol received the Olave Award for their work with refugees.

Outdoor and Environmental Activities
Camping is a popular activity among members of the Association in Portugal. In addition, in 1990 Guides were involved in an environmental project 'Protection of Nature' which focused on the protection and maintenance of protected areas.

Training
In order to meet the need for new leaders, the Association has made training a priority. It runs training camps, correspondence training courses for leaders in remote places, weekend trainings and an annual training.

Communication and Co-operation
Members attend international gatherings and seminars abroad whenever possible, and maintain contact with other Girl Guides/Girl Scouts through participation in Jamborees-on-the-Air.

Recently the Association has been working with São Tomé e Principe to help start Guiding there. Efforts have been met with enthusiasm and the Association hopes to provide assistance until S. Tomé can become a member of WAGGGs.

The Association publicizes its work through displays at conferences and fairs as well as through its newsletter, *O Trevo* (The Trefoil).

The Association co-operates with the Scout Association, the World Health Organization and the Secretaria de Estado de Familia, and is a member of the Portuguese National Youth Council.

Portuguese Guides meet girls from São Tomé e Principe.

Romania

Asociatia Fetelor Ghizi Din Romania

Girl Guiding/Girl Scouting Introduced: 1928
Became Associate Member of WAGGGS: 1993
Membership 1992: 328
WAGGGS Region: Europe

Promisiunea Ghizilor
Promit din tot sufletul să slu-jesc pe Dumnezeu si tara, să a jut pe ceilalti oameni în orice moment, să respect Legea Ghizilor / în functie de credintá.

Legea Ghizilor
1 Intr-o Ghidă poti avea întotdeauna încredere.
2 O Ghidă este cinstită.
3 O Ghidă trebuie să fie de folos celor din jur.
4 O Ghidă este prietena tuturor si sora celorlalte fete Ghizi.
5 O Ghidă se respectă pe sine, îi respectă pe ceilalti si se poartă politicos.
6 O Ghidă iubeste natura si o protejează.
7 O Ghidă este ascultătoare.
8 O Ghidă înfruntă greutătile cîntînd si surîzînd.
9 O Ghidă are grijă de bunurile personale si de cele comúne.
10 O Ghidă este pură în gînd, cuvînt si faptă.

Motto
Fi pregatită

Flower Promise
Promit din tot sufletul să fiu credincioasă lui Dumnezeu si tarii, să a jut pe cei din jurul meu si să respect Legea Florilor.

Flower Law
O Floare este veselă si ascultătoare, nu se gîndeste numai la ea si îi iubeste pe ceilalti.

Flower Motto
Dă mîna

Promise
On my honour, I Promise that I will do my best:

1 To do my duty to God and my country; (according to one's creed)
2 To help other people at all times;
3 To obey the Guide Law.

Law
1 A Guide's honour is to be trusted.
2 A Guide is loyal.
3 A Guide's duty is to be useful and to help others.
4 A Guide is a friend to all and a sister to every other Guide.
5 A Guide is courteous.
6 A Guide loves nature and protects it.
7 A Guide is obedient.
8 A Guide meets difficulties singing and smiling.
9 A Guide is thrifty.
10 A Guide is pure in thought, in word and in deed.

Motto
Be prepared.

Flower Promise
I heartily promise to be faithful to God and my country, to help my fellow men and to observe the Flower Law.

Flower Law
A Flower is cheerful and listens well, she doesn't think only of herself, and loves others.

Flower Motto
Lend a hand.

Age Groups

Seniors	14-18
Guides	11-14
Flowers	7-11

Guide

Flower

Development of the Movement in Romania

Girl Guiding existed in Romania between 1928 and 1938 but activities then ceased and contact was lost. In 1989, following political change in Romania, and on the initiative of Girl Guiding friends in Greece, a group of friends all interested in giving service to the community, formed a committee to start Girl Guiding in the country.

Early in 1990 representatives of the Greek Girl Guides Association visited Romania and met with this committee, introduced them to Girl Guiding and helped them to set up a structure. In the same year WAGGGS representatives travelled to Romania to offer support and participate in the first training for leaders. Following the training four groups were created.

The Asociatia Fetelor Ghizi Din Romania (The Association of Girl Guides of Romania) was established towards the end of 1990 and Guiding gradually grew. During 1992 the Greek Girl Guides Association continued to work closely with Romania, carrying out training sessions and helping the national team create Guide companies and Brownie packs.

The Programme

The programme aims to train girls and young women to become responsible citizens. It focuses on respect for the individual, the family, society and the environment and on developing friendships, team work and service.

A new "Flower" is greeted with an especially warm welcome to the Movement.

Working with the Community

A troop of Guides aged 14-18 visited an orphanage and an old people's home in December 1992 to sing carols and give the children oranges. They had raised the money for the oranges and candles by singing in people's homes. With the remaining money they took 30 orphans to the puppet theatre on a Sunday. Since 1992 the Association has begun weekly visits to a girls' orphanage in Bucharest.

Outdoor and Environmental Activities

The Association has been organizing day trips out of town and big games in parks; they focus on knowledge and protection of the environment.

Training

The Training Commissioner is responsible for the organization of trainings. A preliminary training programme in 1992, run with the help of the Greek Girl Guides Association, resulted in seven newly qualified trainers. In July 1993 the Association organized a training session, with international participation, in Mangalia, which was aimed at leaders and setting up a programme in Mangalia.

Communication and Co-operation

The Association makes every effort to ensure that Guiding is better known within society, schools, government and non-governmental organizations.

Contact is maintained with the Scout Association and with religious and civil authorities as well as with other organizations involved in youth work. Representatives from the Association have participated in programmes organized by UNICEF and UNESCO. The Association works closely with the Ministry of Youth and Sport and the Ministry of Education and Science.

The international dimension plays a major part in the Association. The opportunity to travel extended to several young leaders by other European Associations has been a help and stimulus to all.

A few simple, inexpensive publications have been produced.

Rwanda

Association des Guides du Rwanda

Girl Guiding/Girl Scouting introduced:	**1962**
Became Associate Member of WAGGGS:	**1981**
Membership 1992:	**8,460**
Membership as % of female population:	**0.23%**
WAGGGS Region:	**Africa**

Promesse
Sur mon honneur et avec la grâce de Dieu je promets de faire de mon mieux pour servir Dieu et mon pays, aider les autres en tout temps et observer la loi guide.

Loi
1 La guide n'a qu'une parole.
2 La guide est loyale.
3 La guide se rend utile et aide les autres.
4 La guide est l'amie de tous et la soeur de toute autre guide.
5 La guide est polie.
6 La guide aime et respecte la nature.
7 La guide obéit joyeusement et ne fait rien à moitié.
8 La guide est courageuse et de bonne humeur.
9 La guide est économe et respecte le bien d'autrui.
10 La guide est simple et pure.

Devise
Toujours prête

Promesse Bergeronnette
Je promets d'être fidèle à Dieu, à mes parents, à la loi de la Ronde, et de faire chaque jour un Bon Tour.

Loi Bergeronnette
La Bergeronnette écoute les Grands Oiseaux. La Bergeronnette ne s'écoute pas elle-même.

Devise Bergeronnette
De Notre Mieux

Promise
On my honour and with God's help,
I promise to do my best
To serve God and my country
To help others at all times and
To keep the Guide Law.

Guide

Law
1 A Guide keeps her word.
2 A Guide is loyal.
3 A Guide makes herself useful and helps others.
4 A Guide is a friend to all and a sister to every other Guide.
5 A Guide is polite.
6 A Guide loves and respects nature.
7 A Guide obeys joyfully and does nothing by halves.
8 A Guide is courageous and good-tempered.
9 A Guide is thrifty and respects other people's belongings.
10 A Guide is unaffected and pure.

Motto
Always prepared

Wagtail Promise
I promise to be faithful to God, to my parents, to the Law of the Pack, and to do a Good Turn every day.

Wagtail

Wagtail Law
The Wagtail listens to the fully fledged birds. The Wagtail does not pay too much attention to herself.

Wagtail Motto
The best we can

Age Groups

Eclaireuse	Ranger	17+
Guide	Guide	13-16
Bergeronnette	Wagtail	6-12

Development of the Movement in Rwanda

Guiding in Rwanda began in 1962 with the help of members of the Guides Catholiques de Belgique, but, through lack of support from local leaders, interest in the Movement dwindled after independence later that year. In 1967 Guiding was revived as a branch of the Scout Association.

The Girl Guides set up their own organization, the Fédération des Guides du Rwanda, in 1972, with a national team responsible for administration. The Federation was composed of two Associations, the Association des Guides Catholiques and the Association des Guides Protestantes.

A special dance created for Thinking Day.

A proposal was made in 1974 to form a single Association, and this idea was accepted two years later by the first National Assembly. In 1977 the Constitution was accepted at a general meeting, a permanent national team was appointed, and a work plan was drawn up. The Association des Guides du Rwanda received official government recognition in 1980.

The Programme

A WAGGGS trainer spent five months in Rwanda in 1979 and helped to improve the Association's programme, which involves a wide range of activities designed to assist girls to develop character and civic responsibility, and to get involved in community service. Specific themes and practical training have been developed for each age group.

Working with the Community

Members of the Association undertake community service and development projects, including work in such areas as literacy, primary health care, vaccination, nutrition, hygiene and handicrafts. In the Butare region the Girl Guides of Ruramba run a small agricultural co-operative with a farm and craft studio. Members also carry out projects with the disabled.

Improving the lives and prospects of street girls has become a major programme initiative in Rwanda. In 1990 the Association launched several projects to give girls who fail to profit from school education the chance to learn vocational skills. The main project is run from the Association's headquarters in Kigali where some 50 girls attend classes in singing, literacy, craftwork, gardening and baking. Rwanda Girl Guides Association also runs vocational projects in rural areas for street girls.

Outdoor and Environmental Activities

Camping is a popular activity among members of the Movement in Rwanda. Guides demonstrate their concern for the environment through involvement in re-afforestation projects and conservation of the rural environment.

Training

The training programme is prepared by the training commissioner in conjunction with the training team. Rwanda has one full-time trainer and trainings take place at local, regional and national level. Local training takes the form of short camps and reflection weekends, and regional training is carried out at five-day camps.

Communication and Co-operation

Leaders from Rwanda have attended events at Our Chalet, and have participated in events hosted by other Member Organizations. The Association has co-operated with other Girl Guide/ Girl Scout organizations on specific projects: Denmark has supported water projects through the WAGGGS Mutual Aid Scheme; Germany and Luxembourg, a school leaver project; and Belgium the construction of a Guide office and community centre.

The Association informs the general public of its activities through newspapers, the radio, celebrations for Thinking Day, and events such as dance displays and exhibitions of members' handicrafts. It also publishes a quarterly magazine called *Inganzamarumbo* (Expansion of Guiding).

The Association has been recognized by the Episcopal Conference in Rwanda and leaders participate in meetings of organizations concerned with young people and Catholic action.

Saint Christopher and Nevis

The Girl Guides Association of Saint Christopher and Nevis

Girl Guiding/Girl Scouting introduced:	**1931**
Became Associate Member of WAGGGS:	**1993**
Membership 1991:	**436**
Membership as % of female population:	**2%**
WAGGGS Region:	**Western Hemisphere**

Promise

I promise that I will do my best;
To do my duty to God
To serve the Queen and help other people
and To keep the Guide Law.

Law

A Guide is loyal and can be trusted
A Guide is helpful
A Guide is polite and considerate
A Guide is friendly and a sister to all Guides
A Guide is kind to animals and respects all living things
A Guide is obedient
A Guide has courage and is cheerful in all difficulties
A Guide makes good use of her time
A Guide takes care of her possessions and those of other people
A Guide is self-controlled in all she thinks, says and does.

Age Groups

Rangers	16-18
Guides	11-15
Brownies	7-10

Development of the Movement in Saint Christopher and Nevis

Until 1991 the Girl Guides Association of St Christopher (St Kitts) and the Girl Guides Association of St Nevis were two separate Branch Associations of The Girl Guides Association (United Kingdom). The Movement was introduced in St Kitts in 1931 when four Guide groups were opened in Basseterre. Guiding in Nevis started at the instigation of a teacher from the United Kingdom. The first Ranger company was opened in 1963.

Over the years, with the help of trainers from the Girl Guides Association, United Kingdom, the Girl Guides Associations of St Kitts and of Nevis worked hard to establish themselves in larger towns and some of the villages. In 1989 the two Associations decided to become Members

Brownies on the steps of the Guide headquarters.

of WAGGGS and, as a first step, worked towards becoming one National Organization. In 1991 The Girl Guides Association, United Kingdom sealed a Deed of Transfer making both Branch Associations independent and at the 60th Jubilee celebrations of the Girl Guides Association of St Kitts the two Associations joined to become one entity.

The Programme

The programme aims to give girls the opportunity for self-training in the development of character and service. It is based on the eight-point programme of the Girl Guides Association, United Kingdom and adapted to suit local needs. It enables girls to develop physical fitness, the mind, out of doors enjoyment, homecraft skills, service to others, human relations, creativity and character.

Working with the Community

Community service is an essential part of the programme and projects are carried out by individual companies. Guides visit hospitals and childrens' homes where they distribute toys, books and food packets and entertain the residents. They also help senior citizens by running errands and carrying water.

Outdoor and Environmental Activities

Camping is a popular activity and each pack or company organizes its own camp. The Association held a camp focusing on the environment in 1993.

Training

Three trainers are responsible for overseeing the training programme and a few hours of the monthly leaders' meetings are devoted to training.

Communication and Co-operation

The Association has participated in activities organized by the Caribbean Link of Guiding and attended camps and other activities in neighbouring islands as well as in the United Kingdom.

The Association is well respected by the government and the general public. Relations with the churches very good and individual groups often participate in church activities.

In 1991 the Guides and Brownies participated in a Radio Programme, 'Youth in Action'. Since then the Association has participated regularly in the programme, which is broadcast every three months.

The Association is represented on the Alcoholics Anonymous Committee and has been invited to serve on a steering committee working towards the establishment of a National Committee on Drug Abuse.

Saint Lucia

Girl Guides Association of Saint Lucia

Girl Guiding/Girl Scouting introduced: 1925
Became Associate Member of WAGGGS: 1984
Membership 1992†: 1,543
Membership as % of female population: 2%
WAGGGS Region: Western Hemisphere

Promise
I promise that I will do my best
To do my duty to God
To serve the Queen and my country and help other people and
To keep the Guide Law.

Law
1 A Guide is loyal and can be trusted.
2 A Guide is helpful.
3 A Guide is polite and considerate.
4 A Guide is friendly and a sister to all Guides.
5 A Guide is kind to animals and respects all living things.
6 A Guide is obedient.
7 A Guide has courage and is cheerful in all difficulties.
8 A Guide makes good use of her time.
9 A Guide takes care of her own possessions and those of other people.
10 A Guide is self-controlled in all she thinks, says and does.

Motto
Be Prepared

Brownie Guide Promise
I promise I will do my best:
To do my duty to God
To serve the Queen and my Country and help other people and
To keep the Brownie Guide Law.

Brownie Guide Law
A Brownie Guide thinks of others before herself and does a good turn every day.

Brownie Guide Motto
Lend a Hand

Age Groups

Ranger	15-19+
Guide	10-16
Brownie Guide	7-11

Guide

Development of the Movement in Saint Lucia

The first Guide company in Saint Lucia was started in the capital, Castries, in 1925. In 1926 the Association was registered as a Branch Association of The Girl Guides Association (United Kingdom).

During the early years the headquarters moved several times until, in 1931, the government gave the Association two rooms in the lodge at the botanical gardens in Castries. Building improvements began with a ceremony in 1964 during a visit from the World Chief Guide and work was completed in 1965.

In 1979 Saint Lucia became politically independent and in October 1983 The Girl Guides Association (United Kingdom) signed a Deed of Transfer making the Girl Guides Association of Saint Lucia self-governing in all areas of work.

The Programme
The programme is based on an eight-point programme which gives Guides opportunities to develop physical fitness, the mind, outdoor enjoyment, homecraft skills, service to others, human relations, creativity and character. A general programme is prepared annually by the Executive Committee.

Brownie Guide

Working with the Community
Community service is a major part of the programme and members help in institutions, hospitals and the homes of the housebound, as well as running libraries in schools. Guides participate in national disaster relief projects and in the past have distributed food and clothing to victims of hurricane and fire damage.

Outdoor Activities
Handicrafts are a popular activity at the biennial camps organized by the Association and many articles are made from the raw materials available naturally on the island.

Training
The Association has a team of six members responsible for training. Trainers from The Girl Guides Association (United Kingdom) have given much valuable training assistance and the Association is also supported by specialists from the Red Cross Society and the local police force.

Communication and Co-operation
Saint Lucia is a member of the Caribbean Link, set up for the purpose of consultation and mutual aid among Guide Associations in the Commonwealth countries and islands of the Caribbean. The Association maintains international contacts through visits from members of other Girl Guide/Girl Scout Associations. Contact with neighbouring islands is maintained through camps and joint trainings.

The community holds the Association in high respect and its relationship with the government is good. Schools have been encouraged to promote Guiding as part of an educational plan. The Association works closely with religious authorities, and members participate in monthly church parades.

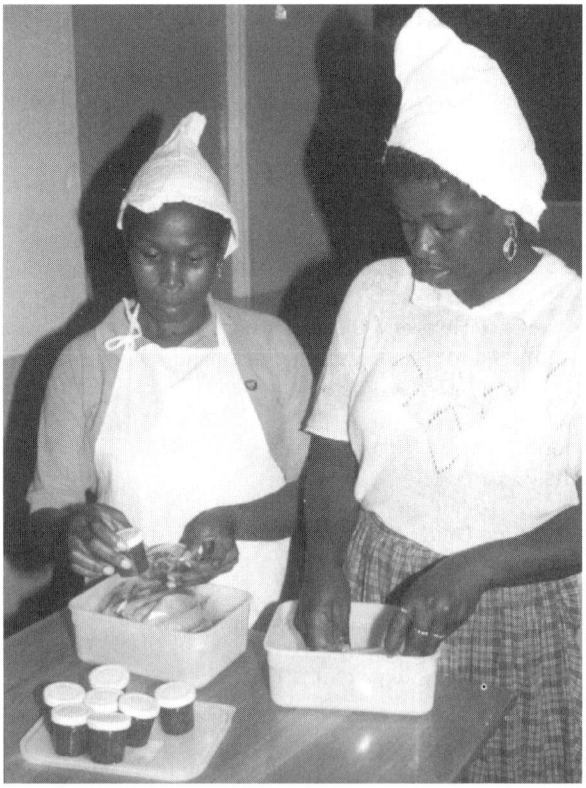

Guides sort out packets to help in institutions – part of community service.

Saint Vincent and the Grenadines

Girl Guides Association of Saint Vincent and the Grenadines

Girl Guiding/Girl Scouting introduced:	**1914**
Became Associate Member of WAGGGS:	**1984**
Became Full Member of WAGGGS:	**1987**
Membership 1992:	**1,240**
Membership as % of female population:	**2.11%**
WAGGGS Region:	**Western Hemisphere**

Promise
I promise that I will do my best:
To do my duty to God;
To serve the Queen and my country
To help other people; and
To keep the Guide Law.

Law
1 A Guide is loyal and can be trusted.
2 A Guide is helpful.
3 A Guide is polite and considerate.
4 A Guide is friendly and a sister to all Guides.
5 A Guide is kind to animals and respects all living things.
6 A Guide is obedient.
7 A Guide has courage and is cheerful in all difficulties.
8 A Guide makes good use of her time.
9 A Guide takes care of her own possessions and those of other people.
10 A Guide is self-controlled in all she thinks, says and does.

Motto
Be Prepared

Brownie Guide Promise
I promise I will do my best:
To do my duty to God
To serve the Queen and my country
and help other people; and
To keep the Brownie Guide Law.

Brownie Guide Law
A Brownie Guide thinks of others before herself and does a good turn every day.

Brownie Guide Motto
Lend a Hand

Age Groups

Ranger	16-19
Guide	$10\frac{1}{2}$-16
Brownie Guide	7-11
Bim-Bim	5-7

Guide

Development of the Movement in Saint Vincent and the Grenadines

Guiding was first introduced in Saint Vincent in 1914 by a Methodist Minister from England and Guide Companies were established in Georgetown and neighbouring South Rivers. Unfortunately the Movement became dormant in the area after the First World War but was restarted again in 1927 in the capital, Kingstown, the new company being registered at Commonwealth Headquarters (United Kingdom) in 1928.

Guiding spread to other towns and later to villages; the first Brownie and Ranger Units were started in 1931. By 1934 the Movement had spread to the Grenadines island of Bequia.

Brownie Guide

In 1983 the Girl Guides Association (United Kingdom) signed a deed of transfer giving the Girl Guides Association of Saint Vincent and the Grenadines self-government in all areas of work.

The Programme
The current programme used in Saint Vincent and the Grenadines was

introduced in 1985 and is based on the development of the individual, the acquisition of skills, the world around us and service.

Working with the Community

Members of the Association are encouraged to undertake service projects. Guides help at child care centres and a school for children with special needs where a unit has been started. They visit and help the elderly and the housebound, entertain the underprivileged and regularly give service in a children's ward of the General Hospital.

Guides are prepared to help out in the event of natural disasters and have taken part in an air disaster simulation exercise organized by the Royal Saint Vincent Police Force.

Outdoor and Environmental Activities

In May 1992 Rangers and Guides participated in the Shell Environment Regional Project. They chose the theme Reduce, Re-Use, Re-Cycle. The Guides were placed second and the Rangers were first in their respective age groups.

Guides and Rangers from Saint Vincent and the Grenadines display the coveted first prize they won in the Caribbean Link Challenge, 1993.

In May 1993 Rangers and Guides also participated in the Caribbean Link Challenge which was aimed at making participants more aware of their culture and surroundings as well as the history and purpose of Guiding. The Guides' presentation of Flora, Fauna and Music earned them the coveted first prize.

Training

The training team, under the Chairmanship of the Training Adviser, is responsible for training all leaders and regularly conducts training sessions at national and district level. A yearly residential training for leaders is also conducted by local trainers and Caribbean Link trainers. Trainers attend conferences and training events organized by the Caribbean Link Training Committee.

Communication and Co-operation

Saint Vincent and the Grenadines has been represented at many international events in the Caribbean, the United Kingdom, the USA and Mexico. The Association has also welcomed many members of the Movement from other countries to the islands and its first international camp, Camp Yourumei, was held in 1988.

Saint Vincent and the Grenadines is a member of the Caribbean Link, set up for the purpose of training and mutual aid among Guide Associations of the Caribbean. It also maintains close ties with Hampshire West (UK) Girl Guides Association. A contingent of two Guiders, five Rangers and six Guides have been invited by the Hampshire West Girl Guides to share in their International Camp Discovery '93 to be held from 6th to 15th August. They will be hosted by the Hampshire Girl Guides after the camp.

The Association has always been an accepted part of the community. The Guides receive much help and support from both church and state, as well as the local media and take part in many national events, including parades.

San Marino

Associazione Guide Esploratori Cattolici Sammarinesi

Girl Guiding/Girl Scouting introduced: 1973
Became Associate Member of WAGGGS: 1993
Membership 1992: 122
Membership as % of female population: 1.08%
WAGGGS Region: Europe

Guide

Promise
With the help of God I promise on my honour to do my best:
to do my duty towards God and towards my country;
to help others at any time;
to observe the Guide Law.

Law
Guides:
- place their honour in deserving trust
- are loyal
- make themselves useful and help others
- are everyone's friends and all other Guides' and Scouts' sisters and brothers
- are courteous
- love and respect nature
- are obedient
- smile and sing even in the face of hardship
- are hard-working and thrifty
- are pure in thought, word and deed.

Age Groups

Rangers	16-21
Guides	12-15
Brownies	7-11

Development of the Movement in San Marino

When Boy Scouting was introduced to San Marino in 1973, the benefits the Movement offered to young people were apparent. With the help of the Associazione Guide E Scouts Cattolici Italiani (AGESCI) a Girl Guide Unit, made up of a Guide Patrol and a Brownie Circle, was opened in 1974. Soon after, the merged Association, now known as Associazione Guide Esploratori Cattolici Sammarinesi (AGECSI) was set up. From 1974 to 1987 all Guides were part of WAGGGS through AGESCI, paying their quota to WAGGGS through the Italian Association.

Guiding continued to grow and in 1976 a mixed Ranger/Rover group was opened and in 1977 the Brownies and Cubs joined together to form a mixed group. In 1987 an Agreement of Co-operation was signed between AGESCI and AGECS allowing AGECS members to wear AGESCI uniform, use its publications, follow its training programme. Expansion in San Marino continued with more units being introduced in 1988. Guiding is now found in all areas of the Republic.

The Programme
The Assembly of Leaders in San Marino draws up the programme used by the Association. The programme's objective is to help its members develop as worthwhile citizens of the country and community. Activities are based on the spiritual dimension, outdoor life, physical development, handicrafts and service. The girls are given several choices and are free to select activities according to their specific interests.

Working with the Community
Rangers take part in community development and service projects. The Association participated in 'Operation Chernobyl' by offering hospitality for a day to children from the Chernobyl Region of the former Soviet Union. The Chernobyl children were the guests of the Emilia Romagna region in Italy.

Guides provide services by helping with civil defence, keeping order at the Olympic Games for the disabled and cleaning up the slopes of Mount Titano.

Outdoor and Environmental Activities
The Roman Catholic Church has given the Association a campsite in Ca'Borgo.

Training
The Leaders Assembly appoints Guide and Scout representatives to be responsible for training for a period of three years. Following the agreement made with AGESCI in 1987, the members of the AGECS work closely with this Association and participate in all training activities organized by the Emilia Romagna region.

Communication and Co-operation
The Association is widening its horizons by participating in various activities organized by other National Organizations. Guides and Scouts are well integrated into the community and their public image is good. The Association enjoys good relationships with the National Government and religious authorities. The Association has contacts with other youth groups and is represented on the National Youth Committee.

AGECS co-operates in the preparation of *Il Foglio*, a periodical produced for leaders in the Rimini area.

A Guide Unit assembles in Borgo Marino.

Senegal

La Section des Guides de l'Association des Scouts et Guides du Sénégal

Girl Guiding/Girl Scouting introduced: 1953
Became Associate Member of WAGGGS: 1981
Membership 1992†: 1,000
Membership as % of female population: 0.03%
WAGGGS Region: Africa

Promesse
Sur mon honneur avec la grâce de Dieu, je m'engage à servir de mon mieux Dieu, l'Eglise et la patrie, à aider mon prochain en toute circonstance, et à observer la loi guide.

Loi
1 La guide est loyale.
2 La guide pense d'abord aux autres.
3 La guide est généreuse, elle est prête à servir.
4 La guide est accueillante, elle a l'esprit d'équipe.
5 La guide, soeur de toute autre Guide, est présente à tous.
6 La guide découvre la nature, elle y voit l'oeuvre de Dieu.
7 La guide doit obéir.
8 La guide ne craint pas l'effort, elle ne fait rien à moitié.
9 La guide aime son travail et respecte celui des autres.
10 La guide est maîtresse de soi, elle est pure et joyeuse.

Promesse des Jeannettes
Je promets de faire de mon mieux pour aimer Dieu, connaître mon pays, dire oui à la loi de la ronde, pour faire chaque jour un plaisir à quelqu'un et apporter la joie à la maison.

Loi des Jeannettes
Une jeannette est toujours propre.
Une jeannette dit toujours vrai.
Une jeannette est toujours gaie.
Une jeannette est toujours active.
Une jeannette pense d'abord aux autres.

Promise
On my honour and with the grace of God, I promise to do my best to serve God, the church and my country to help my neighbour at all times, and to keep the Guide law.

Guide

Law
1 A Guide is loyal.
2 A Guide thinks first of others.
3 A Guide is generous, she is prepared to help.
4 A Guide is welcoming, she has team spirit.
5 A Guide, sister to every other Guide, is at the service of all.
6 A Guide learns about nature, in which she sees God's work.
7 A Guide must obey.
8 A Guide does not fear endeavour, she does nothing by halves.
9 A Guide likes her work and respects that of others.
10 A Guide is self-controlled, she is pure and cheerful.

Brownie Promise
I promise to do my best to love God, get to know my country, accept the law of the Pack, to do a good turn to someone every day and bring joy into my home.

Brownie

Brownie Law
A Brownie is always clean.
A Brownie always tells the truth.
A Brownie is always cheerful.
A Brownie is always active.
A Brownie thinks first of others.

Age Groups

Guide Aînée	Ranger	16+
Guide	Guide	12-15
Jeannette	Brownie	7-12

Development of the Movement in Senegal

Guiding was started in Senegal in 1953 by former members of the Guides de France. It was intended for French girls living in Dakar and was based on the French programme. The Movement soon came to the notice of the Senegalese people, however, and a Ranger company was opened in the Ecole Normale at Rufisque, a teacher training college. Members of this company later went on to become leaders of other Guide companies.

Following Senegal's independence in 1960, companies and packs were started for Senegalese girls in the parishes of Dakar and Thiès. The Association worked together with the Scout Association and in 1962 the National Organization of the Scouts et Guides du Sénégal was officially recognized by the Ministry of the Interior.

In 1964 Guides de France sent a trainer to Senegal for a period of three years. Under her guidance, Guiding was extended to Petit-Côte, St. Louis and Casamance. Until 1967, leadership had been undertaken by non-nationals, but in this year the first Senegalese Guide National Commissioner was appointed, and local leaders took on responsibility for Guiding.

In 1974 a national team was set up with the aim of extending Guiding to more areas of the country and concentrating on leadership training. Guiding and its objectives soon became better known in the country and as a result membership grew and spread to several new areas.

The Programme

The programme is based on development, both at national and local level. Activities are centred on a different theme each year, and although the theme is common to all three branches, each branch has its own programme.

Working with the Community

Guides in Senegal are involved in many community projects related to health, sanitation and literacy. Members also help out in hospitals and homes for the elderly. Guides in Senegal are participating in an expanded child immunization programme and have helped to build village health posts in partnership with UNICEF.

The Association has a training centre at Mboro where income-generating activities include poultry farming and market gardening.

Outdoor and Environmental Activities

A re-afforestation project has been established at the Association's training centre at Mboro.

Training

The Association has a full-time trainer and a training team which meets every month. Weekend trainings and camps are organized at district, regional and national level.

Communication and Co-operation

Senegal is working in co-operation with several other national Girl Guide/Girl Scout organizations. The community development and training centre at Mboro is a product of a twinning project with Luxembourg which was started in 1989. The centre's construction was undertaken by senior sections of the Luxembourg and Senegal Associations. France and Finland have co-operated on health programmes in Senegal and Austria on a re-afforestation project.

The Association co-operates closely with the Scout Associations in Senegal and relations with the government and other authorities are excellent. Finally, the Association is often asked to help at re-education centres and to assist in organizing the annual National Youth Week.

Sierra Leone

The Sierra Leone Girl Guides Association

Girl Guiding/Girl Scouting introduced:	**1924**
Became Associate Member of WAGGGS:	**1963**
Became Full Member of WAGGGS:	**1972**
Membershlp 1992:	**3,967**
Membership as % of female population:	**0.19%**
WAGGGS Region:	**Africa**

Promise
I promise on my honour that I will do my best
To do my duty to God,
To serve my Country and help other people
And to keep the Guide Law.

Law
1 A Guide is loyal and can be trusted.
2 A Guide is helpful.
3 A Guide is polite and considerate.
4 A Guide is friendly to all and a sister to all Guides.
5 A Guide is kind to animals and plants and sees in Nature the work of God.
6 A Guide is obedient.
7 A Guide has courage and is cheerful in all difficulties.
8 A Guide makes good use of her time, money and talents.
9 A Guide takes care of her own possessions and those of other people.
10 A Guide controls herself and is clean in all she thinks, says and does.

Motto
Be Prepared

Brownie Guide Promise
I promise that I will do my best
To do my duty to God,
To serve my Country and help other people
And to keep the Brownie Guide Law.

Brownie Guide Law
A Brownie Guide thinks of others before herself and does a Good Turn every day.

Brownie Guide Motto
Lend a Hand

Age Groups

Ranger	16+
Guide	10-16
Brownie Guide	7-10

Guide

Development of the Movement in Sierra Leone

When Guiding was introduced to Sierra Leone in 1924 most units were attached to schools in the Freetown area. The Association, a Branch Association of The Girl Guides Association (United Kingdom), spread to the rest of Sierra Leone with the establishment of secondary schools in provincial towns and improved communications to remote areas.

The Programme
The Association uses an eight-point programme based on physical fitness, the mind, outdoor enjoyment, homecraft skills, service to others, human relations, creativity and character.

A small Brownie pack and Guide company have been established in the Cheshire Home for disabled children.

A Guide Company has just been opened at the School for the Blind and there are plans to begin one at the School for the Deaf and Dumb.

Brownie Guide

Working with the Community
Service projects are carried out by all age groups and the Association now has two major community development projects.

The one in the Mountain Rural District now stands on its own. The participants who benefited from the Project have now gone on to continue teaching others in their community. The class which was started as a literacy class for small children has now developed into a primary school.

George Brook, a poor suburb of Freetown, became the focus of another Guide community development project in 1989. By 1990, 30 illiterate girls and women had benefitted from classes in handicrafts, sewing, literacy, environmental health, child care and homecrafts.

Another project was started in the village of Lumley in 1990 offering skills training to illiterate women and girls who had dropped out of school. Classes include literacy, typing, sewing, gardening, sanitation and child care.

Outdoor and Environmental Activities

Guides and Rangers attend regular camps and Brownies participate in pack holidays. Guides are involved in tree planting and litter clearance.

Training

The Association now has a National Trainer on secondment from the Ministry of Social Welfare and an Assistant Trainer seconded from the Ministry of Education. This has further enhanced the Training Programme and made it possible for more trainings to be carried out with the help of Voluntary Trainers, who together form the National Training Team.

Communication and Co-operation

The Association encourages members to participate in international activities and many Guides correspond with pen friends in other countries.

In 1988 Sierra Leone hosted a sub-regional community development seminar for the Africa Region which was attended by representatives from neighbouring countries.

In 1989 a twinning project was initiated between the Guide Associations in Sierra Leone and the State of Alberta, Canada. The two community development projects in George Brook and Lumley are products of this co-operation.

The general public in Sierra Leone are informed about Guiding activities through the media. An annual broadcast is given on Thinking Day, and Guides are asked to participate in televised youth programmes. A quarterly circular letter is also published.

Singapore

The Singapore Girl Guides Association

Girl Guiding/Girl Scouting introduced:	**1917**
Became Associate Member of WAGGGS:	**1966**
Became Full Member of WAGGGS:	**1972**
Membership 1992:	**11,229**
Membership as % of female population:	**0.81%**
WAGGGS Region:	**Asia Pacific**

Promise
I promise to do my best: to do my duty to God,
To serve my country and help other people and
To keep the Guide Law.

Law
1 A Guide is loyal and can be trusted.
2 A Guide's duty is to be useful and to help others.
3 A Guide is polite, considerate and respects her elders.
4 A Guide is friendly and a sister to all Guides.
5 A Guide is kind to all living things.
6 A Guide is obedient.
7 A Guide has courage and is cheerful in all difficulties.
8 A Guide takes care of her own possessions and those of other people.
9 A Guide is diligent.
10 A Guide is self-disciplined in all she thinks, says and does.

Motto
Be Prepared

Brownie Promise
I promise to do my best: to do my duty to God,
To serve my country and help other people, and
To keep the Brownie Law.

Brownie Law
A Brownie always obeys and respects her elders.
A Brownie always thinks of others before herself.
A Brownie always tells the truth.
A Brownie is always neat and tidy.
A Brownie always plays and works cheerfully.

Brownie Motto
Lend a Hand

Age Groups

Ranger	16-21
Guide	11-17
Brownie	7-11

Guide

Development of the Movement in Singapore

The first Singapore Guide company was started in 1917 at St. Mary's Home. The Movement proved very popular and soon more companies and packs were formed, holding meetings at girls' schools, the YWCA and in church halls. When war broke out in the Pacific in 1941, active Guiding ceased and the Movement was not revived until 1946.

From then on, Guiding in Singapore was part of the Girl Guides Association of the Federation of Malaya until 1954 when it was registered as a Branch Association of the Girl Guides Association (United Kingdom). With the formation of Malaysia in 1963, the Singapore Association became a State Member in the Malaysian Girl Guides Association. In 1965, when Singapore became independent, the Association drew up its own constitution making it self-governing in all areas of work.

Brownie

The Programme
Singapore has a five-point programme which progresses from the Brownie level through to the Senior branch. It covers a wide range of subjects including service in the home and community, outdoor

activities, international relations, poise, personality, creative ability and health education.

Working with the Community
Members of the Movement in Singapore are involved in various community projects. In 1992, the Association received the Green Leaf Award for its efforts in the re-afforestation project at Upper Peirce Reservoir Park. This year-long project involved the weekly tending and watering of saplings by the Guides.

Outdoor and Environmental Activities
The Association has a permanent campsite situated at the north-western side of Singapore, in front of the Straits of Johore. Many camps are organized annually either at division, district or international level to encourage Guiders and Guides with special needs to come together for a time of fellowship, fun and learning. Training camps are also held there.

Training
Leadership training is emphasized to ensure effectiveness in programme implementation. Training sessions for leaders are carried out by a team of full-time as well as volunteer trainers. In addition to the basic training held annually for new Guide Leaders, trained Guide Leaders are encouraged to return for the skills course.

Training for Patrol Leaders are held annually. The Patrol Leaders are trained to assist their Captains in managing units. They are also encouraged to attend the Patrol Leaders' Kit-making workshops, where the Patrol Leaders are taught to make game kits to be used during meetings.

Communication and Co-operation
Guides and their Leaders have participated in seminars, training sessions, conferences and camps in many other countries. The Association has hosted many international events, amongst them, the 27th World Conference. The Association has also played host to exchange programmes.

Guides demonstrate recycling awareness at a recent Thinking Day celebration.

Slovak Republic

Slovenský Skauting

Founder Member of WAGGGS
Girl Guiding/Girl Scouting introduced: 1919
Membership cancelled 1950
Re-admitted as Associate Member of WAGGGS: 1990
Membership 1992: 2,310
WAGGGS Region: Europe

Promise
On my honour, I promise that I will do my best:
1 To love my native country and to be faithful to it at all times.
2 To fulfil my own duties and to adhere to the Girl Scout Law.
3 To help all my neighbours with all my heart and soul.
Help me, God!

Law
1 A Girl Scout's honour is trustworthy.
2 A Girl Scout is loyal and faithful.
3 A Girl Scout is useful and helps others.
4 A Girl Scout is a friend to all people of goodwill and a brother/ a sister to every other Girl Scout.
5 A Girl Scout is courteous.
6 A Girl Scout protects nature and valuable human creations.
7 A Girl Scout obeys orders of parents, superiors and leaders.
8 A Girl Scout is cheerful and deliberate.
9 A Girl Scout is thrifty.
10 A Girl Scout is pure in thought, in word and in deed.

Leaders Promise
To live and to educate young people in spirit of the Girl Scout Law.

Motto
Be Prepared

Law, Promise and Motto can be worded on particular age levels so that they may conform to their educational aims.

Development of the Movement in the Slovak Republic

The Slovak Republic, or Slovakia, is located in the heart of Europe. It was part of the Czechoslovak Republic between 1918 and 1992. At present it is an independent state.

Groups of Girl Scouts began to form between 1918 and 1922 in various towns in the Slovak region of Czechoslovakia. The Czechoslovak Girl Scouts (and therefore Slovak Girl Scouts) joined the World Association of Girl Scouts in 1928, and so became a founder member of WAGGGS. Girl Scouting in the country grew and progressed until 1939, the start of the Second World War, which brought with it the division of Czechoslovakia. In Slovakia, the government banned Girl Scouting.

But the spirit of Girl Scouting is strong, and survived the war and other persecutions. After the War and the 1944 national uprising, Girl Scouting re-emerged and was recognized by the state of Czechoslovakia.

The Girl Scout movement in Slovakia has over the last 40 years lost the opportunity to reach several generations of children and young people. In 1990, however, the Girl Scouts were once again accepted as members of WAGGGS, and begins to flourish once more. In 1993, when Czechoslovakia split and became the Czech Republic and the Slovak Republic, the Association applied and was recognised as two

Girl Scout

Brownie

Associations. Today Slovenský Skauting is the Association operating in the Slovak Republic.

The Programme
The present programme in operation in the Slovak Republic focuses on the development of the individual and service. It is currently under revision to ensure that it meets contemporary needs. The Association also has plans to develop a Ranger section.

Working with the Community
Service has always played a major part in the Association's programme and projects will be developed as the Association becomes more firmly established.

Outdoor Activities
Camps are held in the month of July, a highlight of the Girl Scout year.

Training
The Association organizes training courses at three levels, a basic leader course at district level; a course for prospective trainers of the basic leader course and a high-level course at national level. Leadership training is being further developed and many qualified trainers and commissioners have also followed refresher courses in neighbouring countries.

Communication and Co-operation
The Association has a tradition of international exchanges and is now anxious to participate in events organized by other Member Organizations and the Europe region. Scouting Nederland has a special link with Slovakia involving an exchange programme and exchange visits have also taken place with Guides from the United Kingdom.

The Association co-operates with other youth organizations and has revived *Skauta*, its former magazine.

Guides meeting in Slovak Republic have fun, too!

Solomon Islands

The Girl Guides Association of the Solomon Islands

Girl Guiding/Girl Scouting introduced: 1949
Became Associate Member of WAGGGS: 1987
Membership 1992†: 569
Membership as % of female population: 0.36%
WAGGGS Region: Asia Pacific

Promise
I promise that I will do my best;
To do my duty to God
To serve the Queen and my Country
and help other people
and
To keep the Guide Law.

Law
1 A Guide is loyal and can be trusted.
2 A Guide is helpful.
3 A Guide is polite and considerate.
4 A Guide is friendly and a sister to all Guides.
5 A Guide is kind to animals and respects all living things.
6 A Guide is obedient.
7 A Guide has courage and is cheerful in all difficulties.
8 A Guide makes good use of her time.
9 A Guide takes care of her own possessions and those of other people.
10 A Guide is self-controlled in all she thinks, says and does.

Motto
Be prepared

Brownie Guide Promise
I promise I will do my best;
To do my duty to God
To serve the Queen and my Country
and help other people and
To keep the Brownie Guide Law.

Brownie Guide Law
A Brownie Guide thinks of others before herself and does a good turn every day.

Brownie Guide Motto
Lend a Hand

Age Groups

Rangers	18-20
Guides	12-18
Brownies	7-11

Development of the Movement in the Solomon Islands

The first Guide company in the Solomon Islands was started in 1949 by a missionary teacher at a school in Santa Isabel but the company disbanded when the teacher moved on. In 1957 the wife of the High Commissioner of the Western Pacific High Commission suggested that Guiding should be restarted in the Solomon Islands. A Commissioner was appointed and a Brownie Pack soon formed.

In 1958 the first Guide Company was registered with The Girl Guides Association (United Kingdom).

After a visit by a trainer from the United Kingdom in 1963, more companies and packs were opened and handbooks, prepared with the help of the Girl Guides Association of New Zealand, were introduced.

Although Guiding has now spread to the larger islands, where the Girl Guides Association of the Solomon Islands hopes to start companies and packs in all schools, the difficulties experienced in communicating with, and travelling to, the smaller islands has hindered the development of Guiding there.

Guide

Brownie Guide

The Programme

The programme is based on the eight-point programme as set out in the Pacific Handbook: keeping the Guide Promise and Law; thinking for oneself; keeping fit; making and doing; being a homemaker; enjoying the outdoors; making friends; giving service. It is adapted as necessary to meet the needs of members in the Solomon Islands.

Working with the Community

During the frequent disasters, such as cyclones and hurricanes which hit the islands, Guides and Scouts help to clear devastated areas, distribute food to victims, and help in general relief work.

Training

The Training Committee, headed by a Training Adviser, prepares a regular calendar of training activities. Trainers are generally responsible for one section – Ranger, Guide or Brownie Leaders. A training programme for Guiders and patrol leaders was launched in 1986 but the Association is experiencing difficulties in extending this programme to the more remote islands and villages.

Communication and Co-operation

There is much contact with other Associations in the Pacific and members from the Solomon Islands take an active part in Pacific Conferences. The Association is held in high esteem by the general public, especially because of the relief work it has carried out following natural disasters.

Several joint projects have been undertaken with the Boy Scouts in the Solomon Islands and both Governmental and non-governmental organizations in the Solomon Islands are very supportive of Guiding.

South Africa

The Girl Guides Association of South Africa

Founder Member of WAGGGS
Girl Guiding/Girl Scouting introduced: 1910
Membership 1992: 33,662
Membership as % of female population: 0.19%
WAGGGS Region: Africa

Gids Belofte
Ek belowe om my bes te doen:
Om my plig teenoor God en my land na te kom;
Om te alle tye my medemens te help;
En om die Gids wet te voldoen.

Gidswet
1 'n Gids is betroubaar.
2 'n Gids is getro.
3 'n Gids is hulpvaardig.
4 'n Gids is vriendelik.
5 'n Gids is hoflik en dink aan ander.
6 'n Gids sorg vir die aarde en lewende dinge.
7 'n Gids is gehoorsaam.
8 'n Gids is dapper en blymoedig.
9 'n Gids is spaarsaam.
10 'n Gids is rein in alles wat sy dink, sê en doen.

Gids Leuse
Wees Gereed

Brownie Promise
Ek belowe om my bes te doen:
Om my plig teenoor God en my land na te kom;
Om te alle tye my medemens te help;
En om die Brownie wet te voldoen.

Brownie Law
'n Brownie het die waarheid lief, is gehoorsaam en opgeruimd.
'n Brownie dink aan ander voordat sy aan haarself dink.

Brownie Motto
Sit hand by

Guide Promise
I promise that I will do my best:
To do my duty to God and to my country;
To help other people at all times;
And to keep the Guide Law.

Guide

Guide Law
1 A Guide is to be trusted.
2 A Guide is loyal.
3 A Guide is helpful.
4 A Guide is friendly.
5 A Guide is polite and thoughtful for others.
6 A Guide cares for the earth and living things.
7 A Guide is obedient.
8 A Guide is brave and cheerful.
9 A Guide is thrifty.
10 A Guide is pure in all she thinks, says and does.

Guide Motto
Be Prepared

Brownie Promise
I promise that I will do my best:
To do my duty to God and to my country;
To help other people at all times;
And to keep the Brownie Law.

Brownie

Brownie Law
A Brownie is truthful, obedient and cheerful.
A Brownie thinks of others before herself.

Brownie Motto
Lend a Hand

Age Groups

Pioneer	Ranger	$16\frac{1}{2}$ - 25
Pioneer Gids	Ranger Guide	$13\frac{1}{2}$ - 17
Gids	Guide	10 - 14
Brownie	Brownie	7 - 10
Teddy	Teddy	5 - $7\frac{1}{2}$

Development of the Movement in South Africa

Guiding began in South Africa in 1910 in Johannesburg. By 1920 it had spread rapidly to all provinces in the then Union of South Africa, and a national body, known as the Girl Guides Association of South Africa was established. The Association, which included members in Basutoland (now Lesotho) Bechuanaland (now Botswana) and Swaziland, was a Founder Member of WAGGGS.

Guides learn new skills from their leaders.

These areas remained part of the Girl Guides Association of South Africa until 1961, but are now Members of WAGGGS in their own right. Upon the independence of Namibia in 1991, another Region became independent, and is now known as the Girl Guides Association of Namibia.

The Programme

The Teddy section, for girls aged 5 - 7 , earn a series of "Paws" for participating in various activities. Teddies do not make a Promise.

The programmes for Brownies, Guides and Ranger Guides encompass challenges relevant to girls from many different backgrounds. Rangers choose their own programme and are encouraged to participate in the Gold Shield Award scheme, a national scheme for all young people in South Africa.

A national development committee has been established with a counterpart in each Region. The aim of these committees is to try to spread Guiding to as many girls and young women as possible. A national "Twin-Pin" membership drive has been launched with the aim of increasing our numbers. As always, finance is a major problem as distances are great and equipment costly.

Working with the Community

Community service is an important aspect of the Association's work. The various branches are involved with their communities in different ways such as providing help for people with disabilities and giving practical aid to the elderly by way of shopping, visiting or providing blankets. Service to national societies such as South African Tuberculosis Society, SSPCA, Child Welfare, children's homes and hospitals are ongoing. A pre-school has been started at the National Centre for children of the local community which offers inexpensive, stimulating day care for those children whose parents have to work.

In rural areas, projects are being implemented to supply clean drinking water, including wells. A National Tea Challenge for the "Help Children Grow" fund has helped to finance many of these projects as well as pre-schools and child health projects.

Literacy Aid, National Eye Care Week, and participation in the WAGGGS Peace and "Water is Life" challenges are all ongoing projects. Guides encourage communities to grow vegetables as a way of promoting improved nutrition. The Association sponsors three projects which teach basic sewing and knitting skills to girls unable to find employment.

Six young women from various parts of the country, usually from economically depressed areas are selected to take part in the "Proteam Project". These young women are housed at the National Centre and are given a one year training in many things, from office skills to driving, so that at the end of the year they will have a greater chance of finding employment.

Outdoor and Environmental Activities

Throughout the country, in both rural and urban environments, outdoor activities attract adventure loving girls. Camping, hiking and environmental trails visits are most popular and outdoor activities form a prominent part of the programme throughout the year. Brownies attend Pack Holidays which are often based on an outdoor theme.

Service camps focus attention on community development, afforestation and conservation. National and Regional events are held regularly and bring together girls of all cultures from all parts of South Africa. Guides also take part in annual World Environment Day and Arbor Day projects.

The effects of deforestation and air pollution are cause for major concern, and for this reason the Association has developed a solar cooker as a non-profit making initiative to assist communities. This cooker enables food to be cooked for a family of approximately six people using the sun as the only source of heat. It is also possible to use the stove to sterilise water in rural areas, and this is being encouraged in a bid to cut down diseases that kill many children.

Training

The Association has both National and Regional Trainers. National trainings are held annually to keep leaders up-to-date with recent developments within the Movement. Regional trainings take place more frequently.

Communication and Co-operation

International Education is promoted in the Regions through a specific programme, and the Post Box links over 1,500 girls a year with members of the Movement in other countries. Travel is encouraged and members of the Association frequently attend international seminars and camps in other parts of the world.

The Girl Guides Association of South Africa informs the general public about activities through newspapers, magazines, radio and television. For its own members it publishes three quarterly magazines, *Look Wide* for adult members, *Good Company* for Guides and Ranger Guides and *Times 6* for Brownies and Teddies.

An audio-visual presentation has been produced to promote Guiding and to make the public aware of all that Guiding offers. There are many languages spoken throughout South Africa and some handbooks have been translated in order to cater for their needs. The Association works in close co-operation with the Boy Scouts of South Africa, and a representative of each Association has a seat on the National Council of the other.

An annual "Biscuit Week", where biscuits are sold to the general public, ensures excellent publicity for the Association and is also a major fundraising project.

Spain

Comité de Enlace del Guidismo en España/ Comitè d'Enllaç del Guiatge a Espanya

Component Federations:
Federació Catalana d'Escoltisme i Guiatge (FCEG)
Federación Española de Guidismo (FEG)

Component Associations of FCEG:
Minyons Escoltes i Guies Sant Jordi de Catalunya (MEiGSJC)
Escoltes Catalans (EC)

Component Associations of FEG:
Asociación Guías de Madrid (AGM)
Asociación Guías de Aragón (AGA)
Euskal Eskaut Gia Elkartea
Associació Guiatge Valencià (AGV)

Girl Guiding/Girl Scouting introduced:	**1929**
Became Associate Member of WAGGGS:	**1959**
Became Full Member of WAGGGS:	**1969**
Membership 1992:	**7,506**
Membership as % of female population:	**0.04%**
WAGGGS Region:	**Europe**

Promesa
Con la ayuda del Creador yo prometo hacer cuanto de mí dependa para amarle a Él y a mi país, ser útil a mi familia y al prójimo en todo momento y vivir la ley guía.

Ley
1 La Guía es leal y digna de confianza.
2 La Guía es consciente de los derechos de los demás y de sus propios deberes.
3 La Guía es generosa y busca la felicidad junto con los otros.
4 La Guía conoce el lugar donde vive y se compromete con su mejora.
5 La Guía es abierta a todos y hermana de las demás guías.
6 La Guía ama la naturaleza y ve en ella la obra del Creador.
7 La Guía aprende a obedecer para saber colaborar.
8 La Guía afronta las dificultades con alegría.
9 La Guía es austera, limpia y ordenada.
10 La Guía sabe dominarse y respeta su persona.

Promesa Alita
Yo prometo amar cada día más al Creador, a mi país, a mi familia; cumplir la ley de las alitas y hacer todos los días una buena acción.

Ley de la Alita
La Alita está siempre alegre.
La Alita es limpia y trabajadora.
A Alita es amiga de todos y les ayuda.
A Alita piensa primero en los demás y procura llevarles su alegría.
La Alita ama la naturaleza y es observadora.
La Alita dice siempre la verdad.
La Alita dice siempre sí al Creador y a los demás.
or
Hablaré con el Creador y le daré gracias por la vida.

Seré amiga de todos y sabré perdonar.
Seré limpia, cuidaré mi persona y todo lo que me rodea.
No cogeré lo que no es mío.
Diré siempre la verdad y no hablaré mal de nadie.
Me esforzaré por hacer felices a los demás y me alegraré de verlos contentos.

Promise

With the help of the Creator I promise to do my best to love Him and my country, to help my family and other people at all times and to live the Guide Law.

Law

1 A Guide is loyal and to be trusted.
2 A Guide is aware of the rights of others and of her own duties.
3 A Guide is generous and seeks happiness together with others.
4 A Guide gets to know the place in which she is living and is involved in its improvement.
5 A Guide is friendly to all and a sister to all other Guides.
6 A Guide loves nature and sees in it the work of God.
7 A Guide learns to obey so she can collaborate.
8 A Guide faces all difficulties with joy.
9 A Guide is frugal, clean and tidy.
10 A Guide know how to control and respect herself.

Little Wing Promise

I promise to love God, my country and my family more each day; to comply with the law of the Little Wings and to do a good deed every day.

Little Wing Law

A Little Wing is always cheerful.
A Little Wing is always clean and hardworking.
A Little Wing is a friend to all and helps them.
A Little Wing thinks first of others and tries to bring them her cheerfulness.
A Little Wing loves nature and is observant.
A Little Wing always tells the truth.
A Little Wing always says yes to the Creator and to others.
or
I will talk to the Creator and thank Him for life.
I will be a friend to all and be able to forgive.
I will be clean, I will look after myself and all that surrounds me.
I will not take what is not mine.
I will always tell the truth and I will say nothing bad about anyone.
I will try to make others happy and I will be glad to see them contented.

Age Groups

The age groups vary among the component Associations. This grouping is the most common.

Guía Mayor	Ranger	16-18
Pionera	Pioneer	14-16
Pionera	Guide	11-14
Alita	Little Wing	7-11

Development of the Movement in Spain

Guiding began in San Sebastián in 1929, and soon afterwards groups of Guides appeared elsewhere in the country, including Zaragoza, Valencia and Madrid. Activities were organized and co-ordinated by the Asociación de las Guías de España.

In Catalonia Guiding started in 1932, the Germanor de Noies Guides developing along similar lines to the Asociación de las Guías de España. Guide companies were quickly formed, followed by Brownie packs and a Ranger section.

During the Civil War (1936-1939) all Guiding ceased in Spain and it was not until 1947 that activities were restarted. By 1955 Guiding had developed throughout the country and the Guides joined to form the Federación Guías de España. In 1962 the Federation was replaced by the Comité de Enlace del Guidismo en España/Comitè d'Enllaç del Guiatge a Espanya (CEGE).

From 1984 the CEGE was made up of two federations: the Federació Catalana d'Escoltisme i Guiatge (composed of Minyons Escoltes i Guies Sant Jordi de Catalunya and Escoltes Catalans) and the Federación Española de Guidismo (formed of the Asociación Guías de Madrid, Asociación Guías de Aragón, Eskaut Gia Elkartea, and Associació Guiatge Valencià). The CEGE aims to maintain mutual aid and co-operation between its two federations.

FCEG Guide

FEG Guide

The Programme

The programme used in Spain varies according to the characteristics of each Component Association. Both federations have a mixed membership of boys and girls and share the aim of promoting equal educational opportunities for both sexes.

Some Associations base their activities on five fundamental points: adventure, team life, nature, development and commitment. They all encourage girls to serve those around them, to make a commitment to their own community and to seek higher spiritual values.

One of the most important aims of CEGE is to develop Guiding in Spain according to the cultural affinities of members in different regions. Each province has a Guide team, and these teams meet annually to prepare for the National Guide Assembly, which reviews progress of the Movement in Spain.

Working with the Community

Spanish Guides are active in the field of community service. Some have worked with gypsies, helping a group of about 50 girls to become self-reliant, to work together with team spirit and to develop a sense of responsibility. Members have also helped people to settle in their new community when moving from one area of the country to another.

Outdoor and Environmental Activities

Members attend regular camps on varied themes such as leadership training and winter sports. Guides in Spain are involved in many environmental projects. In 1987 the Scouts and Guides of Sant Jordi de Catalunya carried out an environmental survey amongst young people aged 15-25 and introduced environmental projects within national parks.

Training

Regular training meetings are organized at national level for branch and unit leaders.

Communication and Co-operation

Brochures have been produced to explain and publicize the Movement. The Component Associations publish magazines for their members including the bi-monthly magazine, *Prisma*, and the quarterly magazine *Rastro*.

Painting a sign to find her way back, this Brownie learns about orienteering.

Sri Lanka

The Sri Lanka Girl Guides Association

Girl Guiding/Girl Scouting introduced: 1917
Became Full Member of WAGGGS: 1951
Membership 1992: 25,403
Membership as % of female population: 0.30%
WAGGGS Region: Asia Pacific

Poronduwa
Maagé argama saha rata ké-ré-hee
Maagé yuthu-kam itukeree matath
Háma-vita-ma anu-nata pihita-vee-matath
Bala-dhak-shika neethiyata kee-karu veematath
Máta pilivan thata - min diri dáree-mata
Mar-ma gaurawa pera-dáriva porondu vemi.

Neethi
1 Baladhakshikava vishvasa kata yuthuya.
2 Baladhakshikava pakshapathaya.
3 Baladhakshikavage yuthukam nam anunata prayojanavath veemath upakara veemathya.
4 Baladhakshikava sáma mithuriyéki an hama Baladhak-shikavakagema, a sohoyuriyeki.
5 Baladhakshikava karunasheeliya.
6 Baladhakshikava sathunge mithuriyéki.
7 Baladhakshikava anata keekaruvei.
8 Baladhakshikava apahasukam madha sinahavemin gee gayai.
9 Baladhakshikava sakasuruvam sahithaya.
10 Baladhakshikava sithinuth, vatchanayenuth, kriyavenuth pivithuruya.

Adharsha
Sudhanamva sittinna

Kuda Mithuriyange Poronduwa
Maagé argama saha rata udesa
Maagé yuthu-kama itu-kiri-matath
Sáma-dhama anunta, vishé-shayén gédera ayata
Upa-kara kiri-ma-tath, haki tha-ra-min uth-saha karana bavata
Mam-ma porondu vemi.

Kuda Mithuriyange Neethi
Kuda Mithuriya vadehitiyangé adhehas salakai.
Kuda mithuriye hithuwak no-kerai.

Little Friend Motto
Kuda Mithuriyangé Adharsha
Udhau kerenne

Promise
I promise on my honour to do my best:
To do my duty to my religion and country;
To help other people at all times;
And to obey the Guide Law.

Law
1 A Guide's honour is to be trusted.
2 A Guide is loyal.
3 A Guide's duty is to be useful and to help others.
4 A Guide is a friend to all and a sister to every other Guide.
5 A Guide is courteous.
6 A Guide is a friend to animals.
7 A Guide obeys orders.
8 A Guide smiles and sings under all difficulties.
9 A Guide is thrifty.
10 A Guide is pure in thought, word and deed.

Motto
Be Prepared

Little Friend Promise
I promise on my honour to do my best
To do my duty to my religion and country
To help other people every day, especially those at home.

Little Friend Law
A Little Friend gives in to older folk.
A Little Friend does not give in to herself.

Guide

Little Friend

Little Friend Motto
Lend a Hand

Age Groups

Jayeshta		
Baladhakshika	Senior Guide	16-22
Baladhakshika	Guide	11-16
Kuda Mithuriye	Little Friend	7-11

Development of the Movement in Sri Lanka

Guiding in Sri Lanka began in 1917 when the first Girl Guide company was opened in the historic hill town of Kandy. The Movement has since created and strengthened ties between the country's diverse groups.

The Programme
Good relationships between people of different ethnic groups are encouraged at all levels, and the Guide and Senior Guide programmes involve learning both official languages of Sri Lanka in order to create better understanding. Many Guide companies exist in schools for children with special needs.

Working with the Community
The Association undertook projects to build wells and sanitation facilities in conjunction with the UN International Drinking Water Supply and Sanitation Decade (1981-1990). Pre-schools have been set up in many areas, with financial help from Girl Guide/Girl Scout Associations in other countries. Programmes have also been introduced for school drop-outs and school leavers. Guides in one area prepare and serve nutritious soup to the underprivileged on a regular basis.

For its efforts, Sri Lanka won the 1986 WAGGGS Olave Award for outstanding, sustained service to the community, for a drug rehabilitation project in Colombo. The project was undertaken in co-operation with the National Dangerous Drug Control Board.

Outdoor and Environmental Activities
The appeal of the outdoors has resulted in widespread camping activities. All age groups are encouraged to conserve natural resources and nature conservation is one of the challenges taken up by Senior Guides in the Prime Minister's Award Scheme. The Earth Keeper's Badge has also been introduced to the President's Guide scheme.

Training
The development and continuity of the training programme is ensured by regular training sessions for potential trainers. To encourage training Island wide, the Association has established its first National training centre.

Communication and Co-operation
Events organized by the Association are given coverage on radio and television, and in the press. The Association publishes a bi-monthly magazine, *The Trainee* and valuable public relations work is carried out on Thinking Day, when Guides clean public places, help in hospital wards and visit homes for the elderly and the underprivileged.

Between 1985 and 1988 the Girl Guides Association (UK) and the Sri Lanka Girl Guides Association were involved in a twinning project focusing on primary health care in Sri Lanka.

The Sri Lanka Girl Guides Association co-operates with other non-governmental organizations and they work very closely with the Sri Lanka Anti-narcotic Association (SLANA). The Girl Guides Drug Abuse Prevention Achievement Badge project, undertaken by SLANA as a pilot project in collaboration with the Sri Lanka Girl Guides Association, concluded with 111 Girl Guides from 11 Districts receiving badges and certificates.

The Sri Lanka Girl Guides Association co-operates with the Family Planning Association in its Population Awareness programme, with the YWCA in family life education projects, with the Sarvodaya Sangamaya on rural improvement, and with the Saukyadana Movement at the Medical Aid Centre during pilgrim seasons and religious festivals. Contact is also maintained with the Scout Association, Lanka Mahila Samiti, the Red Cross, the Sri Lanka Women's Conference and the Women's Bureau.

The Association collaborates with UN agencies and participates in UN international years. UNDP and UNICEF have funded trainings and water/ sanitation projects.

Sudan

The Sudan Girl Guides Association

Girl Guiding/Girl Scouting introduced:	**1928**
Became Associate Member of WAGGGS:	**1957**
Became Full Member of WAGGGS:	**1975**
Membership 1992:	**3,448**
Membership as % of female population:	**0.03%**
Member:	**Arab Regional Group**

Promise
On my honour, I promise that I will do my best
To do my duty to God, my Country and President of the Republic
To help other people at all times
To obey the Girl Guides Law.

Law
1 A Guide's honour is to be trusted.
2 A Guide is loyal.
3 A Guide's duty is to be useful and to help others.
4 A Guide is a friend to everybody and a sister to every other Guide, no matter to what country, class or creed, the other may belong.
5 A Guide is courteous.
6 A Guide is a friend to animals.
7 A Guide obeys orders.
8 A Guide smiles and sings under all difficulties.
9 A Guide is thrifty.
10 A Guide is pure in thought, words and deed.

Motto
Be Prepared

Bluebird Promise
I promise to do my best to do my duty to God, my Country and the President
To help other people every day, especially those at home and to obey the Bluebird Law.

Bluebird Law
1 A Bluebird always does her best.
2 Thinks of others, before herself.
3 Does a good turn every day.

Bluebird Motto
Lend a Hand

Age Groups

Raaidat	Ranger	16-20
Mursheda	Guide	12-16
El Taira el Zarga	Bluebird	7-11

Guide

Development of the Movement in Sudan

Guiding began in Sudan in 1928 when two companies were formed, one in an American Mission School in Atabara and the other in Khartoum. Guiding activities ceased shortly afterwards. However, they restarted some years later when people of many different nationalities worked together to promote the Movement, resulting in companies and flocks being formed in all parts of Sudan.

A headquarters was set up in Khartoum which was opened by the World Chief Guide in 1949. Following the country's independence in 1955, the first Sudanese Chief Commissioner was appointed.

The Programme
The programme covers a wide range of activities including cookery, needlework, home nursing, first aid, hiking and camping. Many fundraising projects are organized, and every year a gala is held to display the girls' work and to raise money to further Guiding.

Bluebird

Working with the Community
Guides in Sudan help out in hospitals in emergency situations and have set up first-aid classes for women in villages and

towns. On Thinking Day Guides carry out special projects with the poor and sick.

The Association has been particularly involved in projects to combat the terrible drought and desertification in Sudan. Guides have helped to resettle people who have been forced to leave their homes and travel to other parts of the country in search of food and water. They have also assisted in a programme to vaccinate the huge number of refugees from neighbouring countries.

Training

Great emphasis is laid on the training of leaders. Due to the shortage of trained leaders in Sudan and the demand for new companies to be opened, leaders meet every week for training.

Communication and Co-operation

A joint project with Denmark has resulted in the establishment of a vegetable farm and leader training centre.

In addition, Sudanese Guides work side by side with the community, helping to keep the traditions and customs of the country alive and, as a result, they have gained widespread recognition and support.

The Sudan Girl Guides Association works in co-operation with other women's organizations in Sudan and with the Sudan Boy Scouts Association.

Surinam

Surinaamse Padvindsters Raad
(Council of the Surinam Girl Scouts)

Component Organizations:
Het Surinaamse Padvindsters Gilde
Gidsen Suriname

Girl Guiding/Girl Scouting introduced:	**1947**
Became Associate Member of WAGGGS:	**1972**
Membership 1992†:	**496**
Membership as % of female population:	**0.23%**
WAGGGS Region:	**Western Hemisphere**

Het Surinaamse Padvindsters Gilde

Promise
I promise to do my very best to serve God and my country, to help others as much as possible and to live up to the Girl Scout Law.

Law
1 A Girl Scout is honest and to be trusted.
2 A Girl Scout is helpful.
3 A Girl Scout is polite and considerate.
4 A Girl Scout is friendly and a sister to other Girl Scouts.
5 A Girl Scout is good to animals and has respect for Nature.
6 A Girl Scout is obedient.
7 A Girl Scout is courageous and remains cheerful in setbacks.
8 A Girl Scout spends her time usefully.
9 A Girl Scout takes care of her own possessions and those of other people.
10 A Girl Scout keeps control of her thoughts, words and deeds.

Motto
Be Prepared

Brownie Promise
I'll do my best to be a real Brownie, to help everybody wherever possible, especially at home.

Brownie Law
A Brownie is truthful.
A Brownie is obedient.
A Brownie is friendly.
A Brownie cares for plants and animals.

Brownie Motto
Let us help

Girl Scout

Gidsen Suriname

Promise
On my honour, I promise, with the help of God, that I will do my best:
to do my duty to God, Church and country,
to help other people at all times,
to obey the Guide's Law.

Law
1 A Guide's honour is to be trusted.
2 A Guide is loyal.
3 A Guide's duty is to be useful and to help others.
4 A Guide is a friend to all and a sister to every other Guide.
5 A Guide is courteous.
6 A Guide is appreciative of Nature.
7 A Guide is obedient.
8 A Guide smiles and sings under all difficulties.
9 A Guide is thrifty.
10 A Guide is pure in thought, word and deed.

Brownie

Guide

Brownie

Motto
Be Prepared

Brownie Promise
I shall do my best, with the help of God, to be a good Brownie,
to help other people at all times, especially at home.

Brownie Law
A Brownie is honest.
A Brownie is obedient.
A Brownie is friendly.
A Brownie takes good care of plants and animals.

Brownie Motto
Tackle the job

Age Groups

Ranger	18+
Guide (senior)	15-18
Guide (junior)	11-14
Brownie	8-11

Development of the Movement in Surinam

Girl Guiding/Girl Scouting in Surinam is carried out under the auspices of Surinaamse Padvindsters Raad (Surinam Girl Scout Council), which was formed in 1968 as the co-ordinating body of the two existing Associations in Surinam: Het Surinaamse Padvindsters Gilde (Surinam Association of Girl Scouts) and Gidsen Surinam (Catholic Guide Movement of Surinam). The Liaison Committee is responsible for dealing with matters which are common to both.

Installation of new leaders is key to being able to meet girls' needs.

Het Surinaamse Padvindsters Gilde was set up in the capital, Paramaribo, in 1947 by the Nederlandse Padvinsters Gilde (an Association from the Netherlands) and subsequently spread to other areas of the country. In 1954, when Surinam became independent, Het Surinaamse Padvindsters Gilde became self-governing in all areas of work.

In 1948 Gidsen Suriname was also set up under the influence of the Dutch and the Association co-operated with Catholic bodies in the Netherlands from the beginning: the Catholic Young Women and the Catholic Young Girls Association.

The Programme
The programme used by Het Surinaamse Padvinsters Gilde was drawn up in 1969 and is based on an eight-point programme which gives Girl Scouts opportunities to develop physical fitness, the mind, outdoors enjoyment, homecraft skills, service to others, human relations, creativity and character.

Working with the Community
The importance of service to others is stressed in Surinam and many service activities are organized. These include taking gifts of food and flowers to homes for underprivileged children and the elderly.

Training
Both Associations place much emphasis on training, and hold regular meetings for group leaders, assistant group leaders and Brownie leaders.

Communication and Co-operation
Het Surinaamse Padvinsters Gilde undertakes first-aid training in co-operation with the Surinam Red Cross. Gidsen Surinam co-operates with the Catholic Boy Scouts Association in Surinam, especially in camp training.

Both Associations have received visits from foreign trainers and WAGGGS' representatives, and have participated in Western Hemisphere events.

Swaziland

The Swaziland Girl Guides Association

Girl Guiding/Girl Scouting introduced: 1924
Became Associate Member of WAGGGS: 1969
Membership 1992†: 1,010
Membership as % of female population: 0.23%
WAGGGS Region: Africa

Setsembiso
Ngetsembisa kwenta lokusemandleni ami:
Kukhonta Nkulunkulu,
Kusebentela iNgwenyama nokusita labanye bantfu,
Nokugcina umtsetfo webaKhanyisi.

Umtsetfo WebaKhanyisi
1 UmKhanyisi wetsembekile katsi futsi lingetsentjwa.
2 UmKhanyisi unelusito.
3 UmKhanyisi unenhlonishp, uyacabangelana.
4 UmKhanyisi ungumngani nadzadze wabo bonkhe baKhanyisi.
5 UmKhanyisi uphatsa kahle tilwane, nato tonkhe tintfo letiphilako.
6 UmKhanyisi uyalalela.
7 UmKhnayisi uinesibindzi, ubeketelela bonkhe bumatima.
8 UmKhanyisi usebentisa kahle sikhatsi sakhe.
9 UmKhanyisi uphatsa kahle timphahla takhe, netalabanye.
10 UmKhanyisi uyatibamba kuko koukhe lakucabangako, lakushoko nalalkwentako.

Motto
Hlala Ulungele

Blue Jay Promise
Ngetsembisa kwenta lokusemandleni ami:
Kukhonta Nkulunkulu,
Kusebentela iNgwenyama nokusita labanye bantfu,
Nokugcina umtsetfo wemaFemfe.

Blue Jay Law
LiFemfe licabanga ngalabanye ngaphambi kokutsi liticabange lona; futsi lenta Sento Lesihle onkemalanga.

Blue Jay Motto
Sita labanye

Guide

Promise
I promise to do my best:
To do my duty to God,
To serve the King and help other people,
And to keep the Guide Law.

Law
1 A Guide is loyal and can be trusted.
2 A Guide is helpful.
3 A Guide is polite and considerate.
4 A Guide is friendly and a sister to all Guides.
5 A Guide is kind to animals and respects all living things.
6 A Guide is obedient.
7 A Guide has courage and is cheerful in all difficulties.
8 A Guide makes good use of her time.
9 A Guide takes care of her own possessions and those of other people.
10 A Guide is self-controlled in all she thinks, says and does.

Motto
Be Prepared

Blue Jay

Blue Jay Promise
I promise to do my best:
To do my duty to God,
To serve the King and help other people,
And to keep the Blue Jay Law.

Blue Jay Law
A Blue Jay thinks of others before herself and does a Good Turn every day.

Blue Jay Motto
Lend a Hand

Age Groups

Ranger/Cadet	15-21
Girl Guide	10-15
Blue Jay	7-10

Development of the Movement in Swaziland

Guiding in Swaziland started in 1924, but it was only in 1950 after a visit from the World Chief Guide that it really began to spread throughout the country. In 1961 the Association was registered as a Branch Association of The Girl Guides Association (United Kingdom). The Ranger section was organized in 1963, and a Cadet company was formed five years later in one of the two training colleges in Swaziland.

The Wayfarers, an organization for African girls working on similar lines to the Guide Association, was also active in Swaziland and soon joined the Guides to form one Movement for all girls in Swaziland. In 1968 girls under 10 became known as Blue Jays and the following year the Girl Guides Association (United Kingdom) signed a deed of transfer making the Swaziland Girl Guide Association self-governing in all areas.

The Programme

The programme is based on eight points: keeping fit, becoming a homemaker, giving service, keeping the Guide Law, getting to know people, enjoying the outdoors, thinking for yourself and exploring the arts.

Working with the Community

Guides and Rangers in Swaziland visit hospitals, clinics and centres for the disabled and have planted trees near bus stops along main roads to provide shade for travellers. Blue Jays hold flower shows to raise money to buy presents for children in hospital.

Outdoor and Environmental Activities

Camping is popular in Swaziland, and events include five-day national camps for Guiders and weekend Ranger camps. In 1989 a camping subcommittee, composed entirely of young adults, was formed to help the camping commissioner organize camps on a regular basis.

In terms of the environment, tree planting is in progress to help prevent soil erosion and to supply a source of fuel.

Training

Adult member training, including commissioners and potential commissioners, is emphasized and residential regional trainings, held once a year in each of the four regions, are open to all members. Training is also carried out by correspondence through training letters prepared for new Guiders.

Communication and Co-operation

In 1987 a Post Box Secretary was appointed to strengthen international education through correspondence with Guides and Girl Scouts from other countries. The Association co-operates with the Swaziland Boy Scouts Association, Swaziland Red Cross Society and UNICEF.

Sweden

Svenska Scoutrådet
(The Swedish Guide and Scout Council)

Component Organizations:
Frälsningsarmens Scoutförbund (FA)
(The Salvation Army Guide and Scout Association)
KFUK-KFUM:s Scoutförbund (KFUK-KFUM)
(The Swedish YWCA Guide and YMCA Scout Association)
Nykterhetsrörelsens Scoutförbund (NSF)
(The Temperance Guide and Scout Association)
SMU:s Scoutverksamhet (SMU)
(The Guide and Scout Organization of the Swedish Covenant Youth)
Svenska Scoutförbundet (SSF)
(The Swedish Guide and Scout Association)

Founder Member of WAGGGS

Girl Guiding/Girl Scouting introduced:	**1910**
Membership 1992:	**69,950**
Membership as % of female population:	**1.62%**
WAGGGS Region:	**Europe**

Löfte
Jag lovar att efter bästa förmåga följa scoutlagen.

Lag
1 En scout visar vördnad för Gud och hans ord.
2 En scout är ärlig och pålitlig.
3 En scout är vänlig och hjälpsam.
4 En scout visar hänsyn och är en god kamrat.
5 En scout möter svårigheter med gott humör.
6 En scout lär känna och vårdar naturen.
7 En scout känner ansvar för sig själv och andra‡.

‡The word 'andra' (others) is a Swedish expression for society, and the clause as a whole means responsibility to the communities in which we live.

Motto
Var redo.

Minior Law
En miniorscout vill vara ärlig och hjälpsam och göra sitt bästa.

Promise
I promise to do my best to follow the Guide Law.

Law
1 A Guide reveres God and His word.
2 A Guide is honest and reliable.
3 A Guide is friendly and helpful.
4 A Guide is considerate to others and trustworthy as a friend.
5 A Guide faces difficulties without complaining.
6 A Guide learns about nature and is concerned with its conservation.
7 A Guide feels responsibility for herself and others.

Motto
Be Prepared

Minior Law
A Minior Guide is honest and helpful and tries to do her best.

Age Groups

Senior Guide	15 - 18
Guide	12 - 14
Junior Guide	10 - 11
Minior Guide	8 - 9

FA Guide and Minior Guide

KFUK-KFUM Guide and Minior Guide

NSF
Guide and
Minior Guide

SMU
Guide and
Minior Guide

SSF
Guide and
Minior Guide

Development of the Movement in Sweden

The first groups of Guides were formed in Sweden as early as 1910 and by 1913 the foundations of Swedish Guiding had been laid.

By the end of the 1950s as many as six Guide and six Scout Associations were active in Sweden. Following the trend towards co-education in the following decade, the Guide and Scout Associations amalgamated to form six Joint Associations within the Svenska Scoutrådet (The Swedish Guide and Scout Council). Two of these Associations subsequently became one, and there are now five Joint Associations working in Sweden.

The Programme

Units are usually open to both boys and girls, although there are also some single-sex units. The programme is divided into four age groups, its aim is individuality and projects are based on the principles of individual development. The planning of programmes and activities has been influenced by the structural changes which have taken place in Swedish society and there is an increased emphasis on adult education, nature conservation and ecology.

Members with special needs are also integrated into companies and packs if possible, and the Association has units for disabled members as well.

Working with the Community

The Swedish Guide and Scout Council encourages participation in schemes to help community development. Members have raised funds for community projects in Sri Lanka, Tanzania and Zimbabwe as well as contributing financially to research work on disabilities, and helping to fund the opening of special homes and schools.

The programme "Scouting for Everyone" aims to involve immigrants and refugees in Sweden.

Outdoor and Environmental Activities

Outdoor activities play an important role in Swedish Guiding and Scouting. Many groups own forest huts and these are used by Guides and Scouts on weekends. Guides and Scouts are trained in tracking and orienteering, skills which are essential for survival in Swedish forests. Summer camping is also very popular and camps vary in size from 20 participants to several thousand. Camps are also organized for the disabled.

Training

Leadership training is carried out at local, regional and national levels.

Communication and Co-operation

Since the beginning of the nineties the Swedish Guide and Scout Council have had an active link with the Guide and Scout Movement in Latvia. Through this project they hope to create possibilities for contacts between local groups in Sweden and Latvia, and to work together with programmes, training and organization.

The Swedish Guide and Scout Council also has a serious commitment to the promotion of world peace and has produced several printed materials on the subject, including posters, cards and booklets.

The Council enjoys good relations with the community. It publishes several periodicals, including *Scout med Ledarbladet*, *Scouting*, *Scout Ledaren* and *Nying*.

The Council has contacts with organizations which work on similar projects including the Svenska Kyrkans Unga (Youth of the Swedish Church) and Sveriges Kyrkliga Studieförbund (The Swedish Church Association for Education), Svenska Röda Korset (Swedish Red Cross), Rädda Barnen (Swedish Save the Children).

Switzerland

Mouvement Scout de Suisse
(Swiss Guide and Scout Movement)

Founder Member of WAGGGS
Girl Guiding/Girl Scouting introduced: 1913
Membership 1992: 24,256
Membership as % of female population: 0.70%
WAGGGS Region: Europe

Girl Scout

Promesse – Premier engagement
Je veux m'engager pour mon groupe et vivre de mon mieux la loi scoute.
Je demande à Dieu et à vous tous de m'y aider.
ou
Je demande à vous tous de m'y aider.

Promesse scoute
Avec l'aide de Dieu, avec votre aide et dans la joie.
ou
Avec votre aide et dans la joie,
je promets de faire tout mon possible pour
- approfondir les valeurs de notre loi scoute
- rechercher les sens de ma vie
- m'engager dans chaque communauté où je vis:
- ...

Loi
Scouts, nous voulons
- Etre vrais
- Ecouter et respecter les autres
- Etre attentifs et aider autour de nous
- Partager
- Choisir de notre mieux et nous engager
- Protéger la nature et respecter la vie
- Affronter les difficultés avec confiance
- Nous réjouir de tout ce qui est beau.

Cette loi nous lie à tous les Scouts du monde. Dans le même esprit nous voulons en particulier:
- ...
- ...

Motto
Toujours prête

Versprechen
Eintrittsversprechen

Ich will mich für meine Gruppe einsetzen und mein bestes tun, nach dem Pfadigesetz zu leben.
Ich bitte Gott und Euch alle, mir dabei zu helfen.
oder
Ich bitte Euch alle, mir dabei zu helfen.

Versprechen
Ich verspreche, meine möglichstes zu tun um
- mich immer von neuem mit dem Pfadigesetz auseinanderzusetzen
- nach dem Sinn und Ziel meines Lebens zu suchen
- mich in jeder Gemeinschaft einzusetzen, in der ich lebe
- ...

Im Vertrauen auf Gott und zusammen mit Euch allen versuche ich, nach diesem Versprechen zu leben.
oder
Zusammen mit Euch allen versuche ich, nach diesem Versprechen zu leben.

Pfadigesetz
Wir Pfadi wollen
- offen und ehrlich sein
- andere verstehen und achten
- unsere Hilfe anbieten
- Freude suchen und weitergeben
- miteinander teilen
- Sorge tragen zur Natur und allem Leben
- Schwierigkeiten mit Zuversicht begegnen
- uns entscheiden und Verantwortung tragen.

Dieses Pfadigesetz verbindet uns mit allen Pfadi der Welt. Wir ergänzen es für uns persönlich und für unsere Gruppe:
- ...
- ...

Little Bee

Motto
Allzeit bereit

Promessa – Primo impegno
Voglio impegnarmi nella mia pattuglia/ nel mio reparto e fare del mio megio per viver secondo la legge scaut.
Chiedo a Dio e a voi tutti di autarmi.
oppure
Chiedo a voi tutti di aiutarmi.

Promessa
Confidando nell'aiuto di Dio e nel vostro aiuto, con gioia prometto di fare tutto il possibile.
oppure
Confidando nel vostro aiuto, con gioia prometto di fare tutto il possibile
- per approfondire i valori della nostra legge
- per cercare di dare un senso alla mia vita
- per impegnarmi a favore di ogni communità in cui vivo
- e per ...

Legge
Noi scaut vogliamo:
- Essere aperti e sinceri
- Ascoltare e rispettare gli altri
- Offrire il nostro aiuto
- Trasmettere gioia attorno a noi
- Condividere
- Affrontare con fiducia le difficoltà
- Saper fare delle scelte e prendere degli impegni
- Amare la vita e proteggere la natura.

Questa è la nostra legge, che ci lega agli scaut di tutto il mondo. Completiamo per noi personalmente e per il nostro gruppo:
- ...
- ...

Motto
Sempre pronto/a

Empermischun d'entrada
jau vi m'engaschar per ia gruppa e far il meglier pussaivel per viver tenor la lescha dals battasendas.
jau dumond a Dieu ed a vus tuts da ma gidar.
u
jau dumond a vus tuts da ma gidar.

Emperischun
Cun l'agid da Dieu, cun voss agid e cun plaschair permet'jau da far tut il pussaivel
u
Cun voss agid a cun plaschair permet'jau da far tut il pussaivel
- per approfundir las valurs da nossa lescha
- per retschertgar il senn da mia vita
- per m'engagaschar en mintga communitad en la quala jau viv
- ...

Lescha battansendas
Nus battasendas vulain:
- esser avertas e sinceras
- enclegier e respectar ils auters
- offrir noss agid
- derasar plaschair enturn nus
- parter in cun l'auter
- proteger la natira e respectar la vita
- far frunt a las difficultads cun confidenza
- trair decisiuns e surpigliar responsabladad

Questa lescha ans colliescha als battasendas da tut il mund. Nus la cumplettain per nus persunalmain e per nossa gruppa:
- ...
- ...

Motto
Adina pronto/a

Promise – First Engagement
I want to pledge myself to my group, and obey to the best of my abilities, the Girl Scout Law.
To this effect, I ask all of you to help me.

Girl Scout Promise
With the help of God, with your help and happily
or
With your help and happily,
I Promise to do my best:
- To study in details the values of our Girl Scout Law
- To search for the meaning of my life
- To be involved in the community where I live:
- ...

Girl Scout Law
Girl Scouts, we wish
- To be true/truthful
- To listen to and respect others
- To be thoughtful and helpful
- To share
- To choose to the best of our abilities and to commit ourselves
- To protect nature and to respect life
- To face difficulties with confidence
- To rejoice in all that is beautiful.

This law binds us to all other Scouts in the world, and in the same spirit we want particularly:

- ...
- ...

Motto

Be prepared

The Law, Promise and Motto can take varying forms according to the age group they apply to.

Development of the Movement in Switzerland

Between 1913 and 1916 nine groups of Girl Scouts were formed independently in different parts of Switzerland. In 1919 these groups joined together to became one association, the Fédération des Eclaireuses Suisses (FES). A major change took place in 1987 when the Fédération des Eclaireuses Suisses and the Scout Association, Fédération des Eclaireurs Suisses, merged together to become the Mouvement Scout de Suisse (Swiss Guide and Scout Movement).

The Programme

One of the main objectives of the Mouvement Scout de Suisse is the formulation of a programme suitable for each branch, with personal development playing a key role. Whenever possible members with special needs are integrated into packs and companies, although separate groups do exist.

Working with the Community

Ranger/Rover activities are based mainly on service and the study of social problems. The lower age groups give help and service wherever they are needed. Service is given in hospitals and institutions throughout the year and service camps are organized regularly, especially in the Calanca Valley.

Outdoor and Environmental Activities

Company camps take place in tents in summer in the mountains and in autumn at lower levels. In winter many companies have skiing camps. Hiking and cycling are also popular with older members.

In 1990 the Association held a seminar to promote environmental education.

Training

Many leaders in Switzerland are young, aged 17-30, and so training is very important. Advanced training is carried out at national level. In 1989 training structures were revised and training content was adapted to meet the new needs of leaders.

Communication and Co-operation

The Swiss Guide and Scout Movement encourages international contacts and exchanges. Each year an increasing number of members go abroad or receive guests from other countries. Development projects, the latest in Zimbabwe and Rwanda, have helped to promote mutual international understanding.

The Swiss Guide and Scout Movement is a member of the National Youth Council, which has consultative status with the government. In addition the Movement plays an active role in various consultative groups where it regularly co-operates with other youth organizations with similar goals.

Taking environmental readings helps Guides learn more about how to preserve a quality lifestyle.

Tanzania

The Tanzania Girl Guides Association

Girl Guiding/Girl Scouting introduced: 1928
Became Associate Member of WAGGGS: 1963
Became Full Member of WAGGGS: 1969
Membership 1992: 17,230
Membership as % of female population: 0.11%
WAGGGS Region: Africa

Guide

Promise
Ahadi za Maskauti wa kike
Natoa ahadi kuwa nitafanya bidii
kutimiza yote yanipasayo kwa
Mwenyezi Mungu na Taifa langu;
kuwasaidia watu wote siku zote;
nakutii kanuni za Maskauti wa kike.

Kanuni za Maskauti wa kike
1 Skauti ni mwaminifu.
2 Skauti ni raia mwema.
3 Wajibu wa Skauti wa kike ni kuwa mtu wa kufaa na kuwasaidia watu kwa hiari.
4 Skauti ni rafiki kwa watu wote na ndugu kwa maskauti wote.
5 Skauti huwa na adabu na heshima.
6 Skauti huwahurumia na kuwapenda wanyama na viumbe vyote vyenye uhai.
7 Skauti hutii amri kwa furaha.
8 Skauti huchangamka hata katika shida taabu yoyote.
9 Skauti ni mwangalifu, na mtuzaji pia huweka akiba.
10 Skauti ni safi kwa mawazo maneno na matendo.

Motto
Uwe Tayari

Brownie

Ahadi ya Kiangaza
Naahidi kwa ya mini yangu kuwa nitafanya bidii,
kutimiza wajibu wangu kwa kumtumikia Mungu, Rais na Taifa langu.
Kusaidia watu wengine kila siku, hasa wale wa nyumbani.

Kanuni ya Kiangaza
Kiangaza huwaheshimu wakubwa wake.
Kiangaza hajipendelei mwenyewe.
Neno Kubwa la Kiangaza

Brownie Motto
Kuwasaidia wengine.

Promise
I promise on my honour to do my best:
To do my duty to God and my Nation;
To help other people at all times;
And to obey the Guide law.

Law
1 A Guide's honour is to be trusted.
2 A Guide is a good citizen.
3 A Guide's duty is to be useful and help others.
4 A Guide is a friend to all and a sister to every other Guide.
5 A Guide is courteous.
6 A Guide is kind to animals and all creation.
7 A Guide obeys orders cheerfully.
8 A Guide is courageous and cheerful.
9 A Guide is thrifty.
10 A Guide is pure in thought, word and deed.

Motto
Be Prepared

Brownie Promise
I promise to do my best:
To do my duty to God and my Nation;
To help other people every day especially those at home.

Brownie Law
A Brownie respects her elders.
A Brownie thinks of others before herself.

Brownie Motto
Lend a Hand

Age Groups

Ranger/Cadet	16-21
Guide	10-16
Brownie	6-10

Development of the Movement in Tanzania

The first Guide company started in the former East African State of Tanganyika in 1928, but it was not until 1935 that Guiding became firmly established following the visit in the same year of the Founder and the World Chief Guide. In 1938 a territorial council and local Association were formed and from 1940 to 1950 Guiding spread to all areas of the country. The first executive committee was formed in 1957. In 1964 the independent states of Tanganyika and Zanzibar united as the United Republic of Tanzania, and the Association was renamed.

The Programme

The Tanzania Girl Guides Association uses a four-point programme based on developing mental and physical attributes, relationships with others, outdoor living and service.

Working with the Community

Guides in Tanzania are engaged in a wide variety of service projects. Members give blood and help in hospitals and dispensaries. Guides also help the elderly and those with special needs and entertain children in orphanages.

The Association runs evening classes for women and in some regions Guides participate in clean-water projects. It also offers vocational training to school-leavers at its headquarters in Dar es Salaam. Vegetable-growing, poultry rearing, cooking, sewing and other handicrafts are among the activities undertaken by the girls. Courses run for two years and aim to make participants financially independent and encourage them to be more responsible citizens.

Outdoor and Environmental Activities

The Tanzania Girl Guides Association encourages participation in conservation projects including tree-planting. Guides also maintain and clean public areas.

Training

The Association organizes a variety of training events including trainings for young adults in order to prepare them to run Guide companies and Brownie packs.

Communication and Co-operation

The Tanzania Girl Guides Association encourages members to correspond with Girl Guides/Girl Scouts from overseas and to participate in Thinking Day activities.

The Association co-operates with the YWCA, the YMCA, the Tanzania Boy Scouts Association and the Salvation Army. Tanzania publishes a quarterly magazine, *Maskauti Wanaitana*.

Guides celebrate Thinking Day.

Thailand

The Girl Guides Association of Thailand

Girl Guiding/Girl Scouting introduced: 1957
Became Associate Member of WAGGGS: 1963
Became Full Member of WAGGGS: 1972
Membership 1992: 19,685
Membership as % of female population: 0.07%
WAGGGS Region: Asia Pacific

Guide

Bluebird

Kum Patiyan
Duey giat Khong Kapajow
Kapajow Kaw Patiyan Ton Wa:
Kapajow ja patibat na-tee un pueng mee taw chart, sassana, pra mahakasat;
Kapajow ja chuey luer poo uen smer;
Kapajow chuer lae ja patibat tam goht kong kana poo bumpen prayote.

Goht
1 Tum ton hai pen tee chuer tue lae wai wang jai dai.
2 Suesat.
3 Tam ton hai pen prayote lae chuey luer poo uen smer.
4 Pen mit gub kon tung lai lae tue pen pee nong gub poo bumpen prayote ruam kana.
5 Supab on nom.
6 Metta karuna taw sut.
7 Chuer fung lae patibut tam kumsung.
8 Oht ton taw kwam yark lumbark duey jai ra rerng.
9 Muttayut.
10 Sujarit prom gai vaja jai.

Motto
Triam prom smer

Bluebird Promise
Kapajow ja patibut na-tee un pueng mee taw chart, sassana, pra mahakasat.
Kapajow ja chuey luer poo uen took wun doye chapaw kon nai bahn.

Goht Bluebird
1 Nok Seefar Kaorop lae cheua Fang Pu Mee Arwuso
2 Nok Seefar Mai Nuck Thueng Tae Ton Eng Tao Nan
3 Nok Seefar cha Tong Pued Tae Kwam Jing
4 Nok Seefar Ja Tong Saad lae pen rabeub
5 Nok Seefar Tam Ngarn lae len duay Jitjai rarueng lae raksa Kotken.

Bluebird Motto
Chuey luer poo uen smer

Promise
On my honour I promise:
To do my duty to my country, my religion and the King;
To help other people at all times;
To obey the Guide Law.

Law
1 A Guide's honour is to be trusted.
2 A Guide is loyal.
3 A Guide's duty is to be useful and to help others.
4 A Guide is a friend to all and a sister to every other Guide.
5 A Guide is courteous.
6 A Guide is a friend to animals.
7 A Guide obeys orders.
8 A Guide smiles and sings under all difficulties.
9 A Guide is thrifty.
10 A Guide is pure in thought, word and deed.

Motto
Be Prepared

Bluebird Promise
I promise to do my best to do my duty to my country, my religion and the King.
I promise to help other people every day, especially those at home.

Bluebird Law
1 The Bluebird respects and obeys the elders
2 The Bluebird does not think of herself only
3 The Bluebird only speaks the truth

4 The Bluebird is clean and in order
5 The Bluebird works and plays cheerfully and orderly.

Bluebird Motto
Lend a Hand

Age Groups

Senior Guide	16-21
Guide	11-15
Bluebird	7-11

Development of the Movement in Thailand

Girl Guiding in Thailand began in 1957 and the Girl Guides Association of Thailand was formally registered in 1958. The Association received visits from World Association trainers and Guiding expanded rapidly with the formation of Guide companies all over the country. In 1962 the Association was granted Royal Patronage by Her Majesty Queen Sirikit.

The Association's headquarters in Bangkok were opened in 1967 and consist of an administrative block with an adjoining hostel. This provides dormitories for trainers, guest rooms, a cafeteria, a shop, a swimming pool and a pre-school centre.

The Programme

The programme for Guides and Bluebirds focuses on four points: character building, health, handicrafts and service. The programme for Senior Guides stresses service; duty to religion and country; international understanding; and the development of skills useful to society and the individual.

The programme for school-leavers emphasises occupational training such as agriculture, fishery skills, weaving and sewing, in addition to the programme outlined above. Law for everyday life and simple arithmetic are also taught, and participants are encouraged to develop leadership qualities, and an awareness of personal health and hygiene.

Working with the Community

Community service is included in the programme of each branch and large-scale service projects are undertaken. Guides help in hospitals, orphanages and day nurseries and work with leprosy patients and those with special needs. They also give service during emergencies and epidemics, and assist with water supply, sanitation and nutrition.

The Association runs a special literacy programme for girls who do not receive a formal education. Skills taught include reading, writing, handicrafts and hygiene.

Guides are learning to make uniforms as an income-generating project. The skill gives them a chance to find jobs.

The Girl Guides Association of Thailand runs a national campaign centred on urban and rural primary health care. Training in primary health care is given to many women's groups and rural villages. The Association has also opened childcare centres in many provinces.

Service in the healthcare area is also very important. Thai Guides support the country's goal of Health for All by the Year 2000 and have implemented a project entitled Promotion of Women as Health Care Providers of Family and Community. The project aims to increase national awareness of the role of women as health care providers as well as promoting women' participation in health and other social development projects.

The Thai Guides and Leaders run annual service camps for underprivileged girls which give young girls from poor families, with little education, a broad general training. The girls have a chance to enjoy themselves, to see new things and to acquire a basic knowledge of their own country.

Outdoor and Environmental Activities

The Girl Guides Association of Thailand is

conscious of the threat of pollution and the need to protect the environment. The Association has held meetings on conservation with other youth organizations in the country, produced anti-pollution stickers and arranged tree-planting campaigns.

Training

The training department at headquarters has full-time trainers. In addition, the Association sends good trainees abroad and to government institutions for further training.

Communication and Co-operation

The Girl Guides Association of Thailand has ongoing exchange programmes with Australia and the United Kingdom and also takes part in an annual tree-planting programme with Girl Scouts from Japan. It also has good press, radio and television coverage, and publishes a newsletter periodically.

It works closely with international organizations and national government agencies. For example financial support for the project Health for All by the Year 2000 came from the World Health Organization and technical assistance from such local government agencies as the Ministry of Public Health.

Girl Guides have created awareness of environmental pollution problems.

Togo

Federation des Guides et des Eclaireuses du Togo

Component Associations
Guides du Togo
Eclaireuses Unionistes du Togo

Girl Guiding/Girl Scouting introduced: 1942
Became Associate Member of WAGGGS: 1963
Membership 1992: 556
Membership as % of female population: 0.03%
WAGGGS Region: Africa

Guides du Togo

Promesse
Sur mon honneur, avec la grâce de Dieu, je m'engage:
A servir de mon mieux Dieu, l'Eglise et la Patrie;
A aider mon prochain en toutes circonstances;
A observer la loi des guides.

Loi
1 La guide est loyale.
2 La guide pense d'abord aux autres.
3 La guide est généreuse: elle est prête à servir.
4 La guide est accueillante: elle a l'esprit d'équipe.
5 La guide, soeur de toute autre guide, est présente à tous.
6 La guide découvre la nature; elle y voit l'oeuvre de Dieu.
7 La guide sait obéir.
8 La guide ne craint pas l'effort; elle ne fait rien à moitié.
9 La guide aime son travail et respecte celui des autres.
10 La guide est maîtresse de soi; elle est pure et joyeuse.

Devise
Toujours prête

Promesse des Jeannettes
Je promets de faire de mon mieux:
pour être fidèle à Dieu, à mon pays, à mes parents, à la loi de la ronde, et pour faire chaque jour un plaisir à quelqu'un.

Loi des Jeannettes
Une jeannette est toujours propre.
Une jeannette est toujours active.
Une jeannette est toujours gaie.
Une jeannette dit toujours vrai.
Une jeannette pense d'abord aux autres.

Devise des Jeannettes
De notre mieux

Promise
On my honour, with the grace of God, I undertake:
To do my best to serve God, the Church and my Country;
To help others in all circumstances;
To keep the Guide Law.

Law
1 A Guide is loyal.
2 A Guide thinks first of others.
3 A Guide is generous: she is prepared to help.
4 A Guide is welcoming: she has team spirit.
5 A Guide, sister to every other Guide, is at the service of all.
6 A Guide learns about nature, in which she sees God's work.
7 A Guide knows how to obey.
8 A Guide does not fear endeavour; she does nothing by halves.
9 A Guide likes her work and respects that of others.
10 A Guide is self-controlled; she is pure and cheerful.

Motto
Always prepared

Brownie Promise
I promise to do my best:
to be faithful to God, my Country, my parents and the law of the pack, and to do a good turn to someone every day.

Guide

Brownie

Brownie Law
A Brownie is always clean.
A Brownie is always active.
A Brownie is always cheerful.
A Brownie always tells the truth.
A Brownie thinks first of others.

Brownie Motto
The best we can

Age Groups

Guide Aînée	Ranger	17+
Guide	Guide	12-17
Jeannette	Brownie	7-12

Development of the Movement in Togo

Girl Guiding in Togo began in 1942 with the formation of the Eclaireuses Unionistes du Togo and in 1956 Guides du Togo was established. Activities of the two organizations were carried out under the auspices of Scoutisme Féminin du Togo. The members of the Eclaireuses Unionistes du Togo were mainly in rural areas of the country, while the Guides du Togo had members in schools and parishes, and also in the countryside.

Guides du Togo

The Association caters for the special needs of Roman Catholic girls.

The Programme
Members of the Association choose a theme each year and programme activities are planned to highlight aspects of it.

Working with the Community
An agricultural project is run by members of the Association at Agou where employment is offered to needy young people. The project has entailed planting maize, gombo, spinach, yam and cassava crops which are sold to buy more supplies to continue the project.

Literacy and basic economics courses are also offered as part of the project. Similar agricultural projects are carried out at Goumoukope and Tsevie where women participate in craft projects and learn dressmaking, embroidery, crocheting and knitting skills.

Outdoor and Environmental Activities
Guides in Togo are involved in re-afforestation projects. They have planted trees around the Association's grounds and have also improved public areas through tree-planting.

Communication and Co-operation
Guides correspond regularly with the Association des Guides du Burkina Faso and work with other youth movements at national level.

Guiding is publicized by the girls themselves, who organize exhibitions of their art, handicrafts and photographs.

Eclaireuses Unionistes du Togo

There had been no news of active Girl Guiding by the Eclaireuses Unionistes du Togo for several years, due to unrest. But now WAGGGS has re-established contact with the Association and the Movement is restarted.

More information about this Association will be available in a future edition of this publication.

Tonga

The Girl Guides Association of the Kingdom of Tonga

Girl Guiding/Girl Scouting introduced: 1952
Became Associate Member of WAGGGS: 1987
Membership 1992†: 205
Membership as % of female population: 0.44%
WAGGGS Region: Asia Pacific

Promise

I promise that I will do my best;
To do my duty to God
To serve the King of Tonga and my Country
and help other people and
To keep the Guide Law.

Law

1 A Guide is loyal and can be trusted.
2 A Guide is helpful.
3 A Guide is polite and considerate.
4 A Guide is friendly and a sister to all Guides.
5 A Guide is kind to animals and respects all living things.
6 A Guide is obedient.
7 A Guide has courage and is cheerful in all difficulties.
8 A Guide makes good use of her time.
9 A Guide takes care of her own possessions and those of other people.
10 A Guide is self-controlled in all she thinks, says and does.

Motto

Be Prepared

Brownie Guide Promise

I promise I will do my best;
To do my duty to God
To serve the King of Tonga and my country
to help other people and
To keep the Brownie Guide Law.

Brownie Guide Law

A Brownie Guide thinks of others before herself and does a good turn every day.

Brownie Guide Motto

Lend a Hand

Development of the Movement in Tonga

Guide

Guiding was started in Tonga at the instigation of Queen Salote in 1952 and the first companies were formed on the island of Tongatapu. In 1955 the consort of the present King became Commissioner of the Association. The first Brownie pack was started in 1957 and, during the next few years, Guiding spread to the islands of Ha'apai and Vava'u, and to the 'Eua in 1971.

In 1986 the Girl Guides Association (United Kingdom) signed a Deed of Transfer which gave Tonga, formerly a Branch Association, self-government in all areas of work.

The geography of the country and the lack of roads make communication between the islands difficult which prevents regular visits and trainings on the outlying islands. At present, Guiding is active only on the main island due to a lack of leaders. Teachers interested in Guiding are currently being encouraged to start units in their schools.

Brownie Guide

The Programme

The Association follows a programme specially prepared for the Pacific Islands. It is based on the eight-point system of the Girl Guides Association (United Kingdom): thinking for oneself, keeping fit, keeping the Guide Law, exploring the arts, giving service, becoming a homemaker, getting to know people and enjoying the outdoors.

Working with the Community

The Guides and Rangers concentrate on activities such as service, health and hygiene, homecraft and first aid.

Outdoor and Environmental Activities

Camps are often held on the grounds of the Association's headquarters. The girls sleep indoors but enjoy camping activities outside during the day. In 1988 the government asked the Association to take responsibility for the care of a 60-year-old tree in the middle of the capital.

Guides learn to make leis.

Training

Three trainers are responsible for running training sessions and testing leaders, and trainings are held at the headquarters once a week for leaders who are new to the Movement. The Association hopes to start refresher courses for the members conducting these sessions.

Communication and Co-operation

From Brownie level, members are trained to appreciate the international nature of the Movement. The Association understands the value of participating in international activities and members have attended events in several other countries.

Girl Guiding is well accepted by the community, and the Association has been invited to assist at several state functions. It is frequently invited to participate in the activities of other organizations such as the Red Cross, and has good relations with Rotary International and Lions International. Guides have assisted at the Lions Club annual Christmas party for children with special needs since 1985.

The Association has a monthly newsletter, *Tautavale*, which is sent to all leaders.

Trinidad and Tobago

The Girl Guides Association of Trinidad and Tobago

Girl Guiding/Girl Scouting introduced:	**1914**
Became Associate Member of WAGGGS:	**1963**
Became Full Member of WAGGGS:	**1969**
Membership 1992:	**2,483**
Membership as % of female population:	**0.4%**
WAGGGS Region:	**Western Hemisphere**

Promise
I promise that I will do my best
To do my duty to God,
To serve my country and help other people,
And to keep the Guide Law.

Law
1 A Guide is loyal and can be trusted.
2 A Guide is helpful.
3 A Guide is polite and considerate.
4 A Guide is friendly and a sister to all Guides.
5 A Guide is kind to animals and respects all living things.
6 A Guide is obedient.
7 A Guide has courage and is cheerful in all difficulties.
8 A Guide makes good use of her time.
9 A Guide is careful of her own belongings and respects those of others.
10 A Guide is self-controlled in all she thinks, says and does.

Motto
Be Prepared

Brownie Promise
I promise that I will do my best
To do my duty to God,
To serve my country and to help other people,
And to keep the Brownie Law.

Brownie Law
A Brownie thinks of others before herself,
And does a good turn every day.

Brownie Motto
Lend a Hand

Age Groups

Young Leader	18-21
Ranger	15-18
Senior Guide	12-15
Junior Guide	9-12
Brownie Guide	6-9

Guide

Development of the Movement in Trinidad and Tobago

Guiding in Trinidad and Tobago began in 1914 and the Association became a registered Branch Association of the Girl Guides Association (United Kingdom). In 1930, the foundation stone of the Girl Guide headquarters was laid by the Founder and World Chief Guide.

The Programme
Trinidad and Tobago, with the other members of the Caribbean Link of Guiding, has introduced a Caribbean Programme suited to the needs of Caribbean girls.

Working with the Community
Much emphasis is placed on service as an important segment of the programme for girls at all levels. Activities include ushering at church services and public functions; escorting children with special needs on outings; cleaning and maintaining homes for the aged; helping the elderly with their chores; assisting with fund raising ventures and visiting and helping patients in hospitals and institutions.

Brownie

Outdoor and Environmental Activities
The Association organizes camps and hikes for Guides, local Association members and leaders as well as pack holidays and nature walks for Brownies at both unit and national levels.
Guides have been involved in tree-planting activities and in helping to make parks and public buildings more attractive.

Training
The training programme is organized into three categories: regional trainings, which are monitored by regional training committees, trainings for Guide leaders, and trainings for trainers and potential trainers.

Communication and Co-operation
The Association's programme emphasizes international education and members attend events abroad when possible. International friendships are maintained through pen friend schemes and participation in international camps. Trinidad and Tobago is a member of the Caribbean Link, set up for the purpose of consultation and mutual aid among Guide Associations in the Commonwealth countries and islands of the Caribbean.

Turkey

Federation Turque de Scoutisme et Guidisme
(Scouting and Guiding Federation of Turkey)

Girl Guiding/Girl Scouting introduced: 1923
Became Associate Member of WAGGGS: 1972
Became Full Member of WAGGGS: 1987
Membership 1992†: 4,625
Membership as % of female population: 0.02%
WAGGGS Region: Europe

And
Tanrıya, vatanıma karşı vazifelerimi yerine getireceğime, izcilik türesine uyacağıma,
Başkalarına her zaman yardımda bulunacagıma,
Kendimi bedence sağlam, fikirce uyanık ve ahlâkça dürüst tutmak için elimden geleni yapacağıma şerefim üzerine and içerim.

Türe
1 İzci sözünün eridir, şeref ve haysiyetini her şeyin üstünde tutar.
2 İzci, yurduna, milletine, ailesine ve izci liderlerine sadıktır.
3 İzci, başkalarına yardımcı ve yararlı olur.
4 İzci, herkesin arkadaşı ve bütün izcilerin kardeşidir.
5 İzci, herkese karşı naziktir.
6 İzci, bitki ve hayvanları sever ve korur.
7 İzci, büyüklerın sözünü dinler, küçüklerini sever ve korur.
8 İzci, cesurdur her türlü şartlar içinde neşeli ve güler yüzlüdür.
9 İzci, tutumludur.
10 İzci, fikir, söz ve hareketlerinde açık ve dürüsttür.

Motto
İzci daima hazırdır

And Yavrukurt
Tanrıya, vatanıma karşı vazifelerimi yerine getireceğime,
Yavrukurt türesine uyacağıma,
Başkalarına her zaman yardımda bulunacağıma,
Kendimi bedence saglam, fikirce uyanık ve ahlâkça dürüst tutmak için elimden geleni yapacağıma, şerefim üzerine and içerim.

Türe Yavrukurt
Yavrukurt, izcinin izinde gider ve her gün bir iyilik yapar.
Yavrukurt çalıskandır, işinde bikkinlik ve bezginlik göstermez.

Motto Yavrukurt
Yavrukurt çok çalısır

Promise
On my honour, I will try:
To do my duty to God and my country,
To obey the Girl Guide law,
To help other people at all times,
To keep myself physically fit, mentally awake and morally honest

Law
1 A Girl Guide's honour is to be trusted.
2 A Girl Guide is loyal to her country, her parents and her leaders.
3 A Girl Guide's duty is to be useful and to help others.
4 A Girl Guide is a friend to all and sister to all other Guides.
5 A Girl Guide is courteous.
6 A Girl Guide is a friend to animals and plants.
7 A Girl Guide obeys orders of her parents and loves and helps those who are younger than herself.
8 A Girl Guide is brave. She smiles under all difficulties.
9 A Girl Guide is thrifty.
10 A Girl Guide is clean in thought, word and deed.

Motto
A Girl Guide is always ready

Guide

Brownie

Brownie Promise
On my honour, I will try:
To do my duty to God and my country,
To obey the Brownie law,
To help other people at all times,
To keep myself physically fit, mentally awake and morally honest.

Brownie Law
A Brownie lives like a Guide and does a good turn every day. A Brownie is industrious and never never shows boredom or laziness.

Brownie Motto
Lend a Hand

Age Groups
Ergin Ízci	Venture Guide	16-21
Ízci	Guide	12-16
Yavrukurt	Brownie	8-12

Development of the Movement in Turkey

Guiding started in Turkey just after the foundation of the Turkish Republic in 1923, following a request from the Ministry of Education that the Movement be introduced into several girls' schools. These companies continued their activities, and in 1936 the Directorate of Scouting and Guiding was founded. This Directorate acted as the central governing body for both Guides and Scouts.

In 1968 the Association was re-organized, becoming a Joint Organization. Men and women have equal rights of election to administrative committees, but programmes for girls and boys remain separate.

The Programme
The programme emphasizes the spiritual and moral values of Guiding as outlined in the Promise and Law. It concentrates on giving girls an interest in other people and in service to the community in which they live, as well as providing opportunities to learn practical skills and crafts.

Working with the Community
The Guide Section is involved in many different fields of service. Members organize literacy classes for adults, and are active in hygiene campaigns. Guides have given valuable assistance in times of natural disasters by providing clothing and shelter for the victims.

Outdoor and Environmental Activities
The Association has access to several campsites throughout the country. A Scout and Guide winter camp, which includes winter sports, is organized at the Bolu Aladag centre.

Training
The Guide Section has both professional and volunteer trainers. The Association organizes a full programme of seminars and gatherings for leaders, trainers and administrators in order to ensure that appropriate activities are run efficiently throughout the country. The seminars include specialized training according to the age group.

Communication and Co-operation
The Guide Section receives good media coverage and also publicizes its activities through newsletters.

Tuvalu

Girl Guides Association of Tuvalu

Girl Guiding/Girl Scouting introduced: 1950
Became Associate Member of WAGGGS: 1990
Membership 1989: 444
Membership as % of female population: 12.57%
WAGGGS Region: Asia Pacific

Guide

Sunbeam

Promise
I promise that I will do my best;
To do my duty to God
To serve the Queen and my country, to help other people and
To keep the Guide Law.

Law
- A Guide is loyal and can be trusted
- A Guide is helpful
- A Guide is polite and considerate
- A Guide is friendly and a sister to all Guides
- A Guide is kind to animals and respects all living things
- A Guide is obedient
- A Guide has courage and is cheerful in all difficulties
- A Guide makes good use of her time
- A Guide takes care of her own possessions and those of other people
- A Guide is self controlled in all she thinks, says and does.

Age Groups

Rangers	15-25
Guides	11-14
Sunbeams	7-11

Development of the Movement in Tuvalu

Guiding was introduced to the Ellice Islands, now Tuvalu, around 1950 by leaders from the neighbouring Gilbert Islands (now Kiribati). The Movement spread quickly and in 1968 the first training was held in Funafuti with the assistance of a trainer from New Zealand. In 1975 the Ellice Islands became Tuvalu. The Association, a branch Association of The Girl Guides Association (United Kingdom) established an Executive Committee and visits from leaders and trainers from the United Kingdom helped Tuvalu to develop its future plans and programme.

In 1989 The Girl Guides Association (United Kingdom) signed a Deed of Transfer giving the Girl Guides Association of Tuvalu self-government in all areas of work. Thus, Guiding is now flourishing in eight of the nine islands comprising Tuvalu.

The Programme
The programme used by the three branches was devised for the Pacific Islands in 1969 and has been regularly reviewed since its introduction. It is based on an eight-point programme which gives Guides opportunities to develop physical fitness, the mind, outdoor enjoyment, homecraft skills, service to others, human relations, creativity and character. Some units are attached to schools, although open units are also found in villages.

Working with the Community
The Association started the Olave Kindergarten in 1986, the only registered kindergarten in the country. About 60 children attend the kindergarten which is run by four trained teachers employed by the Association. This project helps members to appreciate the importance of community development within the Guide programme.

Many service projects are also undertaken such as laying a new drainage system for a village and catering for activities organized by other organizations.

Outdoor and Environmental Activities
All members participate in camping and hiking activities. Guides improve their environment by undertaking to clean public areas.

Training
Training sessions are taking place in Vaitupu pending the completion of the Association's new headquarters. Due to the high cost of travel a national training is held every two years and is attended by all leaders. New leaders recruited between national trainings receive basic training in Funafuti.

Communication and Co-operation
The Association takes an active part in Pacific Island Conferences and in the past members have attended international trainings and camps in New Zealand and Australia.

The Olave Kindergarten has helped to publicize Guiding in Tuvalu and the Association's work is well-received by the public.

The Association is a founder member of the Tuvalu Association of Non-Government Organizations (TANGO) and it works closely with the Women's Handicraft Centre, the Red Cross and the Scout Association. The Red Cross offers Guides first aid courses and members of the Association help the Red Cross in return.

Uganda

The Uganda Girl Guides Association

Girl Guiding/Girl Scouting introduced: 1914
Became Associate Member of WAGGGS: 1963
Became Full Member of WAGGGS: 1984
Membership 1992†: 10,136
Membership as % of female population: 0.12%
WAGGGS Region: Africa

Guide

Promise
I promise, on my honour, to do my best:
To do my duty to God and my country;
To help other people at all times; and
To obey the Guide Law.

Law
1 A Guide is reliable and speaks the truth.
2 A Guide is loyal.
3 A Guide's duty is to be useful and to help others.
4 A Guide is a friend to all and a sister to every other Guide.
5 A Guide is polite and considerate.
6 A Guide respects God's creation and protects plants and animals.
7 A Guide obeys orders.
8 A Guide smiles and sings under all difficulties.
9 A Guide makes good use of time, talents and possessions.
10 A Guide is pure in thought, word and deed.

Motto
Be Prepared

Brownie Promise
I promise to do my best:
To do my duty to God and my country;
To help other people every day, especially those at home.

Brownie Law
A Brownie is truthful, obedient and cheerful.
A Brownie gives in to the older folk.
A Brownie thinks of others before herself.

Brownie Motto
Ready and helpful

Age Groups

Cadet	17+
Ranger	15+
Guide	11-15
Brownie	7½-11

Development of the Movement in Uganda

Guiding in Uganda began between 1914 and 1918 at Toro Girls' School, but it was not until 1922 that the first Guide company was officially recognized and the Movement was firmly established.

Guiding subsequently spread throughout the country and the Girl Guides Association (United Kingdom) sent trainers to Uganda, who helped to organize camps and trainings. In 1956 the World Chief Guide visited Uganda and laid the foundation stone of the headquarters for the Girl Guide and Scout Associations.

During the 1970s membership declined because of the difficult political situation, but since 1981 Guiding has steadily grown and companies and packs which had ceased to function have been restarted.

The Programme
The programme is prepared with the aim of training Ugandan girls to become worthwhile citizens, and activities are based on the development of character, relationships with others, physical fitness, health and hygiene, outdoor activities and service to others. Members include girls with special needs.

Working with the Community
The Association has four major service projects. A school leavers' project at

Brownie

national headquarters offers girls and women training in sewing, cooking, dress-making and embroidery.

An immunization campaign, launched in 1986 in two pilot districts, Kampala and Entebbe, has now been extended to 12 districts. Guides visit homes and educate mothers about the importance of immunization as well as helping to carry children to dispensaries and immunization centres.

Local vegetables are grown at the Association's national camping and training ground at Kaazi to promote nutritional standards among the members of the Association and the surrounding community. The Association plans to extend this project to all districts. In 1990 the Association launched a piggery project at the same site which will also be extended to other areas of Uganda in the long term.

Training

A training programme is prepared annually by the Programme and Training Committee and the Association has two full-time trainers. Trainings for Commissioners are carried out at national level, and leaders' and trainers' trainings are held at district level.

Communication and Co-operation

Representatives of the Uganda Girl Guides Association have attended training seminars, workshops and Conferences hosted by other Member Organizations. The Association has also received much support from other countries, for example, the piggery project at Kaazi supported by the Canadian High Commission.

Guiding is well known throughout Uganda. The Association informs the general public about its activities through radio, television, newspapers, talks and films and the Association publishes a quarterly magazine called *The Link*.

The Association has good relations with the Church and the Government, especially the Ministry of Education, and is invited to government functions. Contact is maintained with several non-governmental organizations in the country, including the Uganda Scouts Association, UNESCO and UNICEF. The Uganda Scouts Association, the YMCA and the St. John's Ambulance Brigade all have representatives on the Uganda Girl Guides Association's National Executive Committee.

Uganda Ranger makes her Promise.

United Arab Emirates

Girl Guides Association of the United Arab Emirates

Girl Guiding/Girl Scouting introduced:	**1973**
Became Associate Member of WAGGGS:	**1984**
Became Full Member of WAGGGS:	**1990**
Membership 1992:	**5,883**
Membership as % of female population:	**1.2%**
Member:	**Arab Regional Group**

Promise
On my honour, I promise to do my best:
1 To do my duty to God then to my country;
2 To help other people in all circumstances;
3 To abide by the Girl Guides Law.

The Law
- A Girl Guide Honour is to be trusted.
- A Girl Guide is loyal to God, her Country, her leaders and subordinates.
- A Girl Guide is useful and helpful to others.
- A Girl Guide is a friend to all and a sister to every other Guide.
- A Girl Guide has a praiseworthy character.
- A Girl Guide is kind to animals.
- A Girl Guide is obedient to her parents and leaders.
- A Girl Guide keeps her smile when facing difficulties and deals with all such difficulties with patience and perseverance.
- A Girl Guide is thrifty.
- A Girl Guide is pure in word and in deed.

Flower Promise
On my honour, I promise that I will do my best:
1 To do my duty to God and my country;
2 To help other people at all times, especially my family;
3 To obey the Girl Guide law.

Age Groups

Senior Guides	16-18
Guides	12-15
Flower	6-11

Development of the Movement in the United Arab Emirates

Guiding in the United Arab Emirates began in 1973 when Girl Guide companies were opened in Sharjah. In the same year the first training for 30 leaders was run by the Arab Training Commissioner and Guiding has since spread to all seven Emirates.

The Girl Guides Association of the United Arab Emirates was officially registered with the government in 1979. Guiding has now reached all educational sectors, including the university, and efforts are being made to extend the Movement to rural areas.

The Programme
The Association follows an eight-point programme based on keeping fit, becoming a homemaker, giving service, keeping the Guide Law, getting to know people, enjoying the outdoors, thinking for yourself and exploring the arts. The programme is carried out in schools and aims to assist girls in becoming good citizens and future leaders, and to serve others.

Guide

Flower

Working with the Community

Community service is a major part of the programme and members entertain patients in hospitals and centres for people with special needs. Guides also visit rural areas to give instruction to women in health care and first aid. Patrols take responsibility for cleaning communal areas in schools, and care for younger children who travel by bus.

Outdoor and Environmental Activities

Overnight camping is not permitted for girls in the Emirates, but day camps are organized and girls follow the traditional camp programme. The grounds at the Association's headquarters in Sharjah provide facilities for some camps and trainings.

The Association's concern for the environment is demonstrated through its involvement in tree-planting and in Traffic Week.

Training

The Association has a committee and commissioner for training, camping and programme activities. The committee meets every two weeks. Each Emirate carries out local trainings and camps and the national trainers organize regional and national events. The Association has four paid trainers and ten volunteer trainers and is in the process of producing a training manual.

Communication and Co-operation

The United Arab Emirates promotes the international aspect of the Movement and activities include joint celebrations of Thinking Day with overseas members of other Girl Guide/Girl Scout organizations. The Association also has good relations with the Emirates Scout Association and works with many national women's organizations.

On the publicity side, the Girl Guides Association of the United Arab Emirates is held in high esteem by the government and the public. The media publicizes the Association's work widely, and members are always invited to official ceremonies.

Flowers learn games as part of learning about their heritage.

United Kingdom of Great Britain and Northern Ireland

The Guide Association

Founder Member of WAGGGS

Girl Guiding/Girl Scouting introduced:	**1909**
Membership 1992:	**707,651**
Membership as % of female population:	**2.41%**
WAGGGS Region:	**Europe**

Promise
I promise that I will do my best
To love my God,
To serve the Queen and my country[‡]
To help other people and
To keep the Guide Law.

‡The words underlined may be replaced by "the country in which I live" for those who do not regard the country in which they live as their own country. Rangers also have a further responsibility to be of service to the community.

Law
1 A Guide is loyal and can be trusted.
2 A Guide is helpful.
3 A Guide is polite and considerate.
4 A Guide is friendly and a sister to all Guides.
5 A Guide is kind to animals and respects all living things.
6 A Guide is obedient.
7 A Guide has courage and is cheerful in all difficulties.
8 A Guide makes good use of her time.
9 A Guide takes care of her own possessions and those of other people.
10 A Guide is self-controlled in all she thinks, says and does.

Motto
Be Prepared

Brownie Guide Promise
I promise that I will do my best;
To do my duty to God,
To serve the Queen and help other people, and
To keep the Brownie Guide Law.

Brownie Guide Law
A Brownie Guide thinks of others before herself and does a Good Turn every day.

Brownie Guide Motto
Lend a Hand

Rainbow Guide Promise
I will do my best to
love God and be kind
and helpful.

Age Groups

Ranger Guides	14-25
Guides	10-14
Brownie Guides	7-10
Rainbow Guide	5-7

Guide

Development of the Movement in the United Kingdom of Great Britain and Northern Ireland

The Guide Association was officially recognized in 1910 and now has four sections – Rainbow Guides, Brownie Guides, Guides and Ranger Guides. The Guide Association has members in the six Regions of England and in the Countries of Scotland, Wales and Northern Ireland. It also has British members in more than 30 countries overseas and represents a number of Branch Associations throughout the world.

The Association is fortunate in the support it is given by the British Royal Family: HRH The Princess Margaret is President of the Guide Association and HM The Queen and HM The Queen Mother are both Patrons.

Brownie Guide

The Programme
Each girl takes part in a balanced and varied programme which encourages her

to develop physically, mentally, emotionally and spiritually so that she can live out her Promise and make a positive contribution to her community and the wider world. The programme, the core of which is common to each section, grows with the girl. Everyone in the unit is encouraged to take a full part in planning the programme and determining its activities. Building on its Forward Plan the Association is offering more and more adventurous activities and opportunities.

Brownies learn to use new computer technology.

Working with the Community

The Association wants Guiding to be available to every girl and woman who wishes to take part and Guiding is adapting more and more to reflect the United Kingdom's multi-racial and multi-cultural society. A Community Involvement and Development group has been formed to encourage the formation of units in areas and communities which might not have traditionally responded to Guiding. Members of the Movement are involved in a wide variety of projects in local communities and undertake fundraising activities to finance development projects in other countries.

Outdoor and Environmental Activities

The Association owns campsites in England and Wales, and in addition runs a centre for outdoor activities in the Peak District, in northern England, which caters for groups of young people and adults wishing to experience and be trained in a variety of pursuits.

Activities to protect and improve the environment form an integral part of the programme. A national recycling project was launched in 1991 in conjunction with a major supermarket chain.

Training

Successful Guiding needs good, supportive training, found in the Leadership Scheme which provides 'in service' training for all Guiders and is tailored to individual needs. A full-time training team operates from the Association's Headquarters and the Association has a series of Country and Region Training and Activity Centres.

The Guide Association Training Licence is recognized by the Council for the Education and Training of Youth and Community Workers as a qualification valid outside the Movement. Commissioners also have a training scheme whereby a new Commissioner is linked with a more experienced Commissioner who acts as her personal tutor. Many young women aged 15-18 take part in the Young Leader Scheme.

Communication and Co-operation

Through both the Girl Guide Friendship Fund and WAGGGS' Mutual Aid Scheme members support and are involved in the development of international Guiding.

Following on the success of a joint Guide Association and UNICEF Primary Health Care Project in Sri Lanka (which was visited regularly), the Guide Association has worked with Rotary International in its PolioPlus campaign. It aims to teach Guides in the United Kingdom about the importance of immunization and primary health care in four developing countries while aiming to eradicate polio and control the five other childhood killer diseases. This project has encouraged further contact with the countries involved, especially Thailand and Jamaica.

International awareness is improved through regular articles, features and competitions in the Association's periodicals. It also maintains a slide library and commentaries on other countries, and has built up a resource centre of games, stories, recipes, activities and information from Commonwealth countries.

Publications and public relations are receiving a fresh new look after a comprehensive overhaul. A new uniform for all sections was introduced in 1990 and the three monthly magazines *Brownie*, *Guide Patrol* and *Guiding* have all been successfully restyled and relaunched.

The Guide Association is a recognized part of the Youth Service and has contact with various 'umbrella' bodies and government departments. The Association co-operates with other organizations for young people, male and female, and particularly with the Scout Association, its units and members. There are four affiliated organizations with which the Guide Association associates in connection with Girl Guiding: the Salvation Army, the Church Army, the YMCA and the Girl's Friendly Society.

Rainbow Guides are some of the youngest members of the Movement.

United States of America

Girl Scouts of the USA

Founder Member of WAGGGS

Girl Guiding/Girl Scouting introduced:	**1912**
Membership 1992:	**3,510,313**
Membership as % of female population:	**2.7%**
WAGGGS Region:	**Western Hemisphere**

Girl Scout

Promise
On my honor, I will try:
To serve God and my country,
To help people at all times,
And to live by the Girl Scout Law.

Law
I will do my best:
- to be honest
- to be fair
- to help where I am needed
- to be cheerful
- to be friendly and considerate
- to be a sister to every Girl Scout
- to respect authority
- to use resources wisely
- to protect and improve the world around me
- to show respect for myself and others through my words and actions.

Motto
Be Prepared

Age Groups

Senior Girl Scout	14-17
Cadette Girl Scout	11-14
Junior Girl Scout	8-11
Brownie Girl Scout	6-8
Daisy Girl Scout	5-6

Brownie Girl Scout

Development of the Movement in the United States of America

Girl Scouting in the USA was established in 1912 by Juliette Gordon Low, who was influenced by the work of the Founder and by the example of Guide companies in England and Scotland. The National Organization was formed three years later. The organization maintains two national centres: The Juliette Gordon Low Center in Savannah, Georgia; and The Edith Macy Conference Center in Briarcliff, New York.

The Programme
Girl Scouts of the USA has made sweeping changes in its programme in an effort to keep pace with society's shifts in values and lifestyle. The programme combines the essential beliefs and principles of the Movement with the expanding role of women and girls. It is designed to help a girl achieve her own highest potential; to develop values to give meaning and direction to her life; to relate to others with increasing understanding, skill and respect; and to contribute to the improvement of her society through the use of her own abilities and leadership skills in co-operative efforts with others.

The nationally distributed Contemporary Issues Series of publications helps girls understand and cope with the many modern-day issues and dilemmas they will face such as substance abuse, teenage pregnancy, literacy, and growing up female.

To provide Senior Girl Scouts with opportunities to develop and use their leadership skills, Girl Scouts of the USA introduced a series of leadership institutes in 1992. Each institute at the Edith Macy Conference Center, focusing on a different theme, such as health and fitness or leadership in a diverse world, is followed by a year-long local council project.

The Girl Scout Gold and Silver Awards, the highest recognitions, challenge girls to use their skills, self-discipline, and determination in order to meet the requirements of leadership, community action and individual development.

Girl Scouts of the USA continually seeks ways to include all girls who want to join. The organization is committed to pluralism and its membership has become increasingly representative of the diverse and changing population in the United States. Girls with special needs are integrated as much as possible, and have participated in Girl Scouting since the organization was founded.

Daisy Girl Scouts, who are five or six years old or in kindergarten or first grade, have been served in Girl Scouting since the mid-80's. The decision to serve girls of this age stemmed in part from the changing patterns of life in the nation, where more women now work outside the home, where there are more single-parent families, and where young children are exposed at an earlier age to pre-primary schooling.

Working with the Community

Since 1990 Girl Scouts of the USA has conducted national service projects as a means of uniting Girl Scouts of all ages across the nation in addressing a critical topic. National service projects have focused on literacy, the environment, and health and fitness. Girls have been given the opportunity to take action and promote positive change in their communities.

Girl Scouts of the USA have supported health care and development projects undertaken by the International Service Association for Health (INSA) since 1982. Activities have included fundraising to help construct schools in Burkina Faso and buy school equipment; assembling first aid kits for Haitian child care centres and making sets of hand puppets and props for use by Indian health workers.

Outdoor and Environmental Activities

Outdoor activities, camping and trips continues to be favourite activities of many girls. Girl Scouts of the USA is adopting a new camping ethic of minimal impact to the environment. This means changing many camping practices to reduce overuse to backcountry areas and adopting new training methods for leaders. Troops are also very active in local recycling, tree planting and community beautification projects. Projects initiated by troops have been adopted as on-going community projects.

Many wider opportunities open to Cadette and Senior Girl Scouts help girls explore careers in natural resource management, environmental protection and habitat protection. Some of these seven to fourteen-day summer opportunities have been made possible through collaborative arrangements with federal and state conservation agencies.

Girl Scouts – from Daisy to Leader!

Training

In order to support the work of volunteers, and their growing desire for acknowledgement and recognition, the organization provides a broad range of training courses at the Edith Macy Conference Centre. Leaders can obtain continuing education credits for these courses.

Communication and Co-operation

Through their contributions to the Juliette Low World Friendship Fund, members of

Girl Scouts of the USA support international understanding and intercultural education by supporting exchange visits between Girl Scouts and Girl Guides; sponsoring seminars and providing scholarships for the World Centres; and contributing to the Thinking Day Fund and to WAGGGS Mutual Aid programmes.

News about Girl Scouting has been carried on national and international wire services, network and cable television programmes, in newspapers, magazines, and by radio and syndicated news outlets.

The organization publishes a quarterly periodical, *Girl Scout Leader*, which provides programme tools and support to adults working with girls. The Association also produces a complete line of audiovisual resources such as training videos for volunteers and promotional films for the general public.

Collaboration with other organizations enhances Girl Scouts of the USA's ability to provide girls with a contemporary programme and to inform other organizations about the work of the Girl Scouts. Girl Scouts of the USA maintains relationships with over 300 national and international organizations and agencies, and national voluntary organizations.

These relations produce direct and indirect benefits for Girl Scouting through financial support, troop sponsorship, mutual support in programme areas, adult leadership and girl membership.

Girl Scouts learn to manage white-water rafting.

Uruguay

Asociación Guías Scout del Uruguay

Girl Guiding/Girl Scouting introduced: 1924
Became Associate Member of WAGGGS: 1966
Membership 1992: 79
Membership as % of female population: 0.01%
WAGGGS Region: Western Hemisphere

Promesa
Con la gracia de Dios, prometo por mi honor, hacer cuanto de mí dependa para servir a Dios y a la Patria, ayudar al prójimo en toda circunstancia y cumplir la Ley Guía.

Ley
1 La Guía es digna de confianza.
2 La Guía es leal.
3 La Guía hace lo posible por ser útil y ayudar a los demás
4 La Guía es bondadosa con todos y hermana de las demás Guías.
5 La Guía es cortés.
6 La Guía ama la naturaleza porque ve en ella la obra de Dios.
7 La Guía sabe obedecer.
8 La Guía es fuerte ante el sufrimiento y se sobrepone a las dificultades.
9 La Guía procura ser económica, limpia y ordenada.
10 La Guía es recta en su forma de pensar y actuar.

Lema
Siempre Lista

Promesa de la Abeja
Prometo hacer todo lo que pueda para ser fiel a Dios, a mi Patria, a los de mi casa y a la Ley de la Colmena, y para darle cada día una alegría a alguien.

Ley de la Colmena
La Abeja piensa primero en los demás; dice la verdad, es alegre, es trabajadora, es limpia y obediente.

Lema de la Abeja
Siempre Ayuda

Lema de la Guía Mayor
Servir

Promise
With the grace of God, I promise on my honour, to do my best to serve God and my Country, to help other people in any circumstance and to comply with the Guide Law.

Law
1 A Guide is worthy of trust.
2 A Guide is loyal.
3 A Guide does everything possible to be useful and help others.
4 A Guide is kind to all and a sister to all other Guides.
5 A Guide is courteous.
6 A Guide loves Nature for in it she sees the work of God.
7 A Guide knows how to obey.
8 A Guide is brave, and overcomes difficulties.
9 A Guide tries to be thrifty, clean and tidy.
10 A Guide is upright in her thoughts and deeds.

Motto
Be prepared

Bee Promise
I promise to do my best to be faithful to God, to my country, to those at home and to the Law of the Hive, and to give someone joy every day.

Law of the Hive
A Bee thinks first of others; she tells the truth, is cheerful, hard-working, clean and obedient.

Bee Motto
Always helps

Senior Guide Motto
Serve others

Guide

Bee

Age Groups

Guía Mayor – Fuego	Ranger	16-20
Guía Mayor – Pre- Fuego	Senior Guide	13-15
Guía	Guide	10-13
Abeja	Bee	6-9

Development of the Movement in Uruguay

Guiding in Uruguay began in 1924 when the 1st Montevideo Company of British Guides was formed. However, it was not until 1955 that the National Association for Uruguayan Guides was established and the first packs and companies were set up. The new Association received help during its formative years from Girl Guide/Girl Scout leaders belonging to international groups in Uruguay.

At the request of the Roman Catholic hierarchy, an Association of Catholic Guides was formed in 1961, which incorporated all existing companies, with one exception. That company became a separate group, and in 1964, as the result of close co-operation between the two groups, they joined together under the name Asociación de Guías del Uruguay. In 1974 the name of the Association was changed to the Asociación Guías Scout del Uruguay.

The Programme

The Brownie programme has been adapted from the programme of The Girl Guides Association (United Kingdom). A team is now working on preparing a new programme for Guides, Senior Guides and Rangers, which is intended to be implemented at the national level.

Working with the Community

Community service activities have included recreation programmes for children in urban and rural areas, helping in a nursery in an underprivileged area and assisting in schools for children with special needs. The programmes aim to incorporate families and thereby consolidate children's education. Members have also made layettes for babies of families in need.

Outdoor and Environmental Activities

Camps are organized for Guides and Rangers, and Brownies go on pack holidays. Members have also attended camps in other parts of North and South America, for example in Canada and Chile in 1988 and 1989. In addition, the Association is involved in conservation projects and took part in the Western Hemisphere Tree Project in 1985 which has inspired further efforts to plant and care for trees.

Training

A new training programme of advanced courses for leaders has recently been put into place.

Communication and Co-operation

Representatives of the Asociación Guías Scout del Uruguay attend international meetings in other countries organized by non-governmental organizations, local youth associations and other Girl Guide/ Girl Scout Associations. The Asociación Guías Scout del Uruguay also co-operates with the Red Cross, the CIEF (Centre for Research and Family Studies) and the Asociación Scouts del Uruguay, the Uruguayan Council for Social Welfare and the Women's Ecumenical Group. In June 1993 the Association worked together with non-governmental organizations for the protection of the environment, promoting the solar cooker. To keep members informed it publishes a monthly magazine called *Ecos*.

Vanuatu

Vanuatu Girl Guides Association

Girl Guiding/Girl Scouting introduced: 1955
Became Associate Member of WAGGGS: 1990
Membership 1992: 632
Membership as % of female population: 0.8%
WAGGGS Region: Asia Pacific

Guide

Brownie

Promise

I promise that I will do my best;
To do my duty to God
To serve my Country, to help other people and
To keep the Guide Law.

Law

- A Guide is loyal and can be trusted
- A Guide is helpful
- A Guide is polite and considerate
- A Guide is friendly and a sister to all Guides
- A Guide is kind to animals and respects all living things
- A Guide is obedient
- A Guide has courage and is cheerful in all difficulties
- A Guide makes good use of her time
- A Guide takes care of her own possessions and those of other people
- A Guide is self-controlled in all she thinks, says and does.

Development of the Movement in Vanuatu

Guiding was introduced to Vanuatu from Australia in 1955. A 12-week training course for leaders, organized soon after its introduction, lead to the enrolment of the first English-speaking Guides and Brownies by the end of the year.

In 1958 the Association des Guide Francophone de Vanuatu was started on the Island of Espiritu Santo. The Guide and Brownie groups, run for French-speaking girls by religious sisters, were administered by Les Guides de France. By 1960 more Francophone Guide and Brownie packs were opened on Efate, Ambae and Pentecost.

In 1962 the English-speaking units in Vanuatu, mostly attached to churches and schools, were registered with The Girl Guides Association (United Kingdom). A constitution was introduced in 1965 and the Association was known as the New Hebrides Branch of the GGA.

During the next few years several visits were made by trainers from the United Kingdom, New Zealand and Australia to help prepare programmes and develop Guiding in the country. In 1980 a full-time trainer/field worker was employed for six months to visit several islands and set up new units.

In 1980 Vanuatu gained independence and the Association des Guides Francophone de Vanuatu started to function independently of Les Guides de France.

Due to the difficult situation in the country, Guiding came to a standstill during the years 1981 to 1984. A subsequent visit from the United Kingdom's Commissioner for Branch Associations helped to revitalize the Movement.

In 1986 the two Guide Associations joined together to form one Association – the Vanuatu Girl Guides Association. In 1989 The Girl Guides Association (United Kingdom) signed a Deed of Transfer giving the Vanuatu Girl Guides Association self-government in all areas of work.

At the moment, communication and transport problems in Vanuatu make it difficult to take Guiding to all areas of the country, so most groups are on the bigger islands of Efate, Santo and Epi.

The Programme

The programme used by the three Branches, the Brownies, Guides and Ranger Guides, is based on an eight-point programme which gives girls opportunities to develop physical fitness, the mind, outdoor enjoyment, homecraft skills, service to others, human relations, creativity and character. It encourages young women in their personal development and helps to elevate the status of women in the country. The Ranger programme, introduced in 1980, is now being studied with a view to making it more suitable for older girls.

Working with the Community

Guides in Vanuatu are involved in various service projects such as cleaning public areas and churches and collecting and distributing gifts for patients in hospitals.

Training

The Training Adviser is responsible for preparing the training programme and ensuring that all training needs are met. A network of committee members, commissioners and trainers fulfil training needs.

Communication and Co-operation

A Thinking Day Service is held each year with the Scout Association and a special project undertaken annually to mark the occasion.

Members of the Vanuatu Girl Guides Association have attended camps and trainings abroad thanks to financial assistance from other National Organizations.

Guiding is well-accepted by the community in Vanuatu and the Association has close links with churches of all denominations.

Radio Vanuatu gives the Association a 30-minute weekly programme which helps communication with the islands, as well as publicizing Guiding activities. The Association also publishes a newsletter periodically.

Venezuela

Asociación de Guías Scouts de Venezuela

Girl Guiding/Girl Scouting introduced: 1958
Became Associate Member of WAGGGS: 1960
Became Full Member of WAGGGS: 1966
Membership 1992: 4,165
Membership as % of female population: 0.04%
WAGGGS Region: Western Hemisphere

Guide

Promesa
Yo prometo por mi honor hacer cuanto de mí dependa para:
Cumplir con mi deber hacia Dios y mi Patria,
Ser útil al prójimo en todo momento y obedecer la Ley Guía.

Ley
1 La Guía es leal y merece confianza.
2 La Guía es útil y ayuda a otros.
3 La Guía es comprensiva y generosa.
4 La Guía es hermana de toda muchacha Guía.
5 La Guía es cortés.
6 La Guía ve en la naturaleza la obra de Dios.
7 La Guía sabe obedecer.
8 La Guía es valiente y animosa en las dificultades.
9 La Guía es económica y ordenada.
10 La Guía es pura en lo que piensa, dice y hace.

Lema
Siempre Listas

Promesa de la Alita
Prometo hacer cuanto pueda por: cumplir mis deberes para con Dios y para con la Patria, hacer buen servicio a alguien cada día, especialmente a los de mi casa.

Ley de la Alita
La Alita obedece y escucha a los mayores.
La Alita complace a los demás antes que a sí misma.

Lema de la Alita
La Alita Ayuda Siempre

Promise
I promise on my honour to do my best:
To do my duty to God and my Country,
To help other people at all times and to obey the Guide Law.

Law
1 A Guide is loyal and deserves trust.
2 A Guide is useful and helps others.
3 A Guide is understanding and generous.
4 A Guide is a sister to every other Girl Guide.
5 A Guide is courteous.
6 A Guide sees in nature the work of God.
7 A Guide knows how to obey.
8 A Guide is courageous and cheerful under difficulties.
9 A Guide is thrifty and tidy.
10 A Guide is pure in all she thinks, says and does.

Motto
Always ready

Little Wing Promise
I promise to do my best to fulfil my duties to God and my Country; to do someone a good turn every day, especially those at home.

Little Wing

Little Wing Law
A Little Wing obeys and listens to her elders.
A Little Wing pleases others before herself.

Little Wing Motto
A Little Wing Always Helps

Age Groups

Ranger	Guía Mayor	15-18
Guide	Guía Menor	11-15
Little Wing	Alita	6-11

Development of the Movement in Venezuela

Guiding began in Venezuela in 1958 when the Asociación de Muchachas Guías de Venezuela was founded in Caracas. In 1959 several companies were formed elsewhere in the country, and the first Guide rally and the first National Assembly were held. In 1972 the Association changed its name to the Asociación de Guías Scouts de Venezuela.

The Programme

The Association has introduced an expansion programme and has been restructured to cater for the growing number of members. The expansion programme includes wide dissemination of information on the Movement throughout the country.

Working with the Community

Community service is very important for Guides in Venezuela. Guides have participated in a project to provide recreational activities for disadvantaged children; in a farming project for young people and in a programme for the inmates of reformatories. Members also visit homes for the elderly and take part in an annual anti-cancer fundraising campaign. Many girls have learnt about first aid, life-saving, fire-fighting and safety in order to give better service to the community. The Association is also involved in a government literacy programme and Rangers have also participated in a special service project in a children's hospital.

Outdoor and Environmental Activities

The Asociación de Guías Scouts de Venezuela has its own school camps at Curupao, which are well-equipped and attended by members from all over the country. In recent years, Guides from neighbouring countries such as the Netherlands Antilles and Trinidad and Tobago have camped there during the summer vacation, and courses for adults and girls of all ages are held there.

Guides work to clean up the camp.

The Association has worked on conservation programmes and has created the 'Billy Phelps' Prize Project, a biennial project to promote awareness of the need for environmental protection programmes. On Thinking Day 1989, members planted an area with fruit trees in honour of Lady Baden Powell's centenary. The trees were donated by the Venezuelan Institute for Scientific Research.

Training

A progressive training plan has been implemented for leaders of all three branches as part of the Association's expansion programme and training sessions and camps are held regularly for leaders, Rangers, and patrol leaders.

Communication and Co-operation

The Association recognizes the importance of involvement in international activities and makes every effort to encourage its members to participate in international events. In 1989 Venezuela took part in a Wider Opportunities Project in Colorado, USA as guests of the Girl Scouts of the USA.

In 1991 two Venezuelan Guiders visited Sangam World Centre for the first time and every year several Guiders and Senior Guides attend the Regular Sessions of Our Cabaña in Mexico. In 1992/93 a Venezuelan Guider worked for six months as a House Assistant in Pax Lodge.

The Association informs the public about its activities through newspapers, radio and television. Guiding has a good image in the community and the Association is aware it needs to keep publicizing the work of Guiding and its value for girls and young women. It publishes a monthly newsletter called *La Guiadora*, a magazine *El Trébol*, and an international newsletter called *Guía-Visión*, which gives information on Guiding at home and abroad.

The Asociación de Guías Scouts de Venezuela co-operates with the Scout Association, the Rotary Club and other institutions including the Fundación del Niño, and Fé y Alegría, which has developed programmes to provide recreational activities for underprivileged children.

Yemen Republic

Yemen Republic Girl Guides Association

Girl Guiding/Girl Scouting introduced: 1962
Became Associate Member of WAGGGS: 1990
Membership 1989: 6,653
Membership as % of female population: 0.97%
Member: Arab Regional Group

Promise
On my Honour I promise to do my best to do my duty to God then to my Country – to help other people in all circumstances – to abide by the Girl Guide Law.

Law
- A Girl Guide's Honour is to be trusted.
- A Girl Guide is loyal to God, her Country, her leaders and subordinates.
- A Girl Guide is useful and helpful to others.
- A Girl Guide is a friend to all and a sister to every other Guide.
- A Girl Guide has a praiseworthy character.
- A Girl Guide is kind to animals.
- A Girl Guide is obedient to her parents and leaders.
- A Girl Guide keeps her smile when facing difficulties and deals with all such difficulties with patience and perseverance.
- A Girl Guide is thrifty.
- A Girl Guide is pure in word and in deed.

Age Groups

Rangers	Juwalat	16-23
Guides	Murshidad	12-15
Brownies	Zahrat	7-12

Development of the Movement in the Republic of Yemen

Girl Guiding has existed in the Yemen Arab Republic since 1962 and in 1972 it was officially organized under one official administrative body. In 1975 the Yemen Scouts and Girl Guides Association was set up, which spread Guiding to areas of the country where it had not previously existed.

Guide

The Association became a member of the Arab Regional Group in 1980. During the next few years trainers from the Arab Bureau helped to prepare leaders and open new companies. In 1986 Yemen successfully hosted the 10th Arab Conference which served as a platform for women leaders within the Association to demonstrate their abilities to government authorities and the public. Women demonstrated that they could hold positions of authority and carry out their responsibilities effectively. As a result the Girl Guides Association became a separate Association working independently of the Scouts.

In 1990 the People's Democratic Republic of Yemen merged with the Yemen Arab Republic. Guiding had previously developed in the Arab Republic but now started to spread to all areas of the newly created Republic of Yemen.

The Programme
The programme incorporates spiritual training, technical guidance, health, handicrafts, the outdoors, campcraft skills, service and community development. It aims to teach members to become useful citizens and future leaders in the community.

Brownie

Working with the Community
The development and advancement of women is a principal concern of the Association and a focus of many projects. The Association organizes classes for women in dressmaking, cookery, home economics, music, and reading and

writing at community centres in several areas of the country. Similar handicraft and recreation classes are offered for girls after school. Income-generating projects are also carried out at three training centres. In addition girls take part in a variety of service projects for the general benefit of the community. They visit patients in hospitals, and care for the aged, orphans and people with disabilities.

Outdoor and Environmental Activities

The Association owns a campsite on the outskirts of Sana'a with extensive grounds. Local customs do not permit girls to stay overnight, but they are able to participate in a variety of outdoor activities at day camps.

Guides also help with the cleaning of public areas and gardens and take part in annual tree-planting campaigns.

Training

The Association has a Training Committee which meets regularly under the Training Commissioner. The Committee is responsible for preparing a training plan and materials and arranging training events for trainers and leaders.

Communication and Co-operation

Yemen encourages exchange visits with neighbouring countries and holds an annual charity bazaar on Thinking Day to create international awareness, raise funds and create publicity.

Several other organizations have supported the Association: Yemen has worked with Scouting Nederland on a home economics and income generating project in Hodeida; UNDP and UNESCO assist in providing special teachers to train girls and leaders in home economics, health care and literacy.

The Association has produced a manual on Family Life Education with the help of UNICEF and a trainer from USA. Financial assistance from USAID has funded the production of four education charts which have been circulated to all members of the Arab Regional Group.

The Association is able to ensure public awareness of its activities by participating in young people's weekly television and radio programmes and making use of space allocated in local papers. Guiding is well received by both government officials and the general public.

Guides work at a local charity fair.

Zambia

Girl Guides Association of Zambia

Girl Guiding/Girl Scouting introduced:	**1924**
Became Associate Member of WAGGGS:	**1966**
Became Full Member of WAGGGS:	**1978**
Membership 1992:	**12,000**
Membership as % of female population:	**0.28%**
WAGGGS Region:	**Africa**

Promise

I promise that I will do my best:
To serve God;
To serve my country and other people; and
To keep the Guide Law.

Law

1 A Guide is to be trusted.
2 A Guide is loyal.
3 A Guide is helpful.
4 A Guide is a friend to all and a sister to all Guides.
5 A Guide considers other people.
6 A Guide is kind to animals and respects all living things.
7 A Guide is obedient.
8 A Guide is cheerful and brave, even in difficulties.
9 A Guide is thrifty.
10 A Guide controls herself in all she thinks, says and does.

Motto

Be Prepared

Lechwe Guide Promise

I promise that I will do my best:
To serve God;
To serve my country and other people;
And to keep the Lechwe Guide Law.

Lechwe Guide Law

A Lechwe is truthful, obedient and cheerful.
A Lechwe thinks of others before herself.

Lechwe Guide Motto

Wide Awake

Age Groups

Guide Cadet	18+
Ranger	14-18
Guide	11-15
Lechwe Guide	7-11

Development of the Movement in Zambia

Guiding began in Zambia in 1924 when the first Guide company was registered in Livingstone, the capital of what was then Northern Rhodesia. In the same year a Ranger unit was opened, and two years later the first Brownie pack was set up.

In 1930 the Wayfarers, an organization for African girls working along similar lines to the Guide Association, was started and by 1936 it was known as the Wayfarer Guides and Sunbeams. After a referendum in 1948, the Wayfarers joined the Guides to make one Movement for all the girls in Zambia. In 1952 all girls under 11 years became known as Brownies and the Association was unified under one Commissioner.

When Zambia became an independent republic within the Commonwealth in 1964, the Girl Guides Association of Zambia, previously a Branch Association of The Girl Guides Association (United Kingdom) became self-governing in all areas of work. In 1966 the first Zambian Chief Commissioner was appointed and the newly-built headquarters were opened in Lusaka.

In 1974 the name Brownie was changed to Lechwe Guide, the lechwe being a species of brown antelope found only in Zambia.

The Programme

The programme is designed to involve girls in a wide range of activities. The Association has companies for blind girls, and produces some publications in Braille. Other girls with special needs are integrated into existing companies and packs.

Guide

Lechwe Guide

Working with the Community

Service has always been important for the Girl Guides Association of Zambia. The Association undertakes literacy and leadership training for young married women in shanty towns and rural areas and has established training centres in Lusaka and Chipata. The centres offer vocational facilities for school leavers, specializing in tailoring. Members run a nursery school in Ndola on the Copperbelt, and the Association sponsors a school for the deaf in the Eastern Province.

Outdoor and Environmental Activities

Camping and outdoor skills are a regular and popular part of the Guide programme. The Association runs a tree-planting project which focuses on forest conservation.

Training

The Association holds a national training twice a year, and divisional trainings once a year.

Communication and Co-operation

The Association is aware of the importance of international contacts, and regularly participates in international gatherings.

On the area of communications, the Girl Guides Association of Zambia informs the general public about its activities through radio and television coverage and the press as well as publishing a monthly newsletter and an annual periodical, *Camp Kudu Magazine*.

The Guides co-operate with the Zambia Boy Scouts Association, the Ministry of Youth and Sport, the Zambia Council for Social Development and other organizations concerned with youth. Work also is carried out with the United Nations, especially through UNICEF and UNESCO.

Zimbabwe

Girl Guides Association of Zimbabwe

Girl Guiding/Girl Scouting introduced: 1912
Became Associate Member of WAGGGS (as Girl Guides Association of Rhodesia): 1969
Became Full Member of WAGGGS: 1972
Membership 1992: 12,284
Membership as % of female population: 0.25%
WAGGGS Region: Africa

Promise
I promise that I will do my best
To do my duty to God,
To serve my country, and other people and
To keep the Guide Law.

Law
1 A Guide is loyal and can be trusted.
2 A Guide is helpful.
3 A Guide is polite and considerate.
4 A Guide is friendly and a sister to all Guides.
5 A Guide is kind to animals and respects all living things.
6 A Guide is obedient.
7 A Guide has courage and is cheerful in all difficulties.
8 A Guide makes good use of her time.
9 A Guide takes care of her own possessions and those of other people.
10 A Guide is self-controlled in all she thinks, says and does.

Motto
Be Prepared

Brownie Promise
I promise that I will do my best:
To do my duty to God;
To serve my country and other people; and
To keep the Brownie Law.

Brownie Law
A Brownie is truthful, obedient and cheerful.
A Brownie thinks of others before herself.

Brownie Motto
Lend a Hand

Age Groups

Ranger	14-20
Guide	10-17
Brownie	7-11

Development of the Movement in Zimbabwe

Guiding in Zimbabwe began in 1912. In 1926 the Wayfarers, an organization for African girls working along similar lines to the Guide Movement, was started. In 1940 the two Movements began to merge, and this process was completed in 1950.

The name of the Association was changed in 1981 from the Girl Guides Association of Rhodesia to the Girl Guides of Zimbabwe.

The Programme
Zimbabwe uses an eight-point programme based on keeping fit, becoming a homemaker, giving service, keeping the Guide Law, getting to know people, enjoying the outdoors, thinking for yourself and exploring the arts. Particular emphasis is placed on keeping the Ranger programme relevant to the needs of today's girl.

Working with the Community
The Girl Guides Association of Zimbabwe recognizes the need for community service, and Guides and Rangers endeavour to respond to the country's needs. For example Brownies, Guides, Rangers and Young Leaders participated in the Literacy Plus Campaign for International Literacy Year, 1990. As a follow up, Rangers run literacy classes for

Guide

Brownie

adults and have given regular service at a home for deaf and blind children for many years.

A Ranger Company was granted the WAGGGS Olave Award for 1990 for their tremendous work during the Literacy Campaign. In addition the Monte Casino Rangers programme which was introduced in 1986, caters for families relocated to the Macheke Resettlement village under a government Resettlement Scheme. Originally from a remote rural area they had little previous experience of either health or education services. The Rangers undertook to educate the parents through classes encompassing literacy, health, sewing, nutrition and forestry.

The Youth Workers' Scheme trained young people selected by their community leaders in skills to improve their quality of life. In 1988 the Girl Guides Association of Zimbabwe was the recipient of a grant from the Zimbabwe Voluntary and Welfare Organizations Trust for income-generating projects. Community-based projects were implemented and are continuing successfully.

Outdoor and Environmental Activities

The Association owns two national training and camping centres, Pax Park near Harare and Rowallan Park in the Matopos Hills near Bulawayo.

Guides are also dedicated to the protection of the environment and participate in tree-planting campaigns. The headquarters, in Harare, is registered as a reclamation depot for scrap glass as part of the CARE campaign (Clean Air, Rivers and Environment). In 1987 the Guides competed in a national conservation awareness challenge and won the premier trophy from the National Conservation Trust of Zimbabwe for their efforts.

The "We Care!" Project is an environmental resource package adapted by the Association for use in Zimbabwe. It is designed for ready comprehension by youth and their leaders and embodies many illustrations and activities throughout the text. It covers a wide range of topics relating to flora, fauna and natural resources with warnings of abuse and recommendations for preservation. The object is to increase environmental knowledge and awareness and to develop positive and caring attitudes.

Training

The Association is continually working to increase the quality of its adult leadership. During 1992 as part of the Association's 80th Anniversary, "The 80 Game" recruited more than 80 new Guiders who completed the Basic Training Course. The introduction in 1992 of graded skills trainings has resulted in an increased demand for trainings and greater expertise amongst Guiders.

Communication and Co-operation

Representatives from the Association attend events abroad whenever possible and the Post Box links members with their counterparts throughout the world.

Zimbabwe has been involved in Zimswede, a twinning project with Sweden since 1984 in conjunction with the Scout Association of Zimbabwe. This has helped to bring clean water, toilet facilities and shelters for playgroups and literacy classes to rural areas, as well as aiding international education and understanding.

The Association participates in many national events and makes its work known through the media and its periodical, *News and Views.* During 1992 the Girl Guides Association of Zimbabwe celebrated its 80th Anniversary.

The Girl Guides Association of Zimbabwe is a member of the Standing Committee of Associations of National Youth Organizations and the Wild Life and Conservation Society. It also co-operates with the Girl's Brigade, the Scout Association, the President's Award Scheme and UNESCO.

Appendix A

Founder Members of WAGGGS

Founder Members of WAGGGS, as indicated in the 5th World Conference Report, 1928, and confirmed in the 6th World Conference Report, 1930:

Australia
Belgium
Canada
Czechoslovakia [1]
Denmark
Estonia [2]
Finland
France
Hungary [2]
Iceland
India [3]
Japan [4]
Latvia [2]
Liberia [5]
Lithuania [2]
Luxembourg
Netherlands
New Zealand
Norway
Poland [2]
South Africa
Sweden
Switzerland
United Kingdom of Great Britain and Northern Ireland
United States of America
Yugoslavia [2]

1 The National Organization of Czechoslovakia ceased to be a member of WAGGGS in the aftermath of World War II, but rejoined in 1990 as an Associate Member. Following the change in national structure, WAGGGS recognized the National Organizations of the Czech Republic and of the Slovak Republic (Slovakia) at the 28th World Conference (Denmark, 1993) as Associate Members, replacing the former Czechoslovakia.

2 The National Organizations of Estonia, Hungary and Latvia rejoined WAGGGS at the 28th World Conference (Denmark, 1993). Lithuania, Poland and Yugoslavia are not currently members of WAGGGS.

3 India in 1928 covered the areas known today as Bangladesh, India and Pakistan.

4 The National Organization of Japan held membership until 1939; on being reorganized it became an Associate Member at the 14th World Conference (Norway, 1952), and a Full Member at the 17th World Conference (Greece, 1960).

5 The National Organization of Liberia held membership until 1931; on being reorganized it became an Associate Member at the 19th World Conference (Japan, 1966), and a Full Member at the 22nd World Conference (United Kingdom, 1975).

Appendix B

Important Addresses

THE WORLD BUREAU

Olave Centre,
12c Lyndhurst Road
London NW3 5PQ
England, UK
Telephone number: +44 71 794 1181
Fax number: +44 71 431 3764

THE WORLD CENTRES:

OUR CHALET
CH 3715,
Adelboden,
Switzerland
Telephone number: +41 33 731 226
Fax number: +41 33 732 082
Telegraphic address: WAGGGS, Adelboden

OUR CABAÑA
Apartado Postal 4-406,
62430 Cuernavaca,
Morelos,
Mexico
Telephone number: +52 73 152 650
Fax number: +52 73 152 897
Telegraphic address: CABAÑAGUIAS, Morelos

PAX LODGE
Olave Centre,
12c Lyndhurst Road,
London NW3 5PQ,
England, UK
Telephone number: +44 71 435 2202
Fax number: +44 71 431 3825

SANGAM
World Centre for World Association
of Girl Guides and Girl Scouts,
Alandi Road, Yerawada,
Pune 411006,
India
Telephone number: +91 212 663 252
Fax number: +91 212 642 354
Telegraphic address: SANGAM PUNE 6

For further information about the World Centres, please refer to *The Story of Four World Centres*, available for purchase through your National Association, the World Bureau, or contact the Guider-in-Charge at the World Centre in which you are interested.

Your National Association

Fill in the name, address and telephone/fax numbers for your National Association below.

Association:

Address:

Telephone:

Fax:

Appendix C

Symbols of the Movement

Many of these symbols, initially introduced by Lord Baden-Powell, have been updated to continue reaching today's girls and young women.

World Trefoil

The Trefoil, used on the World Badge, is the unifying symbol of WAGGGS. Every part has a meaning. The golden Trefoil on a bright blue background represents the sun shining over all the children of the world; the three leaves represent the three-fold Promise as originally laid down by the Founder; the base of the stalk represents the flame of the love of humanity; the vein pointing upwards through the centre of the trefoil represents the compass needle pointing the way; and the two stars represent the Promise and Law. In March 1991, to reflect the forward-looking nature of the Movement, the World Trefoil and other aspects of WAGGGS' corporate identity were updated to give them a fresh, dynamic look.

World Badge

The World Badge was first adopted at the 11th World Conference (France, 1946). Today it features the gold World Trefoil on a blue background. It may be worn by all members of the Movement, girls and adults, in or out of uniform.

World Association Badge

The World Association Badge was first adopted at the 7th World Conference in 1932. It is similar in design to the World Badge. The World Association Badge is worn by members of the World Committee, its sub-committees, World Bureau staff, Guiders-in-Charge at the World Centres, Honorary Associates, and others who carry out special duties for the World Association.

World Flag

The World Flag was also updated in March 1991. The golden Trefoil remains the focal point on a blue background. A new white blaze in the lower, right-hand corner represents WAGGGS' commitment to peace; this is crowned by three golden blocks symbolizing the three-fold Promise. It is used at the World Centres, the World Bureau, WAGGGS' gatherings and by all Member Organizations, often as a unit flag.

The Motto

The Motto, "Be Prepared", shares the Founder's initials and is a practical reminder of the educational purposes of Girl Guiding/Girl Scouting.

Good Turn

The Good Turn symbolizes the service given by all members of the Movement to the community. Younger girls think of ways they can do a good turn every day, while older girls develop this further into service projects at local, national and international levels.

The Left Handshake

The Founder suggested a Left Handshake to recognize other members of the Movement, and it is still used widely. When asked to explain the origin, Baden-Powell related a legend told to him in West Africa: two hostile, neighbouring tribal groups decided to try to live together in peace, and so they flung down their shields, which were carried on the left arm, and advanced, unprotected, to greet each other with their left hands extended in trust and friendship.

The Sign or Salute

In giving the Sign or Salute, Girl Guides/Girl Scouts raise three fingers of the right hand as a reminder of the three-fold Promise.

The World Song

The World Song was adopted at the 13th World Conference in 1950. The music was adapted with the approval of the Finnish composer, Jean Sibelius, from his March, Opus 91b. It was originally composed as the march for one of Finland's oldest Scout companies. First published with English words by Gavin Ewart in 1952, the World Song highlights the principles and spirit of the Movement.

Thinking Day Symbol

The Thinking Day Symbol was introduced in 1975. The World Trefoil in the centre represents the World Association. Arrows pointing towards the Trefoil represents action and direction. The circular design represent the world of the Girl Guide/Girl Scout Movement.

The WAGGGS Peace Symbol

In 1993 WAGGGS developed a special symbol to use during CREATE PEACE WORLDWIDE – THE WAGGGS INITIATIVE, a three-year initiative to highlight WAGGGS' members' commitment to peace. The logo was designed by a former Guide from Brazil. Its special symbolism brings members together in friendship and peace. The elements of the symbol are described as follows:

> Shining over the world, brightening the future, is the WAGGGS Trefoil. The world is linked with golden cords, connecting places and people in friendship and peace. The Guiding knot at the top stands for the strength of Girl Guide/Girl Scout actions to create peace worldwide. The cords embrace a green olive branch, which symbolizes a growing peace for the future.

The WAGGGS Peace Symbol appears on the back cover of this book.